A HISTORY of DIPLOMACY

A History of Diplomacy

Jeremy Black

REAKTION BOOKS

For Harvey Sicherman

Published by
Reaktion Books Ltd
33 Great Sutton Street
London EC1V 0DX, UK
www.reaktionbooks.co.uk

First published 2010
Copyright © Jeremy Black 2010

All rights reserved
No part of this publication may be reproduced, stored in a retrieval system, or transmitted, in any form or by any means, electronic, mechanical, photocopying, recording or otherwise, without the prior permission of the publishers.

Printed and bound in Great Britain by
Cromwell Press Group, Trowbridge, Wiltshire

British Library Cataloguing in Publication Data
Black, Jeremy.
A history of diplomacy.
1. Diplomacy–History.
I. Title
327.2'09-DC22

ISBN : 978 1 86189 696 4

Contents

Preface 7
Introduction 11

ONE
1450–1600 43

TWO
1600–1690 59

THREE
1690–1775 85

FOUR
1775–1815 119

FIVE
1815–1900 151

SIX
1900–1970 180

SEVEN
1970 to the Present 224
Conclusions: The Future 248
Postscript 256

References 265
Selected Further Reading 295
Index 299

Preface

'So I made up my mind that you should be the next American Ambassador to France. I should like to see Mabel's face when she reads the announcements in the papers. A nobody, she called you. Well, the Ambassador to France isn't a nobody.'

J. Wellington Gedge does not subscribe to his wife's use of him to pursue her rift with her late husband's sister. Far from seeking honours or wearing 'uniforms and satin knickerbockers' and cocked hats, he wishes to spend time in California, but his wife seeks to soothe him:

'There's nothing to being an Ambassador . . . It's just a matter of money. If you have money and there are important people like the Vicomtesse de Blissac and Senator Opal behind you . . .'[1]

And so the plot of *Hot Water* (1932) is set in motion. Being a Wodehouse, it dealt more with the course of true love, as mediated by jewel thieves; and the details of the diplomatic life did not feature. Instead, they could be taken as read by a public used to diplomacy as a set of established practices, indeed rituals. Such was the situation which underlay the presentation of diplomats and diplomacy on stage and in fiction, whether serious or satirical, as with Terry-Thomas's central role in the British comedy film *Carlton-Browne of the F.O.* (1959).[2] Indeed, to take the Wodehouse link further, distinguished retired British Ambassador Sir Nicholas Henderson at the lunch on 3 June 1988 following the unveiling of a blue plaque in London honouring Wodehouse, claimed that most foreigners expected British diplomats to behave like Bertie Wooster and that he had aspired to be a mixture of Jeeves and Wooster in order to achieve success.

This world did not exhaust the public perception of diplomacy. Indeed, there was a popular board game of that name, created by Allan

Calhamer in 1954 and released commercially in 1959. When I was an undergraduate in Cambridge in 1975–8, there was a student society devoted to related socializing and to playing the game; a word order that captures the reality of the situation rather than grammatical conventions. *Diplomacy* is a game focused on alliance-making that takes Europe just before the First World War as its subject. In its catalogue, Avalon Hill, the American publisher of the game, described it as the favourite game of both President Kennedy and Henry Kissinger.

The study of nineteenth-century European history inspired Calhamer, but the game scarcely conforms to the idyll of diplomacy mocked in Franz Lehár's comic operetta *The Merry Widow* (1905). Instead, the diplomacy in *Diplomacy* is centrally integrated into what is a war game, or at least one about the use of force. Negotiation acts as a force multiplier, rather than a means of avoiding conflict. The same is true of the commercially released variants, namely *Machiavelli*, set in Renaissance Italy, *Kamakura* (feudal Japan), *Hundred* (the Hundred Years' War), *Art-Rí* (medieval Ireland), *Classical* (the Hellenistic world) and *Colonial Diplomacy* (late nineteenth-century Asia).[3]

Satire and game both illustrate the variety of definitions and approaches that diplomacy offers and suggests. This variety is also the case as far as the more conventional understanding of the subject is concerned, and it is to that that we shall turn. Indeed, this book rests in part on the need to emphasize the range of diplomatic conceptions and activity, especially if non-Western views and practices are considered, and therefore the need to be wary of any account that is overly coherent and schematic.

A meeting with old friends after a significant gap is at once heartwarming, invigorating and disconcerting. The pleasure of friendship in play is matched by the arresting realization of the impact of the years. And so with this book. From the late 1970s to the early 1990s, I was very much an historian of British foreign policy, but, thereafter, my contact was episodic. To think again about diplomacy has therefore been instructive. In part, this process of instruction, through reading the welcome work of others as well as by my own efforts, reflects the extent to which the subject has changed, not least with a greater interest today in the role of non-governmental organizations or NGOs. There is also a shifting interest on my part, not least to diplomacy's role as a form of information gathering and dissemination. Moreover, this book represents a development of my earlier studies in the fields of international relations, diplomacy and related subjects, not least with its critique of established teleological and Whiggish approaches.[4] As such, it is an aspect of a wider attempt to ask questions about conventional accounts of change and modernization.[5]

PREFACE

This book sets out to change the way in which the history of diplomacy is discussed. The standard European-based continuum of diplomatic development until it encompassed the globe during the twentieth century is an insufficient guiding principle of analysis, and it is necessary to change it so that the 'non-West' receives its fair share of attention, both in the way diplomacy was thought about by its users and in the treatment of diplomatic events. The challenge of the 'worldwide' includes not only the need to discuss non-Western notions of diplomacy, but also to consider encounters with Western concepts.

The established chronology is also addressed, not least with the argument that the process of change was always messy and that there were continuities observable well beyond the usual points at which a key shift is said to have occurred. Major themes in the book include the development of professional diplomacy, the tension between ideology and realism, and the impact of the proliferation of states in the twentieth century. There is also discussion of empires and diplomacy, hegemonic diplomacy, diplomacy and totalitarianisms, and the role of both supra-national institutions and NGOs (Non Governmental Organizations). In general there is an emphasis on the complexity of developments, which is intended to offer a warning against over-reliance on synoptic models of any kind. In doing so, there is the formidable challenge of writing history to cover a long time span and a worldwide canvas. This has proved very exciting.

Michael Leaman, the excellent publisher of this series, has reminded me firmly of the need to include a discussion of the conventional topics, such as the rise of diplomatic immunity and of specialized embassy buildings, but, for me, much of the interest has come through being able to discuss these topics in terms of the wider context. Diplomacy should be located not only in terms of developments in international relations but also of those in cultural representation and intellectual thought.

I benefited greatly from the opportunity to discuss this topic and my approach with the late Matthew Anderson and would like to record my gratitude for his encouragement. It is a great pleasure to thank David Armstrong, Peter Barber, Simon Barton, David Braund, Frank Cogliano, David Cohen, Art Eckstein, Glynn Evans, Denice Fett, Robert Finlay, John France, Bill Gibson, David Graff, Sarah Hamilton, Michael Leaman, Michael Levin, Tim May, Peter Onuf, Toby Osborne, Thomas Otte, Michael Prestwich, Matthew Seligman, Edward Tenace, Peter Wiseman, Patrick Zutshi and two anonymous readers for their comments on earlier drafts of all or part of the thesis, and Yiğit Alpogan, Claude Altermatt, Paul Auchterlonie, Michael Bregnsbo, James Chapman, Simon Dixon, Henry Kamen, Tim Niblock, Andrew O'Shaughnessy, Tim Rees, Joe Smith and Simon Stoddart for advice on particular points. None is responsible for any errors that remain. I have benefited from hearing an unpublished paper by Denice Fett and from the permission of Richard Head to quote from the Bland Burges papers. I would like to thank the University of Exeter for supporting relevant research trips.

It is a great pleasure to dedicate this book to Harvey Sicherman, the President of the Foreign Policy Research Institute. I have been associated with the Institute for many years, for several as a Senior Fellow, and this association has always brought me pleasure and interest. Much of both has come from the company and conversation of Harvey, who is one of the most perceptive thinkers and brilliant communicators that I know. That Harvey is also a good friend is a great boon.

Introduction

Executing the envoys of Chinggis Khan did not prove a wise move for Muhammad II, the Khwarizm Shah, who ruled an empire centred on Persia (Iran) though stretching from the Zagros mountains to the Syr Danya and the Indus. The news

> had such an effect upon the Khan's mind that the control of repose and tranquillity was removed, and the whirlwind of anger cast dust into the eyes of patience and clemency while the fire of wrath flared up with such a flame that it drove the water from his eyes and could be quenched only by the shedding of blood.

Ata-Malik Juvaini, the Persian servant of the Mongol Ilkhans of Persia in the late thirteenth century, who recorded this episode, was writing some decades later, but such an explanation appeared plausible to him and was the one he thought it appropriate to spread.[1] In practice, Chinggis Khan had tried to settle the dispute without war. A caravan that the Mongols had sent was massacred by the Governor of Otran. A camel attendant escaped and reported to Chinggis, who, furious, sent diplomats to resolve matters as he still wanted to trade, and was also involved with a major war with the Jin Empire of northern China, a more immediate challenge. Chinggis asked for the offending governor to be sent to him for execution and for the restoration of goods. However, offended by the language of the envoy, who implied that Chinggis was more powerful, Muhammad had the envoy executed and singed the beards of his guards, a clear breach of the etiquette of relations between rulers. This act made war inevitable. In the event, Persia was overrun by the Mongols in 1220.

This episode serves as a reminder that diplomacy takes different forms and has varied consequences. The standard account, one focused on the Western model of permanent embassies, is overly narrow, and that is a theme of this study.

In books, as with diplomacy, it is best to make clear what is on offer. To critics, the skill of being a diplomat rests in part in obfuscation, and similar comments have been made, often with reason, about the misleading nature of book titles and cover descriptions. This book cannot seek to provide a short summary of diplomatic negotiation, even over the last half-millennium. Instead, it focuses on the nature of the diplomacy, in order to throw light on its changing character as well as on key developments in the field of international relations.

As far as this changing character is concerned, the intention is not to provide the standard account of the development of embassies, but rather to see diplomacy as a privileged aspect of general systems of information-gathering, of representation, and of negotiation. As such, the approach is not that of Sir Ernest Satow who, on the opening page of his classic (and much-reprinted) 1917 guide to diplomatic practice, defined diplomacy as 'the application of intelligence and tact to the conduct of official relations between the governments of independent states, extending sometimes also to their reactions with vassal states; or, more briefly still, the conduct of business between states by peaceful means'.[2]

For Harold Nicolson, like Satow a British diplomat at a time when Britain was the leading world power, diplomacy was 'the process and machinery by which . . . negotiation is carried out',[3] a definition that in fact excluded much of the doings of diplomats. More succinctly, the historian Peter Barber defined diplomacy as 'the peaceful management of international relations', although he continued, as others have done, by discussing this in terms of the actions of diplomats,[4] rather than of others involved in these relations.

Leaving aside the key role of diplomacy in preparing for war, notably assembling coalitions and misleading opponents and neutrals, which scarcely equates with peaceful management, this approach is very different to that which, far more loosely, extends diplomats and diplomacy to other forms of representation, power-projection and negotiation, such that, to the theorist James Der Derian, diplomacy becomes 'a mediation between estranged individuals, groups or entities'.[5]

At present, in fact, alongside the expanding agenda of foreign services and diplomacy, and the complex interaction with domestic issues and actors, there is a widespread use of the terms diplomats and diplomacy to include cultural[6] or sporting activities, and indeed, even the concept that anyone, and thus everyone, abroad is a diplomat for their country.

Such concepts have since also been applied retrospectively, for example to the American world baseball tour in 1888, which indeed was the product of the entrepreneurial energy of Albert Spalding, rather than of any government body.[7] Sport in fact can be important for diplomatic links, as with the 'ping pong' diplomacy between China and the USA in the early 1970s: table tennis then served as a demonstration of improving relations.

The range of the use of the term diplomats as a description for others who lacked such accreditation is also shown with the idea of editors, foreign editors or key correspondents of authoritative newspapers, would-be newspapers of record, as diplomats without portfolio. A prime example was Valentine Chirol, the anti-German Foreign Editor of *The Times* from 1899 to 1911, who was received in Japan by the Emperor and was described by President Theodore Roosevelt as the 'godfather' of the Anglo-Japanese treaty of 1902.[8]

Like war, as with 'war on poverty', or drugs, or cancer, diplomacy therefore becomes a term that is widely employed. So also does the use of terms relating to diplomats. In July 2009 Lord Darzi, a recently resigned health minister, claimed that employees of the British National Health Service, the largest employer in Europe, should 'be ambassadors of prevention and wellbeing. . . . They should all be public health ambassadors.'[9] That October, John Bercow, the Speaker, described his role as being 'Ambassador for Parliament'.[10] In September 2009 the film director Joel Coen explained the prologue to the new Coen brothers film *A Serious Man*, a film set in the American 1960s but with a prologue set in nineteenth-century Poland and scripted in Yiddish, by remarking 'We just thought a Yiddish ghost tale would be a good ambassador for what comes after.'[11]

An instance of the use of the term diplomacy that focuses on government policy, but ranges more widely than that of foreign ministries, is that of dollar diplomacy. Initially employed by *Harper's Weekly* on 23 April 1910, to describe the efforts by Secretary of State Knox to secure opportunities for American foreign investment, this term was applied after the Second World War to the provision of economic assistance, especially to Latin American states, and often in return for supervision by American economic advisers. The key agency was generally not the Secretary of State. Yet, however different, the root cause of this support often matched that of more formal diplomacy, namely that of economic and political stabilization and/or the promotion of democracy.[12]

Adopting this approach, diplomacy is loosely defined, becoming political activity at the international level. Such a definition, however, is overly loose and, in particular, underplays the distinctive character of diplomacy as the implementation of policy through accredited persuasion. Nevertheless, there is no clear distinction between the formulation and implementation of policy, while persuasion is not the sole means, nor accredited agents the only ones to play a role.

Moreover, even allowing for a focus on diplomats, the emphasis in discussion of diplomacy is usually overly narrow. The role of diplomacy in opening spaces for cultural exchange is important, and has been highly significant in the past, and not only in Europe[13] but also in East Asia and elsewhere. To take another often underrated aspect of diplomacy, information-gathering is a key role, as government depends on information, and modern government very much so, and the extent of access to accurate material is central to the success of a diplomatic system. As such, diplomats are only part of the process by which information is obtained, and often are not the most important part.[14]

This point serves as a reminder that, whereas diplomacy is an aspect of information-gathering, as also of representation and of negotiation, it is by no means the sole means for any of these. Indeed, part of the history of diplomacy is the account of how far these processes have been conducted through, or under the control of, the formal mechanisms of diplomacy. In practice, this has always been the case only to a limited extent.

Of the three, information-gathering has tended to be least under the control of the formal diplomatic process, although diplomats were often best placed to both validate and trade information, while a key professional skill is that of distinguishing the certain from the doubtful.[15] However, in order both to validate and to trade information, diplomats were highly dependent on the provision of information from their home governments. If they were unable to receive, and thus provide, such information, then they lost credibility and simply did not know what to say. In such a position, they would find it difficult to gather intelligence and to offer the informed counterfactuals that are part of their job-description. This point underlines the mutuality between states that is important to diplomatic processes.

Alternative sources of information on foreign countries have included mercantile and military, both individuals and institutions. Some of the alternative sources have been governmental, but others not, which remains the case to the present. As far as the governmental sources are concerned, this point serves as an important reminder of the degree to which the diplomatic system, understood as that centred on diplomats, does not control the diplomatic process, understood as the management (peaceful or otherwise) of international relations. A similar conclusion can be made about the extent to which the use of force was not simply a matter of the formal military mechanisms of the state.

It was (and is) not only with information gathering that the diplomatic system did not control the diplomatic process as conventionally understood: this lack of inclusiveness was also true of representation and negotiation. The last is the one of the three that has been most under the control of diplomats, although the direct role of sovereigns, heads of state, ministers, and favourites of sovereigns not given diplomatic rank, has tended to lessen this control. The travels of heads of state could be closely linked to diplomacy, as with Raymond Poincaré, Prime Minister of France in 1912–13 and President from 1913 to 1920. He made major efforts to strengthen relations with Russia and Britain, including paying a state visit to the former in July 1914, with René Viviani, the Prime Minister, a visit in which the deteriorating Balkan crisis was discussed. Poincaré backed the Russian position of standing by Serbia.

The visit also showed the problems of travel prior to the age of jet aircraft as Poincaré, who left St Petersburg, then the Russian capital, by sea on 23 July, did not reach Paris until 29 July. During this period, the Germans interfered with wireless telegraphic traffic to and from Poincaré. The end result was that the French were unable to exercise sufficient restraint on Russia in the run-up to the First World War. In contrast, the direct role of heads of state and ministers has increased considerably since with the great improvement in communications stemming from air travel and from the instantaneous dispatch of messages, as is discussed in chapter Seven and the Conclusions.

The concept and practice of representation helps ensure that action against diplomats and embassies is seen as particularly serious. In June 2009 the Cuban and Venezuelan envoys in Honduras were seized during a military coup, leading President Chávez of Venezuela to threaten action if his envoy was harmed. Members of the government that had been overthrown took refuge in embassies, a process that is often seen on such occasions, and that can greatly complicate diplomatic relations. In turn, the new Honduran regime pressed for the breaking of diplomatic relations with Venezuela.

Representation is a concept that may be extended too loosely if removed from the idea of formal accreditation. For example, Intelligence agents can further government policy, but the Syrian agents who assassinated Rafiq al-Hariri, a prominent Lebanese politician and former Prime Minister, in Beirut on 14 February 2005 cannot profitably be seen as diplomats. Conversely, they can be presented as key representatives of a state in which the Intelligence agencies take a central governmental role, and where notions of legality play scant role. Moreover, this assassination can be seen as the crucial way in which Syria, at that juncture, sought to manage relations with neighbouring Lebanon by controlling, or at least influencing, Lebanese politics: al-Hariri was opposed to Syrian influence and to the Syrian-backed President, Émile Lahoud. Such Syrian conduct is against international law, but it is not always helpful to treat this activity as separate to diplomacy, because to do so risks leaving aside from the analysis the conduct of many states across history.

Here, the key point is that these agents pursued state policy abroad, which can be taken as conforming to a functional definition of diplomacy, even though they were not accredited diplomats; while, as an aside, relations between the diplomatic service and Intelligence agencies can be poor, as in the case of France in the 1930s.[16] Moreover, the high level of Intelligence operations seen during the Cold War has continued thereafter, not least with recent and current Russian and Chinese Intelligence operations against Britain and the USA. However, these operations today play a smaller role in the public world of international links than was the case during the Cold War when their exposure was exploited to make political points. Thus in 1984 the KGB resident in Britain was expelled as a result of the arrest of a Briton recruited as a spy, while the following year the defection of Oleg Gordievsky, the KGB Resident-Delegate, led to the expulsion of 25 Soviet intelligence officers.

Not all Intelligence operations conformed to state policy. Notably, the immediate cause of the First World War, the assassination of Archduke Franz Ferdinand of Austria at Sarajevo in 1914, was the product of an alternative foreign policy directed by Colonel Dragutin Dimitrijević, the chief of Serbian military intelligence, who sought both to create a Greater Serbia and to overthrow the Serbian Prime Minister, Nikola Pašić. The latter was unable to block Dimitrijević, but the crisis caused by the assassinations was brought home to Serbia which was attacked in 1914 and overrun in 1915.

To put a determining emphasis on accreditation risks inviting the rejoinder that diplomats have themselves on occasion acted in a manner that similarly resulted in violent and, more commonly, subversive acts. In addition, the role of Intelligence agencies is not simply separate to that of foreign services; they are often intertwined. Moreover, diplomacy and diplomats are frequently affected by the covert operations mounted by these agencies. It is tempting to treat this situation as a matter only of 'rogue' or roguish states, such as Syria, but this approach is misleading. The major role of the CIA in American activity in Afghanistan, Cambodia and Nicaragua in the 1980s, for example supporting the Contra rebels against Nicaragua, indicated that the pursuit of hostile policies toward Soviet-backed governments also had wider consequences for American diplomacy. Diplomacy more narrowly defined as appropriate action similarly risks excluding too much from consideration, not least by taking what was regarded as appropriate in a particular context and applying it more widely. As an aspect, for example, of representation to the wider Cuban public subsequently judged inappropriate, the American embassy in Cuba, during the presidency of George W. Bush (2001–9), prominently displayed an electronic billboard that was used to pass news that breached the Cuban government's censorship. In turn, the Cuban authorities erected barriers and flew flags to block the messages. In July 2009, during the Obama administration, in an attempt to end an irritant in relations with the government, the billboard was switched off.

In this book, within the terms of the approach of treating diplomacy as a privileged aspect of general systems for information-gathering, representation and negotiation, diplomacy will be considered chronologically in order to make possible both discussion of change and qualitative comments about diplomatic processes. The focus is on the last half-millennium, which was the original agreed scope for the study. This period has been taken not because of any belief that modernity arrived with the sixteenth century, but because European expansion substantially increased the pace with which distant societies were brought into contact, creating a greater and more complex need for information-gathering, representation and negotiation, as well as establishing a degree of tension between these functions and goals. Yet it is also important to look to the deep history of diplomacy; not least in order to avoid the customary Whiggish approach to the subject and, in deciding to do so, I have found much of relevance.

In prehistoric periods, gift exchange in various forms suggests personal relations projected through objects, but diplomacy, and thus diplomats, probably required a state apparatus, which would usually go with writing. Thus there are inscriptions and iconography, for example from Egypt and Mesopotamia, that are highly indicative. Diplomacy, understood in the sense of the peaceful management of international relations, furthered by designated agents, can certainly be traced to Antiquity, where it owed much to political contexts that were similar in some respects to those seen with the development of permanent representation in 1440–1550 CE (Common Era or AD), first in Italy and then in Western Europe.[17] This latter development dominates the literature on diplomacy, but it is instructive to consider the earlier situation. In particular, the numerous states in a small area found in fifteenth-century Italy, especially northern Italy, could also be seen in the city states of ancient Sumer (southern Iraq) from about 2400 BCE, as well as in Greece prior to (and after) Macedonian domination in the late fourth century BCE.

It was important for these states to manage relations with each other and to try to advance their interests. It could also be useful for them to co-operate in order to confront external challenges, as some (but not all) of the Greek states did when threatened by major attacks in 490 and 480 BCE by the Persian Achaemenid empire, which stretched to the Indus and included Egypt and Anatolia. In contrast to their own self-image, the Persian practice of diplomacy was presented by hostile Greeks as employing threats and blandishments in order to ensure compliance with their hegemonic pretensions and their expansionist intentions. Acceptance of Persian pretensions was seen as a means of pursuing this expansion. In practice, however, the Persian demand for 'earth and water', a demand for submission, appears to have been accompanied by a subtle diplomacy that in 480 BCE brought over many of the Greek states. Alongside an imperialist outlook, Persia also had a subtler kind of diplomacy, a combination that was also relevant for later empires, such as those of China as well as nineteenth-century Britain.

Nevertheless, to European commentators of the Renaissance and later, the (Ottoman) Turks, who conquered Constantinople (Istanbul) in 1453 CE, and, both earlier and thereafter, expanded into the Balkans and eventually Central Europe, posed a threat that could be given a parallel and historical validation by comparison with the Persians of Antiquity. Indeed, the Persian demand for the symbolic surrender of the essentials of life, one fulfilled when the states that submitted sent embassies literally carrying earth and water,[18] provided an appropriate note of menace.

In turn, diplomacy in the fifteenth and sixteenth centuries could be dignified as a defence of civilization against the barbarians, not least by reference to the Classical Greeks. Indeed, looking back to Greek co-operation against the Persians, and continuing medieval patterns, notably, but not only, those associated with the Crusades, the negotiation of peace between Christian powers could be seen as a way to prepare for conflict with the non-Christian outsider, more specifically the Turks. Moreover, the stereotypes of Antiquity accepted by and from the Renaissance – of peaceful and cultured Greeks, nasty Persians, and bullying (as well as noble) Romans – took precedence over the more significant but mundane differences that did exist, for example in degrees of centralization and scope of state (as opposed to personal) interest, as well as in the extent of *laissez-faire* ideology. These differences were not the ones harped on in later centuries by those with their own axes to grind and their potent cultural assumptions.

The similarities in international conduct between Classical Greece and Renaissance Italy supported, but were not responsible for, the ideological and cultural appeal of the actual (or implied) comparison. Indeed, texts related to diplomacy produced in Europe during the Renaissance, as well as subsequently, made reference to Classical precedents. This practice was particularly the case in advancing rules, as these precedents were seen to bring validation. The French lawyer Pierre Ayrault published in 1576 *L'Ordre, Formalité et Instruction Judiciaire dont les anciens Grecs et Romains ont usé ès accusations publiques conferé au stil et usage de nostre France*, a work in which the idea of extra-territoriality, a key basis for diplomatic immunity, was advanced.

Similarly, as another parallel across the centuries, although not one with a comparable cultural resonance, the larger competing European states of the period of the Italian Wars (1494–1559 CE), notably France, Spain and Austria, can be compared with those of the Fertile Crescent, especially Egypt and Mesopotamia (Iraq), in the first two millennia BCE. The key comparisons were that these competing states were engaged in a struggle for regional hegemony and were in large part an expression of their rulers.

Documents found in Egypt in 1887 CE, consisting of about 350 letters from the mid-fourteenth century BCE between the Egyptian court of the Eighteenth Dynasty and other states of the ancient Near East, some independent but most vassal, indicate the interdependence of the great powers of the period, and also provide evidence of a wide-ranging diplomatic network with a sophisticated level of dynamics and formalities. The correspondence relates to status, ranking and prestige, both in absolute terms, vis-à-vis Egypt, and in relative terms, vis-à-vis each other relative to Egypt.

The root metaphors involved gift-exchange and family/blood/kinship ties, and, although these reciprocities ideally symbolized equality, in reality they did not, not least because the fundamental marriage tie was asymmetrical in favour of Egypt, in a ranking lubricated by prestige considerations. Again there are instructive comparisons with later periods of diplomatic activities. Moreover, royal marriage was to be a theme of abiding central importance for international relations until the nineteenth century.

However, in Egyptian Amarna-period diplomacy, despite frequent references to brotherhood and family, the kings showed little inclination toward problem-solving based on improving the culture of diplomatic discussion. Indeed, by the standards of (later) Classical Greece (not that these were without serious flaws), the diplomacy of the Amarna period was fairly crude, not least because it was unable to sustain a high level of clear and nuanced communication, even in those channels where it flowed most smoothly. Yet the links that existed indicate that in the presence of a balance, or at least sharing, of power among interdependent states, there will be pressure for a diplomacy that can provide a degree of effectiveness; a point that was to be relevant for the subsequent development of diplomacy.

At the same time, and again this was to be a characteristic feature of much diplomacy, the international language of diplomacy and marriage in the late Bronze Age Near East had deceptive aspects:

> The various ethnic and linguistic entities knew that their neighbors had different customs and saw the world from a different (inferior!) point of view. The lingua franca and international marriages allowed sufficient ambiguity and imprecision so that those who

participated as equals could actually appear so on the international stage. But the ambiguity and cultural games allowed each of the Great Kings [of Egypt] to rest satisfied that the others did not really measure up to the stature that each envisioned for himself.[19]

The diplomacy of the Near East, of the Hittite Empire, which flourished in Anatolia from about 1450 to 1200 BCE, for example, as well as of Egypt, is instructive, and also saw the use of diplomatic forms and agents still found today, such as interpreters;[20] but European diplomatic practice should rather be traced to Classical Greece. Indeed, diplomacy takes its name from the diploma (folded letter) of the Greeks. This descent, however, occurred via the intermediaries of the imperial systems of Rome and Byzantium, both of which in practice looked more to concepts of imperial hegemony and rivalry than to the Greek inheritance.

This Greek inheritance included concepts such as neutrality, methods such as arbitration, and practices such as diplomatic immunity for heralds and providing envoys with credentials. The Greek god Hermes (the Roman Mercury) was for a long time to be linked with diplomacy as symbol and protector. He was frequently depicted as a messenger bearing a herald's staff. Immunity for envoys and their accredited staff was taken further by the Romans, although their focus tended to be military.

The Greeks were also well-practised in the diplomacy of alliances, not least through the creation of leagues. As a reminder of the extent to which the diplomatic world of Europe was for a long time a matter of continuity or revival, rather than new departures, these leagues provided an anticipation to the leagues of Renaissance Italy and the Italian Wars of 1494–1559, although there had already been significant anticipations in the Middle Ages, notably with the Lombard League of the late twelfth century. Indeed, Milanese sources of the eleventh century sometimes appealed rather directly to the Roman republican past against the imperial pretensions of the Germans: there was also a ready parallel between the Lombard cities grouping together against the Holy Roman Emperors, with their power based to the north, and the Greek cities seeking how best to resist Persian and, later, Macedonian pressure, the last also from the north. At the same time, in all three cases, there were serious rivalries between the cities themselves, and these interacted to a great degree with the challenge from outside.

Alongside special envoys, the Greeks used *proxenoi* in cities to represent the interests of other city states: for example a citizen of Athens representing Corinth's interests in Athens.[21] Moreover, hostages were for long employed as guarantors of agreements, and indeed were used within European diplomacy in the Peace of Aix-la-Chapelle of 1748 (CE). This continuity might not seem as attractive as some of the other diplomatic practices traced to Antiquity.

At the same time, and as a reminder of the problems posed by the standard account with its teleological drive, there were serious limitations with Greek diplomacy. Given the practice of seeing this diplomacy as an anticipation of that of Renaissance Italy, any emphasis on these limitations may also be taken as offering an instructive approach to the later period. A positive account of the Greek situation would emphasize the basic customs that were normally followed, such as the sacrosanctity of ambassadors, and would note the friendly interactions based on the fictive kinship of states, the trade that occurred between states, and the emergency coalitions of 480 and 338 BCE against the Persians and Philip II of Macedon (the father of Alexander the Great) respectively. The Aetolian League was active in the 200s BCE in opposition to the expansionism of Philip V of Macedon. Attention would also be devoted to the efforts made to improve relations between states, including many attempts at third-party mediation, and even arbitration. Furthermore, there were calls for improved behaviour, including observing treaties sworn to the Gods, from a number of Greek writers such as Thucydides, Plato and Polybius.

Yet these points can also be qualified. For example such arguments stemmed from an understanding that there was something very wrong in the current character of interstate exchanges, with attitudes and practices both at issue, if not fault. In reality, no major ancient state, Greek, Roman or other, accepted mediation, while there were no permanent envoys and the indigenous, unofficial friends in other cities who were used could not remedy the situation: they were unofficial, and also haphazard. In 427 bad and self-interested information from such *proxenoi* helped create a crisis between the city states of Athens and Mytilene. The lack of a continual flow of reliable information from one polity to another ensured a degree of opacity.

Moreover, when resort was had to diplomacy, in the shape of the dispatch of official envoys, it was often only when a crisis in relations had already arisen, and this diplomacy was characteristically bellicose. It often consisted of threats and employed a very blunt diplomatic language. In short, what political scientists term 'compellence diplomacy' was a habitual Greek style. In addition, since Greek societies were slave-owning honour societies, and no one wished to be or to appear to be 'slave-like' by compromising, let alone giving in, the style of Greek diplomacy contributed to the onset of wars; an instance of the key role of cultural factors.

Contrary to later idealized notions, Greek states were regularly imperialistic, Athens, Sparta, Corinth and Thebes proving some of the bigger players, although, compared to Persia, the scale of their imperialism was small. There was a different, but related, strand of diplomacy in terms of the construction of alliances, but alliance systems, such as the Delian League (founded in 478 BCE), the rival Peloponnesian League, and the Achaean League were, in large part, covers for the domination of one-city state (Athens, Sparta and Corinth respectively). Indeed, alongside their development of diplomacy, the Greeks, like the moderns, also invented a critique of it, when Thucydides, the historian of the Peloponnesian War, argued that, whatever they claimed, Athenian diplomacy was actually crude, bullying and, like that of Persia, a touchstone of the unacceptable. Furthermore, the league of 480 (BCE) against Persia was composed of a minority of the city states; the others either tried to remain neutral or, notably Boeotia and Thessaly, compromised with the Persians.[22]

Relations with the states based in what is now Iran also caused problems for the Romans, for, unlike Alexander the Great, they were unable to conquer first the Parthian Empire and then its Sassanian replacement. In his *Life of Sulla*, Plutarch noted how Lucius Sulla, then Proconsul of the province of Cilicia in South-East Asia Minor, in or about 92 BCE, reinstated the pro-Roman king Ariobarzanes in neighbouring Cappadocia. In addition,

> he spent some time by the [River] Euphrates and while he was there he received a visit from Orobazus a Parthian, who came as an ambassador from King Arsaces. Up to this time there had been no relations of any kind between Rome and Parthia . . . It is said that on this occasion Sulla ordered three chairs to be brought out – one for Ariobarzanes, one for Orobazus and one for himself – and that he himself sat on the middle chair and so gave them audience. As a result of this the King of Parthia afterwards put Orobazus to death. As for Sulla, while some people praised him for making the natives[23] eat humble pie, others regarded his behaviour as a vulgar and ill-timed display of arrogance.[24]

The episode indicated the difficulty of establishing appropriate diplomatic mechanisms to deal with states of similar stature, and most particularly for empires not used to dealing with such states.

In turn, consideration of the diplomacy of Byzantium, the Eastern Roman Empire based on Constantinople that lasted until 1453, serves as a reminder of the varied strands in the Classical tradition, as well as of the difficulty in ensuring appropriate conduct. Thus embassies from Theodosius II to the threatening Huns in 412 (CE) and 449 were compromised by attempts to assassinate key figures, including, in 449, Attila.[25] As an instance of continuity across the subsequent medieval/early-modern divide, as well as that between the Classical and medieval worlds, Constantinople was the capital of the (medieval) Byzantine empire and, from 1453, of the (early-modern) Ottoman (Turkish) one.

Alongside the civic and imperial traditions in diplomacy, crudely those of Greece and Rome, came an ecclesiastical one, and again there were cultural consequences. The collapse of the Western Roman Empire in the fifth century, and its replacement by a number of 'Barbarian' kingdoms, such as Francia, left the Church not only as the supra-national body in Western Europe but also as the one disposing of the most educated and politically knowledgeable individuals. Clerics thus played a key role in medieval European diplomacy, and even when others were significant, it was still the case that Christian concepts were very important to the understanding of the nature of international relations.

For the Latin West, there is evidence for a good deal of diplomatic activity in the early medieval period, but the complicating factor is that most of the evidence is based on narrative texts rather than the letters later used as evidence. Liudprand's accounts of his embassies to Byzantium in 950 (very favourable) and 968 (very unfavourable) are an instance of the problem this creates as they reflect the different audience he was writing for, and are thus, in large part, a product of the Italian politics of the period. Born into an Italian noble family, Liudprand was Bishop of Cremona. His father had been ambassador for King Hugh of Arles and Italy. Liudprand was sent to Constantinople in 950 by King Berengar of Italy, being accompanied by an ambassador of Otto I, King of East Frankia. In 968 Liudprand went for a second time, this time as an ambassador of Otto, now Holy Roman Emperor.[26]

Central to Christian concepts about diplomacy was a belief in the unity of Christendom, and thus in a general good, and a related commitment to securing peace. This was frequently expressed in terms of preparing for a crusade,[27] a key episode of international action in accordance with idealistic goals, but with the identity, norms and goals of the international system defined in accordance with Christianity. This commitment provided an exegesis for the role of diplomats that saw them as fulfilling a duty that was quasi-religious, an approach that gave them a necessary defence against obstructions and against more active attempts to hinder diplomacy. This was the approach taken in the first Western European tract solely on diplomats, the *Ambaxiator Brevilogus* [*Short Treatise on Ambassadors*] (1436) by the French diplomat Bernard du Rosier, a cleric who eventually became Archbishop of Toulouse.

This career pattern can be seen with many diplomats, while others came from a legal background. The development of the law was indeed important to that of diplomacy. In the late twelfth and early thirteenth centuries, the growing application of Roman law in legal processes was linked to the ability of those in authority to empower others for specific tasks. As a formal legal act, it became possible to appoint a proctor (*procurator*) who had a mandate which defined his powers to negotiate. Such appointments, which are documented from the early thirteenth century, dealt mainly with litigation.[28] The ability to entrust others readily with the right to commit to agreements was not specifically linked to diplomacy, but was important to diplomatic culture and practice. This development indicates the importance of the medieval period in the evolution of diplomacy. The need for the legal and bureaucratic skills of the age was also seen with the use of the notaries and secretaries of the royal chancellery, who tended to support the more socially exalted diplomats.

An understanding of medieval European diplomacy benefits from an awareness that it was far from primitive and far from unchanging. Instead, there is a need for an appreciation of the dynamic aspects of medieval diplomacy, while noting that evidence of change owes something to changes in the evidence. For example, prior to the middle of the twelfth century, precise information on the methods used by English rulers to communicate and negotiate with foreign heads of state is very difficult to come by, and as a result, no study of English diplomatic practice during that period can hope to offer more than suggestions.

In Europe as a whole, correspondence between rulers seems to have been a key means of diplomacy,[29] while their meetings, such as that of Louis the German and his brother, Charles of West Frankia, in 870, provided a key opportunity for negotiations. The 'summit conference' was already in evidence in the twelfth century, notably with the Peace of Venice of 1177, when Frederick Barbarossa, the Holy Roman Emperor, Pope Alexander III, the representatives of the Lombard League, and the envoys of William II, the King of Naples and Sicily, met to conclude a mutual peace and to end the papal schism begun in 1159. Moreover, the protected status of ambassadors was already established by then, to judge by Barbarossa's complaints when the Byzantine Emperor Isaac Angelos arrested Frederick's envoys in 1189. It is all too easy to downplay the scale and expertise of high medieval diplomacy. The former, for example, is indicated by the intense diplomacy at the papal court and involving Louis VII of France, sparked by the career of Thomas Becket as Archbishop of Canterbury (1162–70).

In part, the dynamic aspects of diplomacy reflected the need to adjust to changing circumstances that had direct implications for diplomacy. Notable instances included the role of the Papacy as an organizing principal, and would-be coordinator, for Western Christendom. Thus Pope Gregory

VII (r. 1073–85) sent An Nazir of Tunis a very diplomatic letter on behalf of the Christians of North Africa. Changing circumstances included the extent to which lay rulers had to define their position with reference to the Papacy, which, notably in Italy, had secular as well as spiritual pretensions, in so far as the two could be separated; and also the developing modes of communication between Byzantium, Islam and the West.[30]

In Western Europe, an understanding by lay rulers of the distinction between foreign and domestic in terms of territoriality was important to a sense of independent political legitimacy, and thus foreign policy.[31] Rulers had to define their position towards the Holy Roman Emperor, which, from its revival under Charlemagne (r. 768–814), claimed an overlordship over Western Christendom. The idea of a Christian empire, as expressed by ninth-century commentators such as Jonas of Orléans and Hincmar of Rheims, became influential as a notion of statehood.

Ideas of overlordship were not restricted to the Holy Roman Empire, and also affected other royal meetings, so that they became occasions for the rituals that marked relationships as well as for negotiations. In 1031 Cnut, king of both England and Denmark, advanced to the River Tay, receiving the submission of Malcolm II of Scotland, which reaffirmed the claims of the Crown of England to overlordship while also securing Malcolm's support against Norway.

Meetings also provided opportunities for the gift-giving and one-upmanship that both expressed and complicated issues of prestige and equality. Within the overall emphasis on dynastic considerations, there was much concern with these factors. As is usual in systems of competitive honour, there was a complex mix of competitive prestige, often on very symbolic and trivial points of honour, within an overall presumption of equality. In practice, this presumption, combined with an ethic of competition, produced a touchy honour in which rulers were constantly vigilant about one-upmanship, yet while also seeking to achieve it. This situation was especially an issue when one monarch claimed that another owed him homage, as in the difficult relations between the King of France and the King of England (as Duke of Gascony) in the lengthy run-up to the Hundred Years War which began in the 1330s.

The search for allies was also an important aspect of medieval diplomacy. For example, successive kings of England, notably from the early thirteenth century on, but also earlier, sought the support of German rulers and the princes of the Low Countries, such as the Counts of Flanders and Hainault, in their frequent struggles with the kings of France. King John in the 1200s turned to Otto IV, the Holy Roman Emperor, in an unsuccessful attempt to defeat Philip Augustus of France, and this as part of a diplomacy that encompassed the Papacy and power-politics in Italy.[32]

Such far-flung diplomacy was also very important under Edward I (r. 1272–1307) and Edward III (r. 1327–77), and continued thereafter. In 1391 Anglo-French negotiations were linked with the possibility of a French invasion of Italy.[33] In 1474 Edward IV sent John Morton, a cleric who was Master of the Rolls, in an attempt to win the support of Emperor Frederick III against Louis XI of France. By the close of the Middle Ages, a sophisticated system of English diplomacy has been detected, although there was less uniformity in detail than a general evolutionary schema might suggest.[34]

In turn, English policy was countered, from the close of the thirteenth century, by the French attempt to create an axis with Scotland. Both sides also pursued allies in Iberia, notably in the late fourteenth century, and with dynastic ambitions intertwined with power politics, especially in the struggle for control of Castile and in seeking to benefit from the troubled relations between Portugal and Castile. Indeed, power politics were often an expression of these dynastic ambitions, which helped explain the importance of marital diplomacy and of meetings between monarchs linked to marriages, such as that of Richard II of England and Isabella, daughter of Charles VI of France, in 1396, a marriage that followed an extension of the truce between the two kingdoms.

Dynasticism was a central issue in medieval diplomacy. The major concerns were who married whom, what marriage agreements looked like, who inherited what, and who else had claims on what they inherited, and what was offered as dowries and how these terms were enforced. Dynasticism also focused on legal claims to territory often drawn from property and family law, a feature central in European diplomacy and one that remained highly significant into the mid-eighteenth century, with important continuities thereafter. Rulers pursued goals that had a basis in law, as with French claims to Naples and Sicily, which were asserted from the late thirteenth to the mid-sixteenth century. Raw force was weak at the expense of other Christian rulers unless supporting a claim, although force was required to enforce these claims. The role of dynastic considerations helps explain why *herrschernähe* (familiarity with the ruler) was a key element in the appointment of diplomats.

The importance of dynasticism can be seen in the way it influenced papal diplomacy. First, popes engaged in dynastic politics for the interest of their own family which remained clearly the case into the seventeenth century, with popes such as Urban VIII (r. 1623–44) providing yet another qualification of the mistaken notion that Renaissance Italy ushered in a sea-change in diplomacy. Notwithstanding rumours about Boniface VIII (r. 1294–1303), most medieval popes after Gregory VII (1073–85) were personally pretty virtuous, especially about sex, but there was no need to be decadent like the second Borgia pope (Alexander VI, r. 1492–1503) in order to try to benefit nephews and other family members. Popes such as Innocent IV (r. 1243–54), who wrote dense treatises on canon law as well as proclaiming the Seventh Crusade in 1244, also engaged in dynastic politics.

The papacy's diplomatic power in part came from its place in the system of marriage and inheritance. In the long term, the pope's ability to interfere in dynastic events, by granting both dispensations to marry within prohibited degrees, a key element given the interrelationship of ruling families, and annulments, was a much more powerful threat to lay rulers than excommunication. Kings and communities could endure the latter for years. England was placed under papal interdict by Innocent III in 1208 and King John was excommunicated in 1209, but he did not give in until 1213.[35] Papal dynastic decisions were not always obeyed, as kings could, and did, ignore papal strictures on matters such as prohibited degrees; but papal stubbornness in granting a dispensation or an annulment could disrupt a monarch's plans for years, as was to be seen with Henry VIII of England, and monarchs might compromise a lot to get what they wanted from the pope in this sphere.

Power politics were intertwined with papal diplomacy, as with the Papal Schism (1378–1417), when, and not for the first time, there were rival popes. Thus it is clear that international combinations and negotiations were matters of considerable complexity and required skill. The permutations of international relations were increased by the range of dynastic interests and by the far-flung concerns of rulers, for example the Mediterranean policy of those of France.

Diplomatic representation played a key role not only in the practical field of negotiation, but also in terms of advancing and securing status. The last was important as a means of pursuing sovereignty but, short of that, there were still important advantages in interests and status to be gained by the use of diplomatic mechanisms.

A classical way to treat the Middle Ages as primitive is to see the usage of such mechanisms in a system of shared sovereignty, presided over by the Holy Roman Emperor and the Papacy, as flawed. In particular, the sharing of sovereignty and the notion of oversight are treated as anachronistic from the perspective of the Westphalian system, the term employed to describe ideas and methods of European diplomacy that prevailed from the Peace of Westphalia in 1648. That approach, however, seems far less secure from the perspective of modern constitutional mechanisms, notably in Europe, where the European Union is, in both theory and practice, a system of shared sovereignty, and thus oversight, and one moreover that opens up a new sphere for diplomacy.

Diplomatic relations developed in the Middle Ages, and not only in Europe, to address needs and opportunities in immediate contexts, rather than to handle the far less common possibility of continuous distant links. There was no single moment or cause of the development of permanent diplomatic contacts in Europe, but the major cause seems to have been the need to improve the reporting of foreign states, rather than to handle negotiations, as the latter did not require such permanence. The relative governmental sophistication of the Italian states in the fifteenth century provided a key context, but it is necessary to balance this with the context provided by their propinquity and acute rivalries and opportunistic alliances, as well as to consider the earlier situation. As so often, it is easy to note changes and to offer explanations, but choosing between these explanations, or, rather, assessing their relative weight, is far more problematic.

The institutional sources for permanent diplomatic contacts were medieval European, part of the wider difficulty in any history of diplomacy of separating the medieval from the early modern. The key source here was the greater frequency and length of the medieval pattern of short-term embassies, combined with specific features of the Papal and Venetian systems. Aside from an extensive issue of papal letters, the Papacy not only had representatives in other courts but also received representatives from their rulers, although the bureaucratic regularity implied by such a description needs to be handled with care. While the role of the papal court, in Rome or Avignon, as the seat of business and the source of (often hard-won) favours, encouraged representation, this process also indicated a lack of specialization that was more generally true of diplomacy as other interests were also represented.

Thus Andrea Sapiti, a notary public for the Frescobaldi banking and trading company of his native Florence, in addition acted for a number of English interests at the Papal curia at a time when the Frescobaldi were the leading company of foreign merchants permitted to do business in England. From 1313 Andrea represented Edward II and Edward III at the papal court of Avignon, but he also helped English petitioners until he was replaced in 1334. Ottone, one of his sons, was to represent the commune of Florence at the papal curia in 1350.[36]

Papal representatives were termed nuncios, a reference to the role of envoys as message-bearers; while representatives from other rulers, proctors (or *procuratores*), were by the fifteenth century occasionally called ambassadors.[37] Proctors were also employed at the courts of other lay rulers, as by the rulers of England, as Dukes of Aquitaine, at the court of the kings of France.

Papal nuncios were a key element in a system that produced large numbers of papal letters, and also included a sophisticated Papal Chancery that was reorganized by Innocent III (r. 1198–1216), a Pope very much concerned with power politics and with extending the power of the Papacy. In part, this extension was a matter of litigation, notably through issuing decretals; and the major judicial role of judges delegate and of papal legates underlines the difficulty of distinguishing diplomacy as a separate activity. Innocent's chancery provided a bureaucratic regularity, hitherto lacking in much papal government, and also helped set a pattern for bureaucratic practice elsewhere in Christian Europe. The registers of letters to and from the Papacy survive from 1198, and provided an institutional memory that was diplomatic as much as legal for the longstanding conflict with the Holy Roman Emperors.[38]

In addition, the original chancery register of Gregory VII (r. 1073–85) survives, as do copies of that of Gregory I (r. 590–604) and of part of that of John VIII (r. 873–82); the latter were almost certainly made during the pontificate of Gregory VII. Under John of Gaeta, Papal Chancellor from *c*. 1089 to 1118, when he was elected Pope as Gelasius II, there was a significant period of reform at the chancery. The role of the chancery serves as a reminder that diplomacy as a bureaucratic system required not only permanent or semi-permanent embassies, but also a directing office enjoying institutional continuity. Separating the two is possible but not always helpful.

The multiple diplomatic role of the Papacy included its financial power, as in granting tithes for royal use. The Papacy also operated at a range of geographical levels. In Italy, there was the diplomacy involved in the protection and aggrandisement of the Papal States, as well as the papal role in giving cohesion to opposition to the Holy Roman Emperors. The Papacy was also able to grant title where none, or not much of one, existed, as when Charles of Anjou was made King of Sicily in 1266. This theme was taken forward in 1494 when, by a papal decree, Alexander VI established the Treaty of Tordesillas dividing the Western Hemisphere between Spain and Portugal. This treaty was pronounced by the Spaniards when they arrived in a new land.

The Venetians also kept representatives abroad, notably the *bailo* at Constantinople. His function was that of commercial agent and representative of the merchant community, but he also reported on developments both at Constantinople and more widely, and thus helped shape policy. The *baili*, moreover, were entrusted with negotiations that were not held to merit a special embassy, a process which was slow as well as expensive.

Knowledge of the papal and Venetian systems probably prompted innovations by other Italian rulers, but their resident envoys also marked an important departure, as their status was different, being that of an envoy rather than a privileged representative. Indeed, the major innovation in the fifteenth century was to come not from the Papacy nor Venice, but from the Italian princes, notably the Dukes of Milan. The first book devoted to resident envoys, *De Officio Legati [On the Office of Ambassador]* (1490), was by the Venetian Ermolao Barbaro, who had served on a special mission to the Emperor Frederick III and as resident envoy in Milan and Rome.

Continuities and discontinuities in diplomacy should not only be probed within Europe. They also pertained in the case of relations with non-Christian powers. The key relationship was that with Islam. The stage of continual conflict between Christendom and Islam passed rapidly, and thereafter, against a background of confrontation and conflict that varied a great deal, there was a need to devise diplomatic practices. Charlemagne had diplomatic relations with the Abbasid court of Baghdad, which lay behind his expedition to Umayyad Spain in 778: the latter rejected the authority of Baghdad.

Diplomatic relations with the Islamic states in Iberia proved of particular importance, and Jews were frequently employed as intermediaries. These links also served as means of cultural transmission as when the future Pope Sylvester II (r. 999–1003) visited Moorish Spain in the 960s and showed an interest in Moorish knowledge. In about 950 Otto I, King of East Frankia/Germany (from 936), of Italy from 951, and, from 962, the Holy Roman Emperor, who ruled the German-speaking lands and northern Italy, sent an embassy to the Caliph Abd-al-Rahman III in Cordova, probably to ask the Caliph to limit raiding from the Moorish base at Fraxinetum in Provence, raiding that threatened Otto's territories in northern Italy. The Caliph's reply, dispatched with a bishop, was regarded as highly offensive to Christianity and the emissaries were detained for three years as virtual prisoners in Germany.

When Otto released them, he sent another letter to the Caliph, one prepared by his brother, Bruno, Archbishop of Cologne. Insulting to Islam, the letter was carried by a monk, John of Görze, who apparently sought martyrdom, a very different goal to that of most modern envoys, and one that demonstrates the need for care when emphasising continuities and tracing developments in the long term. Arriving in Cordova in 953 or 954, Görze's message and attitudes led to an impasse in which John was left in cloistered seclusion, prevented from presenting his letter to the Caliph.

This impasse was solved when Recemundus or Rabi ibn Sa'id, a Cordovese Catholic who held a post in the Caliph's administration, went on a mission to Otto in Frankfurt. As a result, more diplomatic letters were sent back with Recemundus in 956, and John was authorized to provide presents to the Caliph and not to hand over the original letter. Recemundus was rewarded with a bishopric in al-Andalus (Moorish Spain), and later went on missions to Byzantium, Jerusalem and Syria,[39] a reminder of the far-flung nature of the diplomatic links of the major Islamic powers. Similarly, Sallam the Interpreter had travelled widely as the representative of the Baghdad-based Abbasid Caliph in the mid-ninth century. Cordova under Abd-al-Rahman III also received embassies from Byzantium and Baghdad.

The entire episode suggested the need for forbearance in trying to make a success of cross-cultural diplomatic relations. With time, relations between Christian and Islamic states became more predictable,[40] not least as each not only signed agreements with the other, but moreover, notably in Iberia and also in the Crusading East, sought to exploit rivalries among the other bloc by negotiating agreements. This process was seen at the time of the First Crusade. After the crusaders' capture of Nicaea from the Seljuk Turks in June 1097 the Byzantine Emperor, Alexius I Comnenus, advised the crusaders to send a mission to the Seljuks' bitter rival, Fatimid Egypt. In February/March 1098, a Fatimid embassy returned to Antioch, which had by then been seized by the crusaders, and the embassy appears to have come to a provisional arrangement against the Seljuks of north Syria. The crusaders, however, broke this arrangement in May 1099 when they entered the Fatimid lands to seize Jerusalem.

Thereafter, diplomacy remained very important during the crusading period. For example, after the death of Saladin in 1193, his family, the Ayyubids, divided, roughly between Syria and Egypt; and this division was exploited by the crusaders. In particular, the Holy Roman Emperor Frederick II, who embarked on the Sixth Crusade in 1228, achieved the liberation of Jerusalem (where he crowned himself king in 1229) through diplomacy, not conflict, concluding a truce with the Sultan of Cairo which both restored Jerusalem to Christian control and established peace for ten years.[41] Subsequently the crusaders, notably Louis IX of France (r. 1226–70), made intense efforts to achieve an alliance with the Mongols against the local Muslim rulers, especially the Mamluk Sultanate of Egypt, which had overthrown the Ayyubids: there were repeated attempts to enlist the Il-Khanids, the Mongol rulers established in Persia, who indeed fought the Mamluks and were looking for allies against them. Arghun, the Il-Khan, sent embassies to the West in the 1280s and 1290, calling for joint action, and Edward I sent a message in reply in 1292, but by then Arghun was dead, and his successor displayed little interest.[42]

These efforts looked toward Western (in the sense of Christian Europe) attempts to win the support of Timur (Tamerlane) in the 1390s and 1400s, of Aqquyunlu Persia in the late fifteenth century, and of Safavid Persia in the sixteenth and seventeenth centuries, in each case against the Ottoman Turks.⁴³ Timur, who heavily defeated the Ottoman Turks at Ankara in 1402, appeared a particularly good option. The King of Aragon sent an envoy, Clavijo, and Timur used him in his diplomacy with the envoys from Ming China, primarily to offend them by giving Clavijo a higher seat of honour.⁴⁴

Aside from its impact on power politics in the Near East,⁴⁵ the crusading movement lay in the background of much medieval European diplomatic activity, and especially that of the Papacy. Nevertheless, although still significant,⁴⁶ crusading became less important after the death of Louis IX of France in 1270, while the extent to which the popes began to use crusades as a weapon against non-heretical Christians compromised the cause. As with Human Rights today, many leaders and officials probably felt genuinely guilty about not doing more to fulfil their crusading rhetoric; but there were often too many vital interests at stake for them to do more than feel guilty.

At the local level, and with more general reference to the culture and processes of diplomacy, the extent to which both Iberia and the Crusading East were characterized by 'societies in symbiosis', such as thirteenth-century Valencia, was also significant in encouraging a process of negotiation.⁴⁷ Marriage alliances were important to the diplomacy between Christians and Moors, notably in the ninth to eleventh centuries.⁴⁸ Moreover, trade was a powerful motive in encouraging the negotiation of treaties, as between the major commercial republic of Genoa and Tunis in the thirteenth century

On the other hand, there was a clear discontinuity between medieval and early-modern Western contact with the Indian states. Vasco da Gama's arrival in Indian waters in command of Portuguese ships in 1498 marked a new departure. Furthermore, whereas the polities encountered by the Spaniards in the West Indies from the 1490s and by the Portuguese in coastal Africa could be treated, however misleadingly, as less developed than those of Europe, and moreover, attempts could be made to conquer them, in the case of India it was not possible to regard states such as Gujarat in this light.

There were of course distant links between Christendom and non-European societies prior to the late fifteenth century, and these links are worthy of attention. For example, Christendom's search for allies against Islam, or rather, against the most prominent Islamic opponents, led to the pursuit of diplomatic relationships in Asia and Africa, notably with the Mongols and with Abyssinia (Ethiopia), the land of the mythical Prester John. The dispatch of a mission to Europe by Emperor Zara Yakob of Abyssinia in 1450 was welcomed in Europe, but Mamluk Egypt tried to block links. In part, Portuguese maritime expansion to West Africa in the fifteenth century was also designed to secure allies and resources, especially gold, for use against the Moors.

Thus there was no abrupt shift in the sixteenth century toward a more distant diplomacy, but there was a marked quickening of pace as new opportunities were pursued. As a reminder, however, of continuities, this search was in part still directed against Islamic opponents. Morocco remained a key opponent for Portugal, and yet also a sphere for operations including the negotiation of alliances.[49] For Christendom as a whole, however, the major rival was the expanding Ottoman (Turkish) Empire, which controlled the Islamic world bordering Europe from the Crimea (an Ottoman vassal from 1475) to Algiers (from 1528). However, to indicate the complexity of diplomatic relations, both Crimea and Algiers enjoyed considerable autonomy as, in effect, vassals, and negotiated on that basis, both within the Turkish Empire and outside it.

Europeans tended to see and understand the outside world in familiar terms; and there were also powerful, indeed more powerful, continuities in Chinese assumptions of their world. China's ideology, world-view, internal cohesion and foreign policy were scarcely unchanging, not least with varied emphases on overlordship over others. Nevertheless, to the Chinese relations with the Emperor defined the real presence and ranking of foreigners.[50] These relations were maintained by the Chinese in terms of rituals that were very different to those of the great age of European diplomacy in the late nineteenth century, but that, like the latter, very much reflected a common emphasis on established practices and on conventions that maintained and expressed values.

In China the emphasis was much more on the presentation of gifts, reflecting first tribute and then, on the part of the Chinese, approval. This tribute system was intended to ensure minimal foreign relations, and to provide, in particular, for stability in a peaceful system of nominal dependence on the Emperor. The alternative, which was generally not preferred nor sought, was active international relations which would require an active search for co-operation, a process that might compromise the imperial position by implying a need for co-operation. The Chinese system also testified to a more general emphasis on ritual. For example, sacrifices on behalf of the Emperor, as the son of Heaven, to mountains and rivers beyond his rule, represented a claim of imperial sway that included a moral purpose that was seen as a reflection of Chinese superiority.

It is valuable to consider the nature of Chinese tributary relations because they throw light on the range of possible diplomatic cultures and practices during the development of European diplomacy. The position of the Chinese Emperor was confirmed by respect, and this respect was expected from barbarian foreigners as well as the Chinese. Thus a lord and vassal relationship was inscribed as the Chinese view of both domestic and foreign relations. This relationship was seen in the practice of confirming the succession of foreign rulers which ensured, in Chinese eyes, their legitimation as well as their vassalage.

The key relationship was a personal one, between Emperor and tributary rulers; and missions, gifts and letters expressed and confirmed it.[51] In 1044 the Tangut ruler Li Yüan-hao agreed to refer to himself as 'subject' when addressing the Song Emperor, bringing to an end a war that had begun in 1038 when he had proclaimed himself Emperor of the Great Hsia empire and refused to send annual tribute, steps that were unacceptable to the Song.[52]

Similarly in the Mediterranean, concepts of vassalage and tribute were used to demonstrate overlordship and also as the currency of diplomatic links; although the reality of the relationship was frequently different from that expressed in these concepts. From 1269, Charles of Anjou, King of Sicily, referred in diplomatic exchanges to al-Mustansir, the Emir of Tunis, as 'our faithful', but he was certainly not faithful, and the phrase was instead an aspiration to primacy,[53] part of an established diplomatic current. As an acknowledgement of Chinese superiority and suzerainty, each taken as ensuring the other, foreign tributaries wore Ming ceremonial robes. For the Chinese an acknowledgement of cultural superiority was important, and neighbouring peoples were graded by this standard.

Parallels could be found in other imperial systems. Thus Byzantium treated neighbours as barbarians and sought to impress them with display and ceremonial and, in doing so, to bind them within a subordinate relationship in which they accepted the hierarchical notions of Byzantium. Display and ceremonial, for which a classic example is the description in the Russian Primary Chronicle of the reception of an embassy in the 960s, were key elements of the cultural core of Byzantine control, for modern ideas of defined frontiers clearly demarcating areas of distinct sovereignty, each with equal rights, were absent. Instead, the acknowledgement of control or overlordship was crucial to Byzantium. Moreover, display and ceremonial were an aspect of the conspicuous consumerism and pleasure that could help Byzantium achieve its diplomatic goals, notably by providing psychological sway over impressionable visitors, a longstanding theme in the conduct of diplomacy.[54] This sway also reflected the extent to which ceremonial suggested a particularly effective intercessionary role with the Heavens.

The emphasis on majestic court rituals as a means to impress foreign envoys, and also to demonstrate their subjugation, was inherited from Byzantium, like much else, by Muscovy, the self-styled Third Rome, and was practiced there in the fifteenth century.⁵⁵ Yet at the same time, ironically, the Muscovite Grand Dukes had to pay tribute to the Khans of the Crimea.

Display and ceremonial were significant as a means of expressing a world-view, and thus seeking to impose it. Such a culture of diplomacy may appear misleading as well as anachronistic, but ceremony has always been central to the public conduct of diplomacy, and often to its private conduct as well. As far as the former is concerned, tableaux laden with symbolism remain highly significant, as in the placing of leaders in summit photographs, the choice of sites for them to visit, or indeed the dishes and drinks served at state dinners, notably their provenance. Gordon Brown's failure to secure a one-to-one meeting with President Obama during his visit to the USA in September 2009 was seen as a public snub, stemming from American anger over the British release of a Libyan terrorist. The settings of ceremonial have varied greatly, and in the medieval period, it was not only a case of activity inside palaces. Royal hunts were also important, not least, but not only, in Persia, north India and Turkestan.⁵⁶

Although Byzantine notions of international hierarchy offered a coherent world-picture, they could not provide a basis for diplomacy notably – but not only – with states that did not accept their ideology, for example, from the mid-seventh century, Islamic states. In the person of the Caliph, the latter claimed an authority that matched Byzantine pretensions. Indeed, alongside an emphasis on cultural representations of suasion, Byzantium also followed a realist policy, creating a ministry responsible for foreign affairs and containing professional negotiators. Byzantium pursued a very hard-headed, well-informed and practical diplomacy towards its neighbours, largely based on the divide-and-rule principle, especially towards the nomads of the Russian steppe, and later with regard to the Turks in Asia Minor. A handbook for this diplomacy survives in the shape of the *De Administrando Imperio* of Emperor Constantine VII Porphyrogenitus from *c.* 948.⁵⁷ By the reign of Emperor Manuel II (1391–1425), Byzantium had a resident envoy at the Ottoman (Turkish) court, which, however, was also a sign of weakness.

More than cultural and ideological superiority was also at stake for China and, in addition to their notions of superiority, there was a degree of realism in their implementation on the part of the Chinese.⁵⁸ Indeed, alongside the point made earlier that a tributary system was certainly the ideologically preferred mode from Han times (140 BCE–220 CE) onward to the nineteenth century, there were always other precedents that could be applied when necessary. The alternative of an active search for co-operation outside China was adopted on many occasions, as when the Song Emperor Zhenzong reached the Accord of Shanyuan with the invading

Kitan Liao in 1005[59] and when the Song allied with the Jurchens to crush the Kitan Liao on their northern frontier in the early twelfth century.

Much depended on the specific situation and configuration of forces, for Chinese rulers were capable of dealing with other powers in practical terms as de facto equals, and in some periods even approached formal parity in diplomatic practice. Indeed, the Chinese had plenty of precedent for the peer interaction of effectively sovereign states on a basis of formal equality, dating from the long period between the break-up of Zhou rule in the eighth century BCE and the Qin unification in 221 BCE, a period when there had been several states in China, especially in the Warring States period (403–221 BCE).[60]

As with Christian–Muslim relations in the Mediterrean, trade and tribute were related in the complex relations between China and neighbours or near-neighbours, such as Tibet or, in the fifteenth century (CE), the Timurid lands of Central Asia. The offer of goods by envoys and merchants, and the receipt, in return, of Chinese goods provided a way to ensure mutual profit and to disguise official trade. However, this relationship was also unstable, not least (but not only) as it relied on each side finding the same value in the quality or quantity of goods exchanged. This issue, for example, caused major problems in Chinese relations with Central Asia in the early fifteenth century, notably those with Hami and Samarkand.

The Chinese system also faced problems in their neighbours' use of tributary embassies to pursue commercial interests. Thus the Jurchens to the north-east of Ming China (later the basis of the Manchu empire which overthrew the Ming in the seventeenth century) used embassies in order to trade, which both overcame the controlled nature of Chinese trade and also brought profit and prestige to those who took part in the trade. The numbers involved in the embassies posed a problem for the Ming government, which was expected to feed and house them. In this case, the tribute/trade relationship moved against the Chinese, but at the same time it was a way to keep the peace, notably in the early sixteenth century.

In contrast, when there was a breakdown in relations, it frequently focused on the embassies, as in 1466 when the Ming imprisoned and subsequently executed the Jurchen leader, Tung-shan, who had led an embassy to complain about the gifts given by the Chinese in return for tribute. If ritual did not ensure compliance, notably from Vietnam to China, nevertheless the tributary system remained the standard form of Chinese diplomacy, at once rhetoric and technique. Indeed, the ritual of the tributary system could serve to disguise and confirm changes of power that were unwelcome to China, such as Vietnam's conquest of the Cambodian state of Champa in the mid-fifteenth century. In theory, China maintained its moral and practical superiority, but in practice, the tribute system could alleviate tension and anger, which in part was an aspect of the co-existence of contradictory positions, a key skill in diplomatic relationships.

Similar points could be made about other imperial powers, for example Russia. Whereas Russia saw the *shert* as an oath of allegiance by the chiefs of peoples on its frontier, they regarded it as a peace treaty with mutual obligations.[61] Comparable tensions were to arise in relations in North America between Native American tribes and, first, European colonial powers and later the USA.

Yet such a variety of views offered flexibility as well as being a potential cause of tension. In the event, the tributary system was not practised with sufficient flexibility by the Chinese, because they were unable to appreciate the extent to which polities they saw as ruled by barbarians, notably Burma, that were to be defined by the giving of tribute, had in practice become important independent states that had to be taken more seriously. There was also a failure to understand the consequences of the arrival of European powers: their desire for trade ensured that they could be incorporated into the Chinese tributary system, but this process broke down in the nineteenth century.

In the long term, therefore, the Chinese tributary system lacked sufficient flexibility, although the length of time that it lasted suggests that great care must be taken before treating it as an anachronistic ethos and means of diplomacy, and one that was to be proved secondary to, and eventually made obsolete by, that of the Europeans. The last point about obsolescence does not prove that the system was necessarily secondary, or even redundant, in earlier centuries, and a positive re-evaluation of the Chinese system can be seen as an aspect of a more general improvement in Chinese diplomatic history from the 1930s, one characterized by greater Western use of Chinese sources and by a multi-archival approach.[62] In recent decades there has been a greater willingness to appreciate the role of force and militarism in Chinese history, and the extent to which there was a willingness to match methods of conciliation, such as invented kinship arrangements, to claims to universal sovereignty.[63]

Judgements based upon Chinese developments are important as China had a degree of institutional continuity greater than that of other non-Western states; and because similar elements, notably of suzerainty and vassalage, were seen elsewhere, for example in Aztec Mexico and in Ethiopia into the twentieth century;[64] but also as there is a need to address the causes and consequences of Western distinctiveness in the development of residential diplomacy as well as to consider the qualitative value to be attached to it. Outside Europe, there was the diplomacy of special envoys, such as the Khan 'Alam, the Mughal (Indian) envoy to Shah Abbas of Persia in 1613.[65] However, it is argued that the distances separating the major powers (the Mughal and Safavid capitals, Delhi and Isfahan, were separated by the expanses between northern India and western Persia) and the absence of a sense of equality, on the part for example of Chinese Emperors and Ottoman (Turkish) Sultans, affected the use of such envoys and discouraged the development of a comparable system of residential diplomacy. The religious role of these rulers contributed to this situation.[66]

Returning to medieval and early-modern China, international and domestic policies were not clearly differentiated by the Chinese, and this point represents a challenge to any clear-cut discussion of the development of a separate diplomacy, one specific to international relations. For example, across much of China there were large numbers of non-Han people who were only under indirect state control. They were ruled by native chiefs, invested by the imperial government, who provided the state with military service and taxes, and were expected to send tribute missions to Beijing every three years. This situation was scarcely diplomacy as formally understood, and yet it is difficult to see how far this situation can be distinguished from diplomacy in the case of China. To do so implies a clarity about frontiers, independence, the nature of states and the existence of a states system that is inappropriate.[67]

This point about diplomacy within China can be repeated for other non-Western states, for example Mughal India, which very much had internal frontiers,[68] as well as for European states.[69] Indeed, this element in relations and attitudes provided an important continuity in the diplomacy practised by the latter, raising the question of whether foreign policy existed if the bulk of diplomatic activity involved vassals and overlords,[70] and/or relations between neighbouring powers with scant sense of separate statehood.[71] This continuity was notably so as far as 'multiple' states were concerned, those in which monarchs ruled a number of distinct territories, for example the Habsburg monarchy, which, under the Emperor Charles V (r. 1519–56), included Austria, Spain and much of Italy, each in turn divided into many territories with their separate identities and politics.

Yet at the same time as continuities, there were important long-term qualitative developments in the nature of diplomacy within Europe over the last half-millennium that were of eventual importance to the character of diplomacy elsewhere. In part, these developments reflected ideas and practices within an autonomous world of diplomacy, but they were also linked to more wide-ranging themes of bureaucratization including professionalism, specialization, and the acquisition and application of information. The latter relationship, therefore, is one that has to be studied, as are those between diplomacy and globalization, public politics, ideological division and NGOs (non-governmental organizations).

Each of these factors also affected the models that could be employed to analyse or explain both diplomatic conduct and diplomatic duties. There is a tendency to see globalization, public politics, ideological division and NGOs as aspects of the modern world, but this is misleading. For example, to stretch a definition, NGOs were important to the world of ecclesiastical diplomacy, as with the Jesuits or Order of Jesus, an international Catholic clerical order under Papal direction, founded in 1534 as part of the Catholic or Counter-Reformation of the sixteenth century. It had its own structure and negotiated to advance its views and interests within the Church, in the Catholic world,[72] and beyond it, notably in China.

Across the long timespan, it is also important to consider how far the operation and quality of diplomacy helped or hindered the states (and NGOs) that practised it. This question takes on greater weight because states owed success and failure not only to structural factors, such as resources and economic capability, but also to the play of contingency in specific conjunctures.[73] In particular, military success and diplomatic combination interacted, not least due to the role of alliances. These acted as crucial force-multipliers at the same time that they framed and focused commitments, and, therefore, the parameters of diplomatic obligation.

Thus in the Italian Wars (1494–1559), the Habsburgs sought to exploit longstanding English animosity toward France in order to distract French monarchs from their pursuit of Italian ambitions. Simultaneously, the resulting alliances placed the Habsburgs in a situation that had to be managed with care in order to avoid limiting their options. There is a tendency to treat such commitments in 'rational', realist terms, as aspects of a modern states system, but alliances also included dynastic pledges, notably Catherine of Aragon (the aunt of Charles V) as wife to Henry VII of England's two sons, first Arthur (1501) and then, after his death, Henry VIII (1509), as well as Philip II (Charles's son) as husband to the latter's daughter by Catherine, Queen Mary.

Had the latter union of 1554 produced a child, then a new polity would have resulted, with a reshuffling of the cards in the multiple monarchies set. The same was true of the childless union of Francis II of France (r. 1559–60) and Mary, Queen of Scots (r. 1542–87), a marriage (in 1558) that served the French geopolitical goal of fixing Scotland in enmity to England as well as dynastic aims. The failure of these unions to produce either a child or an alliance that survived the marriage serves as a reminder that diplomacy helped make major developments possible but also could only achieve so much.

An emphasis on dynastic considerations could eventually draw attention to an at least latent tension between the sovereign as key player and the development of a sense of political community separate from the monarch. Nevertheless in this period the political system, and thus the designation of goals, remained focused on the monarch. Indeed, royal *gloire* helped to integrate heterogeneous groups into the gradually emergent 'states',[74] and was thus linked to the practice of vassalage at the 'international' level.

Any emphasis on the role of choice in international relations, in commitment, policy and response, necessarily directs attention to specific circumstances, even individuals, and to the ability to appreciate and direct – or at least influence – events. Thus the quality of diplomacy is at issue. This quality relates not only to the insights and ability of diplomats but also to the nature of government, both in general and with specific reference to foreign offices.

There is a Whiggish tendency in many of the synoptic accounts of diplomacy, one that presents a positive developmental model of professionalism and institutional improvement for diplomats and foreign offices, and also reads modern attitudes, goals and systems back into the past.[75] The argument in this book is that this model is insecure. There were changes, but, aside from the customary risk of teleology, judging these changes is made difficult by a lack of clear criteria. For example, a recent account of English diplomacy in the reign of Edward II (1307–27) notes:

> In the light of the later establishment of great power blocs and empires, webs of 'great alliances', and especially modern ideological blocs, much medieval manoeuvring does look short term and ad hoc, but this does not mean foreign affairs were chaotic.

Instead, this account argues that interests were discerned and pursued during that reign with the benefit of effective envoys and appropriate information,[76] an approach that underlines the earlier argument for the previous reign that international diplomacy in this period 'was a skilled and difficult art'.[77] Moreover, it is clear that the characteristics short term and ad hoc also describe much modern foreign policy. The bold ambitions and wide-ranging schemes of many medieval monarchs might appear ridiculous: Henry III of England (r. 1216–72), for example, adding to his interest in securing German help to regain lands lost to France, a project to conquer Sicily as part of an unsuccessful plan to have his brother, Richard of Cornwall, elected Holy Roman Emperor and also to forward a crusade.[78] Yet, albeit presented in different terms, the opportunities, combinations and consequences traced out by many modern leaders are also based on an improbable confidence in their ability to determine events.

Allowing for the caveat that all ages seek a fitness for purpose, there were also improvements in diplomatic practice, but these have to be discussed as part of a complex situation in which attempts to ensure improvement often failed, while diplomatic practices frequently breached institutional standards. These breaches reflected not only administrative faults but also the character of institutions and the nature of politics. To take Brazil, Latin America's leading power, the British envoy in 1907 described the Baron do Rio Branco, a Foreign Minister with a high reputation:

> His slovenliness and untidiness are appalling. His table is covered literally a foot high with documents in their turn covered with dust. This is probably the dust-heap into which disappear many of our carefully prepared private letters and memoranda on pressing matters and possibly even our Notes, of which we never hear anything again.

In 1921 there was another British envoy and another Foreign Minister, but the situation was similar, the former reporting, 'It is difficult to describe the extraordinary sense of ineffectiveness which attaches to all dealing with the Minister.'[79] These flaws, however, did not prevent Brazil from settling its borders with Uruguay, Paraguay, Peru, Ecuador, Colombia, Venezuela, and British, Dutch and French Guiana, nor from playing a role in the First World War and as one of the members of the Council of the League of Nations. Nevertheless, there was scarcely a suggestion that the conduct of the *Itamaraty* (Brazilian Foreign Service) matched the standards that were possible.

Similar comments can be made of the present situation, not least in Britain. Thus Lord Malloch-Brown, United Nations Deputy Secretary General before becoming a Foreign Office Minister in 2008–9, complained that the British government lacked 'strategic thinking' and professionalism.[80]

Such remarks, which can be readily replicated, indicate the need for caution before proposing narratives of clear improvement. Alongside institutional weaknesses, these remarks also direct attention to the primacy of politics in determining diplomatic success. Yet, personal skill also played a part. Jacob Anton van Gansinot, the representative of the Wittelsbach rulers to the United Provinces (Netherlands) from 1716 to 1741, noted in 1728 that it took a long while to win the friendship of the Dutch and required a conformity with their habits, including drinking, eating and smoking. He contrasted his success with that of the recently arrived Austrian envoy, Wenzel, Count Sinzendorf.[81]

Politics in another form, the eventual strength of Western states, and their ability to establish norms, is of consequence because it leads to an obscuring of developments elsewhere. These developments are discussed at some length in this book, in part because of the evidence they offer of differing ways in handling diplomacy and diplomatic roles. Moreover, the continued vitality of non-Western methods into the nineteenth century should qualify the tendency to write of diplomatic method and progress in terms of the diffusion of Western norms.

This tendency also underplays the earlier ability to construct agreements and practices of international law across cultural boundaries without these being based on a clear sense of the superiority of Western models. The establishment of principles of maritime neutrality in the Mediterranean provides a good example, as this neutrality bridged Christendom and Islam and was to be a basis for the declaration on this topic adopted at the Congress of Paris in 1856. These principles were defined and maintained through (Western) European treaties with the North African Barbary powers, although, like the Chinese, the Turks preferred the idea of granting security to Western powers to that of being obliged to come to terms with them.[82] Focus on relations with non-Western powers, on trade, and on the situation at sea, all serve to underline the extent to which the standard narrative of the rise of diplomacy, from Renaissance Italy via the Westphalian settlement of 1648, requires supplementing, which is the key task of this book.

ONE
1450–1600

Diplomatic history is a sphere in which Whiggish ideas of improvability and improvement in a set direction play a key role, and with singularly scant qualification. The standard theme is of improvement understood in terms of bureaucratic processes, notably systematization. This theme is given a particular chronological pattern. In particular, there is a generally negative account of medieval diplomacy and a consequent stress on subsequent new departures. This standard account is heavily teleological, linking the development of modern diplomacy with the theme of strong states, centralized governments and a comprehensive states system.

The most effective exponent of this approach was Matthew Anderson, an expert on the eighteenth century, who, in searching for longer-term development, adopted the standard chronological pattern. Thus, under the heading, 'The origins of modern diplomacy', he began: 'The sixteenth century saw the emergence for the first time of a network of organised diplomatic contacts which linked together more or less continuously the states of western Europe . . . It was in Italy that [the] situation first changed decisively and permanently.'[1]

This approach is in keeping with a more general treatment of medieval and modern, one indeed that can be traced to the Renaissance with its sense of new beginning and its reaching back beyond the medieval to search for appropriate Classical roots, references and models. Yet these judgements have to be qualified both by an understanding of medieval diplomacy, as discussed in the Introduction, and by a consideration of the early modern situation, in so far as the two can be defined satisfactorily.

Indeed, location in terms of late medieval or early modern is not always helpful. There are medieval examples of what are sometimes presented as distinctively modern. Thus, as far as permanence is concerned, there were many years-long embassies by accredited representatives during the Middle Ages[2] and France, for example, had regular diplomatic contacts with Milan, Florence and Naples in the early 1390s.[3] Moreover, some individuals can be seen as diplomatic specialists, knowledgeable about particular countries or dynasties or international negotiations in general. In addition, the reports from medieval envoys could be well informed and observant. Furthermore, there was much discussion of interests, power balances and coalitions. While this discussion tended to be episodic and focused on the immediate situation, and was conducted within a framework that emphasized dynasticism and the politics of status, this situation was also the case as far as the early modern period was concerned.

Yet there were changes in the early modern period. These included the idea that diplomats' work did not put their personal honour at stake, and that they were not supposed to feel personally shamed if their ruler called upon them to lie or if they ended up lying as a consequence of their ruler's actions, which was the position attributed to the Earl of Warwick by Shakespeare (see below). The idea that state (or royal) service could not harm personal honour developed in England about 1500.[4]

The notion that state service removed personal honour from consideration also applied to ideological hostilities, which became very significant with the Wars of Religion within Europe that followed the Protestant Reformation of the sixteenth century. However, underlining the argument in this book that changes in the Renaissance period have been pressed too far by scholars, medieval popes, like their early-modern successors, claimed that normally dishonourable actions in a papally approved cause, for example rebellion against a heretic, did not dishonour the performer of those actions. Furthermore, the continued stress on the appointment of aristocrats as diplomats encouraged, and reflected, a long-standing commitment to personal honour.

Returning to the theme of change, the fragmented political system in Italy, alongside the expansionism of most of the powers, and, more particularly, the determination by seignorial families to establish their position, encouraged conflict. In turn, conflict led to pressure for diplomacy. The Gonzaga and the Visconti played a key role in using resident envoys, with Gian Galeazzo Visconti, Duke of Milan (r. 1378–1402) proving particularly important. His envoys were backed up by an effective chancery which served as an embryonic ministry of foreign affairs. The example of the 'despots' was followed by the republics, notably Venice, and they anchored permanent or resident envoys in a regular system of official diplomatic practice. In 1435 Venice became the first Italian republic to appoint a resident agent, sending Zacharias Bembo to Rome as 'Orator' in order to strengthen the republic against Filippo Maria Visconti.

The lengthy warfare that had followed the collapse of Visconti power with the death, in 1402, of Gian Galeazzo Visconti, culminated in the Peace of Lodi of 1454, which brought the War of the Milanese Succession to a close under the papal mediation of Nicholas V. This peace provided an opportunity for the consolidation of the recent major expansion by Florence and Venice. Like that of Westphalia in 1648, the Peace of Lodi also encouraged a widening of the diplomatic net, as resident diplomacy ceased to be the means to preserve alliances and, instead, was extended to former opponents. The leading Italian states were linked in and by a system of permanent embassies.[5]

This system spread, with the Italians again playing the key role. The coalition politics of war and peace in Western Europe focused on Italy, but bridged with the wider world, not least because of relationships with interests outside Italy. Thus perhaps the first resident envoy was used by Luigi Gonzaga of Mantua at the court of the Holy Roman Emperor, Ludwig (Louis IV) 'the Bavarian' (r. 1314–47). The overlordship the Emperor claimed in northern Italy provided successive Emperors with a major and longstanding role there, a theme that can be traced back to Charlemagne's revival of the Holy Roman Empire in 800.

The Duchy of Milan, which had taken the leading part in developments in Italy, also had a resident envoy in Paris from 1463, followed by one there from Venice in 1479; their first envoys in the London of Henry VII, who made England stronger after the chaos of the Wars of the Roses, arrived in 1490 and 1496 respectively. Sebastian Giustinian was to be an informed reporter on the court of Henry VIII.

The Venetians were to be notable for the writing of *relazioni*, reports from envoys at the end of their mission that offered a complete guide to the state to which they had been accredited, as well as reviewing the nature of its relations with Venice. The first one recorded is Andrea Gritti's on the Turkish empire in 1503. The fame of these reports encouraged a degree of emulation elsewhere, although not on the scale of Venice. The *relazioni* disguised flaws in the Venetian system, including a frequent reluctance to serve as diplomats, and also greatly affected subsequent views on the importance of this period for the development of diplomacy. Material in the Venetian archives relating to Britain was calendared and the calendar published in 38 volumes from 1864.[6] This reflection of contemporary interest in Venice accompanied work on material in the Spanish archives at Simancas in setting a standard for an interest in primary sources that helped define a view on quality and progress in diplomacy.

Alongside the development of permanent embassies came an increase in the diplomatic material preserved in the archives, most notably in Milan; as well as treatises on the new system, and specifically on the character and duties of the ambassador, treatises that reflected a wish to act appropriately and effectively.[7] In turn, this literature helped create a normative pattern.

As far as a consideration of the early modern situation is concerned, it is necessary to appreciate the dynamics of early modern dynastic states, both European and non-European, especially the impact of dynastic considerations, notably precedence, prestige and the succession, and the directing role of the monarch.[8] Thus it is mistaken to criticize the last in terms of muddying the waters of foreign policy management.[9] This latter argument represents a serious failure to understand the nature of early-modern international relations, and in particular, the central role of the princes in creating and sustaining polities that were expressions of proprietary dynasticism, determining their goals, and achieving their implementation. As a related factor, diplomacy, with the exception of Venice, Genoa and other city states, was essentially a princely institution, with loyalty therefore a key element in appointments.[10]

Criticism of the role of monarchs is an aspect of the attempted modernization of pre-1800 diplomacy: the tendency both to search for modern elements and modernizing trends, and to judge the period in terms of how far it conformed with modernization. This approach is anachronistic. So also are other assumptions, such as an exaggeration of the potential role of training, as opposed to social skills, in *ancien régime* diplomacy, and the tendency to downplay religious motivation and ecclesiastical topics in relations. Whether or not anachronism is at issue, it is also reasonable to ask how far the modern assumption, that diplomacy should constitute and reflect a mutuality and equality in representation and negotiation, is one that can be applied in the past without qualification.

Such an assumption is central to modern concepts of diplomacy and the international system, but can be regarded as only one of a number of means of diplomacy, a number that needs to be considered in terms of fitness for purpose and without any sense of hierarchy in quality. For example, the tribute relationship between Korea and first Ming and then Manchu China can be seen as leading to a stable relationship until the 1870s. Vassalage ensured non-interference, the process mediated by the dispatch of treaty envoys. This relationship was ended by Japanese intervention in Korea, which in the event produced not a 'modern' diplomatic system but a different form of imperial relationship as Japan became the colonial power, annexing Korea in 1910.[11]

This transition underlines the danger of treating European patterns and chronology as normative when considering diplomacy on the world stage. Indeed, even in Europe, the international system and diplomatic situation, including the means of diplomacy, would have looked very different to the usual historical summary of European diplomacy had the perspective been one from 1810 or 1941, when Napoleon and Hitler, respectively, were dominant.

More generally, it is important to emphasize the organizational limitations of European diplomacy in the early modern period. The customary emphasis is on modernization through the establishment of permanent embassies, and they bear the brunt of the Whiggish approach. Hamish Scott has written of the 'familiar sense' of diplomacy, 'that of the peaceful and continuous management of relations between states'.[12]

However, aside from the question whether permanence was such a paradigm shift, the majority of rulers did not maintain such embassies for long. This was due to assumptions about how international relations should be conducted, as well as to more practical issues, such as cost, the difficulty of finding suitable diplomats, and the absence of matters requiring negotiation. Emphasis, moreover, on the creation of an integrated diplomatic network through these embassies underplays the extent to which such a network did not in fact exist across all of Europe.

The stress, instead, was often still on episodic bilateral relations, which entailed the cost, risk and delays of travel; and, in place of permanent embassies, rulers might use their courtiers for special missions, share an agent or rely on confidential newsletters. The first reflected the long-standing practice, dating back to Antiquity, that the envoy was a trusted and thus dignified messenger, who was generally expected to return to his court as swiftly as possible. This practice was very much the dominant one in medieval Europe. The expectation that the envoy should have oratorical skills was an aspect of the legacy of his role as a messenger.

More generally, any teleological account of the development of a diplomatic system tends both to overlook the number and role of unaccredited diplomatic projectors who agitated the waters, and to entail assumptions about the calibre and skill of diplomats, which are characteristics that in practice are difficult to assess. This difficulty is especially acute if the necessary social skills are considered, as these did not match theories of bureaucratization. Instead, ability in negotiation was tested less continually than court skills, for the influence of an envoy frequently reflected his ability (and it was always a case of men in this period) to make the right impression at court. Mention of this factor serves as a reminder of the socio-cultural dimension of diplomacy, one that was inscribed in terms of the values of a particular social élite as well as those of the overlapping professional group.

Social prominence, however, came with an attitude of political contractualism between Crown and élite, monarch and aristocrats, and this attitude could affect the behaviour of envoys. Fictional form was given to this ethos in *Henry VI, Part Three*, a historical play of the 1590s by William Shakespeare and others, in which Richard, Earl of Warwick, 'the Kingmaker', denounces Edward IV (r. 1461–70, 1471–83), whom he had served and against whom he rebelled:

> When you disgrace'd me in my embassade,
> then I degraded you from being King,
> And come now to create you Duke of York. Alas,
> how should you govern any kingdom
> that know not how to use ambassadors.[13]

Warwick's embassy, typically, had involved marital negotiations on behalf of Edward as part of a complex pattern of diplomacy encompassing England, France and Burgundy. Warwick had negotiated for a French marriage for Edward, but in 1464 Edward instead secretly married Elizabeth Woodville, a commoner.

Such international marital embassies were conducted by those at the apex of society. In 1466-7 there was fresh marital diplomacy involving Warwick and the future of members of the three ruling families, while, in 1567, Thomas, 3rd Earl of Sussex, visited Maximilian II, the Holy Roman Emperor, to invest him with the Order of the Garter and to negotiate a marriage alliance between Archduke Charles and Elizabeth I, which in the event did not occur. Sussex, who had a military background, also had diplomatic experience linked to marital negotiations: with the Marquess of Northampton to France in 1551, to arrange a marriage between Edward VI and Elizabeth, daughter of Henry II of France, a marriage that did not occur; and in 1554 to Brussels and Spain to further the proposed marriage of Queen Mary and Philip II of Spain, which took place later that year.

The culture of international representation and negotiation affected of course the composition of the diplomatic corps. Both culture and corps can be regarded as anachronistic from the perspective of today, but the values were those of display, prominence and social linkage, and these were important aspects of the *entrée* of the diplomat at court. These values were an expression of the role of the envoy as the representative of, into substitute for, the sovereign, a role underlined by the extent to which rulers also met and engaged in diplomacy in person, as when Richard II of England met Charles VI of France in 1396, and Frederick III, the Holy Roman Emperor, met Charles the Bold, Duke of Burgundy in 1473, while Edward IV of England and Louis XI of France met two years later. The use of the socially prominent in diplomacy also reflected the importance of reputation in sustaining the prestige that acted as a lubricant for international and domestic co-operation.

Furthermore, the role of the social élite captured other utilitarian purposes as well. The shared-costs dimension of government was a key issue. Just as with military command, so with diplomatic representation, there was an important element of entrusting responsibility to those with social position who could bear part of the cost and raise some of the necessary credit. The private and often public correspondence of diplomats was dominated by issues of pay and expenses,[14] both of which were commonly in arrears, while each, especially the latter, was regarded as inadequate. Rodrigo Gonzalez de Puebla, who in 1487 became the first resident diplomat in London, serving Ferdinand, King of Aragon (who also ruled Sicily and Sardinia) there for most of the period until 1508, was constantly left unpaid, and complained accordingly.

Cost was a particular problem at the more expensive and prestigious courts, such as Vienna, where diplomats were expected to maintain a costly state; and this factor was an additional reason to appoint wealthy men, and was openly recognized as such. In general, representation at the capitals of republics, such as Genoa, Venice and the United Provinces (Netherlands), was less expensive than that at princely courts. This situation was true, for example, of the splendour of social occasions and of clothes.

Concern about costs reflected the extent to which much of earlymodern government was under-capitalized. It is of course true that most government in most periods has been short of funds, but, in comparison to the nineteenth and twentieth centuries, governments did not benefit from an important industrial base, the infrastructure of credit was less developed, and government creditworthiness was limited.

A limitation that was more pressing for the conduct of diplomacy as far as contemporaries were concerned was that of communications. Indeed, Fernand Braudel, the great historian of the sixteenth-century Mediterranean, referred to distance as the 'first enemy' and news as 'a luxury commodity'.[15] Rulers and ministers frequently complained (not least to their envoys) that diplomats exceeded or, otherwise, misunderstood instructions, but it was difficult to provide orders that would comprehend all eventualities or, alternatively, to respond adequately to the pace of developments, including negotiations. The slow and uncertain nature of communications ensured that considerable discretion had to be left to envoys if negotiations were to advance speedily.

Special couriers could speed messages, from Milan to Venice in twenty-four hours and from Rome to Venice in fifty in the early sixteenth century. Special galleys could aid at sea, so that a message from Constantinople (Istanbul) to Venice sent on by Corfu by galley could take twenty days. Alonso Sanchez, Charles v's envoy in Venice, reported in 1526 that it took twenty days of hard riding to get a message from Venice to Vienna.[16]

Communications, however, were not only slow by modern standards; they were also frequently such that information and messages could only be confirmed by waiting for subsequent messages. Moreover, uncertainty about the speed, and indeed arrival, of messages ensured that they could be sent by separate routes simultaneously. For example, messages from Constantinople to London in the eighteenth century would be sent both overland and by sea, a method also used to Venice and Paris. The same variety was deemed necessary for messages from colonies, with those from India to Britain being sent to Europe by sea and by a number of overland routes, a pattern that was to be repeated with the establishment of telegraph lines in the nineteenth century.

There were incremental improvements to communications on land in the sixteenth to eighteenth centuries, notably as a consequence of road-building, for example in France, and of the replacement of ferries by bridges, but there was no transformation in communications on land until the nineteenth century. Moreover, although there were significant improvements at sea, especially better rudders, and an enhanced awareness of the position of ships, thanks to the ability to measure longitude, again there was no marked improvement until the nineteenth century. Instead, in the sixteenth, as in the eighteenth and fourteenth centuries, this was a diplomatic world in the age before telegraphs, railways and steamships, with the constraints and practices that might be expected accordingly.

The global diplomacy of the late nineteenth century depended on innovations, such as the rapid movement of messages by telegraph, and of diplomats by railways and steamships, with, as a result, a key separation of the means of transmission for messages and diplomats. Moreover, the possibilities presented by these communications were greatly improved by a range of other developments, such as the use of explosives, especially dynamite, nitroglycerine and gelignite, to create tunnels under mountains, or the improved sounding of waters, which helped navigation.

However, prior to the late nineteenth century, the diffusion of new attitudes, such as those manifested in Revolutionary America or France in the late eighteenth century, as well as bold proposals for far-flung combinations, like the sixteenth-century schemes for concerted action by Portugal and Ethiopia against the Ottoman (Turkish) empire, were necessarily limited in their impact, in part because of the nature of communications. Thus innovations, for example representation in Europe from Christian Africa,[17] or, in the eighteenth century, the reception of South Sea Islanders in Europe, did not have the consequences that might have ensued had communications been more predictable and rapid.

These consequences of limited communications both hindered diplomacy prior to the nineteenth century, and also played a major role in ensuring that it retained its longstanding character. Diplomats were accredited to non-Western powers, Sir Thomas Roe serving James I of England at the Mughal court of India from 1615 to 1618, visiting Persia on his way back, and later serving the English crown at Constantinople from 1621 to

1628,[18] while embassies visited Europe from North Africa.[19] Nevertheless, links with rulers more distant than Constantinople proved episodic.

There were also important conceptual limitations to diplomacy. The nature of the interaction with non-European powers was obscure to most contemporaries. Aside from distance, there was the difficulty of discussing and conceptualizing what was poorly, if at all, understood outside the zone of interaction. There was also the habit of conceiving of the distant world principally as an extension of the nearby, especially of its problems, configurations and patterns of causality. Diplomacy was part of this process, both as a means of contact and as a medium for recording contact. As an instance of the latter, Spanish paintings of the 1690s depicting the conquest of Aztec Mexico in 1519–21 showed Cortés, the Spanish leader, dining with Moctezuma's ambassadors as part of a process of grounding the conquest as a process of legitimate expansion. Moreover, the Europeans extrapolated their patterns of statehood, social hierarchies and sense of cause and effect on to other states, while at the same time often tending to simplify, if not primitivize, the last.[20] Thus European history was scanned in order to understand non-Western societies and states, with the sultans of the Turkish Empire treated as latter-day versions of the pre-Christian tyrants of Imperial Rome, notably Nero, and African polities understood as if they were European states. Diplomacy served to advance Western interests, rather than to understand Turkish society and culture.

This pattern of interaction became more insistent as competition between European states spread into the overseas world, notably in commerce and colonization. As a result, foreign states were understood largely in terms of their alignments with rival European powers, as well as with the pattern of European politics, an approach that greatly underrated the independence of non-European states, while also exaggerating the significance and potential of links with the European powers. Such a pattern extended to the present, not least with the tendency during the Cold War (1945–89) to assess Third World states essentially with reference to the politics of the Cold War. The same was true of the 'War on Terror' in the 2000s.

The nature of diplomatic links within Europe was related to another aspect of the emphasis on limitations discussed above. The deficiencies of governments (and their need for more strength) became more acute in the late fifteenth and early sixteenth centuries, as the leading European states engaged in competition that entailed not only much warfare but also more regular diplomacy for these states. In contrast to the habitual emphasis on supposedly modern, or at least modernizing, states, including the 'New Monarchies' of the fifteenth century (notably the France of Louis XI, the England of Henry VII, and the Spain of Ferdinand and

Isabella), this increase in the regularity of diplomatic links owed little to changes in the nature of states, their strength and government. Instead, the crucial cause for increased regularity was the extent to which the competitive international activity of the period entailed coalition politics, both in diplomacy and in warfare, and moreover a volatile coalition politics that involved a need to keep a close eye on alliances.

After the Italian warfare of the early fifteenth century (see pp. 44–5), another crucial period of conflict was that of the Italian Wars, the name given to a series of wars focused on control of the Italian peninsula and the leading states there that were waged from 1494 to 1559. These conflicts came to involve, directly or indirectly, all the states of Western, Central and Southern Europe. In particular, war proved a way to advance and demonstrate the interests, and maintain the prestige, of the Holy Roman Emperor and the crowns of Spain and France, and thus of the Habsburg (Austria and Spain) and Valois (France) families. Succession disputes, notably, and not only, to Naples, Milan, Castile, and the Burgundian inheritance, all played a major role.[21]

The conflicts saw rapid changes in alignment, especially in their early stages, and the formation of alliances that required diplomacy. The invasion of Italy by Charles VIII of France in 1494 was followed by the creation of the hostile League of St Mark, which included Pope Alexander VI, Ferdinand of Aragon (who was also ruler of Sicily and Sardinia), Venice, the Holy Roman Emperor, Maximilian I, and Duke Ludovico Sforza of Milan. Later alliances included, in a far from comprehensive list, in 1508 the League of Cambrai, organized by Pope Julius II to attack Venice, and including Louis XII of France and Milan; in 1511 the Holy League, by which Julius, Spain, Venice and Henry VIII of England agreed to drive the French from Italy; and in 1526 the League of Cognac, by which Pope Clement VII, Francis I of France, Francesco II Sforza of Milan, Venice and Florence challenged Charles V.

The major role of the Papacy in creating these alliances looked back to medieval patterns of diplomatic activity, but the intensity of negotiations encouraged a stress on permanent embassies, to provide representation and information. Frequent treaties marked the Italian Wars, including Granada (1500), by which Louis XII and Ferdinand partitioned the kingdom of Naples, a longstanding issue in diplomacy; Blois (1505), by which Louis renounced his claims; Noyon (1516), by which the French claims to Naples were to accompany the French princess who was to marry Ferdinand's grandson, the future Charles V, a marriage that never occurred; Madrid (1526), which followed the French defeat at Pavia in 1525 and marked Charles' dominance of Italy; and Cambrai (1529) which affirmed the latter, again after the defeat of French forces.

The personal meetings of rulers played a role in this diplomacy, for example those of Louis XII and Ferdinand of Aragon in 1507, of Henry VIII of England and Francis I of France at the Field of the Cloth of Gold in 1520, and of Charles V and Francis I at Aigues-Mortes in 1538. Meetings between monarchs displayed a different form of protocol and ceremonial to that seen in those involving diplomats, but with a similar emphasis on asserting status, peaceful competition, and the furtherance of business.[22] In both cases, royal courts provided a key setting for the display of an exemplary status.[23]

Diplomacy was intended to ensure profit from the use of force, just as force was seen as the way to pursue diplomatic goals; although in 1528 Francis I rejected Charles V's challenge to a duel. It was not therefore surprising that both standing armies and diplomatic networks developed in the same period. The Italian Wars proved highly disruptive for the Italian principalities and the families who ruled them, some of whom were only newly established. Indeed, the absorption of several Italian territories and principalities by neighbours and foreign powers, notably of Milan and Naples by the Habsburgs, and of the republics of Pisa (for the second time) and Siena by Florence, reduced the number of those able to send envoys.

This situation encouraged the use of diplomacy as a key part of the search for security, let alone aggrandizement, and as an aspect of institutional innovation in an intensely competitive environment. Venice provided a successful example of the value of perceptive diplomacy able to adapt to changing circumstances,[24] although it had to be backed by military force. Furthermore, the dispatch and reception of embassies proved a major way to establish legitimacy, and thus to offset the claims of opponents, notably exiles. Legitimacy and aggrandizement were linked, as when the Medici were able to negotiate themselves into the rank of Grand Dukes of Tuscany.

The Italian Wars encouraged the adoption elsewhere in Europe of the Italian idea of the permanent embassy. With his territories in southern Italy, Ferdinand of Aragon operated as an important bridge between Italy and the rest of Europe, and he appointed the first non-Italian resident envoys outside Italy in the 1480s. France and England each dispatched their first permanent embassies in 1509, and France had ten by 1547. Yet in this period there was no expansion on this scale to include Scandinavia, Poland or Russia.

Limitations did not arise only within Europe. On the global scale, it was the weakness of states, not their strength, that was a crucial aspect of European international relations. At the beginning of the sixteenth century, no European state wielded the power of Ming China nor Ottoman Turkey. These strong states required diplomacy rather less than Tudor

England, Valois France, or Sforza Milan. The European states needed diplomacy to win allies if they had recourse to war and, conversely, to be able to avoid war. The importance of diplomacy thus ensured that weaknesses and failures in the international system that reflected such limitations as the delays or loss of messages led to an actual or potential instability in international relations.

Linked to this weakness was another defining aspect of European international relations: its multipolar character, which provided cause and opportunity for frequent diplomacy. Thus the development of European diplomacy can be located in terms not so much of a theory of modernization through government development as of the contingent nature of a states system that was distinctive, rather than modern. This distinctiveness was readily apparent in contrast with East Asia or the 'pre-contact' (i.e. pre-Spanish) Americas, but was scarcely unique. The development of diplomacy in Antiquity owed much to similar political contexts.

More than the multipolarity provided by several competing states was at issue in European developments. Indeed, it is instructive to contrast the European situation with that in the Middle East where, in 1480–1530, a series of Islamic states, notably the Ottoman (Turkish), Mamluk (Egyptian), and Safavid (Persian/Iranian) empires, sought to define their relations. There was a degree of similarity with the situation in Western Europe. The Ottomans were given a crucial advantage by the inability of the Mamluks and Safavids to co-operate,[25] and this failure can be paralleled in the unwillingness of the Christian states to combine against Ottoman expansion.

Yet there were major differences, not least the extent to which there were not second and third-rank powers in the Middle East comparable to those in Christian Europe; the latter led to needs for diplomacy in order to secure alliances.

There were also important ideological factors at play in the Middle East that limited the development of a comparable international system to that seen in the Habsburg–Valois rivalry. In particular, rivalry over claims to be the true Islamic polity introduced a potent element of hostility, and this rivalry was exacerbated by confessional differences between the Safavids and the Ottomans, and by the willingness of the former to encourage heterodox religious tendencies in Anatolia.[26] Such issues remain significant to diplomacy in the modern Middle East, with the organization of the haj, the annual pilgrimage of the faithful to Mecca, and the safety of the pilgrims, providing a particular irritation.[27]

There were important cultural and practical differences in the early-modern period between Turkish diplomatic relations with Christian enemies and with Muslim enemies, especially Persia. In the latter case, there was an emphasis on rhetoric and cultural abilities, with an attempt to gain prestige by displaying a greater knowledge of verse and Muslim law.[28] Relations between the Turks and the Habsburgs developed in parallel with confrontation and conflict. Ferdinand of Austria sent envoys in 1527 (they were thrown in jail), 1532 and 1533; and the last two embassies included Cornelius Schepper, who was the de facto envoy to Ferdinand's brother Charles V, and ended with Ferdinand concluding a diplomatic agreement with Suleyman the Magnificent over the partition of Hungary.[29]

The multipolarity of European international relations, and the weakness of European states, were challenged by the consolidation, as a result of successful marital diplomacy, of the Habsburg, Burgundian, Aragonese and Castilian inheritances in the person of Charles V, by the expansion of his power in the Americas, and by his policies in Europe. Yet Charles was also repeatedly checked, notably at Algiers in 1541, in Germany and at Metz in 1552. The last left a strong impression of failure, confirmed by the Peace of Augsburg of 1555, which permitted the existence of Lutheran states in the Holy Roman Empire, while the partition of his inheritance between Charles' son (Philip II of Spain) and his brother (the Emperor Ferdinand I) further served to make Christian Europe more like a multipolar system.

As a reminder of the dangers of the anachronistic use of modern concepts of diplomacy, the result of this partition for Habsburg Europe, which indeed comprised much of Western Europe, was a practice of family diplomacy. This diplomacy was partly pursued by a pattern of repeated marriages designed to maintain links between the two branches of the family, while Spanish diplomats also sought to further the interests of the Austrian Habsburgs, or, rather, the views of the Spanish Crown as to what these ought to be.

Moreover, in the late sixteenth century, the Austrian Habsburgs further divided the inheritance, which in turn expanded the range and increased the complexity of this family diplomacy, not least as the inheritance (unlike the divided inheritance of Philip of Hesse) was in turn to be consolidated anew. The Tyrol, which was frequently assigned to a younger son and then reincorporated when his male line of succession came to an end, was in separate hands from 1554 to 1595, 1602 to 1618, and 1625 to 1665. In 1652 John George I, Elector of Saxony, divided his lands among his sons. Such divisions underlined the extent to which diplomacy was so intertwined with the dynastic policies of leading families that it was unsurprising that lawyers were often seen as possessing the skills necessary to be diplomats.

Similar policies were adopted by prominent princely and aristocratic houses, such as those of Guise, Nevers, Orange and Sapieha,[30] the interests of which frequently spanned 'states'. Their policies invite discussion in terms of diplomacy, and certainly in comparison with those of small 'sovereign' territories. This theme of the primacy of family diplomacy can be pursued throughout the *ancien régime* period, for example with Franco-Spanish relations in the eighteenth century when both kingdoms were ruled by branches of the house of Bourbon, or again with relations, friendly or hostile, between the branches of the Wittelsbach family; and this theme needs repeatedly to be borne in mind when considering its diplomatic system. The ideology of hierarchy and lineage exerted pressure on individuals,[31] while there was a clash between the wills of individual sovereigns and so-called fundamental laws governing royal successions.

A focus on dynasticism also amplifies the misleading character of any narrow approach to state-building that stresses the paramount importance of high politics formulated by invisible ministers without personality. Instead, in terms of the latter, it is necessary to emphasize the complex character of politics and élite factions. The international contacts, family links and client networks of these factions also expanded the influence of governments.

This situation interacted with the rivalry between major powers. For example, a study of the leading Savoyard diplomat, Abbot Alessandro Scaglia (1592–1641), indicates the extent to which second-rank states were far from passive but, instead, could manoeuvre with a margin of success, so as best to respond to circumstances. The cultivation of Savoy reflected Bourbon–Habsburg rivalry, a rivalry that helped set the lines of dynastic interaction with Savoy. Since the formulation of Savoy's foreign policy remained the prerogative of Charles Emmanuel I, Duke from 1580 to 1630, this policy reflected dynastic priorities which proved more important than 'material' considerations, such as military resources or geographical location.[32]

Yet, to focus on a feature in European history that captured an element of the modern, the definition of state sovereignty became more of an issue in the sixteenth century, in part linked to the disruption created by the Protestant Reformation. On behalf of their states, rulers, such as Henry VIII of England (r. 1509–47), rejected the authority of the Papacy, and advanced new claims for state sovereignty. These claims at once became an issue in diplomacy and a means by which diplomacy served to assert the ideology of particular regimes. The importance of claims to, and about, sovereign powers underlined the value of appointing lawyers as diplomats.

Diplomacy is, in part, an issue of monopolization: the monopolization of international representation from a given space that is judged sovereign and independent, and thus foreign to others. The ability of states to seize, assert and maintain such a monopolization was a crucial consequence and aspect of state-building. Indeed, the subordination of a territory was expressed in control over its representation. For example, as a key aspect of Muscovy's increasing dominance of the hitherto independent city state of Novgorod, the latter, by the Treaty of Iazhelbitsii of 1456, agreed to submit its foreign policy to the approval of Muscovy. Similarly today, territories that have considerable autonomy nevertheless tend to have their foreign policy under the control of the sovereign power as a key aspect of this sovereignty: this is true, for example, of the relationship between Greenland and Denmark; and between the Channel Islands and the Isle of Man, and Britain.

The emphasis on monopolization helped give diplomacy a wider significance as a means by which a sense of identity was expressed, and by which sovereignty was asserted as a distinctive attribute of a particular level of authority. This process was related to the marked decline in the practice of international diplomacy by non-sovereign bodies, for example individual provinces.

Looked at differently, such diplomacy was now practised within states. This was not least the case with multiple states. Thus Portugal was ruled as a separate state by Philips II, III and IV of Spain between 1580 and 1640, and it continued to have a distinct international identity. Yet, within Spain, a separate identity was also maintained by provinces with particular liberties, notably Catalonia. They practised what in effect was diplomacy, in terms of information-gathering, representation and negotiation, within Spain. The same was true of the estates of the territories of the Austrian Habsburgs. The ability to mediate and reconcile was exceptionally important in imperial and multiple monarchies, with local élites successfully integrated and co-opted through voluntary coalescence.

If international diplomacy is seen as the distinguishing feature, then it can also be noted that provinces could seek to pursue such diplomacy, and indeed did so as part of the process of bargaining within states. Moreover, the distinction between international diplomacy and such activity was not always as clear as it might be. The rejection of Habsburg authority by the Bohemian Estates, and their willingness to elect a Protestant German prince, Frederick, Elector Palatine, as King, was central to the origins of the Thirty Years' War (1618–48).

The Reformation greatly challenged diplomatic practices between, as well as within, states. Although the period saw the development of diplomatic relations with the Turks, with French and English envoys dispatched to Constantinople, in 1535 and 1583 respectively, international links within Christendom were sundered by religious animosity. Moreover, the ability of diplomats to practise a form of Christianity different to that of the state to which they were accredited threatened religious coherence, and was constrained, if not resisted. After 1568, when Philip II of Spain refused to permit the English envoy to have Protestant services in his house there was no resident English envoy in Spain until the war between the two powers that had begun in 1585 ended in 1604.[33] This lack of an embassy removed an important means of communication, as successive Spanish envoys in London were compromised by their willingness to conspire against Elizabeth I. Moreover, in 1589 Philip closed his embassy in Paris because he was unwilling to recognize the Protestant Henry IV as king.

Looking ahead to later periods of ideological foreign policy, the lack or weakness of channels of communication was less significant than it might seem, as much (but by no means all) foreign policy was very much driven by ideological factors, and with scant interest in compromise. Motivated by what Geoffrey Parker has termed a 'messianic imperialism', Philip II, in particular, lacked flexibility, believing that his constancy testified to his devotion and his mission. Opposition to him, in Philip's view, was largely a matter of heresy, and heresy of opposition; and this confessional viewpoint restricted the room for manoeuvre, both in domestic and in international issues, in so far as they could be separated.

All too often, the service of God was the means as well as the goal of policy, while the justification of war in confessional terms made it difficult to end it, other than by proposing to focus on a more serious threat, as when Philip moved, in the 1570s, from war with the Turks to confronting the Dutch rebels. Despite the skills of Spanish envoys, such as Dom Bernardino de Mendoza (Paris) and the Count of Olivares (Rome), diplomatic failure was therefore simply an aspect of a more general unwillingness on Philip's part to relate goals to practicalities.[34]

A stress on the role of confessional considerations suggests a degree of modernity, one that looks toward more recent emphases on ideology and subversion. There were indeed important parallels, although the context of diplomatic activity was very different. Parallels and contrasts will emerge through the discussion in the following chapters.

TWO
1600–1690

Religious strife, or strife that could be explained in confessional (religious) terms, proved to be a key feature affecting the diplomacy of the period, as it threatened the idea of a network of relationships providing a basis for representation and negotiations. Instead, religious strife helped ensure that diplomatic relations were often limited. The association of religious animosity with attempts to depose hostile rulers proved a particularly serious bar to good relations, and the involvement of diplomats in conspiracies was at times a significant issue, notably in Anglo-Spanish relations in the 1570s–80s,[1] and, to a lesser extent, Anglo-French relations in the early 1560s.

Such involvement was believed to be common, and this belief proved an aspect of the paranoia of the period, such that diplomats were centrally inscribed in the picture of threat. Indeed, Pope Pius II (r. 1458–64), Louis XI of France (r. 1461–83), and Henry VII of England (r. 1485–1509) had each sought to block the presence of resident envoys at their court. Concern about their possible role in sedition exacerbated the longstanding anxiety that diplomats were dissimulators, if not spies, and made their treatment in this light a more important topic in the details of diplomatic life. Furthermore, in terms of intellectual positioning, the challenge that diplomacy posed for humanist values was one that could compromise the *virtù* of the envoy.[2] As envoy for Henry VIII of England, Sir Thomas Wyatt sought in the late 1530s to kidnap or assassinate Cardinal Reginald Pole, the Papal legate, who was seen as a key figure in organizing Continental opposition to Henry.[3]

In 1604 Sir Henry Wotton, en route to take up his embassy at Venice, inscribed his name with the sentence 'An ambassador is an honest man sent to lie abroad for the good of his country', a remark that earned James I's anger. Other diplomats also referred to themselves as following the trade of espionage, for example Rochefort, the French consul in Hamburg in the 1710s.[4]

Moreover, this critique of diplomacy as dishonest and duplicitous, a critique that continued despite attempts to present a better account of the task, cohered with the suspicion arising from the practice of foreign relations as a 'mystery of state' and as a prerogative of the sovereign that must necessarily remain secret. This practice encouraged public concern about the policies of one's own, as well as foreign states; and this concern fed into the critique of diplomacy that has been so insistent a theme, and notably over the last half-millennium. Thus in England in the 1620s and 1630s there were suspicions, in part justified, that the Stuart Court was following pro-Catholic policies, at home and abroad; and anxiety on each head contributed to exacerbate the other. Suspicion of Spanish diplomacy led to a hostile depiction of Diego, Count of Gondomar, the recently departed Spanish envoy, in Thomas Middleton's play *A Game at Chess* (1624).

Such fears in England revived in the case of France with rumours about the agreement reached by Charles II at Dover in 1670, an agreement in which the key negotiations were very much inside the royal family; indeed with Charles' sister Henrietta, Duchess of Orléans, wife of Louis XIV's brother.[5]

The consequences of religious division, however, were less serious than might be imagined from this paranoia, and, to make a comparison with a very different age, less grave than those in the 1950s, during the height of the Cold War. Indeed, the most serious consequence was that the role of Rome as a centre for diplomacy declined because the representation of the Papacy was restricted to Catholic courts. In contrast, the peace treaties of 1598–1609 that ended conflict in Western Europe, notably France–Spain in 1598, England–Spain in 1604 and Spain–the Dutch in 1609, were followed by the establishment of resident embassies across confessional lines, for example Dutch envoys in Paris and Venice, and a Spanish embassy in London.

This strengthening of the network of resident embassies was important to the general character of Western diplomacy. It also provided listening posts that left correspondence[6] from which a cartography of diplomatic concern and reporting can be charted today. Other than for ceremonial occasions, notably royal marriages, lavish, large special embassies now appeared anachronistic, as with the unsuccessful English attempt in 1619 to mediate in the European crisis: the embassy of James, Earl of Doncaster, which contained 150 people (delaying progress), cost £30,000, and was mocked for its size.[7] Nevertheless, such embassies were also seen as a way to honour the recipient, which encouraged Charles I of England to send Thomas, 2nd Earl of Arundel, to the Emperor Ferdinand II in 1636 in an unsuccessful attempt to have his nephew, Charles, restored to the lands of the Elector Palatine. Moreover, large embassies featured prominently in Rome during the seventeenth century.

English diplomacy under James I (r. 1603–25) in part arose from his search for a Christian reunion, which was linked to a desire for peace. The former entailed a wish for an ecumenical church council.[8] Such aspirations, which represented a continuation of medieval papal calls for peace within Christendom, reflected not only the range of diplomacy, but also the extent to which broader ideological drives played a role. Thus relations between churches continued to provide the cause for a distinctive type of diplomacy, and one that had parallels with secular diplomacy, not least in terms of the interplay between claims to universal authority and the need to adapt to the quasi-sovereignty of the individual churches.[9]

The impact of religious factors was limited because of the willingness to ally across confessional divides, again a factor seen in the medieval period (see p. 25). Thus French rulers frequently allied with Protestant powers against the Habsburgs. Just as Henry II of France had successfully allied with a number of leading German Protestant princes in the 1550s, so Louis XIII allied with the Dutch and Swedes during the Thirty Years' War (1618–48), and indeed encouraged Gustavus Adolphus of Sweden to invade Germany in 1630. Although there was a sense within the French Church and political élite that Catholic France should not fight other Catholics, Cardinals Richelieu and Mazarin, the leading ministers in 1624–61, were largely responsible for the strong anti-Habsburg policies of the period, and they selected diplomats accordingly, as indeed they needed to do. Negotiations with the Turks, which the French had pursued from the 1520s, fitted into this pattern, although widespread cultural suppositions about their inappropriateness at a time of a serious Turkish threat to Christendom limited the willingness of the French to pursue formal links.

A major way of finessing the confessional issue was to distinguish between relations with foreign rulers of a different confession, relations that could be good; and animosity toward subjects of another confession. The latter were seen as challenging the authority of the Crown, and therefore as deserving correction, but this view was not the attitude taken toward foreign rulers. This distinction helped defuse the impact of religious animosity, although, in turn, a willingness by diplomats to intervene on behalf of co-religionists could harm relations or at least create an unwelcome atmosphere. The revocation in 1685, by Louis XIV of France, of the Edict of Nantes (of 1598) that had guaranteed certain rights for French Protestants became an issue in diplomacy, at once an irritant and an expression of a wider hostility between Louis and what was presented as a coherent Protestant Europe.

Anxieties about diplomats persisted throughout the period; but they were also useful as a means of communication and source of information, and reflected lustre on a court. To refuse to receive envoys was to call into question one's place in the international order; and new palaces, such as those at Versailles, Schönbrunn (near Vienna), Stockholm, Berlin, Dresden and Turin, were in part designed to provide monarchs with exalting settings in which to receive diplomats and where the reception could be recorded on canvas.[10]

Given this situation, it is not surprising that notions of diplomatic immunity developed. In the sixteenth century, there had been significant infringements of the idea that the person of a diplomat was free from assault, imprisonment and legal action, but nevertheless the idea became more common and was increasingly extended to the envoy's house. As a result, envoys who had acted in what was seen as a hostile manner faced expulsion rather than imprisonment. The Turks followed the practice of incarcerating envoys as an aspect of a declaration of war, but expulsion was the norm elsewhere.

Instead, envoys had rather to fear a lack of pay, and resulting civil action by creditors. Financial problems led to the imprisonment in 1708 of Andrei Matveev, the Russian envoy, in a London debtors' prison, a step that had serious diplomatic consequences. Some envoys abused their position, using their exemption from customs duties to smuggle goods for others; shield their servants from legal action, as in 1725 when the Portuguese envoy in London protected his coachman from arrest on a charge of assault;[11] or provide criminals with shelter in their houses; but such practices served as irritants, rather than undermining the system of immunity.

A less benign scholarly approach can be taken by emphasizing the interception of diplomatic correspondence, including by attacking couriers, as when English agents disguised as highwaymen took dispatches from the Spanish envoy in London in 1562. Seven years later, another Spanish envoy was confined to his embassy in London on the grounds that he was taking a hostile stance; all his Catholic servants were dismissed and all his couriers were stopped.[12] In 1739 a Swedish courier was murdered by Russian agents keen to ascertain the nature of negotiations between hostile Sweden and Turkey, which was already at war with Russia.

Alongside the development of notions of diplomatic immunity, another aspect of standardization that helped reduce difficulties was the practice within Europe of assuming that rulers who dispatched envoys, rather than host countries, would pay the costs of diplomats; although non-Western envoys continued to expect that they would receive the payment of all expenses, and this indeed remained the pattern, for example for

North African envoys in London. This was also the assumption of Russian envoys, for example Vasili Posnikov, who came to London in 1687, which could create difficulties: in his case, because, on top of the money that was paid him by the English government, he sought an additional subsistence allowance which was rejected.

The Thirty Years' War (1618–48) represented a high point in sustained religious animosity within Europe, especially prior to full-scale French entry into the conflict in 1635 against the (Catholic) Habsburg powers, Austria and Spain. At the same time, however, the war encouraged diplomacy. Peace negotiations continued during the conflict, often in tandem with military operations and being affected by them or by reports and rumours about them, a situation that put a premium on Intelligence.[13]

The search for allies also encouraged diplomacy. Thus in the case of Denmark, in place of temporary, ad hoc diplomatic missions, there came, from the 1620s, the emergence of diplomats residing permanently at a foreign court. The first was in Stockholm, from around 1630; moreover, there were permanent residents in Paris and in The Hague, and in the 1640s there were also permanent Danish residents at Vienna, Madrid and Brussels, although the latter were consular rather than political in function.

The great distances spanned by alliances, negotiations and operations put pressure on diplomacy. Problems with communications accentuated the issue of how far diplomats could act with authority on their own initiative, not least committing their rulers to agreements without explicit instructions to do so. This issue played a part with the Treaty of Regensburg (1630), as Richelieu claimed, disingenuously, that the French envoys had acted beyond the scope of their instructions in agreeing that France would not assist the enemies of the Emperor and in signing the treaty with the Emperor, Ferdinand II; and he repudiated the treaty.

The war ended in 1648 with treaties signed at Münster and Osnabrück that are collectively known as the Peace of Westphalia. This peace is seen as a key marker in the development of international relations, and therefore in that of diplomacy. Indeed, the Westphalian settlement is frequently presented as the beginning of the modern state system. There was an important grounding of sovereign independence, with Spain acknowledging Dutch independence, bringing the Dutch Revolt that had begun in 1566 to an end, while Austrian Habsburg control over their dominions, notably Bohemia, was accepted, ending the ability of these dominions to pursue autonomous courses, with the important exception of Hungary.[14]

The view of Westphalia as a key departure in the establishment of the modern state system also owes much to the acceptance in the treaty that German princes were free to pursue their own foreign policy. This acceptance marked an effective end to the pretensions of Christian unity provided since the ninth century by the Holy Roman Empire. The decline of the Imperial ideal has been seen as a transition from medievalism to modernity. Indeed, the Westphalian notion of sovereignty, and the Westphalian state system, are terms that have been extensively used. They hinge on the idea that the individual state is a sovereign body answerable to none. This idea is contrasted to supra-national institutions and theories, such as those supposedly advanced by exponents of Imperial ideas (those of the Holy Roman Empire) prior to 1648 and by liberal universalists in the 1990s.[15]

This analysis, however, places too much weight on the changes brought by Westphalia, making it another equivalent to the dawn for a new diplomacy already seen in much of the discussion of the Renaissance period, and notably of the development of resident embassies. In each case, there are instances of the pronounced historical preference for crucial turning points (usually the subject of the author's research) and the repeated belief that major developments must be marked by a key occasion of transition.

In practice, the impact of the changes in Germany was limited, while their wider consequences are unclear. Effective autonomy had long existed for the princes within the Empire, and they had negotiated accordingly; while the process of imperial disunity and the effective sovereignty of individual princes had been greatly advanced as a result of the Protestant Reformation. Thus the changes brought by Westphalia represented the adaptation of a weak federal system, in which what in effect was interstate diplomacy had already occurred, rather than a turning point. The latter bears little reference to the more circumspect shift in the relationships between Emperor, Empire, and Princes actually seen in and after the Peace.[16]

Moreover, many of the German states were too small to pursue an independent foreign policy seriously; and this, in part, explained the continued role and importance of the Emperor and the Empire. Indeed, if there was a limited parallel between earlier conceptions of the Holy Roman Empire and Chinese assumptions about their world, elements of these earlier conceptions continued, and notably of the superior prestige of the Emperor.[17]

In addition, a belief in restraint on the part of the German states was indicated by the clauses in the Peace of Westphalia that allowed princes to ally amongst themselves and with foreign powers to ensure their preservation and security, in other words not for offensive purposes. Moreover, these alliances were acceptable only on condition that the alliances were not directed against the Emperor, the Empire, or the terms of the treaty. During the War of the Spanish Succession, the Electors of Bavaria and

Cologne, France's allies, were placed under the Imperial ban in 1706, depriving them of their rights and privileges, and they did not regain these until the war came to a close with the Treaty of Rastatt in 1714.

Less seriously, Philip, Count Sinzendorf, the Austrian Chancellor (and the First Austrian Plenipotentiary at the Congress of Soissons in 1728), declaimed in 1727 against French envoys in the Empire as spies. His wish that they not be suffered to continue[18] represented an implicit threat to the diplomatic position of the princes of the hostile Wittelsbach family, notably Charles Albert, the Elector of Bavaria. More generally, international relations in the century after Westphalia were not too different from those in the preceding century.

Rather than Westphalia representing a new departure for European diplomacy, it was the need to address current and new issues in the second half of the seventeenth century that encouraged the use of diplomats for reporting and negotiation. The creation of an English republic in 1649 and its subsequent international activity under, first the Rump Parliament and later, from 1653 to 1658, Oliver Cromwell, provided an important early challenge. This challenge was accentuated by a sense of England as unstable, as well as a dynamic player in international relations. Christer Bonde, a Swedish ambassador in the mid-1650s who spoke good English and was friendly with Cromwell, reported: 'this regime is riddled with intrigues and with such jealousies that I have some reason to doubt whether there may not be those who deliberately confuse sensible policies so that matters may go ill'.[19] In turn, Cromwell exploited the conflict between France and Spain in order to win the alliance of France which had hitherto supported the English Royalists.[20]

The need to address new issues was notably the case with the threat from the policies and pretensions of Louis XIV, who took personal control of French policy in 1661, and their implications within the European system. For example, the interrelationship between Austro-Turkish and Austro-French relations were such that the policies of the Turks were seen as having a direct consequence for power relationships in Western Europe.

Moreover, rather than emphasizing the innovative character of Westphalia, it is appropriate to focus on a less teleological approach. More particularly, the Thirty Years' War had interrupted the development of the system of resident diplomacy,[21] only for it to resume thereafter. In turn, the reciprocal character of representation encouraged the spread of the system of resident diplomacy, although it was also far from comprehensive. For example, the representation of Italian states in London in 1665–72 was patchy.[22] Furthermore, notions of bureaucratic development in the conduct of foreign policy, notably in France, have been questioned by research indicating the plasticity of administrative practice and the extent to which regular forms were shot through by the impact of personal connections and related factional politics.[23]

Westphalia, however, began a sequence of lengthy peace congresses ending major wars, and these congresses demonstrated the value of diplomatic skill. The congresses, and the diplomacy that led to them, also encouraged a continuing appreciation of the multiple interactions of states comprising an international system that was not only multilateral, but also where distant issues could have a direct consequence for those not directly involved. The congresses, moreover, led to an emulation of the style and method of French diplomacy, methods which were seen as particularly effective.[24]

These congresses also reflected complex shifts in emphasis in the political culture of international relations, with a greater belief in the value of arbitration within what should be a naturally benign international system, as well as a need to respond to changing legal ideas on war.[25] Ideas advanced in works such as Samuel, Freiherr von Pufendorf's *De Jure Naturae et Gentium Libri Ôcto* [*Eight Books on the Law of Nature and Nations*] of 1672 contributed to these developments. Indeed, the views of jurists of international law were significant in shaping political thought and the norms of international relations.[26] The implications for diplomacy included a strengthening of its practice as a means for relations with all other states, rather than solely between allies and, thus, generally at the expense of others. Equality as a basis for negotiations proved important at congresses, and notably to the procedures adopted there.[27]

Just as Westphalia should not necessarily be seen as a new departure, so the same was true for the violent replacement of the Ming dynasty in China in the mid-seventeenth century by the Manchu, a dynasty that brought together Chinese and non-Han traditions and influences. The Manchu rulers maintained the basics of the Ming view of the world, with the Emperor, as Son of Heaven, presiding over an orderly civilization to which respectful barbarians were to be admitted. Korea had already recognized the Manchu ruler as the tributary overlord in 1636.

A key bridge, as before, was the role within China, alongside the bureaucratic administrative hierarchy, of a feudal-type suzerainty enjoyed by the Emperor over vassals within his dominions. The latter practice was then extended to the outside world, where all powers were seen as tribute-offering vassals. These assumptions made the 1593 demands of Hideyoshi, Japan's new ruler, for equal status with the Wan Li Emperor a major challenge. He wished to be invested with the title King of the Ming (as a way to legitimate his seizure of power in Japan), as well as to receive the privileges of tribute trade. In contrast, the Chinese wanted Hideyoshi to accept a more subordinate status, for example equivalent to that of Altan Khan, the Mongol ruler, but their attempt to achieve this outcome was rejected in 1596 when Hideyoshi ascertained what was really on offer from China, terms that the Chinese envoys had sought to keep obscure in order to avoid the breakdown in negotiations. Similarly, in 1889 Menelik II of Abyssinia (Ethiopia) rejected the Italian use of a different text in the Italian version of the treaty signed that year, a text employed to enable Italy to claim a protectorate.

Rather than the crisis of the seventeenth century ushering in a new system in China, as it did to an extent in Europe, virtue in China continued to reside not in the norms and actions of an international system of sovereign states, which became the European model, but rather in the meritorious example of the Son of Heaven, the Emperor. Barbarians honoured this merit by bringing tribute and performing due obeisance, especially kowtowing, and thus maintained the idea of an order expressed in and maintained through a universal kingship.

Alongside the theory, the practice of Chinese diplomacy included elements that would have been familiar to Western rulers, such as playing one barbarian off against each other. Another comparison was provided by the extent to which negotiations sought to ensure peace by what can be seen as a deceitful bridging of contradictory pretensions and claims, but what was also an attempt to save face and status by this deceit.[28]

Saving face was not only a key goal for China's diplomacy. Rejected by the Chinese refusal to accept any equality of status, Japan both used diplomacy, specifically the sending and receiving of envoys, to assert the legitimacy of the Tokugawa shogunate in 1689, and was able to save face in part by restricting its diplomatic links in the seventeenth and eighteenth centuries largely to Korea and to the conquered kingdom of Ryukyu.[29] This drawing in was also seen with a marked curtailment of links with European powers. The Portuguese were expelled from Japan in 1639, and links with the Dutch were curtailed in 1641. In contrast, the Europeans sought trading privileges in China, as with the embassy from the Dutch East India Company received in 1656. This embassy was described (and illustrated) by Johann Nieuhof in *Legatio Batavica*, part of the process by which diplomacy led to an expansion of information about the outer world.

By the late seventeenth century, most major important Western and Central European states reciprocally maintained permanent embassies in peacetime, and together these constituted the diplomatic corps. This corps was an increasingly defined and self-conscious world, with particular privileges and modes of operation. It attracts attention in discussion of the development of a diplomatic system, but, rather than focusing solely on the forms, it is also necessary to understand the degree to which this system developed and adapted in response to particular needs and anxieties.

The three major exceptions in Europe to the development of a network of peacetime embassies were Russia, which only established its first permanent embassy, in Poland, in 1688; the Turkish empire; and the Papacy, whose representation was restricted to Catholic courts. Russia began diplomatic links with England in the 1550s and sent an envoy to Paris in 1615 and an agent to Stockholm in 1635–6; but such links were generally ad hoc and on the earlier pattern of only for specific purposes and a limited period.

Although the major Christian states maintained embassies in Constantinople, the Turkish empire did not decide to establish permanent embassies until 1793, preferring, earlier, to send individual missions for particular negotiations. In 1689 one such reached Vienna in an unsuccessful attempt to negotiate peace in a war in which the Turks were being seriously defeated. The mission was headed by Zulfikar Efendi, the head of the Chancery, and Alexander Mavrocordato, the chief interpreter to the Imperial Divan, a choice that reflected the seriousness of the effort, and also the extent to which the dispatch of a special embassy could signify and convey more than a resident envoy.[30] Some prominent Turks saw foreign envoys as spies.[31]

Relations with the Turks were complicated by issues of status. Thus Russia accepted peace with Turkey at the end of 1739, but unresolved articles, including the titles by which the Sultan and Tsar would be addressed, as well as the exchange of slaves, border demarcation and the demolition of the fortifications of Azov[32] were not resolved until May 1741, and the treaty was not ratified until that September. Envoys from the Sultan of Morocco represented another instance of the diplomacy of Islamic powers with Europe.

Other powers, rather than being different, often used the same method of individual missions, even when they maintained permanent embassies. This method was employed to deal with important negotiations and to fulfil ceremonial functions, such as congratulations on accessions, marriages and births, or installations with chivalric orders.

Diplomatic choice was twofold: where to send envoys and whom to send. The central issue, as far as the first was concerned, was the nature of relations. If they were poor, then diplomatic links were broken or downgraded, which ensured that the range and nature of representation were greatly affected by periods of conflict. There were also other types of dispute that led to the severance of diplomatic links.

In deciding where to send envoys and whom to send, reciprocity was an important factor and was central to the issue of honour, for honour was implied by reciprocity. A failure to maintain representation led to anger, as when Charles Emmanuel III of Sardinia (whose key dominions were Savoy and Piedmont, r. 1730–73) threatened to withdraw his envoy from The Hague because the Dutch had ended their representation at Turin. Aside from this issue of mutuality in deciding where to send envoys, there was also that of effectiveness.

The majority of rulers did not, however, maintain permanent embassies in more than a few capitals, if that. This was because of the cost, the difficulty of finding suitable diplomats, and the absence of matters requiring negotiations. Thus, the idea of an integrated diplomatic network ignores the rulers who had no, or very few, permanent embassies.

Some minor powers were better represented than the large number of weak, but sovereign, princes and cities, but not to the extent of their major counterparts. The minor powers tended to maintain envoys, if at all, at Vienna, whose Imperial position and law court attracted German and north Italian envoys; Paris; The Hague; Rome, if they were Catholic; and Madrid, for the Italian states. London did not reach this rank until after the Glorious Revolution of 1688–9 led to a more assertive foreign policy. Thus, as today, there was a hierarchy of representation, one that reflected custom, emulation, the specific needs of particular rulers, and the specific requirements of individual conjunctures.

As far as the Swiss Confederation was concerned, there was no permanent agent appointed by the Confederation or any of the thirteen sovereign cantons or any of the allies, notably Geneva, the Bishop of Basel, the Abbey of St Gall, the Valais and the principality of Neuchâtel. The complicated structure of the old confederation, which possessed only one common organ in the Diet (*Tagsatzung*), was the main factor in this. The Diet and the thirteen sovereign cantons, or coalitions of cantons, had received diplomatic representatives from abroad since the fifteenth century, and had had permanent representations from abroad since the sixteenth century. However, they did not maintain their own legations at foreign courts and republics, but simply sent extraordinary missions as required. The achievement of full Swiss independence from the Holy Roman Empire, through the Peace of Westphalia in 1648, changed nothing in the lack of any reciprocity in diplomatic missions.

The capitals that attracted diplomats were important not only as political foci but also as cultural centres. This role underlined the extent to which courts were in competition; with prestige linked to the conspicuous display of cultural patronage. Stylistically the Baroque, the major cultural form of late seventeenth-century Europe, lent itself to this competition. The centres of diplomatic activity, especially Paris and Rome, were also production and marketing centres for luxury industries. These industries provided opulent and high-quality goods that were sought by rulers, such as mirrors, furniture, watches, clothes, paintings, mathematical instruments, pictures and books. These purchases, which often overlapped with the financial encouragement provided by major powers, for example France to the Wittelsbachs,[33] underlined the extent to which the personal concerns of rulers dominated diplomacy. Embassies, moreover, were significant points of cultural exchange, which remains true today, especially for states not at the front rank and where the commercial cultural sphere is limited.

Cultural exchange took a number of forms. Diplomats were generally able to secure desired goods and to avoid customs duties and restrictions. In 1685–6 Gaspar Fagel, the Grand Pensionary (leading minister) of Holland, asked Anthonie Heinsius in London for plants from the Apothecary's Gardens at Chelsea for his country estate. The Bavarian envoy in Paris sent substantial quantities of furniture and clothes to Munich for the Elector in the 1720s and 1730s, Louis XV ordered both hunting dogs and condoms from London through diplomatic channels, while in 1764 the Palatine envoy in Vienna was asked to send Turkish coffee to the court in Mannheim.[34]

Art played a major role. Justus Alt, the Hesse-Cassel envoy in London, purchased paintings for the Landgrave in the mid-eighteenth century, as well as a small pocket telescope. Catherine the Great of Russia used her diplomats to acquire art, notably the Houghton collection from Britain.[35] Diplomats could also be expected to purchase works of art for prominent individuals other than the sovereign.

It was not only a question of purchases. In the early seventeenth century Peter Paul Rubens, a famous painter, had played a major role in the world of diplomacy, notably in Anglo-Spanish relations, providing a key instance of its overlap with that of the arts. Furthermore, cultural patronage served as a way to gain and display status. Thus the court of Savoy used patronage to underline its identity as a leading European court. The diplomat Alessandro Scaglia was a major patron of Van Dyck, who himself was part of the world of diplomacy, and Scaglia was also linked with other artists, including Jordaens, Seghers and Snyders.[36]

Personal links were also seen in the expectation that diplomats would look after the interests of well-connected compatriots and others enjoying the protection of their sovereign. The latter would include the local community, as well as prominent travellers who would be presented at court, introduced into local society, and protected from onerous legal issues and government regulations. In general, the protection provided by diplomats was an indication of the role of personal connections in what was still essentially an élite milieu.

The capitals to which minor powers sent envoys became the general places of negotiation with them as, however widely spread their embassies might be, major states generally did not retain permanent envoys to these minor powers and usually lacked business sufficient to justify special embassies. The French, for example, maintained permanent embassies at only a few German courts, although these embassies were expected to handle relations at neighbouring courts as well, a practice that could also be followed in Italy, and that is seen today, for example with British representation in Africa (see p. 169).

A system of one-sided representation did not always encourage the clear transmission of opinions, but it did enhance the diplomatic importance of particular capitals, especially Paris, where there were numerous envoys. For example, Anglo-Wittelsbach negotiations in the winter of 1729–30 were conducted in Paris: Britain lacked envoys at the Wittelsbach capitals, and in 1735 the Hesse-Darmstadt agent in Paris was able to press the British envoy there on the future of the territory of Hanau.[37] Moreover, The Hague was termed 'the whispering gallery of Europe' (a reference to Sir Christopher Wren's St Paul's Cathedral) for its ability to register and repeat reports from throughout Europe.

Continuity in representation did not entail permanent embassy buildings. The reasons were not simply those of cost, although that played a role, as it also did with the decision to send envoys.[38] There were also assumptions different to those of today. Permanent buildings existed, notably for ecclesiastical and related bodies, for example the constituent 'nations' of chivalric orders, such as those of the Order of St John, the Knights of Malta, in Valetta. Yet representation by a sovereign was seen to rest with the envoy, rather than the embassy. This situation entailed gaps in representation, as envoys left before others were appointed, as well as differences in the needs, connections and affluence of individual diplomats. The latter rented or bought houses (and contents) which they parted with at the end of their mission. A measure of continuity was provided by diplomats continuing the rental or purchasing the property. Less commonly, from the late seventeenth century, a few buildings were acquired as permanent embassies.

As diplomats represented their sovereigns, who were themselves conscious both of their own rank within a monarchical hierarchy, and of the need to grade representation carefully, the senior diplomatic ranks remained dominated by the aristocrats and reflected this hierarchy. This system, however, did not work well outside Europe, as the basic assumptions were not shared. Thus, the Spathar-Milescu embassy from Tsar Alexis to the K'ang-hsi Emperor of China faced the fundamental problem that Spathar-Milescu refused to kowtow; a mark of deference that

Europeans correctly saw as taking due respect to the point of humiliating subservience.[39]

Within Europe, the most senior grade, Ambassador, was allocated only to a small number of courts, generally Paris, Madrid, Vienna and Rome, although the situation was far from rigid. The rest of the diplomatic hierarchy, from Envoys Extraordinary through a series of grades including Ministers Resident, down to Secretaries of Embassy and unaccredited agents and secretaries, provided a large number of ranks.[40] This differentiation permitted distinctions in relations to be made and reciprocated through the choice of representation. Thus George II of Britain showed his regard for Charles Emmanuel III when he sent Algernon, 3rd Earl of Essex, to Turin in 1732, the first British Ambassador to the court, while, the following year, George expressed his pleasure that Karl Philipp, the Elector Palatine, had sent 'une personne de condition'.[41] Similarly, monarchs devoted great care to the forms of address with which they honoured other rulers, and, even more, to those forms that they expected to receive, in case they infringed their status. In turn, royal favour was important for not only the diplomats chosen, but also for the rank at which they were chosen.

The extent of diplomatic expertise remains a topic open to varied assessments. Many aristocratic envoys held military posts in wartime, and peacetime diplomacy was therefore an aspect of fairly continual service to their monarchs, as well as providing a role for these men. The frequent appointment of military men reflected not simply the absence of notions of specialization and technical training in diplomacy, but also the sense that such envoys were especially appropriate for particular courts, notably Berlin where successive monarchs were especially interested in military affairs. Both factors still remain the case. The appointment of military men was also pertinent when wartime co-operation was at issue or when drawing on memories of such alliances. Similarly, such individuals frequently had experience of the coalition diplomacy that military operations often entailed.[42]

Privileged servants of the Crown, rather than officials of an impersonal state, aristocrats also represented the principle that diplomacy was not taught, but was an adjunct of gentility. *El Embajador* (1620), by Juan de Vera, a Spanish nobleman, an influential work that was translated and reprinted, argued the case for envoys as well-bred and gentlemen. These characteristics were particularly important for ceremonial embassies, such as the dispatch to Vienna in 1688 of Nicholas, 2nd Earl of Carlingford, in order to bear James II's congratulations to the Emperor Leopold I on the election of his son as King of the Romans, the next Emperor. In what was an instructive example of the difficulty of separating out diplomatic functions, the French government was concerned whether Carlingford had anything else to negotiate, and he had to deny rumours that he was negotiating a settlement between Austria and Turkey, an outcome that would have made it easier for Austria to oppose French goals in the Empire.[43]

Aristocrats were particularly appropriate for the lavish hospitality and court ceremonial necessary to the sustaining of royal *gloire* and for the character of diplomacy as political performance, while there was a sense that affecting the fate of dynasties and nations was a role that required envoys of distinguished status. Moreover, the friends of rulers and those they trusted most were likely to be aristocrats, for example Everard van Weede van Dijkveld, who was used by William III (William of Orange) for a number of embassies.

A few envoys at this level and rank were permanent or semi-permanent career diplomats, although that was much more common at the more junior ranks. There, longevity in service was important because, as in most spheres of public life, training was on the job. Experience was crucial. For resident envoys, experience played a role in fostering the values of ability and personality, as with Sir Isaac Wake, English agent in Turin from 1615 until 1623, envoy to Savoy and Venice from 1624 until 1630, and to France from 1630 until his death in 1632. Wake was able to play the role – 'alert to the power of rhetoric, well versed in the art of flattery, and given to conspicuous display' – but he also benefited in his commitment to the continued security of the Protestant Swiss and Genevans from a combination of consistency, energy and ability.[44]

Some diplomats gained training and patronage through posts on the staff of envoys. Indeed, in 1724 Count Andrei Osterman, the Russian Foreign Minister, recommended that diplomats be trained first by being attached to the Central College (Ministry) and then to Russian embassies.[45] Moreover, the private papers of envoys sometimes included the dispatches of predecessors that were clearly obtained as a form of information.[46]

Reading past dispatches was useful for understanding the background to both negotiations and reporting on developments. Judging between these two functions is difficult. Scholarly attention tends to concentrate on diplomats as negotiators, because it was then that their activity, perception and ability were most significant, and also apparent to contemporaries, both within and outside the government structure. Yet most of the time diplomats were reporters, and this role has left the biggest trace in the archives, although it tends to be understated by scholars. To the government of this time this role was far more important than is generally allowed in scholarship, and thus more significant in the assessment of individual diplomats. They were expected to provide a gloss on the news in order to make it explicable, and experience helped greatly in this contextualization. Distinguishing between what was doubtful and what certain was seen as a key attribute of diplomatic ability, and the difficulty of evaluating information vied with the need to make frequent reports.

Distinguishing between reporting and negotiating should not be pursued too rigidly, as they were both aspects of a continuum of activity. Moreover, there could be significant overlaps, as when conversations between diplomats and ministers, a key aspect of reporting, were used to comment on the state of relations and, in doing so, to suggest changes, an aspect of negotiations. Thus in March 1688 Bevil Skelton, English envoy in Paris, was left in no doubt that James II's refusal to commit himself diplomatically was unwelcome to the French:

> some discourses I heard yesterday at Court from some of the ministers, who making reflections upon the States' [Dutch] ill usage of his Majesty [James II] . . . say that they would not dare to do it were they but made more sensible of the amity and good understanding that there is between the two Crowns, and 'tis the assurances which His Majesty sometimes gives the Spanish minister of his being in no manner of engagement with France, that makes the States thus insolent; I have nothing more to say to it than to tell you what are the discourses of the most considerable men here as well as of Monsr de Croissy, who again told me his Majesty might depend upon all the services this Crown was able to do him.[47]

The employment of clerics, rare, although not unknown, in Protestant Europe, was increasingly uncommon among Catholic states, with the prominent exception of the papal nuncios.[48] The complicating consequences of confessional factors in diplomacy[49] may well have discouraged the use of clerics, although in 1774 the Palatine envoy in Vienna was to recommend (unsuccessfully) that he be succeeded by a cleric, not least because the latter could be recompensed with a benefice, which would not cost the Elector anything.[50] Consular posts were dominated by merchants, and these posts were crucial to the protection of commercial interests and privileges.

Aristocrats were disinclined to accept formal training, while the prevalence of French as a diplomatic language helped reduce the need for wide-ranging linguistic competence. In the seventeenth century, French was already one of the leading diplomatic languages, although German, Italian, Latin and Spanish were also all important.[51] When Sir William Temple negotiated with the Prince-Bishop of Münster, they spoke Latin, as Temple did not know German.⁵² Towards the end of the century and even more in the eighteenth, French went on to become close to an international diplomatic language over much of Europe; for conversation, and indeed treatises on diplomacy, if more slowly in diplomatic correspondence.

Political developments played a role in this change. The weakness of Spain during the reign of Carlos II (r. 1665–1700), the attention and prestige that Louis XIV (r. 1643–1715) brought France, the greater role of Paris as a diplomatic centre, the decline in papal prestige and the weaker relationship between Rome and Europe by the late seventeenth century,⁵³ and the importance within the Empire of German dialects all helped to ensure that by the time of the negotiations for the Peace of Utrecht (1713), French was the leading diplomatic language in Western Europe. The Peace of the Pyrenees of 1659 was signed as two peace treaties, in French and Spanish separately, but no Latin original was produced.⁵⁴ Whereas, at the international peace conference at Nijmegen in 1678, the Franco-Spanish treaty was drawn up in French and Spanish, and the Austro-French treaty was in Latin, at Rastatt (1714) the Austrians used French.

Moreover, French-style diplomacy was increasingly influential across Europe, and was thus encoded as the normative standard in what was, by its nature, a repeating, indeed repetitive, form of activity. French ease was contrasted with Spanish-style formality and circumspection,⁵⁵ and the former proved generally more attractive and fashionable; a development that had cultural as much as political causes. It has recently been argued by Heidrun Kugeler that Louis XIV's France became the pace-setter of diplomatic practice because it was the first state to adapt its diplomatic apparatus to the new states-system, although that argument fails to give due weight to other factors making France influential and also underplays the extent of adaptation elsewhere.⁵⁶

The greater prestige of France in the world of diplomacy was ironic, as opposition to France proved one of the biggest drives in the development of more regular diplomacy. William III of Orange, Stadholder of Holland from 1672 to 1702 and ruler of Britain from 1689 to 1702, used French in much of his correspondence, despite being a bitter rival of Louis XIV. In particular, Louis was increasingly seen from 1673 as a threat to the interests of others and indeed to a wider sense of the interests of Christendom, such that he was referred to as the Christian Turk.

Louis himself used religion as an aspect of his foreign policy and diplomacy, both in Europe where he competed with the Austrian Habsburgs in presenting himself as the champion of the Catholic Church, and further afield. Louis's attempts to develop a relationship with Siam (Thailand) owed much to his desire to present himself as a champion of the Church. This theme was probably far more important to him than expanding France's trade. In 1685 Louis sent Abbé François-Tomoléon de Choisy to Siam in an unsuccessful attempt to convert its ruler, Phra Narai. Choisy also failed to gain the privileges he sought for missionaries and converts, while commercial hopes proved abortive. Nevertheless, seeking aid against the Dutch, a Siamese embassy was sent to France, being received in Versailles in January 1687, and in 1687 Louis ordered the dispatch of a new embassy.

However, in 1688 a coup ended Louis's scheme for an alliance. Phra Narai fell and his successor, Phra Petratcha (r. 1688–1703), put a stop to hopes of any relations.[57] This coup was provoked by the arrival of Simon de La Loubère at the head of the second French embassy. Yet, rather than seeing this as a blow to the idea of diplomacy, it appears that the crucial issue in arousing hostility was the dispatch of 636 soldiers with La Loubère in order to occupy the key positions of Bangkok and Mergui. The kingdom was then closed to Europeans, except for a Dutch trading post, and official French contact did not resume until the nineteenth century.

In Europe, as also overseas, Louis used the processes of diplomacy not only to advance his specific interests but also to proclaim his *gloire*. Indeed, triumphal palace architecture, notably at his palace of Versailles, was in part designed for the reception of foreign envoys in a way that impressed them with the majesty of the king, while the decorations recorded his victories.[58]

Louis also took an aggressive stance over diplomatic representation and, notably, precedence. The latter was a longstanding issue, not least because the honour of sovereigns was believed to be bound up in issues of protocol and appearance. This theme continues to this day and helps ensure that the activities of diplomats constitute a distinctive form of representation and negotiation, a form characterized by an almost ritualistic style.

The problems posed by precedence as well as titles and visits led to often complex issues of protocol. Some could be solved by insisting on equal treatment, as with eighteenth-century peace conferences in which envoys entered the conference chamber through different doors at the identical moment, sat down at the same instance, and signed their copy of the treaty as one. Not all issues, however, could be addressed this way, notably the order in which envoys appeared in processions, an order that was generally understood to equate with precedence.

John Finet, the Master of Ceremonies in the English court in the early seventeenth century, discussed some of the clashes in his posthumous *Finetti Philoxenis* (1656). The problem led to attempts to settle precedence, as in John Selden's *Titles of Honour* (1614), which focused on the antiquity of monarchical rank, although that issue itself led to quarrels, including over claims to the inheritance of kingdoms, such as Jerusalem, which enjoyed distinction and antiquity. In his *A Discourse Concerning the Precedency of Kings . . . Whereunto is also Adjoyned a Distinct Treatise of Ambassadors* (1664), James Howell, the English Historiographer Royal, managed to present Britain as a 'Royal Isle' even prior to the Roman period. In part Howell, who declared that he was happy to have gentry rather than aristocrats as envoys and also saw a potential for women in that role,[59] was seeking to establish precedence as opposed to France and Spain.

An emphasis on ceremonial and protocol can make the diplomatic culture and ideology of the period appear remote and redundant, and notably if both are seen as non-functional and anachronistic. This approach, however, is very much the outsider's view, and one held of a time, unlike today, when alternatives were not at offer. In practice, far from being redundant, ceremonial and protocol – and a wide range of ideas, assumptions and practices are understood by the terms – were the focus of a diplomatic world for which they served as a means of asserting and defending status and interests. Senior diplomats represented their masters in the sense that when acting in a formal capacity they were to be seen as the sovereign, most clearly when they acted by proxy for their master in royal marriages.

The focus on ceremonial and protocol was perfect for a competitive world that wished to have an alternative to conflict. The role of ceremonial ensured that considerations of status played a major role in the choice of diplomats and in the allocation of diplomatic rank. Moreover, 'being', and particularly 'being' in an appropriate fashion, was important alongside 'doing'. Envoys lay down their stomachs, as well as their purses, for the cause of their sovereigns.

In 1661, the year in which Louis XIV came to exercise royal authority in person, a dispute over precedence between the Count of Estrades and the Baron of Batteville, the French and Spanish envoys in London, erupted into a serious clash, with the Spaniards forcing their way ahead of the coach of the French envoy at the celebration of the arrival of a new Swedish envoy. Two servants were killed. Louis at once convened an extraordinary council. It unanimously advised moderation, but Louis, instead, decided to push the issue. He expelled the Spanish envoy and obliged Philip IV of Spain, his father-in-law, to recall Batteville and to have his new envoy in France declare publicly before Louis in a formal audience that all Spanish diplomats had been instructed not to contest precedence with their French counterparts, a key expression of the use of the diplomatic world to establish status. The thirty other diplomats accredited to Louis were present at the audience and, to underline his triumph, Louis issued a medallion depicting the audience to celebrate his victory.[60]

When in 1662 a dispute between papal guards and the armed following of the French envoy in Rome, the Duke of Créqui, resulted in violence, Louis broke off diplomatic relations, expelling the nuncio and withdrawing his envoy. His threat of military action led Pope Alexander VII, vulnerable to French action both in Italy and, more particularly, in his principality of Avignon, which was surrounded by French territory, to make concessions in 1664. This quarrel was not solely about prestige but related also to wider considerations, especially French hopes of weakening the Spanish position in Italy.

The use of the position of diplomats as the representative of their ruler was rarely as blatant or violent as by Louis XIV at the expense of the Pope, and it would be mistaken to draw a causal link from such intimidation to the failure of Louis in the long term to mould Europe to his will. Instead, French diplomats frequently proved adroit in negotiation, as well, until the early 1680s, as in intervening in domestic high politics in order to advance French interests. Thus, in the United Provinces (Netherlands) in the early 1680s, D'Avaux was able to exploit the anti-Orangeist feeling of the Louvestein party and the apparently justified sense that Spain and England, the alternative allies to France, were broken reeds. Yet more was at stake at this juncture. For example, favourable French tariff charges, and the consequent revival of trade, influenced Dutch opinion.[61]

Despite their adroitness, the efforts of such diplomats were undermined by the extent to which the weakness of potential opponents encouraged Louis to press on with his aggressive schemes. Intimidation appeared to be an end as much as a means, the result of a situation in which diplomacy did not seem necessary for Louis other than to cement military gains.[62] This situation prefigured that under Napoleon and, indeed, Hitler.

The result under Louis was the pursuit of agreements aimed against France, a pursuit that led to the diplomacy required for alliances and coalitions, the latter considerably more complex than the former. The formation of the League of Augsburg in 1686 was a crucial episode and was followed by the Grand Alliance in 1689. This alliance of Austria, Britain and the United Provinces served as a key strand in European diplomacy over much, but by no means all, of the following six decades until the Diplomatic Revolution of 1756 (see p. 108), with negotiations required not only to establish the alliances but also to sustain them, not least in often fraught discussions over the supply of troops, the provision of funds, and military goals.

The mix that led to such alliances was a matter of principles, adroit diplomacy, and the movement by rulers keenly aware of shifts in the wind. French diplomats urging, in reply, the cause of Louis's *gloire* and honour, and the need to overawe opponents,[63] failed to provide accurate information on a shift in European opinion or to define the situation in terms of French interests that could be advanced through negotiations.

Equally, arguments for caution were scarcely part of the political culture of Louis XIV's diplomacy, and certainly not at crisis moments.[64] Indeed, this political culture requires more general probing because it raises the question of how far diplomats were (and are) constrained by the presuppositions of their state. This is a key element as such constraint affects the gathering of information, the process of representation, and, indeed, the compromises necessary in any negotiations; a situation that links past to present. There are also significant institutional constraints on diplomats and foreign policy, not least as part of the bureaucratic, cultural and ideological moulding integral to oversight and control. Indeed, there is the argument now that foreign ministries have become somewhat redundant because they have been overly bound by their institutional practices, notably as élite representatives of established views, and therefore have not been able to adapt to the public politics of the present day.

To a certain extent, the process of constraining diplomats by the presuppositions of their ruler was true of Louis XIV's diplomacy and diplomats. Louis's determination, expressed in 1661, to be his own principal minister was demonstrated by his ordering that no dispatches or orders were to be sent by the Secretaries of State without permission or signature.

French diplomats and ministers failed to adapt to the extent to which not only their policies were unwelcome but also the way in which they were perceived to do business. Indeed, there was the development, notably, but not only, in Britain and the United Provinces, of what would later be termed the 'public sphere'. This sphere did not only provide a key forum for the expression of anti-French remarks; it also served as a forcing-house for these views. Descriptions and arguments applied earlier against Spanish diplomacy under Philips II, III and IV, notably the 'Black Legend' about Philip II, were used against that of France.

In contrast to the developing 'public space', French diplomacy under Louis XIV generally focused more on relations with small and known groups, although there was also the publication of manifestoes and other attempts to reach out to the public. French policy and diplomatic style proved unsuccessful, in part because shifts in the wider public politics interacted with, and were exploited by, those in the governing groups in the United Provinces and Britain, notably with the rise of William III in both.[65] Nevertheless, such a focus on small and known groups was the normative one in the age of 'courts and cabinets'. This focus provided much of the character of diplomacy, but also an indicative guide to its potential weaknesses. These included the danger of political oblivion if allies fell.[66]

The widespread opposition to Louis XIV in the late seventeenth century was striking. By the end of 1690, Austria, the United Provinces, England, Spain, Savoy-Piedmont, and most of the German princes, including Brandenburg, Hanover, Hesse-Cassel and Bavaria, were at war with Louis in the Nine Years' War; also known as the War of the League of Augsburg and as King William's War. This list was a product not only of French failure but also of the ability of diplomacy to advance a new international order designed to ensure a form of collective security focused on the enforcement of Louis' observance of his treaties. Although Victor Amadeus II of Savoy-Piedmont was, characteristically, bought off by Louis in 1696, most of the allies fought on until peace was negotiated at Rijswijk in 1697.

At the same time, and the point is more widely applicable when judging claims of the success of diplomacy, the coalition was not solely a product of negotiating skill. In addition, the force that could be deployed by the respective sides was important in winning success. For example, the Marquis de Villars, sent by Louis in late 1688 to win the alliance of Elector Max Emanuel of Bavaria, reported that the Bavarian government was frightened by Austrian ministers who said that the Electorate would be overrun if it opposed Leopold.[67] Such considerations were particularly pertinent for Villars, an experienced officer who had already served as a peacetime envoy to Bavaria but, in doing so, had accompanied Max Emanuel on his successful campaign against the Turks in 1687.

The coalition of the 1690s can be linked to a developing trend in international relations, that toward a public diplomacy in which information was more explicitly designed for an audience that would respond, and respond in ways different to those elicited by spectacular ceremonial. Already in 1659 public interest in the Peace of the Pyrenees was such that many copies were printed and private individuals could buy them.[68] Earlier, at least 42,000 copies of the Peace of Westphalia were printed within a year of its signature in 1648.[69] Publication reflected both commercial opportunity on the part of printers and the governmental desire to win support, as with the English publication of the peace terms with Spain in 1630; although the latter excluded the contentious clauses relating to colonial issues.

Following interest in individual treaties came that in compilations, as in the six volumes devoted to French treaties from 1435 to 1690 that were profitably published in 1693 by Frédéric Léonard, the printer to Louis XIV. He had started in 1668 when he published a copy of the Treaty of Aix-la-Chapelle. Also in 1693 Gottfried Leibniz published a *Codex Juris Gentium Diplomaticus*.

The public debate over policy was an attempt, at both the national and the international level, to demonstrate the appropriate nature of decision-making. As such, the debate was also an aspect of the growing concern with the need for self-consciously instructed policy-formation. This need can be related to the drive for what was termed 'political arithmetic', as well as to the Scientific Revolution. The advances in chemistry associated with Robert Boyle (1627–91) and in physics with Sir Isaac Newton (1642–1727) encouraged a sense that predictable rules or laws existed in the natural world, and that these could, and should, be discovered and harnessed. The preference for systemic approaches was one in which relationships of cause and effect were rational, clear and subject to measurement.[70]

This argument linking diplomacy, the public sphere and science might appear persuasive, but it contains an element of teleology, not to say triumphalism. Aside from doubts over the scale, coherence and impact of *the* public sphere, it is worth pointing out that there was already a well-developed (albeit different) public[71] sphere in the sense of confessional politics. Indeed, in the 1680s–90s, as during the Thirty Years' War, there was tension between calls for a confessional diplomacy and attempts to justify a different form, the latter based on opposition to a ruler with allegedly hegemonic tendencies. In 1688 Louis called for a Catholic league in the face of Protestant aggression, while James II sought the support of Catholic powers on the basis of his domestic pro-Catholic policies.[72] Had William III not been committed to opposition to Louis, then Leopold I's attitude to William's invasion of England might well have been different, and Catholic internationalism might have been more important.

The centrepiece of the new-found desire for a progressive secular system, as far as international relations were concerned, was the concept of the balance of power. This was a porous concept that was both associated with political arithmetic and Newtonian mechanics, and was seen as the necessary protection against the imperial pretensions of other powers and, therefore, both as helping ensure the cycle of history in which empires rose and fell and in protecting against these empires when they were at their height.

Reason in the form of intellectual speculation tended to suggest a benign order, in which well-meaning states ought to co-operate, but this approach was not the best basis for the cut-and-thrust of self-interested diplomacy that appeared to prevail. Indeed, the sense that powers had interests that should be combinable to produce a coherent and rational states system carried with it the consequence that, if they did not act as anticipated, then this was a consequence of error: a foolish or wilful failure to understand interests. As a result, there was a frequent complaint about the views of individual members of foreign governments and, thus, an interest not so much in what would now be termed regime change, but rather in the removal of specific flawed ministers. This approach accorded with the use of the idea of evil ministers in Classical thought and domestic history.

The balance of power had considerable influence as far as diplomacy was concerned. It brought an apparent precision to the relations between states, or, at least, encouraged a sense of normative behaviour. Due to this concern, there was a premium on accurate information about other states.

This premium was fostered by a lack of certainty about what was actually being measured, a lack which reflected the extent to which the balance was more appropriate as a device of political argument than as a basis for precise policy formation.[73] Different assessments of strength were based on such criteria as population, area, army, size and financial resources. All this encouraged a drive for information, which was accentuated by the relative absence of reliable information compared to subsequent centuries. Diplomats were expected to produce information on national strength, although, in general, in a less systematic fashion than their Venetian counterparts. As a Papal equivalent, in 1622 the Sacred Congregation 'de Propaganda Fide' was established in Rome not only to coordinate all missionary activities, but also to centralize information on foreign lands.

Demands for information were linked to another task: attempts to control the flow and dissemination of unwelcome material. These attempts stemmed from sixteenth-century concern about the political possibilities of print and the subsequent need by governments to counter the publication of hostile political and religious material. The role of diplomats in such issues is a reminder of their varied commitments. In part, this role was simply another aspect of the obligation on diplomats to represent, to the best of their ability, their governments, but concern with critical publications indicated the extent to which this obligation was not confined to the world of courts. Nor were the sources of information thus confined, although, in contrast to the modern situation, envoys (and their staff) travelled singularly little within the states to which they were posted. As a result, they did not gain information by that means. It was fairly remarkable for Hop, the Dutch envoy in London, to go as far as Norfolk in 1739.[74]

However, the provision of information by diplomats was but part of the process by which knowledge was acquired about the capability and intentions of foreign powers. Espionage, much of which involved postal interception and deciphering, was significant, not least for spying on foreign diplomats. Human intelligence (rather than SIGNIT or signals intelligence) was also important, with spying directed to foreign armies and navies and largely organized through army and naval commands.

Yet this espionage provided information on capability rather than intentions. The inchoate, usually secretive, nature of policy-making by small groups of individuals made it difficult to understand the latter. Instead, it was necessary to develop links with courtiers, ministers and the diplomats of other powers. Sometimes, these 'agents of influence' were rewarded financially, and such action, once discovered, could lead to judicial and other action. Abraham van Wicquefort (1606–82), a talented Dutchman who served a number of powers, including the United Provinces, as a diplomat, was imprisoned in France in 1659 for supplying official secrets, and again in 1675 when a diplomat for the Duke of Brunswick in the United Provinces. His claims to diplomatic immunity were trumped by the view that a national working in his home country for a foreign power was not entitled to such protection; but Wicquefort also suffered from his opposition to the Orangeists and his links to Johan de Witt, the Grand Pensionary in Holland, overthrown and killed in 1672 when William III seized power. Wicquefort was to escape in 1679, but imprisonment fired him on to assert the need for legal privileges in his *Mémoires touchant les Ambassadeurs et les Ministres Publics* (1676–9) and his *L'Ambassadeur et Ses Fonctions* (1681), both important works in the growing literature on diplomacy.

In general, those who provided information cannot be regarded as spies gained by bribery. Instead, the willingness of courtiers and ministers to offer information reflected the nature of politics, with struggles over power, patronage and domestic factional considerations making it possible for foreign diplomats to find allies in divided courts and ministries. In some cases, this process was pushed very far and diplomats intervened actively in domestic politics; again a situation with modern parallels.

More frequently, diplomats took a less active role, but the factious nature of court politics still provided them with significant sources of information. This material is usually found in the reports of envoys. Thus, rather than being any sharp break between diplomatic and intelligence material, the two were closely intertwined, a situation that owed much to the absence of equivalents to modern espionage institutions. Thomas, 2nd Earl of Ailesbury, observed in 1704 'that the name of Ambassador was most honourable, however they are ever regarded as spies for their masters'.[75]

Information gathering and espionage as aspects of the same process serve as a reminder of the severe challenges states faced, and of the extent to which mistakes could lead to, or exacerbate, danger. This point elides what might otherwise have been a more substantial gap between diplomacy and espionage. Linked to this characteristic is the folly of thinking of states as coherent blocks with diplomatic services that were separate and competing. Instead, the intertwining of diplomatic service and domestic politics was matched by an interpenetration of states and, more specifically, of these diplomatic/political nexuses.[76]

The possibility of creating a potent alliance against France suggested a crucial future for diplomacy, even, ironically, if the language of discussion was commonly French. Thus diplomacy was playing a key role in maintaining Europe as a multipolar system. This alliance looked toward the peace treaties of 1713–14, and to subsequent co-operation in the late 1710s and 1720s in creating a new diplomatic order that incorporated France.

THREE
1690–1775

At one level, it is appropriate to move forward from the stress in the last chapter on international co-operation against France through diplomacy in order to consider the leagues and peace congresses of this period in Europe. The development of ideas and practices of collective security is particularly impressive and, indeed, looks toward nineteenth- and twentieth-century usage, as well as towards the situation today. These ideas were related to the idea of a European system guided by common rules. The value of such a system was outlined by many commentators. This situation was especially the case after the post-Westphalian reduction of persistent religious hostility at the level of international relations in the late seventeenth century encouraged a search for secular rationales of diplomatic policy: or, at least, a search for a language of politics and purpose that could encompass Protestant and Catholic Europe. To some commentators, the maintenance of *the* [not *a*] balance of power in such a European system became the end of diplomacy, or at least the crucial means in securing a more benign future.

The apparent precision and naturalness of the image and language of balance greatly contributed to their popularity in an age in thrall to Sir Isaac Newton and his exposition of mechanistic physics, as well as to Classical notions of order and balance, not least as revived in the Renaissance with the idea of a balance of power between the Italian cities.[1] Furthermore, balance served as an appropriate *leitmotif* for a culture that placed an emphasis on the values of moderation and restraint, and on an international system and diplomatic culture organized around principles of equality between sovereign powers, or at least on the absence of hegemony, which was regarded as un-European and uncivilized. These assumptions were crucial to a major strand in European political culture.

States were seen as sovereign, but linked as if within a machine. This system was perceived as self-contained, and as part of a static and well-ordered world. The concept was based on the model of the machine which, in turn, was regarded as well ordered and enabling its parts to conduct activities only in accordance with its own construction. The mechanistic concept of the system of states was well suited to the wider currents of thought, specifically Cartesian rationalism, as well as its successors.

These currents of thought provided not only an analytical framework, but also a moral context for international relations. A key instance is that of balance-of-power politics, which, as generally presented, appear selfishly pragmatic, bereft of any overarching rules and lacking any ethical theoretical foundations. In practice, however, the situation was somewhat different. There was a widely expressed theory of the balance of power, and rules for its politics, outlined in tracts, pamphlets, doctoral dissertations and explanations of the reasons for the resort to war. The relationship between such theoretization and rules on the one hand, and decision-making processes on the other, is obscure, and clearly varied by ruler and minister, but such discussion set normative standards that helped shape policies and responses.[2]

Moreover, diplomatic correspondence frequently responded to the idea of policy shaped by information, and thus as rational. Seeking in 1752 to persuade the Emperor Francis I, husband of Maria Theresa of Austria, of the wisdom of co-operating with Britain to push through the Imperial Election Scheme designed to secure his succession as Emperor by his son, Archduke Joseph (the future Joseph II), the British envoy, John, 3rd Earl of Hyndford, countered the idea that French opposition represented a block. He told Francis to 'examine France, on the side of its interest, whether it be so, or not, at present to begin a war when neither its trade, marine, nor finances have recovered their strength, when Louis XV's expenses exceed by a third the expenses of Louis XIV'.[3]

Yet as a reminder of the problems posed by constructing the history of diplomacy from the theories of the time, the mathematical approach to policymaking, while suggested by the language of the balance, was not however one that commended itself to most rulers and ministers. Instead, they tended to make an intuitive response to the situation and then, in seeking allies, to push forward the reasons that seemed most persuasive; a situation very similar to that today.

Moreover, without denying a central role for notions related to the balance of power, it is necessary to complement them with an awareness of organic assumptions. These were important not so much at the level of the international system (until the nineteenth century), but at that of individual states. Furthermore, these assumptions helped provide a dynamic component that is generally lacking with the more structural nature of the mechanistic themes. This dynamic component was vitalist in intention.

In particular, there was a sense of a state as the expression of a nation, of the latter as linked in a national character, and of this character as capable of change and as prone to decay. The belief in the possibility of decay looked in part to cyclical accounts of the rise and fall of empires which drew much of their authority on the commanding role of Classical Rome in the historicized political thought of the period, but there was also a strong input from ideas of health. Thus, a traditional sense of the nation as akin to a person remained important.

This idea translated into the international sphere with a sense of nations as competitive and as under threat from challenges that were foreign as well as domestic in their causation and mechanism.[4] For example, as far as the Seven Years' War (1756–63) was concerned, anti-Catholicism was crucial in affecting British attitudes towards their ally Prussia and their enemy France,[5] and this point is worth underlining because it encouraged a sense that the struggle should be persisted in, even in the face of news that was very negative, which was the case in the early days of the war.[6] Anti-Catholicism led to a sense of existentialist and metahistorical struggle.

In 1769 William Robertson, a Scottish historian with a reputation across the West, argued, in his critically and commercially successful *History of the Reign of the Emperor Charles V*, that the balance of power was a product of:

> political science . . . the method of preventing any monarch from rising to such a degree of power, as was inconsistent with the general liberty . . . that great secret in modern policy, the preservation of a proper distribution of power among all the members of the system into which the states of Europe are formed . . . From this era [the Italian Wars of 1494-1516] we can trace the progress of that intercourse between nations, which had linked the powers of Europe so closely together; and can discern the operations of that provident policy, which, during peace, guards against remote and contingent dangers; which, in war, hath prevented rapid and destructive conquests.[7]

'Intercourse between nations' and 'provident policy'. Robertson's book provided empirical and conceptual underpinning for the notion of contemporary Europe as a system that had devised a workable alternative to hegemonic power. The latter type of power was seen as the antithesis to diplomacy as well as the product of a more primitive political culture, more primitive whether identified with Europe's past or with non-Western cultures. There was also a tendency among European envoys in

Constantinople to argue that Turkish policy arose from court intrigues, was inherently changeable and could not serve as the basis for a solid system. Thus Turkey could not be a reliable part of an international system.[8]

Furthermore, the European alternative was regarded as better not only because it facilitated internal development within Europe, but also because competitive, but restrained, emulation, it was believed, gave Europe an edge over non-European powers, an aspect of what would later be termed Social Darwinism. Thus Edward Gibbon, a Member of Parliament as well as an influential historian, argued that:

> the balance of power will continue to fluctuate, and the prosperity of our own or the neighbouring kingdoms may be alternatively exalted or depressed; but these partial events cannot essentially injure our general state of happiness, the system of arts, and laws, and manners, which so advantageously distinguish, above the rest of mankind, the Europeans and their colonies. . . . The abuses of tyranny are restrained by the mutual influence of fear and shame. . . . In peace, the progress of knowledge and industry is accelerated by the emulation of so many active rivals; in war, the European forces are exercised by temperate and indecisive contests.[9]

This perspective, a European version of universalism, described the ideal vision of the diplomatic world of Europe between the Peace of Westphalia of 1648 and the start of the French Revolution in 1789. The perspective was expressed in such diplomatic concepts and devices as collective security and the congress system. Moreover, under Peter the Great (r. 1689–1725), Russia was integrated into European diplomatic practice, with the establishment of regular relations. This represented, as Gibbon pointed out, a major extension of the European international system, and one that was important because Russia's greater power would otherwise have made it a potentially dangerous outside force.

There was scant need for a comparable expansion to take note of new states within Europe, although the kingdom of Naples became one after Spanish conquest from Austria in 1734. The peace settlement following the end of the War of Polish Succession in 1735 led to it becoming an independent state ruled by Don Carlos, a younger son of Philip v of Spain. With Naples a royal court, it gained diplomatic representation.

Just as Gibbon's account excluded the 'barbarians' from his 'one great republic' of Europe, so also the diplomatic world was brittle, at least in terms of what was to come later. That this world excluded women and the bulk of the male population, and also reflected the system of orders and privilege that dominated and manipulated society, is scarcely surprising, but nevertheless helped to ensure that revolution, nationalism, peoples' warfare and peoples' diplomacy all posed serious challenges to it. However, criticizing on these grounds a diplomatic system that was fit for purpose to contemporaries can justifiably be regarded as anachronistic.

The same point can be made about administrative sophistication as judged in modern terms. Indeed, diplomacy, both in terms of the activities of diplomats and of the conduct of foreign policy, can be located in part with regard to a tension over the character not only of government, but also of political society. From the late seventeenth century, and more particularly, from the 1710s, many intellectuals and some rulers and ministers hoped that by using and also transforming government, they would be able to reform society. The French economist Jean-Claude Vincent de Gournay coined the term 'bureaucracy'. Demands for more, and more readily accessible and useable, information, drove what has been seen as an information revolution.[10]

Yet the call for stronger and more centralized administration had general implications that clashed with traditional conceptions of government. The latter were mediated through a system reflecting privileges and rights that were heavily influenced both by the social structure and by the habit of conceiving of administration primarily in terms of legal precedent. As a rules-based system, diplomacy was very much located in the latter context, not least with the emphasis on protocol. Rulers varied in their willingness to exchange the traditional foundations of authority and power, in legal precedent and a particularist social order, for a new conception of government. Diplomacy, however, shared in a general situation in which many of the reforms can best be understood not as administrative transformations, but in habitual terms, both as the response to established problems and also as the attempt to make existing practices work better.

To call, from the perspective of today, for administrative revolution in the period, as indeed in many other periods, is misleading. New institutional bodies were created in the eighteenth century for foreign policy (see p. 113), but these were societies that put a premium on continuity and order, in part as a reaction against the political, religious and social turmoil of *c.* 1520–*c.* 1660. The search for order based on stability and consensus (albeit socially circumscribed in both cases) was related to a functional dependence on the landed élites and their urban counterparts.

The long-term consequences of the Peace of Westphalia can also be located in this context. An emphasis on mutuality between sovereign states bore a relation to the anti-hegemonic direction of policy, rhetoric and coalition diplomacy that had led to opposition to the Habsburgs during the Thirty Years' War and to France from the 1660s. Thus there were again idealistic and functional components to the goals of diplomacy, just as there were to its organization and social composition.

The emphasis on continuity, order, stability and consensus in the political culture of the age (European but also Oriental) had another important consequence in that there was a reluctance to engage with rebels as key interlocutors in international relations. There were naturally exceptions, but this point seems apparent, certainly when compared to the earlier period of confessional warfare or, more usually, confessionally linked warfare.

The relative decline of the religious factor in international relations within Christian Europe played an important role in encouraging the development of a diplomatic world incorporating all the (European) states. Although all contexts are different, this situation looked toward the change in European diplomacy after the end of the French Revolution toward the development of such a world, and, in contrast, the much more difficult situation after the close of the Cold War, at least at the global level, although not at the European one.

There was not only continuity in the character of international relations within *ancien régime* Europe. Outside Europe, there was also considerable continuity in Western diplomacy, notably in North America, West Africa and South Asia. In North America, the British and French negotiated actively with Native American tribes as they sought to establish and expand their colonies and, crucially, to make headway against each other. Land, trade, presents (including guns) and alliances were the key issues in these negotiations. Alongside wide-ranging European claims to territory, for example for the British colony of Carolina west into the interior, there was a reality of seeking to win Native support, and thus of adapting to Native goals.

The situation was very different, but there was a parallel with the contrast between the claims made by the Chinese and the reality of a more difficult relationship on the ground. The 'middle ground' between Native Americans and Europeans was a shifting one, but the longer trend of European expansion, however damaging, did not in the short term condition the extent to which Natives were able to negotiate their own advantage, often from a position of strength. At the same time, relations with the Native Americans indicate the need to understand the role of varied circumstances, which ensured that the 'middle ground' meant very different situations.[11] The place of individuals in mediating relations was clear in the co-operative role of James Oglethorpe and Tornochichi in ensuring good relations between the new colony of Georgia and the neighbouring Creeks in the 1730s. There was a clear contrast with the more hostile situation in the Carolinas.

Co-operation was important because there were major cultural differences between the two sides that threatened to accentuate specific points in dispute, not least conflicting notions of diplomacy. Whereas Europeans and European–Americans viewed treaties as permanent and absolute contracts, which moreover applied to all members of the nationalities that had accepted the conditions, Native Americans saw them as temporary arrangements that would remain in force until conditions or leadership changed and, also, that were binding only among the participants who were involved in the process of making those arrangements. At the same time, this contrast has to be qualified as the colonists frequently repudiated earlier treaties in their quest for land. In the case of the British and the Creeks, there were also the challenges posed by differing British views about the most appropriate governmental form for the new colony of Georgia, as well as the dynamic provided by the other players involved, notably other Native Americans and other European colonists.[12]

The Western representatives in North America were not diplomats accredited in London, Paris and Madrid, but the agents of colonial governments. The chain of command in dealing with the Native Americans was less than clear, and the individual colonies, Superintendents for Indian Affairs, the Board of Trade, the army and other branches of the government had different, and often competing, agendas. Further complicating the issue was the diversity of relations the Crown and each colony had with the various tribes, as well as the enormous range of knowledge the competing groups had of the Native Americans.

At Albany in 1755, the British colonial delegations negotiated with the Mohawks, notably the headman Hendrick, in an effort to maintain their alliance, but this was handicapped by rivalries between the colonial delegations, each with their own agenda, notably for acquiring land. These rivalries were an ironic comment on plans, actively pushed by Benjamin Franklin, to create an intercolonial union under the British Crown. The meetings among the delegates failed to agree these plans, but they indicated the multiple processes and goals of negotiation at play.[13] Even when the Native Americans were most united against the British, in 1763 several tribes remained on the British side. Through diplomacy, they could be pacified, removed or employed.

In West Africa, European trading posts, of which one of the principal exports was slaves, were not held by sovereign right but by agreement with local powers, and rent or tribute was paid for several posts. It was necessary to maintain a beneficial relationship with numerous local *caboceers* (leaders) and *penyins* (elders) through an elaborate, and costly, system of presents, dashees and jobs. As in India, the limited sovereignty enjoyed by Western interests did not, however, prevent active intervention in local politics.[14]

The European position as far as North Africa was concerned was a complex mixture of force, threats of force, and more co-operative commercial relations. Diplomacy was often conducted by military and naval commanders. The cost of receiving embassies was such that in 1783 Sir Roger Curtis Knight, sent as British envoy to Muhammad III of Morocco, was instructed to discourage the dispatch of any envoy. In return for good relations, Muhammad was offered the gift of a frigate.

Cultural differences played a role. In a report from the fashionable spa of Tunbridge Wells, *Mist's Weekly Journal* of 20 August 1726 noted 'the Morocco Ambassador, who (notwithstanding his strange dress, which causes a stupid amazement in the country people) is really a fine gentleman, and very much respected for his polite behaviour'. Less easily, in Vienna in 1774, a Turkish diplomat had to be persuaded to have three of his servants found in a brothel beaten rather than executed.[15]

In India there was an important transition in relations due to the fall in the power of the Mughal Emperor. In theory, all powers, Western and local, were subject to the Emperor. However, the fluid state of Indian politics, in which the power of the Emperor greatly declined from the early decades of the century, notably after the death of Aurangzeb in 1707, entailed problems in determining how best to negotiate and to define legal settlements with Indian rulers, not least as the latter, in turn, were developing new governmental and political practices.[16]

At the same time, European and native practice in diplomacy was converging and Europeans had little difficulty in adjusting to an established system of *vakils* (agents) at courts. Prior to Lord North's Regulating Act (1773), the three presidencies of the British East India Company – Bombay, Calcutta and Madras – each received *vakils* and conducted their own relations with the Indian princes, with the Company's ad hoc Secret Committee and the Court of Directors providing distant supervision. The Company, a body established by royal charter, had the right to negotiate and sign treaties, wage wars, and send and receive envoys. The *vakils* dealt personally with the Governor or Governor General. The latter, in turn, appointed Residents at Indian courts, who dealt with ministers, rather than directly with the ruler.

The official language on both sides was Persian, and William Kirkpatrick, Resident to the Maratha Prince Sindia in 1786–7 and to the Nizam of Hyderabad in 1794–7, wrote a *Grammar of the Hindro Dialect and an Arabic and Persian Vocabulary* (1782), which was published with the support of the East India Company. European Residents also had to understand Indian courtly etiquette. In some respects, this was a parallel to the dominance of francophone styles in European diplomacy.

Similarly, the British had relied for a long time on the Company's agents to represent them in the Persian Gulf. There was, for example, no envoy or consul in Persia, the capital of which was not a port. Instead, a Company Resident in the port of Bushire was the senior official, and was answerable to the Governor of Bombay.

After the Regulating Act of 1773, Calcutta was given a vaguely defined supervisory authority over the foreign relations of Bombay and Madras, and the Company was required to show despatches and consult the Cabinet in London on matters regarding war, peace and other crucial issues. The following year, its position was clarified with the publication of *Treaties and Grants from the Country* [Indian] *Powers to the East India Company*.

The system established by the Regulating Act led to problems, not only when the Cabinet, which was especially distracted by North America from 1774, knew little and cared less about Indian affairs, but also when Bombay and Madras failed to accept Calcutta's supervision and, instead, appealed to London. The origins, course and settlement of both the First Maratha War (1778–82) and the Second Mysore War (1780–84), in each of which the British forces experienced serious defeats, showed instances of Madras and Bombay conducting their relations with the Indian princes independent of Calcutta. Also in the late 1770s, Calcutta and Madras each had their own representatives at the court of the Nizam of Hyderabad, the key power in central India. Force played a key role in the relationship with Indian rulers, and some Residents maintained control of military forces.[17] The interaction of military and diplomatic responsibilities was seen in many careers as with Walker, the Resident at Baroda from 1802, who was also Deputy Master General for the Bombay army.

There was no comparable interaction between European and local powers elsewhere in Asia; and Japan, in particular, was far more closed to European diplomacy. As far as China was concerned, there were European merchants at Canton and the Portuguese base at Macao.

There was also considerable continuity in relations between Russia and China along one of the longest frontiers between Christendom and the non-West. There had been difficulties in establishing good relations between the two powers, notably because of Chinese opposition to Russian expansion in the Amur Valley, expansion that led to conflict in the mid-1680s. The dispute was referred to negotiations, but these posed problems, notably the lack of qualified interpreters on both sides. As a consequence, the dynamic K'ang-hsi Emperor turned to two Jesuit missionaries in China, Jean-François Gerbillon and Tomé Pereira, who were each given the temporary rank of colonel. Their knowledge of Latin and Manchu ensured the success of the negotiations at Nerchinsk in 1689,[18] and the resulting agreement was the key to Russo–Chinese relations until the 1850s, which were good.

The Russians abandoned the Amur Valley to the Chinese, but there was no retreat to Lake Baikal, so that Russia retained a Pacific coastline on the Sea of Okhosk, from which it was able to expand in the early eighteenth century to the Aleutian Islands and, subsequently, Alaska. The Jesuits in the Amur Valley were a product of their impressive Mission to China, a Mission that reflected an engagement with Chinese culture and language greater than that of any diplomatic representation.[19]

The Treaty of Nerchinsk was followed by the dispatch of a Russian mission to Beijing that showed the role of trade in European diplomatic links with Asia, but also the extent to which the formal control by the European state of these links varied. Isbrants Ides, a merchant, suggested a mission to Beijing in order to create a trade route to China that was seen as a source of great profits. Indeed, the East as a basis of lucrative trade had helped drive European negotiations with Russia, Persia, the Ottoman Empire and China for centuries (for example those of England with the first three in the sixteenth century), acting as a counterpart, and, on occasion, consequence, to maritime exploration across the Atlantic and into the Indian Ocean. In contrast to the diplomacy of the East India Companies, Ides' expedition was turned into an embassy on behalf of Peter the Great, being given diplomatic weight when the government provided a military escort and official interpreters, as well as the credentials that affirmed its status and whose presentation provided an opportunity to establish a legitimate role, and one that distinguished Ides from an ordinary merchant. Looked at differently, this process fitted Ides into the existing pattern of Chinese relations with the outer world.

In turn, Ides spread knowledge of his embassy by publications, which included an edition in English: *The Three Years Land Travels of His Excellence E. Ysbrand Ides from Mosco to China* (1705). Similar publications provided an image of diplomacy as a form of unpicking and exposition of distant cultures. Thus Paul Rycaut, England's able consul in Smyrna (Izmir) from 1667 to 1678, produced *The Present State of the Ottoman Empire* (1668) and *The History of the Turkish Empire* (1680), both of which were to be influential.[20] John Bell, a Scottish doctor who, between 1715 and 1722, accompanied the Russian embassies to Persia and China and in 1737 was sent to Constantinople, left a *Travels from St*

Petersburg in Russia to various parts of Asia (1763) that was also published in a French edition in 1766.[21]

Diplomatic relations were scarcely close, but the Chinese were willing to co-operate with Russia. In 1712 the K'ang-hsi Emperor was prepared to have an envoy in St Petersburg 'conform to the customs and ceremonies' of the Russians, although, in the event, there was no embassy, while in 1720–21 his response to the Izmailov mission to Beijing was favourable. Moreover, Turkish practice was not static. Thus in 1742 a new protocol procedure had been introduced in which, for the first time, a foreign ambassador presented his credentials directly to the Sultan rather than to the Grand Vezir.

In 1727 the Treaty of Khiakta settled the border between Russian-held Siberia and the recent Chinese conquests in Mongolia, extending the Nerchinsk agreement. The Russians were also permitted a presence in China, with a trade mission every third year, a church in Beijing, and Russians in their hostel there allowed to study Chinese, Manchu and Mongol. No other European power had such a presence. Acceptable relations with Russia were significant as the Manchu dynasty put its emphasis in the eighteenth century on policy toward Inner Asia, and in particular did not want Russian support for the hostile Zhunger Confederation based in Xinkiang to the south of Siberia.

China and Russia were helped in the definition of their diplomatic links by the extent to which they were each keen on acting as defined sovereign states with precise boundaries. This approach, however, caused problems for both states when dealing with polities that lacked such a commitment to precision, for example those who clung to a degree of power-sharing and/or favoured imprecise frontiers. In the eighteenth century this situation affected Chinese governmental policy in South-West China, as well as that of the Russians in Central Asia and, indeed, the position of the British as far as the Native Americans were concerned in North America; although, once French Canada had been conquered in 1758–60, the British found it easier to cope with a degree of power-sharing with the Native Americans.

Returning to Europe, alongside issues of conceptualization and imperial diplomacy it is necessary to emphasize other powerful strands of continuity both during the period covered in this chapter and with the earlier chapters. The essential parameters were unchanged. In particular, communications remained uncertain as well as slow. Couriers could regularly travel from The Hague or Paris to London, or vice versa, in three days, but adverse winds would prevent the packet-boats from sailing. In particular, persistent westerlies, winds from the West, could leave the ministry in London waiting for several posts from each of the capitals of northern Europe, with the packet boat to Harwich unable to sail and confined to the Hook of Holland (Helvoetsluys).

These were not the sole problems. The ordinary post from St Petersburg (then the Russian capital) to Hamburg took seventeen days in 1745, but floods and bad roads made the posts very irregular. Rainfall affected the roads particularly badly in the Empire (Germany), Poland and Russia, and there were often insufficient post-horses on the major road routes, and notably so in Eastern Europe. In 1739 Sir Everard Fawkener, the British envoy in Constantinople, noted that the routes from there to Vienna 'are very bad'.[22]

Moreover, many rivers were crossed, as in northern Italy, by ferries rather than bridges, and both snow-melt and heavy rains could make their passage impossible, with the water flowing too fast and the river valley flooding. Rivers were also affected by drought, freezing and weirs, mountain crossings, notably of the Alps, by ice and snow, and sea routes by ice, heavy winds and, in the case in particular of the Baltic, poor charts, which increased the risk of running aground, especially on the approach to ports. No pass across the Alps was open to wheeled traffic until the improvement made to the route through the Col de Tende between Nice and Turin in the 1780s, and that route was not very useful to diplomatic traffic.

Heavy rain affected nearly all posts in Western Europe in mid-January 1728, and ice had a similar effect in the Baltic five years earlier. Winter cold could be better than spring thaw and autumn rain, but summer travel could also be difficult. In 1731 Marshal Villars, a member of the French Council, commented on dispatches that took over 39 days to arrive from Constantinople (Istanbul) to Paris, mostly by sea. Alongside speedy voyages, the journey times of dispatches sent by sea could be greatly affected by wind direction, and were therefore uncertain. The net effect of these and other problems was that the frequency of correspondence with many diplomats was low, which exacerbated the problem that they often did not know if their dispatches were arriving.[23] Especially in distant postings, such as Constantinople, diplomats were often left essentially to their own devices.

Moreover, delays and uncertainties were worse in wartime, including for neutrals. The news of Charles XII of Sweden's total defeat at the battle of Poltava in Ukraine on 9 July 1709 took six weeks to reach Paris, and it arrived first through Dutch newspapers. The uncertainty of sea routes when war with Austria broke out in 1733 (the War of the Polish Succession) led Louis, Marquis of Villeneuve, France's able envoy in Constantinople, to prefer to send his mail across the Adriatic to Ancona in the neutral Papal States, a short crossing, rather than along the Adriatic to neutral Venice, a route that increased the risk of interception by Austrian ships from Trieste. Distance and time were emphasized by the Austrian government when explaining why they could not stop their Russian ally from invading Poland.[24] In 1734 the news of the surrender of Danzig (Gdansk) to the Russians on 30 June reached the Russian envoy in Constantinople on 17 August.

Ten years later, during the War of the Austrian Succession, the hazards of voyages by sea, combined with the danger from hostile British warships, left the French envoy in Genoa without messages for up to three weeks at a time, and led to the hope that Nice, then a possession of the rulers of Savoy-Piedmont, would be captured by French forces so as to improve communications. On an overland route, two successive French couriers from Naples were taken by Austrian hussars.[25] In 1757 the packet boat link between Ostend in the Austrian Netherlands and Dover was severed by the Austrian government[26] because the two states were in opposing blocs, although not at war; an example of the range of international relations with which diplomacy had to deal.

Even if war was not imminent, the desire to avoid the dispatch of couriers via hostile lands could exacerbate the problems of distance. In 1725 the 'great distance' between Vienna and Madrid was regarded as affecting negotiations between the two powers, with the need to send couriers from Genoa to Barcelona by sea, rather than via France, a considerable aggravation.[27] Yet an alliance was negotiated.

It is not surprising that details of the movements of letters and couriers, and of their all-too-frequent mishaps, occurred frequently in the diplomatic correspondence, nor that diplomats posted at any distance often felt forced to respond to developments without obtaining fresh orders. There was progress. In particular, the postal network spread. In 1693–4, for example, the Saxons inaugurated a weekly post from the United Provinces and improved the service with Hamburg so that a reply could be received in eight days: a valuable link between the continental interior and a major port. A new service to Nuremberg was opened in 1699. Portugal signed postal conventions with England in 1705 and Spain in 1718.[28]

Moreover, communications were affected by a general improvement in the second half of the eighteenth century, notably with road-building, for example in France, and by an improvement in the predictability of maritime links. Journey times were cut. The improvements made on the St Petersburg-Moscow road between the death of Peter the Great in 1725 and the 1760s, including the construction of bridges, reduced the journey time over its 825 kilometres from five weeks to two. Nevertheless, there was no comparison with the changes that were to follow in the mid-nineteenth century with railways and steamships. In addition, there were major gaps in road links, for example between Provence and Genoa, that prevent any depiction of an integrated system.

Diplomats as well as messengers could be quick, a British King's Messenger taking seven days in October 1733 to travel from Turin as far as the Calais-Dover packet,[29] but were also delayed due to problems and accidents with methods of transport. Leaving St Petersburg in June 1726, the boat carrying Campredon, the French envoy, ran aground.[30] Philip, 4th Earl of Chesterfield, the British envoy to The Hague, left Harwich at 10 am on 19 January 1745, arriving at Helvoetsluys at 2 pm on 20 January, 'a good deal disordered' after his 'rough voyage'.[31] The voyage to Constantinople in 1755 of Charles, Count of Vergennes, the new French envoy and later the foreign minister, was affected by contrary winds, taking 41 days from Marseille, and that at a time of rising international tension. The time taken led to a determination to send envoys on their way, as in 1755 when Sir Charles Hanbury Williams, who had been appointed to St Petersburg, was informed by the Secretary of State, 'I am particularly commanded by the King [George II] to press your departure, as every day may be of the utmost consequence in the present critical state of Europe'.[32]

Journey times to and from St Petersburg and, less commonly, Moscow were of increased importance because Russia played a more central role in European international relations from the reign of Peter the Great (1689–1725). Although initially a junior member of the league against Charles XII of Sweden that began the Great Northern War (1700–21), Peter rapidly became more important than his beaten Danish and Saxon allies, and he played the key role in defeating Charles, notably at Poltava in 1709. Russian ambitions, real or feared, were soon a key element in international speculation and negotiation. However unwelcome, Russia was seen as a European state, unlike the view of earlier powers from the east such as the Mongols in the thirteenth century, and of their successor groups, notably the Crimean Tatars. Moreover, a major Russian role was sought by other powers. By increasing the pressure on France, the movement of Russian troops into Germany was a key element in bringing the Wars of the Polish and Austrian Successions to an end in 1735 and 1748 respectively, while Russia was co-guarantor with France of the Treaty of Teschen (1779), which brought to an end the War of the Bavarian Succession.

Russian diplomats became permanent envoys at the leading European courts and were highly regarded,[33] helping, for example, to ease Anglo-Russian relations.[34] There were however problems with protocol, due to the Russian claim to imperial status. At times, this claim led to precedence disputes, as with the French envoy in London in 1769. In 1781 the Austrian Chancellor warned the Emperor, Joseph II, that any concession made to Russia would be demanded by other states.[35]

In general, disputes over precedence were less common than in the seventeenth century, but they still occurred. Thus the Dutch and French envoys in London clashed over precedence in 1732;[36] there was a dispute at The Hague in 1753, when the new French ambassador expected the other envoys to visit him 'in ceremony'; a row over precedence involving the Spanish Ambassador in Turin in 1755; and concern in France in 1763 about Austrian and British pretensions.[37] Diplomatic conduct in ceremonial matters was still seen as important, not least for future behaviour,[38] and diplomats sought to vindicate royal dignity through the magnificence of their conduct.[39]

Despite the unwelcome cold,[40] Russian postings became important for career diplomats, as with Sir Charles Whitworth, who served for Britain in St Petersburg from 1705 to 1712. However, his mission was initially almost entirely concerned with commercial matters, which proved far from easy. His experiences negotiating with Peter's ministers on merchants' grievances in general and the tobacco trade in particular were both painful and largely unsuccessful.

Whitworth's posting also indicated the significance of diplomats for reporting on the unfamiliar. The 'Summary Account of Russia as it was in the Spring of 1710', that he drew up and gave to three leading ministers, was published in 1758, and is revealing for its account of rapid change. Whitworth noted the introduction of Western dress and Peter the Great's unpopular attempt to make Russians shave off their beards, and he argued that the brutal form of public punishments demonstrated the essential barbarity and backwardness of Russia. Whitworth suggested that Peter had deliberately set out to weaken the power of the old nobility and that there was much public discontent, not least from increased taxation. He was in no doubt that the Westernization policies were poorly handled as well as unpopular.[41]

The integration of Russia into the European diplomatic system was aided by the extent to which its relations with the Asian powers were episodic. This characteristic was not simply a factor of distance, for the issues in negotiation were different while there were also vexed questions of procedure, notably, but not only, with China. Nevertheless, distance was an important factor; a distance that, in part, reflected serious difficulties in communications, especially the absence of roads. The Russian embassy to Persia that left St Petersburg on 15 July 1715 did not reach Isfahan, the capital of Persia, until 14 March 1717, in turn leaving there on 1 September 1717 and returning to St Petersburg on 30 December 1718. Similarly, the Russian embassy that left Beijing on 2 March 1721 reached Moscow on 5 January 1722; its outward journey had taken over a year.

In contrast to Russia, the place of the Papacy in international affairs dramatically declined,[42] compared for example to the major role of Innocent XI in the 1680s in organizing opposition to both Louis XIV and the Turks. In part, this decline occurred as a consequence across Europe of the diminished importance of confessionalism in government policies at home and abroad.[43] Instead, the Papacy was pushed onto the defensive in diplomacy, being forced to respond to pressure from Catholic rulers for greater control over the Church in their countries, pressure that included the successful campaign for the papal dissolution of the Order of Jesus (Jesuits), which was achieved in 1773.[44]

An emphasis on continuity was true in, and of, the background and training of diplomats. Moves towards training diplomats were episodic, which was in keeping with the nature of much (but far from all) administrative reform in this period. With the exception of the Pontifical Ecclesiastical Academy, founded in Rome in 1701, governmental training establishments were short lived. The *Académie Politique*, established in 1712 by the experienced French foreign minister (and former diplomat), Torcy, to train diplomats, was affected by his fall in 1715, and disappeared in 1720, having had only limited success in placing its products.[45] Regius Chairs of Modern History were created at Cambridge and Oxford in 1724 to help in the training of possible recruits, but few British diplomats were obtained this way. Peter the Great sent Russian nobles abroad to increase their knowledge,[46] especially of foreign languages, but the composition of the Russian diplomatic service was eclectic and included a number of foreigners; which was also true of the military.

Later in the century, over 150 Russians studied in the diplomatic school at Strasbourg founded by Johann Daniel Schöpflin in 1752. This well-attended school drew pupils from across Europe, including France, Germany, Russia, Poland, Scandinavia and the Austrian Netherlands (now Belgium), and was responsible for the publication of useful manuals. The school flourished until the French Revolution, which put an end to it. Products of the school played a major role in European diplomacy, notably in France, but also in Russia and elsewhere.[47]

The use of foreigners as diplomats was a common, albeit decreasing, feature of many diplomatic systems, one reflecting the personal nature of service to a sovereign, and thus of the extent to which diplomatic service was both cosmopolitan and based on notions of personal loyalty and service, rather than being national. The use of foreigners was a product of the ability of rulers to pick whom they wished, which also manifested itself in the large number of foreign military officers. In particular, many Italians and Germans found employment in the service of major rulers. Italians were employed by, among others, Augustus II of Saxony-Poland, while La

Chétardie and Saint-Séverin both served Louis XV of France in senior posts. George I of Britain employed Swiss Protestants at Paris and Vienna.

Emigrés could also be appointed. The Jacobite Lord Marshal of Scotland was appointed envoy in Paris by Frederick II (the Great) of Prussia, while John, Viscount of Tyrconnel, another Jacobite, was his opposite number in Berlin, both choices that angered George II, whose position on the British throne was contested by the Jacobites. As an instance of the complex interplay of family strategies, personal careers and choice by monarchs, James, Duke of Liria, the son of a bastard of James II (the Catholic king driven from Britain in 1688–9), was appointed Spanish envoy to Russia in 1727 when both powers were opposed to Britain. The following year, his cousin, James, Lord Waldegrave (another of James's illegitimate grandsons), who had decided for the Hanoverian dynasty and not for the Stuart exiles, arrived at Vienna as British envoy. From 1730 to 1740 he was to be a highly successful envoy in Paris.

Hiring foreigners, some of whom had already obtained relevant experience, was one way to acquire talent. It was particularly useful for Russia, which was short of native diplomats capable of speaking French. Like the use of foreign military officers, this method was employed more persistently than training establishments. Nevertheless, by the mid-eighteenth century, it was increasingly common to hire natives. In Sweden, for example, such posts were reserved for natives by a regulation of 1723. After 1727, Britain only tended to have foreigners in minor posts.

At the same time, the British, like other governments, made use of friendly diplomats as sources of information, and even as intermediaries, and notably when formal links were broken, as with Vienna in 1727: the British then used Danish, Dutch and Portuguese diplomats. Brunswick-Wolfenbüttel diplomats also served then as intermediaries, notably with St Petersburg. The Dutch retained diplomatic links with France in the War of Austrian Succession after they had been severed between Britain and France in 1744, until France invaded the United Provinces in 1747. Charles Emmanuel III of Sardinia remained neutral in the Seven Years' War (1756-63), and his able envoy in London, Francesco, Count of Viry, later a Foreign Minister, both provided the British ministry with information on French plans and, in combination with his colleague in Paris, acted as a valuable intermediary in Anglo-French negotiations, despite the problems posed by frequent changes in the British government.[48] Such advantages help explain anger when the diplomats of friendly powers failed to assist as expected, a situation that remains the case today. There was also the hope that friendly envoys could provide representation at courts where relations were acceptable, but there was no coverage; for Britain, the Dutch in 1737 at Mannheim, the court of the Elector Palatine.[49]

The calibre of diplomats is difficult to assess. Social skills were certainly important, especially if there was nothing particular to negotiate and the envoy was instructed to make himself agreeable.[50] In 1728 Waldegrave's ability at cards had commended him in Vienna to Prince Eugene, a noted card-player as well as a key Austrian minister.[51] Frederick II of Prussia complained in June 1753 that a French diplomat lacked 'politesse', and that was a quality much in demand, and one for which the French were usually noted. Influence often reflected the ability to make the right impression at court, whether hunting or taking part in the evening smoking and drinking sessions of Frederick William I of Prussia (r. 1713–40), or paying court to the Queen's chamber woman whom Clermont d'Amboise, the French envoy, believed was influential at Naples in 1777. The following year, both he and the Austrian envoy sought to have compatriots appointed to teach the heir to the throne.[52]

The appeal of diplomats with a military background remained strong, and notably at certain courts, especially Berlin. In wartime, some diplomats turned to a military career, most dramatically in 1734, when Count Plelo, the French envoy in Copenhagen, joined a French expeditionary force being sent to relieve Danzig (Gdansk), then besieged by the Russians. The expedition was unsuccessful and Plelo was killed.

Thanks to the significance of Court conduct, training in skills such as riding, as well as in general demeanour, made aristocrats the most suitable choices as senior diplomats, while they also benefited from patronage ties,[53] and from their continued role as exemplary representatives. Monarchs continued, as Henry VIII of England had done, to send trusted members of the court as envoys as pledges of friendship.[54] Some aristocratic envoys disgraced themselves, the well-connected Louis, Duke of Richelieu, a libertine, having to leave Vienna in 1728 for his supposed involvement in black magic rites, but most represented their monarchs in the expected manner.

Their ability in negotiation was often tested less continually than their court skills. Not all diplomats were comparably effective in negotiation, but this situation could, in part, be compensated for by accentuating the role of the respective ministers to whom they reported and, thus, treating the diplomats more as gilded messengers. The ability and experience of ministers responsible for negotiations varied greatly. Many, including Bestuzhev, Choiseul, Kaunitz, Lionne, Pombal, Stormont, Vergennes and Wall, were experienced former diplomats and thus well aware of the problems of diplomacy. Between 1688 and 1713, both Portuguese Secretaries of State were former diplomats, as was the case of later Secretaries such as Mello. Yet some active foreign ministers had little or no diplomatic experience, for example Germain-Louis de Chauvelin, the French Foreign Minister from 1727 to 1737.

In 1731 Anne-Théodore Chavignard de Chavigny, the French envoy at Regensburg claimed that Villebois, his colleague at Cassel lacked the talent of pleasing and of gaining confidence, and 'cette considération personelle qui font la moitié des affaires'.[55] Thus it would be mistaken to suggest that social skills were necessarily incompatible with ability in gaining information and in negotiation. Indeed, a determination to align these underlined the emphasis on the education of diplomats in the eighteenth century, and was linked to the growing tendency for nobles to be the residential diplomats.

In the sixteenth century there had often been a contrast between lower-ranking residential diplomats, and nobles sent for prominent but short-term missions. The latter continued in the eighteenth century, but nobles were increasingly resident diplomats. Sparre, who was recalled from London in 1735, noted that he had been Swedish envoy there for seventeen years, and claimed that his posting had cost him 20,000 ecus of his own money.[56] Aristocratic diplomats often owed their influence to the belief that they were well connected at home. Personal links were important here, as in 1730 when the Marquis of Castelar was sent as Spanish envoy to Paris in an effort to put the Treaty of Seville of 1729 into effect: his brother, José Patiño, was the most influential minister. Patiño appointed other relatives as diplomats.

In 1749 Benjamin Keene, the experienced British envoy, reported from Spain that 'as the ministers here have no great experience in foreign affairs, and there being no council to digest and assist in their political transactions, this court must principally govern itself by the relations of their ministers abroad, and consequently much depends upon the cast of their views and dispositions'.[57] Although some diplomats complained about the courts to which they were accredited, in general they were concerned not about the competence of the ministers there with whom they had to deal, but about these ministers' lack of power or consistency in the face of court politics and monarchical views. Certain monarchs, such as Philip v of Spain (r. 1700–46) and Frederick William I of Prussia, acquired justified reputations for being difficult to deal with. Each played a key role in policy, but the first was unstable and the second irascible to the point of mania. In those circumstances, it was not sufficient to reach an understanding with their ministers. Moreover, in states with powerful representative institutions, notably the United Provinces, Sweden, Poland and Britain, there was the additional hazard that ministries or policies might be overturned or qualified in light of unexpected domestic pressures.

Whatever the political system, there was the continual need for accurate reports. Thus in 1755 Gaston, Duke of Mirepoix, the French envoy in

London, correctly assessed the position of George II when he wrote that the king did not care much about the North American colonies and did not want war, but that he had no intention of trying to improve the situation for his native Electorate of Hanover by making concessions over North America, and indeed had no power to make such a suggestion.[58] To have failed to grasp this point would have exposed French policymakers to the risk of serious error.

The personal nature of monarchical authority repeatedly underlined the role of individuals.[59] Ferdinand VI of Spain (r. 1746–59) resisted French pressure to act against Britain and warnings that the Spanish colonies would follow those of France.[60] Far from being driven to align with France by fear of British expansion or by dynastic links, Ferdinand was reasonably close to Britain. In contrast, his more active half-brother, Charles III (r. 1759–88), was concerned about a fundamental shift of oceanic power towards Britain. This shift in Spanish policy greatly encouraged French firmness in abortive Anglo-French peace negotiations in 1761, because it gave this firmness point.

Meanwhile, British success helped transform not only attitudes there, but also those of Britain's opponents. This sense of strategic culture as dynamic is one that needs to be captured. It is particularly appropriate when considering the latter years of the Seven Years' War (1756–63), for the parameters of debate in Britain were very different to those at the outset. In part, this development reflected the consequences of campaigning, but there were also key external developments in the shape of the new political environment surrounding the accession in 1760 of a new king who was determined to see through changes. There was an important interaction, with choices in relations with Prussia and Spain seen in political terms. George III, his key adviser, John, 3rd Earl of Bute, and Thomas, Duke of Newcastle, the First Lord of the Treasury, had decided to seek to revive the 'Old System' of pre-war alliances. This revival entailed distancing themselves from their wartime ally, Prussia. However, as a powerful reminder of the impact of ideas, and thus conjunctures and contingencies in opinions, George and Bute did not envisage the extensive and costly commitments of Newcastle's pre-war diplomacy. The defence of Hanover, which George never visited, was no longer to be a central feature of Britain's Continental policy.

The role of monarchs underlined the unpredictabilities relating to their lives, for example Louis XV's attack of smallpox in 1728 which led to an intense, albeit brief, period of international concern and speculation. He recovered, unlike Peter II of Russia two years later. The extent to which events and policy were responses to specific conjunctures created problems for those seeking predictable order.

Moreover, a profound challenge was posed by that of personal diplomacies, in which envoys received instructions and correspondence from ministers and advisers other than the foreign minister. This practice, a frequent one in diplomacy, links the modern age of intervention, by heads of state in particular, to that of the *ancien régime*, again establishing a continuity in foreign policy that can be overlooked in teleological accounts. Thus the Austrian diplomatic service under Charles VI (1711–40), the Saxon under Augustus II (1696–1733), and the Prussian under Frederick William I (1713–40) were all characterized by such personal diplomacies, as was the British diplomatic service for periods during the eighteenth century, for example the mid-1740s.

A key element in personal diplomacy was provided by the furtherance of dynastic links. Thus, in 1714, Giulio Alberoni, the envoy to Spain of the Duke of Parma, successfully advocated the Duke's niece, Elizabeth Farnese, as the second wife of Philip V. He went on to become Philip's first minister, a major promotion for the envoy from a minor power. In turn, Jan Willem Ripperda, the former Dutch envoy in Spain, who had converted to Catholicism, become a director of royal textile factories and married a Spanish woman, was able to persuade Philip to send him to Vienna as envoy in 1724, in order to negotiate an alliance between the former enemies, an alliance, based on treaties signed in April–May 1725, that soon extended to the possibility of a marital agreement. In turn, Ripperda, who was very much one of the diplomatic mavericks of the age, was created a Duke and made head of the Spanish government, only to fall in 1726 as his new diplomatic system unravelled.[61]

The practice of personal diplomacy indicates that any presentation of foreign policy in terms of bureaucratic regularity is questionable. This was also true, more generally, of the overt intervention of other ministers in diplomacy, a practice that reflected the absence of collective ministerial responsibility. As a result, uncertainties were left for historians. For example, Johann Daniel Schöpflin, later the founder of the noted diplomatic school at Strasbourg, visited London in 1727–8, but little is known of his mission. He was clearly sent in order to report on the state of British politics, and Schöpflin produced a memorandum that is in a supplementary volume in the archives of the French Foreign Ministry.[62] He was linked to a prominent and influential courtier, the Marshal d'Huxelles, former head of the Council for Foreign Affairs; but it is unclear whether the Foreign Minister approved of the mission.

Indeed, it is frequently the case that, in addition to their obscure relationship with politics at home, little is known about individual missions. Most diplomats that were not of the first rank excited little comment. Thus, for late 1727, when Schöpflin arrived, the mission of the

Württemberg envoy, Count Gravanitz, who also arrived then and who negotiated an agreement, is obscure, and his dispatches do not survive.

This obscurity was even more the case for unofficial missions and for agents who lacked diplomatic rank and who often served a variety of masters. Giovanni Zamboni, an Italian, acted in the 1740s as London agent for the Duke of Modena, the Landgrave of Hesse-Darmstadt, and the government of the Austrian Netherlands, among others, and he had earlier performed that function for Augustus II of Saxony-Poland. Such individuals could serve as the 'very Jack all of news for the more speculative sort of foreign ministers'.[63]

Aside from pay, agents could benefit from diplomatic privilege to circumvent commercial regulations and to sell posts that conferred immunity from arrest, which was particularly useful to indebted tradesmen. An entire diplomatic subworld flourished in many capitals. In London, Italian diplomats were notorious for helping traders to evade import duties and prohibitions, and they were far from alone in doing so. Moreover, diplomatic privileges could interact with sexual desire and the use of violence.[64]

The political dimension at home was frequently crucial to the appointment, credibility and activity of diplomats. For example, ministerial divisions in France were often related to clashes between French diplomats. Thus in 1728 Chavigny, the firmly and energetically anti-Austrian envoy at the Imperial Diet, was encouraged by what he saw as a more favourable attitude by Chauvelin, the French Foreign Minister, than from André Hercule de Fleury, the elderly French first minister; but, in the event, the second stayed in power for longer and also corresponded with French envoys behind the back of successive Foreign Ministers.[65] Personality also played a major role. In Russia in 1742–5, the French Ambassador, La Chétardie, clashed with the Minister Plenipotentiary, D'Alion. In many cases, social distinctions played a role, as when Count Philip Kinsky, the Austrian envoy in London, complained about a lower-ranking Austrian representative in 1734, first mentioning his own 'quality, the social cachet of his family, and the fact that he did not need to serve'.[66]

Such clashes were exacerbated by the extent to which envoys were accompanied by representatives of a more junior rank who often reported on them or disagreed with them. This was a particular problem at the time of the French Revolution, but not only then. In the winter of 1746–7, during the War of the Austrian Succession, Louis, Duke of Richelieu, then Ambassador at Dresden, sought to win Saxon help for an Austro-French reconciliation without keeping the Marquis of Issarts, the Envoy Extraordinary, informed.

Mid-century French foreign policy was responsible for the most famous secret diplomacy, the *Secret du Roi*. Beginning in 1745, this was initially directed to furthering the possibility of the Prince of Conti becoming the next King of Poland (an elective monarchy) and, more generally, seeking to limit Russian power in Eastern Europe, power that was perceived as threatening France's traditional allies, Sweden, Poland, Turkey, and also the international order. Louis XV supported his relative Conti, but insisted that the scheme be kept separate from the foreign ministry and the Council. Diplomats were appointed who were expected to report not only to the ministry, but also, separately and secretly, to Conti and Louis. Envoys were also given secret instructions to facilitate the *Secret*.

The *Secret*, which continued to play a significant role into the 1770s, led to difficulties for both diplomats and ministers, difficulties that are more generally true of personal diplomacies and of the related failure to focus diplomacy on agreed procedures and systems. For example, in 1754, the foreign minister congratulated the envoy in Vienna for rejecting pressure from members of the *Secret* that he should correspond with the *Voivode* of Wallachia, a Turkish client ruler. He warned that any such correspondence would have been soon discovered by Austria,[67] Russia's leading ally, harming French attempts to improve relations with Vienna. In 1755 Vergennes at Constantinople received cautious official instructions that differed from his secret orders from Louis XV to secure a treaty of friendship with the Turks, a treaty moreover that included a secret article committing the Turks to support Polish 'liberties' against Russian aggression. In 1757 the French confidential agent Douglas was disavowed for agreeing certain terms with Russia that did not conform to the *Secret*;[68] and so on. The *Secret* also involved some questionable individuals, such as the cross-dressing Chevalier d'Eon as Secretary of Embassy in St Petersburg and London.

The *Secret*, which was only abandoned when Louis XVI came to the throne in 1774, itself eventually became both cause and means of criticism and opposition to the official government diplomacy within the court, ministry and diplomatic service. Indeed, this criticism fed into a more general critique not only of French foreign policy, but also of supposed secret links between the court and foreign powers, a criticism much directed against Louis XVI at the time of the French Revolution, although largely unfairly in so far as the pre-Revolutionary period was concerned.[69] Louis XV was also involved in other secret diplomacies, as in his secret compact of 1753 with the King of Naples.[70]

Private links could be seen in other diplomatic services, even if they lacked the fame of the *Secret du Roi*. In the late 1720s, aside from the private correspondences of the Prussian minister General Grumbkow with

Prussian envoys,[71] two leading Austrian ministers, Philip, Count Sinzendorf, the Chancellor, and Prince Eugene, the War Minister, maintained an extensive private correspondence with Austrian envoys. Sinzendorf had close links with Mark, Baron de Fonseca, one of the Austrian Plenipotentiaries at Paris, whilst Eugene had similar links with, among others, Count Seckendorf (Berlin), Count Philip Kinsky (London), and Count Wratislaw (Moscow), as well as with foreign envoys such as Diemar, Hesse-Cassel envoy in London, and ministers, for example the Saxon Count Manteuffel. The range of Eugene's system allowed him to follow a private diplomacy of his own, often in opposition to that of the Chancery under Sinzendorf. This situation was compounded by additional distinctive policies, notably by Marquis Ramon de Rialp, Secretary of Charles VI's Council of Spain, and by Count Friedrich Karl von Schönborn, the Austrian Vice-Chancellor.

The effect of this confusion was that most Austrian envoys received contradictory instructions, and were uncertain about what to do. Bad relations were not restricted to rival systems. For example, those between Kinsky and Seckendorf, both protégés of Eugene, were notorious. Seckendorf's claim that most Austrian envoys, himself naturally excepted, were unaware of the true intentions of the Austrian governments, was partially true, although it begged the question whether there were any concerted views at Vienna.[72]

Such a 'system' can be seen as the attempt to retain royal and/or ministerial direction over an increasingly or, at least potentially, autonomous process, but, conversely, it also draws attention not only to more general problems with the idea that governmental organization led to bureaucratic regularity, but also to the tendency to expand the supposed modernity, linked to, and derived from, Westphalia, to cover the entire field of diplomacy. The continued role of royal favourites compounded the problem. For example, alongside the formal Austrian approach to France that led to the Diplomatic Revolution of 1756, the move from enmity between the two powers to alliance, there was a private diplomacy, notably with the Chancellor, Prince Wenzel Anton Kaunitz, approaching Louis XV through his influential mistress, Madame de Pompadour.[73]

There was not always a situation comparable to that of Austria in the 1720s or the *Secret du Roi*. For example, Catherine II, the Great, of Russia (r. 1762–96) did not seek to short-circuit her diplomats. She had her own innovative ideas, including the anti-British Armed Neutrality of European states in 1780, but nothing like the *Secret de Roi*. Foreign envoys in St Petersburg were subjected by her to a very effective charm offensive, but otherwise largely bypassed. All the most important business was done through her envoys, and she seems not to have been particularly choosy about them, at any rate not for the less significant postings such as Dresden. Envoys sent to London included not only her close friend, Ivan Chernyshev, but also the much longer-serving and talented Count Simon Vorontsov, whose aloof family she had every reason to dislike and mistrust.[74]

Nevertheless, it is appropriate to draw attention to the secret diplomacies because they undercut theories of bureaucratization or, rather, showed how difficult it was to match the practice to the reality of court politics. Moreover, these secret diplomacies raise a question mark about the tendency to adopt a teleology of modernization in which Westphalia plays a key role. In doing so, these diplomacies also subvert the teleology more profoundly by looking toward an account of the present situation in which institutional forms cannot contain more disparate diplomacies. Lastly, the secret diplomacies of the eighteenth century helped lead to the revolutionary criticism and rejection of established conventions in the 1790s, a criticism and rejection that were to be important to the long-term Western debate about diplomacy.

Secret diplomacy encouraged intelligence operations. A key aspect of the application of science in diplomacy was the development of code-breaking in so-called Black Chambers. Although the use of cryptography was longstanding, the rise of the Black Chambers was basically an eighteenth-century phenomenon, being introduced for example in the United Provinces in 1707, in part in response to events in the War of the Spanish Succession and to changes and tensions in inter-allied relationships.[75] The range of the highly successful British interception system was such that in 1726 alone they were able to read Austrian, Dutch, French, Hessian, Modenese, Parmesan, Sardinian, Saxon, Spanish, Swedish, Tuscan and Venetian diplomatic correspondence.[76] In turn, the British were concerned about the skill of other decipherers.[77] Often the bribery of members of the staff of foreign diplomats was a significant source of information. The French had access to the correspondence of the Prussian envoy in Paris in the 1720s and 1730s.

Deceit by governments and/or the secretive role of hidden agencies was frequently cited by diplomats when seeking to explain policy or their failure to anticipate or influence moves, but that was by no means the sole reason why they made mistakes in assessment. Instead, there was a tendency, as in the British and French reporting of the United Provinces (Netherlands) in the early eighteenth century, to explain policy in terms favourable to the foreign power, and thus to underplay the autonomy of attitudes and policy in the state in question,[78] a point that recurs to the present day.

Both secretive roles and mistakes in part arose from the nature of foreign policy. The absence of distinct and unpolitical agencies for the conduct of foreign policy, and the close relationship in most states between foreign policy and domestic politics, ensured that, despite the bland assurances of theorists such as Callières on the need for diplomats to harmonize different interests, diplomats had to face difficult choices, choices that are still relevant today. Should the diplomats lend support to domestic opponents of governments following antagonistic policies? Should they seek to gain the support of the reversionary interest: then generally the heir to the throne, today what appears to be the next government? In 1725 Catherine I was concerned that some Russian diplomats supported the interests of the future Peter II,[79] while in 1737 George II informed diplomats in London, via his Master of the Ceremonies, Sir Clement Cotterell, that it was his wish that they should not go to the court of his elder son, Frederick, Prince of Wales,[80] and subsequent instructions to envoys took note of this view.[81] Similarly, the British had to be careful about approaching Crown Prince Frederick of Prussia (the future Frederick the Great) because his father was very opposed to such links.[82]

Instructions to diplomats were often ambiguous and outdated. What can be presented as over-commitment to local interests can also be seen as a response to opportunities and as a policy informed by the potential of the situation. Furthermore, if envoys were possibly over-associated with particular factions or politicians, allowances must be given for partisanship and for the difficulties posed by exclusion from specific circles. In many cases, diplomats intervened actively in domestic politics.[83]

Meanwhile, there were important shifts in diplomatic life and the diplomatic system. The position of French as the European diplomatic language became more pronounced. In Eastern Europe, German and Latin continued significant, while, in Constantinople, Italian, remained important until the 1830s. Although, under George I (r. 1714–27), French had been extensively used by the British foreign service, thereafter it employed English. However, in Europe as a whole, French became the first language of diplomacy. It was thus generally used in Danish, Sardinian, Saxon and Wittelsbach (Bavarian and Palatine) diplomatic correspondence. This need affected the choice of diplomats. A lack of knowledge of French among high-ranking Spaniards encouraged the use of Italians and other foreigners in the Spanish diplomatic service which did not become a permanent Spanish career-service until late in the eighteenth century.[84]

Austria under Charles VI (r. 1711–40) largely used German and Italian, although some French was also employed in confidential correspondence. Because George Woodward could not understand 'perfectly' the message in German ordering him to leave Vienna when relations with Britain were broken off in 1727, he was told to leave in French.[85] Under Maria Theresa (r. 1740–80), French became more commonly used by Austrian diplomats. Moreover, with the accession of Frederick II, also in 1740, French largely replaced German for Prussian diplomacy, although German was also used. In Russia, alongside the continued use of Russian, and that of German by diplomats from the Baltic provinces, there was also an increased use of French.[86] French was also employed for most treaties and diplomatic notes.

At the same time, a sense of distinct spheres ensured that German remained the language generally employed in handling German affairs, for example at Vienna, Copenhagen and Hanover.[87] In part, this use reflected the prominent role of the institutions of the Holy Roman Empire in a system of shared sovereignty, and the extent to which diplomacy therefore had a legal aspect, as claims were advanced in the Imperial courts. In 1755 France was urged to send an envoy to Munich who knew German as he would be better able to explain policy to those who were influential.[88]

The prominence of French reflected the international character of diplomacy and its interrelationship with monarchical and aristocratic society. The development of accepted conventions of diplomatic immunity, notably immunity from civil proceedings and the jurisdiction of the host state, increased a sense of distinctiveness. The immunity from civil proceedings was particularly important, given the extent to which the delay in settling diplomats' arrears in pay and expenses, and diplomats' reliance therefore on their own financial resources, ensured that many were in debt, and thus subject to civil action, including imprisonment, on behalf of their creditors. Aside from diplomatic immunity, the increased ability to overcome confessional and precedence barriers further helped to create a united diplomatic world. Indeed, issues of precedence and rank were pushed less hard in the late eighteenth century than had been the case a century earlier.

In part, this reflected a mid-century shift in sensibility from the Baroque to the Enlightenment. This shift was also seen in the decline in the emphasis on ostentatious show, for example dramatic entries by newly arrived envoys to the capital where their embassy was located. The Coach Museum in Belém, west of Lisbon, contains some lavish examples of Baroque coaches designed for diplomatic entries. Such ceremonial scarcely ceased, but it became less ostentatious and less prominent in diplomacy, and was regarded as of less significance. Similarly, envoys were affected because the monarchs to whom they were accredited tended to adopt a style of conduct and life that was at once utilitarian and domestic.

There was also a difference in tone between the most influential late seventeenth-century work on diplomatic conduct, Abraham van

Wicquefort's *L'Ambassadeur et ses Fonctions* (1681), which stressed diplomatic status, notably legal privileges, and the more pragmatic works of the early eighteenth century, Francois de Callières' *De la Manière de Négocier avec les Souverains* (1716) and Antoine Pecquet's *Discours sur l'art de Négocier* (1737). The article in the 27 September 1757 issue of the London newspaper the *Centinel* which proposed the creation of a political academy to teach diplomacy outlined 'the Ambassadors School; where I would have Monsieur Wiquefort's book upon the functions of that high office carefully explained to the students', but English, German, Italian and Russian editions of Callières appeared in 1716, 1717, 1726 and 1772 respectively.

Callières' book has been described in terms of providing 'the discussion of diplomacy with a focus of political interest, around which its precepts and practices could acquire fuller coherence', as having diplomacy emerge 'as a principle and institution of order', and as conceiving of power politics and civilized behaviour as in unison.[89] In short, like most writing on diplomacy, including the diplomatic common-place books that could serve as manuals,[90] the book lacked originality and was important precisely because it restated views and explained practices in terms of the language of the present. The cultural hegemony of France was such that it was appropriate that Callières was French and wrote in that language. Callières, who had served as a diplomat between 1670 and 1700, pressed for career diplomats, rather than high-ranking amateurs, an argument linked to the establishment of the *Académie Politique* in 1712 and to his own quest for a job.[91] Similarly, the need for French diplomats knowledgeable in the German constitution as well as in social skills was pressed by the influential Brunswick-Wolfenbüttel minister, Baron Johann Christoph Schleinitz.[92]

The diplomatic world was closely related to, but also, at the level of individual diplomats, often in an uneasy relationship with, the growth in specialized national departments for the conduct of foreign affairs. In many states, these departments became more distinct, larger and sophisticated, notably with greater care being taken to ensure that there were permanent specialized staff, translators, maps and archives. France led the way,[93] and set a model for other states. The link was clear in Spain where Louis XIV's grandson, Philip, Duke of Anjou, came to the throne as Philip V in 1700, with a 'Despacho Universal', or cabinet council, dominated by the French ambassador, created the following year. In 1714, at the close of the War of Spanish Succession, Philip created a Secretariat of State, while the Secretaryship of State for Foreign Affairs established in Savoy-Piedmont in 1717 also owed much to France. The latter became an impressive and effective foreign office.[94]

In Russia in 1719, as part of Peter the Great's modernization of government, the old Department of Embassies was replaced by the College of Foreign Affairs, which became a significant ministry. In Prussia, the reorganization of central government also saw the establishment of a Department of External Affairs in 1728; in 1733 it became known as the *Kabinettsministerium*. In Portugal, a separate office for foreign affairs was created only in 1736, although it had been considered desirable earlier. In Austria, the relevant dates were 1742 and 1753, as a result of which a transformed State Chancellery was established.

As a significant aspect of the creation of new ministries, they were given distinct buildings, which helped provide them with a sense of coherence. This sense was true not only of those who worked in the ministries, but also of the envoys answerable to them and of the foreign diplomats who had to deal with them. A specialized diplomatic culture was becoming more grounded in a more developed governmental structure.

Increasingly, the institutional conduct of foreign affairs was segregated. In 1698, the authority of the French Secretary of State for the Marine over diplomats was defined and limited. In Britain, the office of Foreign Secretary was founded in 1782, replacing the earlier system by which two, sometimes competing, Secretaries of State, the Secretaries of State for the Northern and Southern Departments, had been responsible not only for foreign affairs but also for a host of domestic matters, including public order.

At the same time, it would be misleading to take an emphasis on institutionalization so far as to lead to an underrating of the primacy of politics. Thus, in France, in 1716–18, the Marshal d'Huxelles, the head of the Council for Foreign Affairs, was opposed by the Regent, the Duke of Orléans, and his confidant, Guillaume Dubois, who was to serve both as envoy and as Foreign Minister.[95]

Ministers had to consider individual appointments as part of a system, at once a system of patronage that included domestic politics and government, and also a foreign service in which there should be some notion of training, career development and promotion; in addition to the key issues of establishing and attracting representation and reciprocity.[96] Equally, diplomats saw themselves as being chosen within a diplomatic system. Those who sought to pursue a career were well aware of having to respond to, and manoeuvre in, this context. Thus concern about rank was not simply a matter of remuneration, which became more closely linked to rank and posting, but also of social politics and status, and of institutional preference.[97] The last was linked to the development of a career structure within a more self-conscious diplomatic service, a structure that reflected the multiplication in the number of grades (see p. 72).

There was also concern to gain posts and tasks that could yield repute. This concern was especially true of the men of business, seeking promotion, in the diplomatic service or through service as a diplomat, rather than of the envoys of title who were more likely to see representation as their key task and to regard their presence and manner as the crucial requirements of this representation.

Such 'envoys of title' commonly had little notion of a career in diplomacy, and were more likely to focus on service to the sovereign, and thus on issues, and rewards, of rank and prestige. Much of the problem in judging diplomacy derives from the habit of putting both groups together in order to produce an overall judgement. Although in many cases the differences were readily apparent, there was no rigid divide between the groups. Nevertheless, the presence of these two contrasting groups makes questionable any overall judgement that does not make reference to this issue, an issue that remains pertinent today.

As so often when discussing diplomacy, it is important to be aware of developments but also wary of teleology. Thus alongside an important degree of specialization it would be misleading to exaggerate the scope or extent of the administrative changes in the period 1690 to 1775. Many polities lacked specialized institutions and the notion of bureaucratic service and, where the institutions existed, their staff was generally small (and tended to remain so until the late nineteenth century), and were only trained on the job, a practice that underlined the conservative character of diplomacy. The British Foreign Office, founded in 1782, had a far smaller staff than its French counterpart.

Furthermore, the influence of such institutions was limited by the continued direct intervention of monarchs and other ministers. The comment, in the instructions drawn up in 1725 for a Saxon envoy to Spain that, without an appreciation of the internal state of a court, it was impossible to understand its foreign policy,[98] was equally true throughout the period, and led to complaints accordingly.[99] Augustus II ordered another of his envoys, Friedrich, Count Watzdorf (London, 1730–32), to take care to match the tone and views of the government to which he was accredited, and to have no truck with its opponents.[100]

More generally, aristocratic envoys were used to getting their own way, both because they were aristocrats and because many had only limited diplomatic experience and had not been habituated to the system. The personal representative of the sovereign, well-connected envoys felt able to ascribe orders they disliked to particular political combinations, and thus to justify following their own views instead.

Many diplomats had little interest in advancing commercial goals, a situation that reflected the social politics of diplomacy, as well as the degree to which these matters required an unwelcome mastery of detail. There were also institutional issues. French envoys in Constantinople, such as Villeneuve in the 1730s, criticized the Marseille Chamber of Commerce over its prominent role in the organization of the Turkey trade. Criticism of merchants could also be related to disputes between envoys from the same state, notably with their identifying with the governments to which they were accredited. Consuls were apt to be closer to merchants, both literally and figuratively, than envoys, and to be readier to support their interests, not least because their appointment and pay often depended on mercantile favour. The Count of Montaigu, the French envoy in Venice, was recalled in 1746 for a number of reasons including poor relations with the consul, as well as sending inaccurate reports.[101] Envoys, nevertheless, could turn to consuls for advice, and consuls were particularly responsible for preserving commercial rights and privileges.[102]

Envoys from a consular background, such as Paul Rycaut, who served as British Resident Minister in Hamburg and the Hanseatic towns from 1689 to 1700, were particularly concerned about the commercial situation. His correspondence with William Blathwayt, Secretary-at-War and Commissioner of Trade, provided detailed economic, political and diplomatic material, including warnings about privateers fitting out in the Hanseatic ports.[103] The latter serve as a reminder that diplomatic activity for much of the period 1688–1763 was very much affected by conflict or its likelihood.

In warning against teleology, there is also a need to qualify any suggestion that, after Westphalia, diplomacy was an aspect of a secular international system. Seeking his recall from Vienna in 1704, the British envoy, George Stepney, reported on the problems arising from having been instructed to support the Hungarian Protestants:

> I have had repeated orders to solicit earnestly in favour of the Malecontents in Hungary, which I have done with all the zeal I could, and thereby have lost the good looks of most of the ministry, though I barely discharged my duty, which is and ought to be my first consideration. However, I perceive a change in the Imperial Court towards me upon that account, and for that reason am of opinion it may be no less for her Majesty's service than for my private satisfaction, that somebody else be found for that employment.[104]

Such support was an aspect of a more general engagement on behalf of co-religionists,[105] one that linked diplomacy to imperial and domestic attitudes and policies.[106] The Catholic equivalent included support for the Jacobites, while confessional issues continued to play a role in alliance politics, as in 1757 when France was keen to win a Protestant ally among the German princes.[107] However, yet again, realist considerations of power politics played an important part in affecting the support provided and shown.[108] Moreover, with their emphasis on legitimacy, rulers often faced ideological as well as prudential difficulties when it came to considering whether to support opposition in other states, let alone insurrections; and this situation could lead to a reluctance to offer support.[109]

It would also be inappropriate to think of an administrative revolution in diplomacy or its oversight in this period. The nature of diplomatic processes did not conform to the bureaucratic assumptions entailed by the term diplomatic service in the late Victorian period. Moreover, by 1775, the significant development that had occurred in terms of specialization of function, the creation of a system of promotion by merit and seniority, bureaucratic professionalization (as opposed to learning on the job), and an infrastructure of buildings, staff and well-defined records, was far from universal across Europe.

The important role of courts in diplomacy, as sites of activity and sources of reports and policy, complicated the situation. On the one hand, this role helped ensure the value of aristocratic envoys who could play a major part in the life of courts. Yet, the relationship between court politics and government processes could be difficult, as the *Secret du Roi* amply demonstrated. Moreover, these difficulties underlined the extent to which practical problems (such as communications) alone were not responsible for the failure of diplomatic systems, practices and mechanisms to realise their potential.

As diplomacy did not require the implementation of policy across the localities of Europe, it avoided many of the drawbacks of government in the period, but there were still serious limitations. Nevertheless accepting these limitations and the inchoate processes involved in recruitment, pay and, to an extent, ministerial control, there were, alongside more defined institutions than in the seventeenth, let alone sixteenth, centuries, many envoys who acquired considerable experience through long service and thus became professionals, while most diplomats operated effectively.[110]

There were also more specific achievements. Russia had been successfully integrated into Europe's diplomatic system, both with envoys in St Petersburg and with Russian envoys across Europe. As another aspect of success, it was possible to negotiate wide-ranging diplomatic combinations, such as the Alliance of Vienna system created in 1725–6, which joined Spain, Austria, Prussia and Russia; the rival Alliance of Hanover system, which initially joined Britain, France and Prussia, subsequently (in 1726–7) losing the last but gaining the Netherlands, Denmark and Sweden; the anti-Prussian coalition of France, Austria, Russia and Sweden, constructed in 1756–7; and the anti-British League of Armed Neutrality, established by Catherine the Great in 1780.

Moreover, most European diplomats filed regular and comprehensive reports. If they tended to concentrate on court and ministerial factions, this practice was an understandable response to the sources of power and policy. In addition, a failure to devote much attention to broader social and political developments arose from a lack of resources to do so. The information was not readily available and it was generally believed to be of slight significance.

Partly because of the effectiveness of most European diplomats, there was little pressure for new methods, either from within or, even more, from outside the diplomatic system; although the mechanism for expressing such criticisms was restricted. The system was fit for purpose, in terms of a combination of regular reporting and ad hoc negotiating; and fitness for purpose was a key achievement. Alongside deficiencies and failures, there was a steady competence.[111]

European states increasingly moved away from a dependence on the monarch, at least for government, although not for politics. Administrative institutions developed a measure of autonomy and in some states, especially – although very differently – Britain and Russia, there was a considerable gain in governmental capability and sophistication. Yet if the modern world is to be understood in a functional light, in terms (at least in part) of big government able to execute planned policies in a predictable fashion and also capable of integrating feedback readily into decision-making and policy execution, then modernity was still absent. This definition, however, is less convincing in the 2000s than it would have been three decades earlier, because now there is less certainty about the values of centralization and state control. Where, however, such a re-evaluation leads diplomacy is unclear, as there seems scant viable alternative to such a system of control for the organization of international links and foreign policy. Current talk of transnationalism, like earlier support for 'peoples' diplomacy', underplays the confusion that can result from such practices; and confusion, or 'noise', in the international system is a key cause of dispute, if not conflict.

The complexity of modernity, and thus modernization, in any account of diplomatic culture and practice is thus apparent, and this complexity subverts any teleology based on such criteria. In addition to this key conceptual point, there is also the danger of underplaying elements of the situation in the eighteenth century that scarcely conformed to modern notions of bureaucratic operation and effectiveness. The role of factionalism was crucial here, and was referred to in 1736 when Thomas Robinson, envoy in Vienna, and a central figure in British diplomacy, who was to become Secretary of State in 1754, wrote to Andrew Stone, one of the Under Secretaries. With regard to the latter's superior, he wrote 'belonging both of us to the Duke of Newcastle'.[112]

FOUR
1775–1815

'I saw, at once, that the ulcerations in the narrow mind of that mulish being left nothing to be expected on the subject of my attendance.'
—An ambassador is received, Thomas Jefferson.

In his autobiography, written thirty-five years later, Thomas Jefferson painted a picture of an ungracious reception from George III of Britain at his *levée* on 17 March 1786. In practice, there are no contemporary accounts of the meeting, and it is likely that Jefferson's description was over-dramatized, if not totally misleading. Linked to this response was the fact that Jefferson mistakenly blamed his failure to negotiate a trade treaty on George, which exaggerated the latter's role in commercial diplomacy.[1]

A very different impression, that of wise and honest courtesy, was made when George received John Adams on 1 June 1785 as the first American minister to the Court of St James. Adams recorded George as saying:

> I have done nothing in the late contest [the War of American Independence, 1775–83] but what I thought myself indispensably bound to do, by the duty which I owed to my people . . . I was the last to consent to the separation; but the separation having been made, and having become inevitable, I have always said, as I say now, that I would be the first to meet the friendship of the United States as an independent power . . . let the circumstances of language, religion, and blood have their natural and full effect.

George, who, Adams noted, was 'much affected, and answered me with more tremor than I had spoken with', was revealed as informed and relaxed. With 'an air of familiarity, and smiling, or rather laughing', he astutely teased Adams by saying 'there is an opinion among some people that you are the most attached of all your countrymen to the manners of France'. The wrong-footed Adams stood on his dignity. 'Surprised' and 'embarrassed', he responded that he had 'no attachment but to my own country'; which George, 'as quick as lightning', courteously trumped, saying 'an honest man will never have any other'.[2]

Revolutions could be followed by good relations between the opponents, but, at the time, they disrupted diplomacy, as they still do. The personnel of the French diplomatic service, the most prestigious in Europe, were to be made fully aware of this truth. During the French Revolution, which began in 1789, the chilly injunction 'the French nation counts on the zeal and fidelity of its foreign agents'[3] in part reflected the difficulty of matching the views of diplomats to the volatile politics of Paris. The Foreign Ministry itself was placed under the scrutiny of the Diplomatic Committee that the National Assembly created in July 1790. Furthermore, difficulties between French diplomats were exacerbated by accusations of obstruction, disobedience and treason.[4]

At the individual level, the reality was often painful. Charles Flüry, Secretary of Legation at Munich, joined the *émigrés* after his father was killed in the storming of the Tuileries in Paris by the Revolutionaries in August 1792. He then returned to Paris where, in 1793, he was appointed Secretary of Legation at Dresden. Unable, owing to the war, to take up the post, he became, in 1793–6, Secretary of Legation to the Republic of the Valais, a French client state in what is now Switzerland. Denounced as disloyal in 1796, Flüry, nevertheless, was appointed Consul General to Wallachia, Moldavia and Bessarabia.[5]

The impact of the American and French revolutions on the European diplomacy of the period was accentuated by the extent to which much of this diplomacy arose from them and, in particular from 1792, from opposition to the French Revolution. Moreover, in terms of the teleology of diplomatic history, the revolutions, and especially the French Revolution, which began in 1789, have been located as an important move towards modernization.

These revolutions were indeed significant and will be discussed, but this discussion requires prior qualification, notably by drawing attention to features of the diplomatic world of the period that were far from radical and, conversely, by noting other aspects of change in the period that can be seen as of consequence. A key element in the former was the continued slowness of communications, a slowness that helped define the parameters of control from the metropole versus initiative by the diplomat, an issue that became more important with American independence and notably at the time of the Anglo–American War of 1812.

To take a well-established route, Constantinople to Paris, Marie, Count of Choiseul-Gouffier, the French envoy, wrote to Montmorin, the French Foreign Minister, on 25 April 1787, and again the following day. The first dispatch was received on 26 May, the second, sent by sea, on 3 July. Those of 11, 15, 16, 25 January, 10, 23 February, 10, 17, 24 March, 10, 25 May and 9 June 1787 arrived on 11 February, 6 April, 29

March, 26 February, 11 March, 25 March, 8 April, 31 May, 24 April, 9 June, 23 June and 7 July respectively.[6] Choiseul-Gouffier was to be recalled in June 1792, but he refused to return to Paris and, horrified by the reports of the imprisonment of Louis XVI and the September Massacres in Paris, he resigned and transferred his responsibilities to the Turkish government.

As a further indication of the general situation, dispatches of 18 and 25 June and 24 July 1787 from St Petersburg were received in Paris on 12 and 19 July and 17 August.[7] The situation was not to change during this period. Increased trade meant more sailings, which helped increase predictability, but the constraints of climate and weather remained pressing.[8] In 1794, having sailed on 29 November and 'had a favourable passage to the mouth of the Elbe', Morton Eden was able to reach Vienna on the night of 13 December.[9]

From 1792 Europe and the Atlantic world endured a sustained level of conflict with all the disruption that entailed for communications, including the interruption of packet-boat sailings. Some developments that might seem to offer possibilities, notably manned balloon flight from the 1780s and semaphore networks from the 1790s, were not exploited to aid diplomacy, and, in the state they were then in, neither lent themselves to such an end.

Nevertheless, an important degree of innovation arose from the extent to which the sustained and wide-ranging nature of the conflict between the leading European empires from 1778 to 1783 and 1793 to 1815 entailed attempts to bring non-Western powers into the European diplomatic system. Indeed, the alliance between France and the Americans negotiated in 1778 in part represented a French attempt to strike at the British. A more sustained effort was made by France to win alliances with Asian rulers. These alliances were designed to strike directly at the British empire, especially in India, but also to develop French interests that could serve as the basis for an empire of influence, trade and power. Beneficial in its own right, such an empire would also provide key advantages in any conflict with Britain.

The key partner was the Sultanate of Mysore in southern India, as its rulers, Haider Ali and then his son Tipu (r. 1782–99), were energetic rulers whose expansionism clashed with British interests. Haider Ali, a mercenary who had succeeded in becoming a territorial ruler, epitomized the changes occurring in India, changes that affected the nature of diplomacy. The decline in the power of the Mughal Emperors was rapidly followed by a collapse in their authority. Provincial governors gained effective control, as in Hyderabad, and the autonomous actions of India's provincial rulers led to a situation akin to that in the post-Westphalian

Holy Roman Empire. In India, as in Germany, a central issue was that of negotiations by such rulers with foreign powers.

Meanwhile, for France, as for the other European powers, there had been a longstanding tension between links developed by local agents, notably those of the East India Companies, and initiatives coming from the government at home. The former tended to focus on local interests, both trade and security, and the latter on broader-brush ideas of the use of empire, frequently in pursuit of great-power initiatives. The wars of the period 1775–1815 encouraged a focus on initiatives of the latter type, and, therefore, a more sustained governmental interest.

This situation was not only true of war years. Indeed, in the interwar period between the War of American Independence and the outbreak of the French Revolutionary Wars, 1783–92, France made a major attempt to enhance its position to the east. In 1785 France signed an agreement with the beys who wielded most influence in Egypt, opening the Red Sea route to India to overland trade over the Isthmus of Suez and worrying British commentators. The previous year, Choiseul-Gouffier, the envoy in Constantinople, was instructed to improve French relations with Persia, both for commercial reasons and in order to facilitate trade with India, while an embassy under the Count of Ferrières-Sauveboeuf was sent in 1784 to Isfahan, the capital of Persia. Attempts were also made to develop relations with Said I of Oman. In India France sought to train forces for friendly native rulers, such as Nizam Ali of Hyderabad, this proving a key means to establish and sustain better diplomatic relations, while in 1787 France acquired a claim to bases in Cochin China in what is now Vietnam.

Similarly, the British government took a direct role in Asian diplomacy by sending a mission to China. The first envoy, the Hon. Charles Cathcart MP, died en route in 1788, but it was decided to send a replacement. William Grenville, the Home Secretary, wrote in 1789 of the importance of governmental representation, rather than by the East India Company:

> great part of the hopes which are entertained of the success of this mission rests on the greater degree of attention which, it is supposed, the Government of China will show to a person coming there, as authorised by the King, than if he came, only in the name of a trading company.[10]

This policy was felt to be especially necessary because the East India Company was opposed to any initiatives that might affect the monopoly of its factory (commercial station) at Canton. George, Lord Macartney, who had earlier served at St Petersburg, replaced Cathcart. His journey showed the problems posed by distance. Macartney embarked at Spithead on 21 September 1792, although he did not sail until the 26th due to adverse winds. It was not until 20 June 1793 that his flagship anchored at Macao. Macartney failed to obtain the desired commercial advantages. The British sought to add additional harbours where they might trade in China, to end the raising of tariffs, which to them were a system of fraud, to increase the volume of exports, and to receive permission for a British envoy to be permanently stationed at Beijing, the last an inversion of the Chinese means of diplomacy.

Aside from a long tradition of contempt for non-Chinese peoples, who were seen as at the margins of a Sino-centred world, China, like Britain, was a tremendously successful power in the eighteenth century, and saw scant reason to make concessions or gestures that suggested equality. There was no parallel to the arrival in London in 1793 of Yusuf Agah Efendi, the first Turkish resident envoy, who began a representation that lasted until the early 1810s. The Chinese, in contrast, received tribute from most of their neighbours, although not from Russia. They expected envoys to be dutiful, and in 1795 the Dutch mission kowtowed often while seeking a more favourable trade regime.[11] Sir George Staunton, the Secretary to the Macartney embassy, reported from China:

> the Emperor of China receives tribute from princes not very distant from the Caspian Sea. I saw above eighty Tartar princes come to pay their obeissance or rather make their adorations on the Emperor's 83rd birth day.[12]

At the same time, far from being rigid, Manchu control of the Chinese empire reflected an ability on the part of the Emperor to respond to different identities. This response entailed not only a careful managing of policy and image, but also a process akin to diplomacy within the realm, as in the tours to southern China of the Ch'ien-lung Emperor, the Emperor who had been unforthcoming to Macartney, and who was depicted in James Gillray's caricature (cartoon) of the embassy.

The dispatch of a British mission to China might not seem a world away from medieval European attempts to recruit the support of distant rulers, but it took part in a very different context. By the late-eighteenth century, European commerce was truly global. In 1791 the British bought 17,250,000 pounds of tea at Canton and by 1793 India was contributing £500,000 per annum to the British Exchequer. As a result, there was a standardization of the chain of authority and process of diplomacy in India. After Pitt's India Act of 1784, the Governor-General was legally responsible for the East India Company's relations with Indian princes.

The Governor-General, in turn, reported to the now statutory Secret Committee of the Company which wrote despatches dealing with war and peace and relations with other powers at the behest of the Board of Control, a committee linked through overlapping personnel with the Cabinet.

From 1784 within India, all matters regarding relations with the princes were channelled to Calcutta, and the Residents posted to the major powers, notably the Peshwa of Pune/Poona, the Nizam of Hyderabad, and Sindia, received their instructions from the Governor-General. In contrast, routine affairs with minor powers, most notably those between Madras and both Arcot and Tanjore, and between Bombay and the Malabar chieftains, were handled by the Governors under the supervision of the Governor-General. In such dealings, Madras and Bombay received and negotiated with *vakils* and instructed Residents.

Initiatives outside Europe by Britain and France were developed during the subsequent years of war between the two powers. Military links with Indian rulers were pursued as a means of gaining diplomatic influence as well as military advantage. Moreover, Shah Fath Ali of Persia (r. 1797–1834) was seen by Britain and France as a key player against India or, maybe, Turkey or Russia, replicating Turkey's traditional role against Austria and subsequently Russia. In 1807 a Persian envoy reached Napoleon, while a French military mission charged with reorganizing the Persian army was dispatched. France and Persia signed the Treaty of Finkenstein in 1807.

These and other steps encouraged the British to respond in turn, prefiguring a process that was to be seen frequently during the nineteenth century. The interacting pressures of fear and opportunity helped drive forward an engagement with the non-Western world, notably to deny resources to opponents. In 1798 the Governor of Bombay appointed Mirza Mehdi Ali Khan, a Persian exile in his employ, to be the Company's Resident in Bushire on the Persian shore of the Persian Gulf. Like the dispatch of European envoys to distant courts in the medieval and early modern period, this mission was designed to find support in order to put pressure on an opponent from the rear, in this case to win Persian support against the Afghans whose expansionism posed a longstanding problem to northern India.

As a reminder of the problems of duplication within systems that were far from bureaucratic, the Governor-General, Richard, Marquess Wellesley, sent in 1799 a Company officer, Captain John Malcolm, to Tehran to negotiate an alliance, which he did. In turn, in 1804 Samuel Manesty, the British Resident at Basra, sought promotion to become Envoy to Persia, arguing that such a mark of royal favour would be beneficial to British interests in the Near East. Equally, Manesty's requests indicated the role of turf wars, careerism and jealousy in representation, and the possible tensions arising from control at a distance. On the spot, and away from authority, Manesty volunteered to go to Tehran when Wellesley's envoy, Jonathan Lovett, having reached Bushire, relinquished his post due to failing health. Manesty assembled a sizeable entourage, but fearing reprisals from Wellesley for doing so without permission, and with ideas about the shape that Anglo-Persian relations should take, he thought that royal credentials would protect him from the Governor-General's wrath. Whereas Lovett was entrusted to deliver a letter of condolence on the death of a Persian diplomat at Bombay, Manesty proposed to settle Russo-Persian differences, unauthorized conduct that was condemned by Wellesley.[13]

In 1808 Malcolm, sent again to Persia by the new Governor-General, failed in his mission. In contrast, Sir Harford Jones, who was sent by the Foreign Office, was able to negotiate a preliminary Treaty of Friendship in 1809; he had been assistant and factor for the East India Company in Basra (1783–94) and its Resident in Baghdad (1798–1806).[14] Yet there was tension between Calcutta and London over control of relations. Angered by Harford Jones, the Governor-General sent the arrogant Malcolm anew in 1810, only for him to be thwarted by the dispatch of an Ambassador, Sir Gore Ouseley, who spoke Persian. Jones' success had led Persia to send Mirza Abul Hassan to London in an effort to settle relations. His mission posed the problems of the unfamiliar, which were challenging to the status-conscious world of diplomacy. Thus there was worry about whether Hassan was the equivalent to a chargé d'affaires or, as he in fact was, an envoy.[15]

This was an aspect of the problem of arriving at a shared understanding of the meaning and content of representations and agreements. Overlapping with and in addition to this process, there was an attempt to project the values of Western diplomacy. Issues of rank had to be negotiated anew outside Europe. In some respects, the situation was similar: diplomatic rank was often seen as dependent on, and necessarily flowing from, social rank. However, it was difficult to circumvent the issue by dispatching high-ranking envoys as such diplomats were very reluctant to leave Europe. This situation created problems. In 1804 the Dey of Algiers took the 'low degree' of the new British Consul at Algiers as an insult and refused to receive him.[16]

In turn, the career of Mirza Abul Hassan indicated the spreading world of diplomatic links. He went on from London to St Petersburg in an unsuccessful effort to obtain more favourable terms than those in the last treaty, returned to London for a second mission in 1819, and in 1824 became Persia's first Foreign Minister, serving to 1834 and again from 1840 to 1846. Persia's diplomatic net slowly improved, with Russian,

Turkish and French legations established in 1828, 1849 and 1855 respectively, the first after defeat by Russia.

Discussion of such initiatives can overlook the problems faced by diplomacy outside the European world. Distance was a key factor. Thus frequent contact in the seventeenth century had helped define relations with both Turkey and the Barbary States of North Africa, and the latter were happy to accept bilateral agreements that conformed to established European practice.[17]

Greater distance, however, could lead to serious delays. The Treaty of Versailles of 1787, by which France acquired a claim to bases in Cochin China and the valuable possibility of increased trade through them with China, was negotiated with the son of Nguyen Anh, one of the claimants to Cochin China, whose cause was supported by Pigneau de Béhaine, bishop of Adran and Vicar-Apostolic of Cochin China. Distance, however, acted as a deterrent. In 1785 Pigneau de Béhaine had appealed for help to the Governor of Pondicherry, the leading French base in India, but, by the time the treaty had been signed, France had been humbled by Britain in the Dutch Crisis of 1787, and hopes of bold moves had to be retrenched. In place of royal forces, Nguyen Anh received only a small number of Frenchmen, hired thanks to French merchants. Similarly, in 1787 Tipu Sultan of Mysore sent an embassy to France in search of military assistance, but it did not reach the French port of Toulon until June 1788, and it proved impossible to reach agreement.

If distance was a problem for relations with the European powers, nearby China was unable to dominate Vietnam, and, indeed, a Chinese invasion force, seeking to overthrow the new Emperor of Vietnam, Nguyen Hue (r. 1788–92), was defeated by the Vietnamese in 1789. The entire episode threw light on the extent to which traditional notions of Chinese imperial prestige played a role in deciding what policy should be pursued in responding to developments. Looked at differently, the Chinese sought to use force to maintain their longstanding links with the Le emperors of Hanoi, who had been displaced by Nguyen Hue, and they failed.[18]

Distance and competing concerns were also problems in French attempts to develop relations with Persia. Pierre-Amédée Jaubert, who was sent to Persia in the spring of 1805 in order to offer military help, did not reach Tehran until the following year. He left Tehran on 14 July 1806, but did not reach Paris until 21 June 1807. The same difficulty had affected Louis XIV's hopes of alliance with Siam (Thailand), and also eighteenth-century French plans for co-operation with Indian rulers.

Different cultural suppositions and political practices were also a problem, as the British discovered when they sent the Macartney mission to China. These factors accentuated the difficulties created by the tensions within any alliance or potential alliance. Thus in 1807 Persia and France had clashing goals: the Persians wanted help in driving the Russians out of Georgia, which they had recently conquered, while Napoleon wished to see Persia exclude British influence and hoped that it could be a base against British India. Another complication was created by the rival response of other would-be friendly European powers. For example, Catherine II of Russia, with whom France sought better relations, was angered by the French mission to Persia in 1784.

The establishment of new diplomatic systems by radical new states, as a result of the American and French revolutions, is the topic that dominates attention for this period. The American Revolution (1775–83) was the first revolution seeking independence (as opposed to rebellion) by a European settler colony, which helped make it a radical step. This revolution represented not so much a rejection of the European world, one that could be fitted into the existing pattern of relations with non-Europeans, but rather a new type of European state, the first indeed of the new Western world.

The very determination of the Americans to have relations with the European states thus created issues. This determination was linked not only to a striving for legitimacy for the new regime, with the Declaration of Independence (1776) asserting a right to statehood among other states, but also to a practical desire to acquire resources. In particular, France and Spain were key sources of arms and funds for the revolutionaries.

The importance of legitimacy in what was an independence struggle helped ensure that the diplomatic recognition of the new state, in turn, became a fundamental issue in relations between Britain and other European states. The British government sought to block recognition, and treated the reception of American diplomats as an hostile act, prefiguring the response by the Union in the American Civil War (1861–5) to the treatment of Confederate representatives, notably by Britain. Indeed, the signature of treaties between Louis XVI of France and the Americans in 1778 was correctly regarded as a sign of imminent hostilities with Britain.

Lacking an equivalent to the ancestral aristocracies of Europe, the Americans pursued a different diplomatic model to that of Britain. Indeed, the departure from the latter was part of the rejection of the British *ancien régime*. The international model seen as most pertinent in America was that of the United Provinces (Netherlands); and, in fact, republicanism as a diplomatic ethos was well established in Europe, with the Dutch taking forward the achievement of the Venetians.

In practice, however, the basis for American diplomacy was the system by which individual colonies had maintained agents in London. This system provided the necessary experience, and there was an overlap in representation between the colonial and early Republican periods, as with Benjamin Franklin. He proved a considerable success as American envoy in Paris, although Franklin was helped by the popularity there of his cause and of the idea of New World virtue that he was held to represent and that he carefully cultivated.

As the American position was regularized, the volume of Franklin's surviving correspondence increased: in March–June 1779, the first full months of his tenure as sole American envoy in Paris, he wrote on average fifty letters a month. As a reminder of the extent to which diplomacy attracted individuals of talent and was a key source of intellectual and cultural activity, Franklin also acted as a man of the Enlightenment, delivering a paper on the Aurora Borealis to the Académie des Sciences, becoming involved in an attempt by Jean-Paul Marat to challenge conventional views on the nature of science, staying in touch with the British intellectual and scientific world, establishing a type foundry and press, and writing an essay, *The Morals of Chess*, which included 'we learn by chess the habit of not being discouraged by present bad appearances in the state of our affairs, the habit of hoping for a favourable change, and that of persevering in the search of resources', a fitting description of his embassy.[19]

The previous volume of his published correspondence, covering November 1778–February 1779, indicated the continual disputes between the American agents in Europe and, more especially, France, and the amount of time that had to be devoted to shipping disputes and related diplomatic issues and legal quarrels. A particular issue was how French ships captured by the English and recaptured by American privateers should be treated.[20] In 1779 Franklin, an ever-busy diplomat, went on to design a script typeface for passports.

American relations with the French government were often difficult, as assistance was rarely as unreserved as required, while there was justified concern about France's pursuit of its own national interests, not least in terms of French territorial goals in the West Indies. Alongside the customary tensions of any alliance, especially one that linked two powers with such dissimilar objectives, there were also the problems of introducing a new revolutionary state into the world of *ancien régime* diplomacy, and of acting as military and financial agent for America.[21]

The rival British diplomatic system proved weak in its response to the American Revolution. In part, this situation was a matter of the limitations in Britain's international position and the deficiencies of its foreign policy, but there were also weaknesses in its diplomacy, weaknesses that were seen in particular in a failure to understand the tempo of Britain's increasing isolation. In mid-century, Sir Charles Hanbury Williams had suggested that envoys should not leave until their replacements arrived, but such a system was not adopted, and Hugh Elliot complained to a fellow diplomat in 1776:

> The Germans, Russians and French in general fix Secretarys of Legation at the most considerable posts, whose duty it is to give a new Minister every information he requires, and this constant residence and experience in business enables them to do so much more effectually than the most voluminous collections in writing.
>
> It is also common for foreigners to have resided some time without character at a post they are destined to fill.
>
> In England the original establishment for foreign ministers does not seem to have been founded with so much caution as on the continent. An English minister often arrives at his station with no better assistance than what a private secretary of his predecessors can give him, that is copying papers, cyphering etc. Information from home may be worded with the greatest clearness. It can no more convey an adequate idea of the situation of a court and of its principal inhabitants, than a map can of the high and low grounds of a country. Ten days conversation upon the spot with his predecessor would forward a newcomer at least a twelve month in his knowledge of men and things and enable him to take up the thread of intelligence where it had been left.[22]

As another instance of limitations, in this case of a not particularly advanced bureaucratic mechanics, in 1789 James Bland Burges received the congratulations of Edward Mason on becoming joint Under-Secretary in the Foreign Office, as well as the offer of a key item built in 1750:

> I have got a piece of *secretarial* furniture of mahogony [sic], which was of the greatest use to me, when I was in office. . . . It consists of 48 pigeon holes, or two of alphabet, the one for letters, placed in them according to the initial letters of the names of the writers of them. The other alphabet for miscellaneous papers, according to the subject matter.[23]

Once independence was won in 1783, American diplomats found their cause less fashionable in Europe and the nature of representation and negotiation more onerous. Although they tended self-consciously to dress with less show, as part of an ideology of diplomatic conduct directed against luxury, and to pride themselves on being the representative of a democratic people and a republic, some American diplomats adapted well to the *ancien régime*.

Others maintained a more critical response. Jefferson, who served as envoy in France, Secretary of State, Vice-President and President (1801–9), generally favoured diplomatic initiatives over warfare and/or coercion, which in part possibly represented the comparative weakness of the USA, although he took a robust line toward the Barbary States, with extensive consular representation in the Mediterranean linked to the deployment of American warships. At the same time, Jefferson, like other Americans of his Republican viewpoint, was concerned that American diplomats might be corrupted by living amongst the wicked Europeans.[24] Jefferson discouraged the development of the American diplomatic service, which, whatever the quality of individual diplomats, retained a relatively amateurish approach until the reforms of the 1940s.

Another basis of American diplomacy was that entailed in federalism. The representation of the individual colonies was especially important as the Constitution was being negotiated and put into practice. Indeed, the Constitution was a diplomatic agreement between and among the sovereign American states. Thereafter, this representation remained a factor in American politics, with senators, in particular, serving as akin to diplomats, notably in negotiating on behalf of their constituencies.[25] This issue was pushed to the fore when regional interests were especially at issue, as in the Jay–Gardoqui negotiations of 1786 when the states of New England and New York were willing to forego the right to trade on the Mississippi, thereby selling out the interests of the then South West, in exchange for favourable trade relations with Spain.

Regional interests were again at stake in 1814–15 when the states of New England took a different stance during the War of 1812 [1812–15] with Britain, leading to their representatives meeting in the Hartford Convention, which was a form of anti-war Federalist diplomacy.[26] Moreover, the commissioners at Ghent who negotiated the peace treaty with the British in late 1814 were also seriously divided over the terms, which underlined the difficulty of creating an effective diplomatic practice. Subsequently, there were to be attempts to ensure that American diplomats represented regional interests, most obviously with pressure for the appointment of supporters of slavery from Southern interests and politicians, such as Secretary of State John Calhoun.[27]

Due to earlier opposition from the slave states, it was not until most of them were effectively disenfranchised by their rebellion in the Civil War that the independence of Haiti and Liberia were recognized: in April 1862. Congress authorized the dispatch of American envoys. Opposition to recognition was led by Senator Garrett Davis of Kentucky who claimed to be able to imagine no sight so dreadful as that of 'a full-blooded negro' in Washington society. Diplomatic relations with the Dominican Republic followed in 1866.[28]

As far as international relations were concerned, it took time for American political practice and theory to define a workable response to the needs of diplomacy. For instance, as a result of the Longchamps affair in 1784, in which a French diplomat was attacked, the Supreme Court was given jurisdiction over international law, and the authority of the individual states was subordinated.[29] It also had to be subordinated in the case of regulating foreign trade.[30] In 1796 the disclosure of diplomatic papers relating to Anglo-American relations became an issue for the House of Representatives.

The key point as far as American diplomacy was concerned, both during the Revolution and thereafter, was that it was republican, not radical.[31] This was shown in particular by the refusal to recognize Haiti once it won freedom from French rule. A black state proved too much for the influential slaveholding interests in the USA.

The French Revolution, which began in 1789 and led to the declaration of a republic in 1792, posed different issues to its American counterpart, as France was already an independent state whose position was universally recognized. The question, instead, was that of a change in regime and ideology, one that greatly affected diplomacy. While not the first revolution in Europe, it had a particular impact because it occurred in France, the leading land power in Western Europe, overthrowing a prestigious dynasty, the Bourbons, which had ruling branches elsewhere, and was very radical, indeed self-consciously so.

The French Revolution was more disruptive to the European system than were links with the outside world. In part, this was because the Revolution self-consciously sought to strike not only a new tone in foreign policy but also to pursue different goals. In particular, there was a determination to reject the conventions and practices of *ancien régime* international relations. As was the case during and after the First World War (see p. 188), secret diplomacy was decried in favour of its supposed open opposite.

There was also talk of reaching out to people, not governments, prefiguring a theme of the twentieth and twenty-first centuries. There was a challenge to the monopoly of representation that diplomacy seeks. Links between foreign governments and French *émigrés* were an issue, as were those between foreign radicals and the French government. Efforts to align states under the banners of revolution and the rights of man represented an attempt to infringe the autonomy and authority of governmental control over the diplomatic process, a process that could not be matched on behalf of counter-revolution as the latter respected the rights of established governments, although not that of revolutionary France.

The French Revolutionaries rejected traditional rules as at one with the international world of established privilege; and this rejection was given added force by the extent to which the Revolutionaries incessantly attacked the Austrian alliance, an alliance that had been in force since 1756 and that had concrete dynastic form in the shape of the marriage of Louis XVI to Marie Antoinette, the daughter of Maria Theresa, ruler of Austria from 1740 to 1780. Speakers in the National Assembly in 1792 returned frequently to the theme of a link between domestic and foreign enemies: each allegedly made action against the other more necessary. The actions of the *émigrés*, the real and rumoured Austrian connections of the royal court, and the obvious hostile sentiments of most foreign monarchs, lent apparent substance to such accusations.

In turn, the violent overthrow of the French monarchy in August 1792 led to a breach of diplomatic representation in Paris, as the removal of executive power from Louis XVI ensured that diplomatic credentials to him were no longer valid. It was unclear who was now wielding authority in Paris and what the effect of advancing Prussian and Austrian troops would be. The British, Danish, Dutch, Polish, Spanish, Swedish, Swiss and Venetian envoys all left, as the new republican government was not acknowledged.

The new French ideology of international affairs did not impress others. Pierre Lebrun, the Foreign Minister, might declare in November 1792, 'Policy and justice are two ideas that have for too long been separated, but the Republic has firmly decided never to separate them.'[32] The response elsewhere was less forthcoming. William, 1st Lord Auckland, the experienced British envoy in The Hague, noted of his French counterpart that June, 'M. de Maude made a long visit yesterday to the Grand Pensionary, and uttered nothing but classical phrases, natural philosophy, and belles lettres'.[33]

The new nature of the discussion, formulation and execution of French policy ensured that the suggestion that allies be sought was not pursued consistently; that it was compromised by attempts to inspire political change elsewhere, if not also political and social radicalism; and that the new universalist rationale of the French policy, its mission and ideology, made ad hoc French attempts at compromise with other states, and at the retention of aspects of the *ancien régime* diplomatic system, unconvincing. Once unconvincing, there was little mileage in them, for a degree of certainty about the intentions and consistency of a partner in negotiation was as important as the apparent nature of those intentions, an issue that for a long time had affected states with powerful representative institutions.

Diplomacy by declamation challenged the existing international architecture, and deliberately so, a situation that looked toward its more recent usage. For example, in November 1792 the Executive Council decreed that the Austrians (with whom France was at war) should be pursued wherever they retreated, a threat to neutrals, and also that the estuary of the River Scheldt was to be open for navigation, a clear breach of the Peace of Westphalia of 1648, when a closure had been insisted on by the Dutch in order to protect their commercial position. Four days later, these decisions were ratified by the National Convention. The logic of their new ideas and of their rejection of the past made the French radicals unwilling to accept the apparent denial of the natural right of the inhabitants of the Austrian Netherlands (the Belgians-to-be) to trade from Antwerp, which had been enforced by the closure of the Scheldt.

Asserting the importance of the independence of nations, Lebrun outlined the implications of the new diplomacy. He argued that he was not seeking to harm the rights of the Dutch, but that the Belgians were not obliged to maintain the engagements made by their former Habsburg masters, whose yoke had now been overthrown by the French.[34] The Spanish Habsburgs had ruled Belgium at the time of Westphalia and it had been transferred to the Austrian Habsburgs under the Treaty of Utrecht (1713).

This argument indicated Lebrun's wish to dramatize the breach between *ancien régime* and revolutionary diplomacy, as did his offer of support for the transfer of the Caribbean island of Tobago to Britain with the caveat that the consent of its inhabitants was necessary.[35] French decrees demonstrated the nature of the new diplomacy, and notably the attempt to empower the notion of the people. On 19 November 1792, in response to appeals for help from radicals in the German state of Zweibrücken and Mainz, the National Convention passed a decree declaring that the French would extend fraternity and assistance to all peoples seeking to regain their liberty.

As a general principle, this measure was subversive of all international relations, as well as unrealistic. The decree also challenged other states, as their refugees in Paris continually pressed for action on their behalf. Thus, in early 1793, Tadeusz Kościuszko, a leader of the Polish patriots opposed to the Russian dominance of Poland, visited Paris. The role of such refugees constituted an important part of what was an alternative diplomacy. This looked toward other aspects of alternative diplomacy, notably radical episodes such as the Comintern, or Communist International, as well as the radicals of the 1960s (see pp. 133, 191, 192, 195). In January 1795 the Dutch government sent two commissioners to negotiate neutrality with the victorious French only to find that the radical Holland 'Patriots' had sent two representatives who offered full submission.

Yet it would be misleading to ignore the extent to which alternative diplomacies were not restricted to radical movements. For example, Jacobitism, the cause of the exiled Stuarts, was supported by such a diplomacy from 1689. Nor was the French Revolution the first period in which diplomatic action was taken on behalf of people in other countries. Instead, as a result of the Reformation, it was a longstanding practice from the early sixteenth century.

The willingness of the French to sponsor, or encourage, discontent and sedition in the 1790s was seen as an indication both of the essential objectives of French policy and of the means by which they sought to effect them. Noting the belief that the French wished to force 'tout l'univers' to adopt their new regime, Montmorin, still Foreign Minister in May 1791, instead argued that it was up to each nation to judge what was best for itself. By late 1792 the French appeared to have bridged the two propositions by defining other nations in terms of revolutionary and pro-French populaces, and, indeed, the support of such elements compromized French diplomacy.

The French government might complain of misleading and hostile images spread by *émigrés*, but the course of the Revolution appeared to justify them. The actions of French diplomats was a crucial source of distrust. The interception of Maulde's dispatches revealed that his protestations of good intentions towards the Dutch government did not inhibit his encouragement of sedition. Such action suggested that no French diplomacy could be trusted. If individual French diplomats, or indeed ministers, differed in private from the more alarmist aspects of French policy, as many did, that was of limited consequence because they were unwilling and unable to stop it in the National Assembly, the electric public forum that was crucial to its development.

Indeed, French declarations, and the debates they sprang from, reflected the application of philosophical idealism to international relations, with all the cant and self-righteous response to the views of others that was to be anticipated. The new society that was being advocated and created in France was not essentially designed to be formed with reference to the concept of the territorial states. In practice, in so far as the new politics and ideology illuminated the policy of French governments, they did not encourage the limitation of policy aspirations nor compromise with the interests of territorial states. Diplomatic instructions revealed an unwillingness to accept the validity of other perceptions, and there was no consistent willingness to compromise with other states to any serious extent.

The context within which French diplomats – and thus the diplomats of other powers – operated was very much affected by the nature of politics within France. In particular, there was no sustained attempt to explain the views of other powers to the National Assembly and (later) the Convention. Instead, the creation of these institutions was part of a political culture that encouraged both the public expression of specific views on foreign policy, and attempts to influence policy with these. Ministers and politicians who wished to fight were encouraged, while their more hesitant colleagues became cautious about expressing their opposition and lost the ability to push through their own ideas.

The fevered nature of the crucial debates, the declamatory style and extravagant arguments of the speakers, and the frequent interventions of the spectators on the side of action and against compromise, all combined to produce a context in Paris within which it was difficult to conduct not just diplomacy as conventionally understood, but also any negotiations in which mutual comprehension and concessions were to play a role. The reading of dispatches in the National Assembly angered French diplomats and their contacts.[36] There was also concern that their dispatches appeared in the French press.[37] The discussion of foreign states in both the National Assembly and the press also proved troubling.[38] Envoys, moreover, worried about the negative impression created by instability within France.[39] Montmorin was dismissed in November 1791, in part because the Diplomatic Committee of the National Assembly did not accept his argument that he should not publicly reveal all the details of various negotiations. He was executed in 1792

Problems were also created for foreign powers, problems that looked toward twentieth-century issues. In April 1792 William, Lord Grenville, the British Foreign Secretary, wrote to George, Earl Gower, the envoy in Paris, concerning a recent clash between frigates off India: 'You will observe that my dispatch is drawn with a view to public discussion, as I imagine that considering the present state of things in France, *that* can hardly be avoided, however desirable it would have been.' In this case, however, a clash was avoided. The French were then far more concerned about the breakdown in relations with Austria. Thomas, 7th Earl of Elgin, another British diplomat who was then in Paris, heard and was pleased by the minister's report to the National Assembly on the episode.[40]

Foreign powers also had to confront the problem of deciding how to deal with the variety of groups claiming to represent France. These included *émigrés* of various stripes, as well as different interests within France; and foreign powers faced the difficulty of assessing their credibility as well as legitimation. Louis XVI and his wife, Marie Antoinette, were closely linked to the Austrian envoy, the Count of Mercy-Argenteau, and had a secret diplomacy separate from and often opposed to that of the *émigrés*.[41] Suspicions of their attitudes and actions fed into a popular

Austrophobia that affected the public debate over policy.[42] The agents of the *émigré* princes, such as the Chevalier de La Bintinaye, sought to create a counter-revolutionary league.

There is a tendency to seek elements of continuity between *ancien régime* and Revolutionary France, but the Revolution very clearly represented a break from *ancien régime* diplomacy.[43] The Revolutionaries thought of themselves as acting in a new and therefore better fashion, and not least in response to a culture that was primarily reverential of and referential to the past. In 1792 Lebrun sought to free France from 'miserables querelles d'etiquette' and argued that the phrase '*pacte de famile*' (family pact) 'shall be removed from the political vocabulary of France. The Republic knows no family other than the great family of the state', while, from London, the envoy, Francois, Marquis de Chauvelin, referred to 'credentials signed in the name of 24 million free and victorious men'.[44]

The argument that treaties entered into by rulers could not bind people was subversive, while the subordination of foreign policy and the foreign minister to control by a committee of a popular assembly was new: control passed from the executive to the legislature.[45] Partly as a result of such attitudes, diplomatic relations, procedures and personnel were all disrupted, and this also affected the consular service.[46]

Nevertheless, the eventual willingness of other powers to negotiate with what was from 21 January 1793 a regicide regime was striking. Notably, the Treaties of Basle between France and Prussia, the United Provinces and Spain (1795), were followed by the Franco-Sardinian Armistice of Cherasco (1796), the Franco-Austrian treaties of Campo Formio (1797) and Lunéville (1801), and the Anglo-French Treaty of Amiens (1802). In large part, these treaties reflected repeated French success on the battlefield, Lunéville, for example, following French victories at Hohenlinden and Marengo in 1800, but traditional interests and objectives can also be stressed in the diplomacy of the 1790s, as other states sought to adjust to the reality of French power and tried to use it to pursue these interests.

Continuity can also be emphasized if an effort is made to distinguish clearly between on the one hand revolutionary ideologies and ideals, and on the other, the actual policies pursued by French diplomats and ministers, for however radical the speeches made by revolutionary orators, many of the presuppositions underlying government policy were to a large extent traditional. Thus, although revolutionary emotion altered much of the tone of French policy, it had much less effect on its substance; and the situation was rather one of the pursuit of aims, which were not in themselves new, by greatly extended means.

Moreover, it would be mistaken to imagine that *ancien régime* diplomacy was in some way static and inconsequential. There is an element that appeared like the latter, in part because of the pursuit of local judicial issues in the context of the fragmented Holy Roman Empire. Thus in 1787–8 Karl Theodor, Elector of Bavaria, disputed with the Prince-Bishop of Friesing the issue of constructing dykes on the river Isar, as well as the regality of mines in a contested county, while the Elector also had to consider how best to respond, as Protector of a church and Duke of a neighbouring principality with relevant rights, to an appeal from the church chapter against the Dutch government in Maastricht.[47]

Such issues certainly seem inconsequential, although the modern world has its equivalents, including the longstanding Spanish refusal to accept the British position in Gibraltar. As a reminder, however, of the range of *ancien régime* diplomatic methods, the activity of Count Simon Vorontsov, the Russian envoy, in encouraging opposition to the British intimidation of Russia in the Ochakov Crisis in 1791 is notable. Vorontsov, who had threatened the Foreign Secretary, Francis, 5th Duke of Leeds, with stirring up a popular outcry that would block ministerial schemes, played a major role in a busy press campaign against government policy. He also provided Opposition parliamentary speakers with arguments about the war, and encouraged the Russia Company to act as it indeed did.[48] As an instance, moreover, of the extent to which diplomatic links were not simply with accredited envoys, Catherine II gave a better reception in 1791 to Robert Adair, the agent of the Whig opposition, than to the accredited British envoy, William Fawkener.[49]

British concern over Russian expansionism around the Black Sea, the source of the crisis, saw the diplomacy of the period produce an important result in the shape of up-to-date information on the area in dispute. William Lindsay, Secretary of Legation in St Petersburg, provided the government with a detailed memorandum 'respecting the Black Sea, the peculiarities of its navigation, the geographical situation of its ports, their various degrees of importance, the produce usually exported from them, and the views of the court of Russia with respect to their future commerce. I have, at the same time, endeavoured to state all the circumstances which are likely to promote, or militate against, the accomplishment of their projects.'[50]

Ancien régime diplomacy could also deliver results, as in the Partitions of Poland between Austria, Prussia and Russia in 1772, 1793 and 1795. Indeed, there is a parallel between the underplaying of the vitality and effectiveness in *ancien régime* diplomacy and misguided attempts to see change and modernity in warfare as resting in the forces of Revolutionary France;[51] an account that is seriously flawed.[52]

Against this must be set the changes arising from the heightened element of distrust in international relations that the Revolution introduced, a distrust that was paranoid, linked alleged domestic and foreign threats, and echoed the fevered anxieties of relations at the time of the Reformation. The distrust that characterized the Revolutionaries and their opponents, as well as neutral powers, affected the content and character of foreign policy and international relations. Louis XIV and his diplomats had aroused considerable distrust elsewhere in Europe (as had Peter the Great), but they posed less of a threat to the affairs of other countries, especially Catholic countries, than the Revolutionaries.

Moreover, revolutionary ideals and the logic of domestic politics pushed France towards war in a fashion that was totally different from the impact of domestic pressures elsewhere. Thus, whereas it had proved possible for France to avoid war with Austria over the Scheldt crisis in 1784, and with Prussia and Britain in the Dutch crisis in 1787, such a process of compromise was not possible in 1792–3. In the end, however, the decree of 19 November 1792 was revoked by the Convention on 14 April 1793, Georges Danton pointing out that it would oblige the French to assist a revolution in China.

The French Revolution invites discussion of the thesis that an episode of revolutionary foreign policy is necessarily short and will be abandoned, both because the distinctive form of the revolutionaries' diplomacy results in an isolation that can only be escaped by this method, and as an aspect of the more general consolidation of revolutions.[53] This thesis is a matter not only of historical curiosity, in the shape of its application to the late eighteenth century, but also has relevance due to the frequency of revolutions over the last century, as well as the extent to which modern states, notably, but not only, China, Cuba, Iran and Libya, look for their legitimacy to such revolutions.

This issue raises the general question of the applicability of historical episodes. All revolutions are distinctive, and the similarities between, say, the French and Chinese revolutions, or those in Cuba and Iran, are limited. As far as the French Revolution is concerned, there is a need to contrast the (very varied) stages of reform with the particular, more extreme, radical pulse of 1793–4. Much in the former represented a change to usual *ancien régime* practice, but nevertheless drew on reform pressures and ideas already present. The radical impulse of 1793–4 was far more extreme. Yet this impulse led, in the month of Thermidor in the new revolutionary calendar, to a reaction in 1794, a reaction essentially due to domestic political factors; and it is to this specific reaction, rather than to any general rule about the trajectories of revolutionary foreign policies, that changes in French foreign policy in 1794 should be traced.

Moreover, far from rejecting the Europe of courts, and only seeking alliance with fellow revolutionaries, the latter, prior to Thermidor, proved willing to seek alliance with other states, a process encouraged by the impact of war, which had a major effect on all states, revolutionary or other. In 1793 French defeat at Neerwinden on 18 March and the loss of recently conquered Belgium back to the Austrians led to a more cautious approach to annexation and the spread of revolution, and resulted in stronger interest in peace. The Girondins fell in June 1793, and the Jacobin coup gave power to Danton, who sought a return to more conventional diplomacy. In order to obtain peace, he tried to create a powerful league. Prussia, Sardinia, Switzerland and Tuscany were offered terms that were designed to weaken the relative position of Austria. Danton also sought a negotiated peace with Britain in late 1793.

At that stage, neither military nor international developments made this an attractive prospect for other powers, but in 1795 the situation was different. The Thermidorean regime that succeeded the Terror in July 1794 played a role, but so too did the French victories in Belgium that year, and the degree to which Austria, Prussia and, particularly, Russia were increasingly concerned about Eastern Europe, especially Poland.

Meanwhile, once war had begun in 1792, the processes of diplomacy, as in previous wars,[54] were designed to serve the cause of conflict, reporting military information and negotiating alliances. In 1793 Edmond Genet, the new French envoy to the United States, was instructed to dispatch agents to Kentucky in order to arrange an invasion of Louisiana, then under the rule of France's ally Spain.[55] This mission was unwelcome to the USA, as was Genet's attempt to undermine backing for President Washington and the commissioning of privateers which, sailing from American ports, harmed relations with Britain.[56] The war also led to the breakdown of diplomatic relations and the movement of diplomatic posts. In January 1795 the British, Prussian, Sardinian and Spanish envoys left The Hague on the approach of French forces. In 1796 the residence of the French Consul General in Morocco was transferred from Salé to Tangier, so that he would be able to report on naval movements in the Straits of Gibraltar. French advances led to the cutting of postal services, which affected the information available to diplomats, including neutral diplomats.

At the same time, the weakened control of the government over France's generals, combined with the extent to which French policy focused on territorial expansion and strategic opportunism, ensured that powerful generals became key figures in a foreign policy that was distinctly not diplomatic. Neutrals, for example, were systematically bullied. French military successes also gravely limited the extent of rival diplomatic systems, as powers intimidated by France were obliged to break off relations with its enemies.

Napoleon proved a prime instance of this process of the general as policymaker, first in command in northern Italy, where he forced Austria to accept the Truce of Leoben in 1797. There, and later elsewhere, Napoleon proved particularly adept at the principle of compensating victims at the expense of others, a policy later followed by both Hitler and Stalin.

Once in command of the invasion of Egypt in 1798, Napoleon revealed the full extent of the militarization of French diplomacy, notably the absence of the sense of mutual understanding that is crucial to the successful operation of an international system. He assumed that the Turks, the imperial overlords of effectively autonomous Egypt, could be readily intimidated or bribed into accepting French action. Napoleon's sense of grandiloquence and autonomy, and his belief that both French policy and the Orient were designed to serve his views, emerged from his recollection:

> In Egypt, I found myself freed from the obstacles of an irksome civilization. I was full of dreams . . . I saw myself founding a religion, marching into Asia, riding an elephant, a turban on my head and in my hand the new Koran that I would have composed to suit my needs.[57]

Reality was to prove otherwise. The French cultural supposition of superiority and their arrogance of power led to a lack of sensitivity that caused Sultan Selim III to declare war.

The ensuing international crisis provoked the formation of the Second Coalition against France and, ironically, its pressures prepared the ground for Napoleon's seizure of power in a coup in November 1799. At one level, this coup reflected a return to *ancien régime* patterns of diplomatic activity, notably as the inexorable scope of Napoleon's ambition, and his vainglorious capacity to alienate others, can be seen to repeat those of Louis XIV. Moreover, just as Napoleon's regime marked a limitation of radicalism within France, so it also reflected and sustained the abandonment of revolutionary objectives and methods in international relations already anticipated with Thermidor. In particular, open diplomacy was replaced by pragmatism.[58]

This shift would suggest that a fundamental divide occurred in diplomacy (and indeed international relations), not with the (two) overthrows of Napoleon and the Vienna peace settlement, all in 1814–15, but rather with Thermidor in 1794 and Napoleon's rise to power in 1799. Such an approach can be taken further by arguing that therefore there was a fundamental continuity throughout the nineteenth century, one, indeed, that lasted until the Russian Revolution of 1917.

Such a continuity, however, did not mean that the return of France to a monarchical system under (eventually) Napoleon I entailed a reversion to an *ancien régime* system of diplomacy. Instead, one major development that continued was the focus on the nation. This focus was true both of the French, whether Revolutionary or Napoleonic, and of their opponents. Moreover, nationalism was understood both as a positive force for identity and cohesion, one leading diplomacy in a certain direction and, in addition, giving it particular force, and also as a negative xenophobic response. The latter was directed both against other nation states and also against incorporating international forces, most obviously Napoleonic France, as in Spain from 1808.

Partly as a result of such nationalism and xenophobia, the very process of diplomacy took part in a more volatile context, one indeed that looked towards the situation in recent decades. For example, in 1797 the residence of the French envoy in Rome was occupied by papal police during a riot; the rioters had taken refuge there. In the ensuing disorder, General Leonard Duphot, an aide to the French envoy, was killed. Given, however, that the French had sought to provoke a revolutionary uprising, their conduct was less than exemplary, while the crisis was exploited by Napoleon in order to occupy Rome in February 1798 and to proclaim a Roman republic. In 1798 the tricolour flag of the French embassy in Vienna, prominently displayed on an Austrian national holiday by a provocative envoy, led to a crowd demonstration. Leaving Vienna, the envoy demand reparation. Such a use of diplomatic symbols and incidents as the occasions for complaint and action looked toward modern conduct, notably by totalitarian regimes of left and right. Looked at differently, these episodes represented a repositioning, away from dynastic monarchy and towards a new concept of the state, of the long-established concern for status, seen for example in controversies over precedence (see p. 153).

As a reminder that chronologies of change were (and are) complex, alongside nationalism in the 1790s and 1800s came, in the 1800s, a very traditional dynastic aggrandisement. Dynastic prestige played a major role in Napoleon's creation of kingdoms and principalities for his family. Napoleon's stepson, Eugène de Beauharnais, became Viceroy for the new King of Italy, who was none other than Napoleon. The Dutch made Louis, one of Napoleon's brothers, King in 1806, in order to avoid annexation to France, not that that subsequently prevented this annexation. Another brother, Joseph, became King of the Two Sicilies the same year. In 1808, after Louis turned it down, Joseph was given the Spanish crown, and was in turn replaced in the Sicilies by Joachim Murat, Napoleon's brother-in-law, while another brother, Jerome, became King of Westphalia, a new state created by Napoleon that reflected his dominance of Germany.

Far from these new rulers serving the cause of their nations (although Louis sought to do so), these rulers were all subordinate to Napoleon, who not only deployed the force that maintained them in position but also was senior to them as Emperor, a status he had awarded himself in 1804. As such, it was appropriate to his status that his marital diplomacy culminated in 1810, when Napoleon married into the Habsburgs, now the Austrian imperial family as the Holy Roman Empire had been extinguished in 1806. His bride, the Archduchess Marie Louise, was a spoil of war from Austria's defeat by Napoleon in 1809. She was intended to cement Austria's new relationship with France, as well as to provide an heir who would carry through this relationship. In the event, their heir, Napoleon II, the King of Rome, was not to rule.

Napoleon's family aggrandisement helped produce a diplomacy that was at once dynastic and imperial. The latter was characterized by very uneven relations, such as those also seen between Napoleon and states that were clients or that he saw as clients. Napoleon certainly sought to direct and even conduct diplomacy in person. He travelled considerable distances, notably to Central and Eastern Europe in 1805–7, 1808–9 and 1812–13, and to Spain in 1808. However, as his government and diplomacy were intensely personal, a government of personal empire rather than of France, the policymaking process was an adjunct of his travels, rather than being greatly hindered by them.

Yet Napoleon was a total failure at diplomacy. As under Louis XIV, the problem of European alliances was evaded because neither ruler really sought allies. Instead, they were interested in clients: powers that could be manipulated, if not controlled. When Napoleon, like Louis, was given the challenge of sustaining an alliance in which compromise played a role, he failed, and he did so repeatedly. Alexander I of Russia's respect for him encouraged Alexander to try to build on their agreement at Tilsit in 1807, but Napoleon's failure to reciprocate helped to wreck such hopes.

Napoleon was happiest with a diplomacy of force. His character, views, ambitions and ambience did not lend themselves to accommodation, other than as a short-term device. Napoleon's will to dominate was both personal and a continuation of that of the Revolution, as was a refusal to countenance limits in the shape of diplomatic conventions. Treated as spies, foreign envoys were embarrassed, threatened and imprisoned. Sir George Rumbold, the British Chargé d'Affaires to the Hanse towns, was seized by French troops in 1804, although in independent Hamburg. Although Napoleon was probably not involved, Benjamin Bathurst, British envoy to Austria, disappeared, probably murdered, en route home in 1809.[59]

Typically, Napoleon expected his own envoys to be well treated. Napoleon's will and attitude ensured that peace treaties were imposed and that, once they were made, the French sought further benefits, while their defeated opponents felt only resentment and a determination of reverse the settlement. It was indicative that Napoleon took further the tendency, already seen with France in the 1790s, to employ soldiers in diplomatic roles and as heads of missions abroad.[60]

This tendency contributed to an increasing militarization of the conduct of French policy. Thus General Count Antoine-François Andréossy was sent to Austria to enforce a diplomacy of bullying after Prussia had been defeated at Jena in 1806, while General A.-L.-M.-R. Savary, the envoy sent to St Petersburg in 1807 after the Peace of Tilsit, was arrogant and difficult. The following year, Savary was sent to Madrid in order to prepare for the French seizure of power. General J.-A.-B. Law de Lauriston succeeded Caulaincourt (who was not a general) in St Petersburg in 1811, and failed to maintain the latter's careful and cautious approach to relations with Russia; although it was Napoleon who was responsible for the failure of the Franco-Russian entente established in 1807 by the negotiations at Tilsit. The use of generals was not new, and had been frequent under the Bourbons, but it became more insistent under Napoleon. It was also an important aspect of a failure to appreciate that an effective diplomatic service must produce reports and ideas that might be challenging.

Darwinian ideas of the operation of international systems suggest that developments by one power are matched by others as they compete to survive and succeed. Yet, as with the example of Napoleonic warfare, it is unclear how far this process operated; as opposed to an alternative process in which the *ancien régime* states essentially followed their existing practices with greater effectiveness. The latter interpretation would put less of an emphasis on any transformational results from the French Revolution or Napoleon, and this conclusion seems pertinent if the composition, institutions and character of the diplomacy of France's opponents are considered.

The principal changes they had to address were those of war, not diplomacy. The length of the warfare beginning in 1792, and, in particular, the major changes in alliances as coalitions were created and brought low, led to a tempo in diplomacy that was notable. War, its presence, changes and consequences, set the pace for the diplomacy of all states. Much of this diplomacy became a matter of keeping rival coalitions together. The major powers continued and, with the exception of France and Spain, under the same dynasties; but there was considerable change at the level of the secondary powers. States disappeared, notably Poland, Venice and the Netherlands, while others, particularly Spain and Naples, saw a change in dynasty as a result of conquest.

Thus many of the players and pieces were removed from the board, and this removal constituted a major change in the diplomatic world. Not all of it was a consequence of the actions of France. Poland was partitioned out of existence in 1795 by Austria, Prussia and Russia, completing a process that had begun in 1772; while Austria played a major role in the territorial changes in Germany and northern Italy, as (for Germany) did Bavaria, Saxony and Württemberg. Nevertheless, France played an instrumental role in most of these changes.

At the same time, the possibility of change was checked. Most obviously, the calls for national risings for liberty that, albeit often cynically, had characterized the 1790s, became less common. Napoleon called on the Hungarians to rise for independence from Austria in 1809, talked of an Italian national spirit in the Kingdom of Italy, and sought to profit from Polish nationalism and anti-Russian feeling in the Grand Duchy of Warsaw; but in general he avoided international populism.

The Napoleonic system was destroyed on the battlefield in 1812–15, and the legacy was cleared up in the peace conference held in Vienna in 1814–15. In some respects this conference, in which the negotiations were conducted in French, simply took forward the diplomacy by means of which the Sixth Coalition against Napoleon had been assembled and had then arranged its affairs. Indeed, diplomats became used in 1813–14 to following the rulers to whom they were accredited as the latter accompanied their armies in the successful campaigns against Napoleon. The Vienna conference was designed to follow the peace of Paris of 30 May 1814 which had settled France's borders: Vienna was designed to work out the detailed provisions for Germany, Italy, Switzerland and the Low Countries.

There were parallels between Vienna and *ancien régime* peace congresses, notably Nijmegen in 1678–9 and Utrecht in 1713, but, spanning Europe to include Russia, Vienna was more comprehensive in composition, as in intention, than its predecessors. It also took forward the peace treaties of Paris (1763) and Versailles (1783), in including the disposition of trans-oceanic colonies by global powers, with Britain, as at Paris, benefiting greatly.

The diplomacy at Vienna was also not restricted to the cartography of rearranging boundaries. Instead, there was a determined effort to restrict the spread of radical ideas and practices. This effort looked toward postwar interest in maintaining a conservative ideological order, not least by enforcing its goals in countries that did not conform. These themes had parallels in the diplomacy of the Cold War. Significantly, the Congress found time to codify diplomatic arrangements, issuing a regulation on the precedence of diplomatic agents in March 1815. This step was a key measure affirming the resumption of pre-French Revolutionary diplomatic concerns and the desire for agreed conventions.

Indeed, the Congress symbolized this resumption with its return to the eighteenth-century system in form and content. The former included the social whirl of parties organized on the basis of aristocratic society, as well as the interaction of informal and formal negotiations, an interaction that had not been followed by the Revolutionary French nor by Napoleon. In part this was because they had scant time for the diplomacy of compromise that rested on the mutual concessions encouraged by this interaction.

Yet, at the same time, there were changes. The location of the Congress in Vienna, a capital city, and the presence of sovereigns and leading ministers, looked less back to the congresses of 1648–1748 than forward to a different form of meetings, seen for example at Berlin (1878) and Paris (1919), in which diplomacy was directly handled by rulers, or first or foreign ministers, and not by diplomats. Moreover, the tensions at Vienna, notably between Prussia/Russia and Austria/Britain/France over the fate of the kingdom of Saxony, which had remained loyal to Napoleon until nearly the end, led to fear of a resumption of hostilities, and indicated that the conventional diplomatic system was not necessarily better able to prevent disputes than it had been to thwart the challenges it had finally seen off after over two decades of struggle.

In the event, Napoleon's return from exile in Elba played a key role in facilitating the negotiations at Vienna. On 7 March 1815, the delegates knew of his escape from Elba, and on 11 March of his arrival in France. Napoleon's return united the powers, which had been very divided over the future of Saxony. Indeed, Louis XVIII of France had joined Austria and Britain, in a Triple Alliance concluded on 3 January 1815, in opposing Russo-Prussian pressure for the Prussian annexation of Saxony. This alliance was seen by Charles Maurice de Talleyrand-Périgord (Talleyrand), the French representative, as a way to create a new diplomatic order in which France could have greater influence in Europe, as well as specific benefits on her frontiers. There was also tension between Prussia and William I of the Netherlands, with the Prussians demanding that the Dutch surrender the key fortress of Maastricht and the lands on the east bank of the River Meuse/Maas, and refusing to hand over Liège, which they had occupied, until the Dutch did so.

Opportunities for France to become an ally in European power-politics were lost with Napoleon's return. Instead, on 13 March the powers assembled at Vienna declared Napoleon's invasion an illegal act and offered help to Louis XVIII. The presence of Tsar Alexander I and Frederick William III of Prussia in Vienna eased tensions among the allies and speeded deliberations.

In letters to the Allied sovereigns of the Seventh Coalition, Napoleon pledged to observe existing treaties, and affirmed peace with the rest of Europe, but his rhetoric within France toward the other powers was hostile and bellicose. Armand de Caulaincourt, Napoleon's last foreign minister, now back in office, wrote to Robert, Viscount Castlereagh, his British counterpart, on 4 April to inform him of the return of Napoleon and that Napoleon hoped for peace; but Caulaincourt was also ordered by Napoleon to create a new league with the lesser powers, including Spain, Portugal, Switzerland and the minor German and Italian states, a proposal which was a testimony to Napoleon's lack of realism. So also was his confidence that the people elsewhere who had known his rule would reject war against France whatever their rulers thought. This diplomacy to peoples, a throwback to the French Revolution, and one accompanied in brutal practice by the harsh demands of French power, led Napoleon to order the publication of appeals to foreigners who had served in his forces to rejoin them. These foreigners included many German, Belgian and Dutch soldiers. Thus, military needs and international attitudes combined for Napoleon.

On 25 March 1815 the Vienna powers had renewed their alliance in order to overthrow the restored emperor, promising indeed to support France against Napoleon and inviting Louis XVIII to sign the treaty. Austria, Britain, Prussia and Russia each promised to provide forces of 150,000 men, with Britain being permitted to provide some of its contribution with money that was to be used to subsidize the forces of allies or to hire troops from rulers lacking the necessary funds. This division of responsibilities was an appropriate recognition of the respective strength of the powers. Lesser states were also allocated contributions, Brunswick and the Hanseatic cities, for example, 3,000 troops each, and Mecklenburg-Schwerin 3,800 troops.

Moreover, the threat from Napoleon led to a settlement of differences at the Congress, a key event in the formation of the strategic context for the campaign. Had disagreements continued then Napoleon's options might have been better, indeed very much so. Instead, the Prussians and Russians had already backed down over Saxony in an agreement on 18 February 1815, but Saxony still had to be brought to accept terms under which Frederick William III of Prussia was still ceded about 58 per cent of Saxony. Dissension over Saxony complicated the issue of control over the Saxon contingent in the Allied forces deployed against Napoleon. The Allies also disagreed on whether to restore Louis XVIII or to search for other expedients, such as the Duke of Orléans, who indeed became king in 1830; but all agreed that they did not want Napoleon as ruler nor a French general such as Soult.

Victory for the British and Prussians under the Duke of Wellington and Field Marshal Blücher at Waterloo on 18 June 1815 confirmed the decisions of the international peace congress of Vienna, a congress that both set the seal on Britain's triumph over France and marked the beginning of a period in which the British empire was faced with no effective threats. The after-impact of Napoleon's defeat would probably have been different had it been achieved by Austrian and Russian forces, not least in terms of their subsequent role in Western Europe. Instead, Napoleon's return and defeat ensured the British a more satisfactory result. Already, by the Peace of Paris, British control of a host of wartime gains, mostly from France and its allies, including Cape Colony, the Seychelles, Mauritius, Trinidad, Tobago, St Lucia, Malta, the Ionian Islands, Sri Lanka, Essequibo and Demerara (the last two the basis of British Guiana), had all been recognized. Victory at Waterloo strengthened Britain's claim to have a strong say in developments in Western Europe.

As a result of its gains, Britain ruled far more than just the waves, and this empire was a far more widely flung congeries of possessions than any other empire in the world, either then or previously. This empire was also very much one that had been tested in war, and that, if necessary, was ready for further conflict, as its fleet was the largest in the world and its public finances the strongest.

British territorial gains ensured that she had a system of bases to protect her trade while denying others positions, such as Cape Colony, a conquest from the Dutch, that would potentially be a threat in hostile hands. British naval interests have also been as playing a role in the European territorial settlement, with shipbuilding ports that would be a threat in French hands put in those of British allies: Trieste and Venice with Austria, Genoa with the Kingdom of Sardinia (Piedmont), and, crucially, Antwerp with the new Kingdom of the United Netherlands created by the Netherlands (formerly United Provinces) including Belgium. The fact that the Savoyard state (the Kingdom of Sardinia) was not only restored in 1814 but actually gained greatly by acquiring the republic of Genoa owed much to Britain, but diplomacy also works by combining interests, and the abilities of the Sardinian envoys in London and elsewhere were important.

As a reminder of the dynastic theme, the British royal family also gained great prestige as royal status for their possession of Hanover (hitherto an Electorate), proclaimed by the Prince Regent in October 1814, was swiftly recognized by the Congress. Thus, the status of the Hanoverian ruling family in Germany now matched those of Prussia, Bavaria, Saxony and Württemberg. Moreover, Hanover gained territory, notably East Friesland, Hildesheim and Osnabrück, as well as part of the former prince-bishopric of Münster, so that in 1815 it was the fourth largest state in

Germany, after Austria, Prussia and Bavaria. The gains reflected not just dynastic ambition but also the extent to which there was a general share out of German territories, one in which Prussia particularly benefited.

Napoleon's return and subsequent defeat also ensured that France received worse terms than those initially imposed by the Congress. The Second Treaty of Paris, signed on 20 November 1815, stipulated an occupation of northern France for five years (it ended in 1818), a large indemnity of 700 million francs, and the cession of the towns of Beaumont, Bouillon (both to the Netherlands), Landau (to Bavaria), and Saarlouis (to Prussia). Moreover, by the Quadruple Alliance of 20 November 1815, the four great powers – Austria, Britain, Prussia and Russia – renewed their anti-French alliance for twenty years, a step designed to limit the chances of France disrupting the peace.

Napoleon had failed, totally. His legacy was a weaker France, with Russia, the power frequently seen by French politicians over the previous century as a barbarian threat, now dominant in Eastern Europe. Indeed, in September 1815, in a dramatic display of power, Alexander I reviewed a parade of 150,000 Russian troops east of Paris, in the Russian occupation zone, alongside Francis I of Austria and Frederick William III of Prussia, each of whom was also dressed in Russian uniform. Earlier, on 10 July, the three monarchs had entered Paris.

In Europe, in place of Napoleon, came an attempt to develop a practice of collective security through a Congress system, and, from September 1815, Tsar Alexander's Holy Alliance of Christian monarchs (or at least those of Russia, Austria and Prussia), designed to maintain the new order. Within France, the new political order, supervised in practice by the Russian Ambassador, very much matched the ideas of the Holy Alliance, which in turn helped consolidate and affirm the success of the new international order; and in doing so contrasted with the deficiencies of the settlement after the First World War, notably in Russia and Turkey.

The Congress of Vienna was to be seen as a classic instance of a *realpolitik* characteristic of the resumption of *ancien régime* diplomacy in a new nineteenth-century order. That view, however, underplayed the ideological character of that order in terms of an opposition to revolution and, indeed, to significant domestic change. Yet, that reactionary characterization can be qualified by noting the extent to which the Vienna Settlement represented a degree of consensualism based on an acceptance of differing interests within a context in which law was to be the basis of international life and the balance of power was to rest on a mutual trust arising from mutual respect for everyone's rights.[61]

The theme of nineteenth-century *realpolitik* was to be taken up by Henry Kissinger, a historian of nineteenth-century international relations who became a 'defence intellectual', publishing *Nuclear Weapons and Foreign Policy* (1957), and later Nixon's National Security Adviser. Like most holders of that post, Kissinger sought to direct affairs from the centre, with trips in person to key occasion for negotiation, a position reminiscent of the central figures in 1814–15, notably Castlereagh and Metternich, the British Foreign Secretary and the Austrian Chancellor.

Kissinger, like them, left a major role for diplomacy because he placed the emphasis on national interests rather than ideological drive, with these interests traced to long-term geographical commitments within a multipolar and competitive international system. Just as the delegates at Vienna associated ideology, emotionalism and ostentatious moralizing in foreign policy with Revolutionary France, so Kissinger, a refugee from the anti-Semitism of Nazi Germany, associated them with the Germany he had fled. All of them favoured a statesmanship based on rational calculations of national self-interest in which the stress was on order and security.[62]

Diplomacy, which from the late eighteenth century was understood in Europe in its modern meaning of the management of relations between states rather than, as earlier, with reference to the study of documents or diplomas,[63] was required to understand the interests of other powers, and to try to reconcile differences. Macartney pressed the value of diplomacy in the journal of his Beijing embassy:

> nothing is more likely to contribute essentially to the promotion of our interests than having a King's Minister, or a Company's Minister with a King's Commission, always resident at Canton, totally unconcerned with trade of any kind and clearly known to be so. . . . It is no small advantage arising from the embassy that so many Englishmen have been seen at Pekin, from whose brilliant appearance and prudent demeanour a most favourable idea has been formed of the country which had sent them. Nor is it any strain of vanity to say that the principal persons of rank who, from their intercourse with us, had opportunities of observing our manners, tempers and discipline, very soon dismissed the prejudices they had conceived against us, and by a generous transition grew to admire and respect us as a nation and to love us as individuals. . . . Dispositions like these, an able Minister would not fail to improve . . . he would be able to excuse irregularities and clear up mistakes. He would discover the proper seasons for advancing or receding, when to be silent with dignity and when to speak with confidence and effect. But above all the King's Commission would authorise him to write to, and entitle him to be heard by, the Court of Pekin, a circumstance probably alone

sufficient to awe the regency of Canton and keep them within the bounds of justice and moderation.[64]

Moreover, turning to Europe, the argument that states were largely motivated by concern for their national security put a premium, within a conservative international order, on diplomatic skill in understanding and reconciling security goals. This premium was accentuated by a view of the importance of historical experience. Thus the conceptual background for the nineteenth century was put in place in 1814–15. However, this was a worldview to which it was going to be difficult to accommodate new or renewed ideological currents, particularly that nationalism that could not be reconciled to imperial systems.

FIVE
1815–1900

Two diplomatic orders clashed in China in August 1816. In an effort to address issues in Anglo-Chinese relations, notably the conditions under which British merchants operated in Canton, as well as to put relations on a proper footing, Britain, the imperial power of the Western world, sent William, Lord Amherst as envoy. Having sailed in February 1816, he arrived in Canton that July, a voyage that reflected the relatively slow nature of diplomacy in the age before steam. The Chia Ch'ing Emperor, however, saw no reason to yield the prerogatives of superiority. In successive meetings, Amherst refused to accept the resulting position of subordination. At Canton he was unwilling to communicate, except through his secretaries, with the mandarins sent to receive him because they were of inferior rank. At Tientsin, the presents he brought from the Prince Regent (later George IV) were referred to as tribute, which was not the British intention, and he was pressed to perform the kowtow (the striking of the forehead on the ground in obeisance nine times) when he met the Emperor. Amherst, however, was only willing to promise to bow nine times. Differing views over what had happened when Macartney was received in 1793 played a role: the Chinese claimed that he had kowtowed, while Macartney said he had only gone down on one knee and bowed his head.

With such preparation, it was scarcely surprising that the audience to which Amherst was summoned on 29 August 1816 did not go according to plan. Fearing that he would be pressurized into an act of submission, Amherst refused to attend, claiming to be too ill. The Chinese sought substitutes from his staff, only to be told that they were also ill. Seeing this as an act of discourtesy, the embassy was sent home, with the Prince Regent's letter returned unopened.

The parallels with the fate of Otto I's envoy in the 950s (see p. 30) are interesting, and the aftermath was also instructive. Amherst was to go on, not to further diplomatic positions, but to be Governor-General of India from 1823 to 1828, during which time he waged the first Anglo-Burmese War (1824–6), which was the product of a failure on both parts to manage differences, as well as intervening with force in the Indian state of Bhurtpore (1826). Meanwhile, also on 29 August 1816, the Dey of Algiers had confirmed his acceptance of the terms, including the end of Christian slavery, that Admiral Sir Edward Pellew had extorted by means of a prolonged and heavy naval bombardment on the 27th after negotiations had failed.[1] The Emperor, however, saw the Chinese position as unassailable. He wrote to the Prince Regent claiming that Amherst had broken a promise to kowtow, but that this was not taken to compromise George's clear willingness to communicate veneration and devotedness, and to send items of tribute. The Emperor continued by writing that Britain's great distance was such that messages of obedience sufficed and that it was unnecessary to send envoys, a decision significantly delivered in the form of an Imperial mandate sent to vassals.[2]

Given the subsequent enforcement of a different order, with China, in 1842 and, even more, 1860, treated by Britain as Algiers had been in 1816, this mandate can be treated as a curiosity. Robert Kennaway Douglas, writing Amherst's entry in the *Dictionary of National Biography* (1885), was in no doubt that Amherst was in the right. His tone, at this moment of British high-Victorian confidence, was clear: 'the commissioners, who, like all Asiatics, bow only when conscious of weakness, assumed an arrogant tone in their dealings with the envoy. . . . a breach of the commonest diplomatic courtesy . . . the insolent manner of the messengers . . . the true cause of his want of success was duly recognised by his countrymen'.[3] Yet it was through force, not consent, that the Western diplomatic order was to be established.

The period 1815 to 1900 can be seen as the high point of the old diplomatic order, but only if that is presented in Western terms. Other old orders were brought low. As far as the West was concerned, the century saw negotiating rights largely monopolized by state authority, not least as chartered companies, such as the East India Companies, lost that right. From 1804 the Levant Company no longer paid the British Ambassador in Constantinople as it had done from the inception of the embassy in 1583, albeit very much not to the satisfaction of the envoys in the eighteenth century.[4] Exceptions to the process of governmental control were viewed with increasing criticism. The most conspicuous was the new kingdom of the Congo, a state ruled as an independent territory by King Leopold II of Belgium, and one that was being carved out by force. Leopold obliged Belgian diplomats to double as agents of the Congo state.[5] The harshness of his rule and the anomalous nature of his position aroused criticism, and in 1908 the Congo was annexed to Belgium.

This monopolization of negotiating rights by states was linked to other aspects of government policy, for example the banning of privateering and moves against mercenaries. More generally, the role of enterprising individuals operating outside the ambit of the state was greatly limited. A key turning point was the failure of the American adventurer William Walker to seize Nicaragua in 1857 and Honduras in 1860. The American navy actively thwarted Walker's activities in 1857, and in 1860 a British warship turned him over to the Hondurans: he was shot. Filibustering, in what John Brathwaite had seen in 1792 as 'an era of speculation' and 'speculators', was now only acceptable at the behest of the state.[6]

Moreover, aside, in addition, from the strengthening of the diplomatic network and the prestige of a bureaucratic diplomacy in Europe, there was also a massive expansion of Western diplomacy, notably with independence for Latin America and with the drawing in of states that remained outside the ambit of the West – Japan, China, Thailand and Abyssinia – into what was now a global diplomatic order. What was intended to be continuous French representation in Addis Ababa, the capital of Abyssinia, began in 1897, the British following a year later. Such competition was typical, and in the case of Abyssinia was linked to rival British and French ambitions in neighbouring Sudan.

The background to such activity and expansion was provided by the confidence of Western states and peoples in their role, culture and diplomatic practices. The last were in part a product of the strength of Western states and economies, but also of their ability to co-operate through diplomacy, or at least to co-exist using its methods. Diplomacy was thus an aspect of the strength of the West, as well as recording the extension of its power. Moreover, aside from seeking co-operation in particular episodes, efforts were made to ground a culture of such co-operation.

A key achievement was that of the Congress of Vienna (1814–15) in settling issues of precedence, a central point in representation by polities that were acknowledged as sovereign. The *Reglement sur le Rang entre les agens Diplomatique* divided diplomatic representatives into ranks, establishing precedence by rank and by the date of presentation of the credentials, rather than in terms of the rank of rulers. The new system allowed the representatives of minor powers a degree of relative status that was important to the sense of equality that provided a culture for a system that in practice was driven, instead, by the major states, and more particularly their leading ministers, for example Castlereagh, Talleyrand, Metternich and Palmerston. Indeed, with these and similar ministers directing foreign policy, the activity of diplomats was distinctly secondary, which made their relative status of lesser importance. Yet although dominated by the major states, the practice of Western diplomacy also encouraged a liberalism that left room for others, not least because Britain, the most powerful state certainly until the 1870s, had both liberal tendencies and a liberal political culture that greatly affected its diplomats.[7]

Moreover, again widening the margins for action by those who were not representatives of major states, revolutionary exiles, such as Giuseppe Mazzini, sought to use agitation to create a basis for change. This agitation involved both negotiations with countries granting them refuge, notably Britain, and attempts to create international links for action.[8] Diplomacy was also a means by which independence was asserted, both by new states like Greece, which won recognition of its independence from Turkey in 1829–30, and also by existing ones, such as Japan, keen to have their sovereignty and interests acknowledged. Thus, the one-time colonies of Spain and Portugal, which gained their independence in the 1820s, followed the USA in sending and receiving envoys to and from Europe. Commenting on news that British consuls were to be appointed to South America, the *Birmingham Chronicle* of 2 October 1823 noted, 'though the consuls intended to be appointed, it would seem, are merely commercial appointments, still it must be viewed as one important step taken towards a formal recognition of the independence of those states, which, if once made, would effectually prevent the meditated designs of France' to help restore Spanish rule, a step to which Britain was opposed.

Competition between the Western powers was certainly at issue in the spread of recognition. The dispatch of British representatives to Latin America owed something to anxiety about American influence,[9] as the Americans had moved speedily in 1822 to recognize the new independent states. In response, for example, Woodbine Parish was appointed British Commissioner and Consul-General to the United Provinces of the River Plate, sailing to Buenos Aires in HMS *Cambridge*, a necessary display of sovereign power. Parish negotiated a treaty of friendship and trade, signed in 1825, the first such treaty with the Latin American states. As a result, Parish was promoted to be Chargé d'Affaires, a post he held until 1832. During his posting, Parish, alongside John, Lord Ponsonby, who became Envoy Extraordinary at Buenos Aires in 1826, played a major role in negotiating an end to the war between Brazil and Argentina, one that led to Uruguay becoming independent in 1828. Ponsonby then took up a post at Rio de Janeiro as envoy to Brazil. Earlier, Charles Stuart had played a key role in negotiating the independence of Brazil from Portugal.[10]

The changes on the world scale were such that, whatever transformative impact is attributed to the French Revolution, the *ancien régime* of European international relations and diplomacy was coming to a close. If the revolutions in Latin America can be linked to the French Revolution in terms of influence and consequences, this was not the case with the expansion of Western diplomacy to handle more non-Western states. This process was not limited to Europe, as the USA played a major role in developing links with the Orient, and notably with Japan in the 1850s.[11]

The conceptual background to the expansion of the Western diplomatic system was complex as it entailed the range of attitudes influencing relations with the non-West. To a considerable extent, Classical literature provided the basic frame of reference, explicit or implicit, for extra-European relations. Europeans appropriated Imperial Rome as a model for comparison, and officials, both colonial governors and diplomats, were apt to adopt a proconsular role, regarding themselves as bringers of civilization, assumptions also seen with American expansionism.

These values, removed from the suppositions affecting diplomacy in the West, could encourage aggressive attitudes. Thus even though territorial goals in relations with non-Western powers could be limited, certainly prior to the mid-nineteenth century, the mechanisms for establishing a comprehensive settlement were poorly developed, and policy was generally not in the hands of diplomats seeking a compromise. If no native state was acknowledged, then European officials and settlers could take advantage of established conventions, looking back to Roman Law, relating to land seen as waste or desert. Thus, like the practices of settlers,[12] the arrangements made between the Western states made scant reference to local sensitivities. In 1871, when the Dutch sold their forts on the Gold Coast of West Africa to Britain, the views of the King of Asante, Kofi Kakari, who saw them as trading bases under Asante sovereignty, were neglected, helping lead to war in 1873, a conflict that was to be won by Britain. An Anglo-Italian protocol of 1894 placed Harer in the Italian sphere of influence, treating Abyssinia (Ethiopia) as an Italian protectorate, a view rejected by Menelik II.

Arguments or approaches based on Roman Law were scarcely valid in India or East Asia, but the officials of the British East India Company had become less willing from the second half of the eighteenth century to accept local notions of political conduct and sovereignty. Instead, an absolutist concept of sovereignty was increasingly advanced, and implemented by force.[13] These assumptions became more pronounced over the following century. In part, this change was a reflection not only of the major cultural and ideological divides that existed, but also of a decreasing willingness to accept that differences did not mean inferiority. The combined effect of Eurocentric ideologies and a diplomacy of force and coercion was to ensure that, as Western horizons widened and relative power increased in the nineteenth century, it remained natural to resort to violence. The benefits to the West proved short-term, but many of the problems are still with us today.

The more assertive diplomacy was apparent not only in the case of relations with states that were newly encountered, at least as far as diplomatic relations were concerned, but also where such relations were long-standing, as with Turkey and Morocco. Previous rules of procedure were discarded as past accommodations were recast in a way that ensured that non-Western rulers lost face. For example, as far as Tunis was concerned, European and American diplomacies abandoned from the French Revolution and, even more, from 1815, the earlier restraint that had governed relations. In particular, the French were determined to demonstrate that the Bey of Tunis was not an equal to their sovereign.[14]

This process of Western assertion was not restricted to the non-West. Notably, both European powers and the USA employed a diplomacy of pressure, if not coercion, in pursuing interests in Latin America with, in addition, the USA referring to the Monroe Doctrine to justify opposition to activity by European powers, as in 1849 when E. George Squier, the envoy to Nicaragua, opposed British pretensions there.[15] The preference for pressure reflected the sense of Western cultural superiority that led, particularly on the part of the French, to an active promotion of their culture,[16] as well as the difficulty of ensuring that Latin American governments respected agreements, notably in repaying loans, such as those Mexico raised in London in 1824 and 1825. Defaults and restructurings ensured that there was no final settlement until 1888, and the Committee of Mexican Bondholders became a vocal lobby group affecting bilateral relations.[17]

Aside from loan agreements, trade was a key aspect of diplomatic relations with Latin America. Thus in 1852 Sir Charles Hotham, who had defended British trading interests in the Plate Estuary in the 1840s as a naval officer, was sent back to the region to arrange trade treaties. He negotiated them with Argentina and Paraguay, before being sent to Victoria, Australia in 1854 as a Lieutenant-Governor.[18]

Coercion was also a response to what was perceived as instability. Mexico's repudiation of international debts led Britain, France and Spain to intervene with troops in 1861–2 in an unsuccessful attempt to secure repayment that proved the prelude to the French attempt to take over the country on behalf of Napoleon III's protégé, Archduke Maximilian of Austria. Intractable Mexican opposition and, from 1865, American pressure resulted in an end of this attempt and the withdrawal of the French forces. In turn, in 1902–3, American intervention led Britain, Germany and Italy to end their blockade of Venezuela in pursuit of unpaid debts. The Americans, however, were to prove keen interventionists in Mexico, Central America and the Caribbean in subsequent decades.

Diplomacy within Latin America often overlapped with violence, and both were encouraged by the failure to sustain several of the large entities that emerged from the end of the Spanish empire in America. Greater Colombia, incorporating modern Colombia, Venezuela, Panama and Ecuador, ended in 1830, and the United Provinces of Central America came to an end in 1838. Texas successfully rebelled against Mexico. In contrast, Argentina and Brazil each maintained their unity against separatist tendencies.

Border disputes between the Latin American states were often pursued by force, as between Ecuador and Colombia in 1862–3, while there was a close intertwining of international conflicts with internal disaffection and civil wars, as in the Paraguayan War of 1865–70.[19] Ideology, in the shape of struggles between Conservatives and Liberals, played a major role in Latin American domestic politics and international relations, although there was no link between these conflicts and the more sustained revolutionary diplomacy that was to be associated with the Russian Revolution.[20]

Independence for Latin America, followed by the collapse of the larger states that were created out of the Spanish colonies, ensured that the size of the Western diplomatic system grew in terms of numbers of states. So also did the retreat of the Turkish empire in the Balkans, which led to independence for Greece (1830), Romania (1878), Serbia (1878), Bulgaria (1908) and Albania (1913). Further west in Europe, there was also the creation of new states: Belgium (1830) and Norway (1905), from the Netherlands and Sweden respectively; although, in turn, German and Italian unification greatly lessened the number of independent powers.

There was moreover a development in the diplomatic network of other powers. Thus the first permanent Swiss diplomatic mission was established in 1798 in Paris, when the Helvetic Republic was dependent on French power. While in 1848 the newly established modern federal state of Switzerland kept the two legations taken over from the former state, the consolidation of the system of permanent Swiss diplomats only occurred in the 1860s when a small network of four legations was established. A modest further expansion occurred on the eve of the First World War, with the number of legations increased to eleven, mostly staffed with career diplomats. A small foreign ministry was established in Berne.

As far as the West and the non-West were concerned, interacting pressures of fear and opportunity helped to drive forward diplomatic engagement. The problems of arriving at a shared understanding of the meaning and content of representations and agreements were increasingly subordinated to the projection of the values of Western diplomacy. For the Western powers, diplomacy with the non-West created problems, but the extension of the range of Western diplomacy was an aspect of a newly gained great power status. This development was also a facet of modernity, although that term has to be employed without suggesting a teleology, or even more a beneficient disposition.

In some cases, Western powers were willing to acknowledge existing polities as states, but often they were not. Thus in Africa they tended to group kingdoms into new colonial territories. Within these territories, many local rulers were left in place, but relations with them were handled by the agents of colonial government, rather than by diplomats.[21] Looked at differently, the former conducted diplomacy at a different level.

In turn, non-Western powers responded rapidly by adopting the methods of the West. This was not only a matter of diplomatic procedures, with Turkey re-establishing permanent embassies in Paris, Vienna and London in 1835–6: a *chargé d'affaires* appointed to London in 1832 was followed by a special envoy in 1834 and an ambassador in 1836. In addition, the Treaty of Paris of 1856, which ended the Crimean War, consolidated Turkey's position in the international order by formally admitting it 'aux avantages du droit public et du concert européens'. In doing so, an omission arising from Turkey's absence from the coalitions against Napoleon, and thus from the Congress of Vienna, was remedied, and in a way deliberately designed to limit the Russian expansionism that was unwelcome to other European powers and that had helped cause the Crimean War.

The contents of diplomacy were also important to the process of adopting the methods of the West. Notably, there was a move towards precise frontiers.[22] This move proved a factor not only in relations between Western colonial powers and non-Western states, but also between the latter, especially, but not only, as a result of Western intervention. For example, in the early nineteenth century Britain and Russia came to play a greater role in the affairs of Persia and Turkey and, in particular in their vexed relationship with each other. Disputes over the Perso-Turkish frontier in Kurdistan resulted in 1843–4 in the formation of a quadripartite Turco-Persian Boundary Commission involving the two powers, as well as Britain and Russia. Extensive negotiations led, despite the reluctance of Persia and Turkey to compromise, to the Second Treaty of Erzeroum (1847), and to an Explanatory Note of 1848 that dealt with ambiguities in the Treaty. The entire land boundary was allocated, although the territorial limit was loosely defined along the east bank of the Shatt al Arab River.

It proved difficult, however, to delimit the boundary on the ground, and disagreement continued, which in turn ensured that both powers had to continue to participate in international negotiations dominated by Western assumptions and interests. The latter culminated in 1907 with Britain and Russia agreeing on spheres of interest in Persia. There were similar issues elsewhere, although many also related to delimiting the respective territorial interests of the Western empires as far as their colonial bounds were concerned.[23]

The need to participate in international negotiations dominated by Western assumptions was also true of the diplomacy linked to Western attempts to expand trade, notably by free-trade provisions. Britain proved a key player in this respect. As the leading industrial producer, the British needed other states to open their markets, and vulnerable foreign powers were persuaded or coerced into accepting free-trade agreements that did so: Turkey in 1838, Egypt, Persia and Shewa (Showa, part of Abyssinia) in 1841, China in 1842, Morocco in 1856, Siam (Thailand) in 1857, and Japan in 1860. Pressure for transit rights was an aspect of the demand for free trade, and it took particular form with railway diplomacy,[24] and with the agreements that led to canal schemes, most successfully the Suez and Panama Canals, but also, for example, with the earlier plan for a canal between the Atlantic and Pacific across Nicaragua.

Free-trade agreements were the symbolic and practical apex of a more general process by which Britain's growing and more extensive trade, the largest in the world, led to an enormous range of diplomatic activity on behalf of interests and individuals. British diplomacy in China had to take particular note of the role of trade, in part due to the parliamentary influence of the 'Pig-tail Committee', which represented the case for commercial interests in China. Such diplomatic activity was also seen with the British in Europe. Reports on economic developments there[25] were of greater significance than in the eighteenth century.

In large part, this activity was linked to the growing professionalism and, in particular, bureaucratization of the British Foreign Service, and notably with the consuls. At the same time, such representation was not only under the Foreign Office. There was also a parallel commercial (and non-commercial) representation and diplomacy around the Indian Ocean, including in the Persian Gulf, that was under the authority of the government of India: the representation organized by the East India Company became more systematic after the Company's position was replaced by that of the British government in 1858.

Britain's presence in the Persian Gulf region was part of a more general system of political influence that played a major role in the protection of India, and yet also in the projection of the strength of the British Indian empire. As in India, so in the Gulf, this system greatly depended on co-operation with the locally prominent and on working through existing political systems, notably the use of local 'native agents', many of them Indians. In part, this use was due to the pressures of the environment, notably the debilitating climate and disease-ridden living conditions. The Government of India's need for economy contributed to the same end.

The British entrusted non-European agents with greater responsibilities as the century progressed.

The choice, as agents in the Persian Gulf, of locally established, affluent, influential merchants with whom the rulers were financially and politically interdependent, encouraged the rulers to collaborate with the British, which in turn helped strengthen the agents. The use of non-European agents enabled the British to tap into indigenous intelligence networks. This multi-national imperial mechanism proved effective, not least by offering a necessary flexibility. The indigenous side of informal empire thus had an important diplomatic dimension. At the same time, the oversight of activity, whether or not defined as diplomatic, posed a serious problem in the wider Indian Ocean region with competition between the system controlled by the Foreign Office in London and those under the governments of India and Bombay.[26]

The readiness to rely on local expertise was characteristic of imperial systems, but became less so of their formal diplomatic processes; while British advisers also played a major role within the imperial system, for example in the Malay states. In part, this trend away from local expertise, seen for example in the personnel of the Dragomanate of the British embassy in Constantinople, reflected a concern that non-nationals would have divided loyalties, but there was also a stronger engagement with the idea of diplomacy, like military service, as a representation of the nation-state. This point serves as a reminder that the professionalism of diplomacy in the period had a clear cultural and political dimension, with ethnicity being an important element.

As a parallel to the pressure for free trade, the major effort made by the British government to end the slave trade both led to a spread in representation and to the development of a new bureaucratic department, the Slave Trade Department, within the Foreign Office in London.[27] The granting of British recognition to the states that arose after the collapse of Spain's Latin American empire depended on their abolishing the slave trade. Recognition of the then-independent Republic of Texas in 1840, a step that alarmed the USA, was made on the same basis. Pressure was also brought to bear on the Spanish colony of Cuba – enough for David Turnbull, the Consul, to be accused of inciting slave risings.[28] In 1842 George, 4th Earl of Aberdeen, the Foreign Secretary, who had had a conventional diplomatic background as an envoy to Vienna in 1813–14, described the attempt to end the slave trade as a 'new and vast branch of international relations'.[29] This branch involved British negotiations with other European powers, the independent states of the New World, African powers, and those of South-West Asia. Thus in 1880 a convention with Turkey was concluded, although it was not ratified until 1883.[30]

Enforced trade was a key element in the diplomacy presented to the Orient. The context for diplomacy with China was transformed by the First Opium War of 1839–42, which arose from the Chinese attempt to enforce their prohibition on the import of opium, the profit from the rising export of which was important to the financing of British imports from Asia. Moreover, the seizure of opium held by British merchants, and their expulsion from Canton, led to pressure within Britain for a response, pressure that a weak government sought to accommodate in order to bolster its political position.[31]

The Chinese and British diplomatic systems could not meet such needs, not least because there was no structure of mutuality. Indeed, a key element in the crisis was provided by the shifting nature of British demands for representation. The East India Company had supervised Anglo-Chinese trade until its monopoly ended in 1833, and the company, whose logic was commercial, had proved willing to accommodate Chinese expectations for precedence by communicating with the Chinese authorities through the Hong, a group of Chinese merchants in Canton.

The end of the monopoly transformed the situation, as the head of the new British trade commission at Canton was a representative of the Crown, and the British government expected an acceptance of equality that was not only unwelcome to the Chinese but also a clear defiance of their expectations of international order, and, indeed, of the nature of being. In practice, British expectations entailed the replacement of the Hong by direct representation, while the head of the commission was not permitted to use the Chinese character 'pin' at the head of any document, because such usage implied a petition to a superior.

The resort to force arose as the pressure for Chinese compensation for the seizure of opium was backed up by coercion, while the Chinese demanded the handing over of a British seaman accused of murdering a Chinaman. For both sides, honour was a key consideration. The war culminated in 1842 with the British advance on the capital, Nanjing, a particularly blunt form of the representation of power.

The challenge to Chinese suppositions was acute, and left the Chinese negotiators responsible in 1842, in the Treaty of Nanjing, for having to finesse the differences between the British and the court at Beijing. The latter was reluctant to accept the British demand that Chinese negotiators should be able to make major commitments by treaty, an approach that offered the practicality of utilitarianism in place of the conventions of the tribute system.

Indeed, from its inception, the new treaty system represented a shock, in terms of both form and content. Thus the treaty signed by the British was written in Chinese, but with equality given to Britain and China by means of an equal raising of characters. The treaty permitted the opening of five Chinese ports to trade, with a British consul at each. Consular jurisdiction provided a degree of extra-territoriality. Lower tariffs on British goods were enforced at the expense of China's right to regulate its economy and society, while compensation was granted for the opium destroyed by the Chinese in 1839, and Hong Kong, which had been captured, was ceded to Britain.

Replacing the protected trade of privileged traders on Chinese terms, the treaty opened up trade to all British merchants, while at the same time bringing the activities of the latter under the control of the British government. This was an aspect of the more general situation by which diplomacy in this period represented a nationalization in which commercial, military and political activities were brought under state control.

The Chinese government sought to limit the transition represented by the treaty, notably in protocol and terminology.[32] At the same time, the British had led to a change, with concessions to the Americans and French following. Thus the American–Chinese Treaty of Wanghia of 1844 stipulated that American citizens (a loosely defined category) could only be tried by their consuls, while Chinese subjects who wished to bring legal claims against them had to turn to consular courts. This measure was intended to ensure standardization in the treatment of Westerners on a Western basis.

In the 1850s relations deteriorated anew: Britain pressed for an extension of commercial rights, while the Chinese refused to accept a revision of the treaty. The incident that led to hostilities was the arrest in Canton, on charges of piracy, of the crew of the *Arrow*, a Hong Kong ship with a Chinese crew said to be flying the British flag; although whether it was or not, it had no right to do so. This crisis was exploited by Henry Parkes, the acting consul in Canton, who sought conflict.[33]

The British also demanded a transformation in the diplomatic system, with James, 8th Earl of Elgin, the British envoy, pressing that the Chinese negotiators have 'full powers', similar to his, in order to produce a lasting settlement of Anglo-Chinese relations. Elgin also wanted to see a British envoy appointed to the Chinese court in order to protect any new agreement. This demand was unacceptable to the Chinese as such an envoy would not only not kowtow but would also demonstrate an equality of sovereigns. Thus the Chinese world system was at risk, while the concessions demanded by the British appeared to threaten a loss of prestige that would undermine both state and society, and at a time when the Chinese political order was gravely challenged by the large-scale Taipeng Rising.

In the event, in order to prevent the British from advancing on Beijing, a treaty was signed at Tientsin in 1858, granting the right for a resident envoy, as well as extending British commercial rights. The envoy was a key issue, and in 1859 the Chinese sought to make it optional, rather than an obligation. The American minister, John Ward, was willing to travel to Beijing in traditional, tribute, style; and the Chinese government wanted Britain and France to follow suit. The Chinese abrogated the Treaty of Tientsin, and seized the British negotiator, Parkes, and his party, subsequently executing some of these hostages. In response, the British forces pressed on, occupying Beijing and forcing the Chinese to ratify the treaty by means of the Beijing Convention of October 1860, although the Emperor's refusal to return to Beijing meant that the question of whether foreign diplomats would kowtow was avoided.

The threat of force was also used to 'open up Japan' in the 1850s. American naval pressure in 1853–4 extorted diplomatic representation, as well as commercial concessions there, supported by the designation of two treaty ports, Kobe and Yokohama.[34] As in China, these 'unequal treaties' left deep grievances.

Power was a fundamental constraint on the old diplomatic order. Not only did Western forces coerce China and Japan, but they also brought an end to traditional practices of Oriental diplomacy by extending their rule. Between 1860 and 1894 tribute was presented to China from Korea in 25 years, Vietnam (Annam) in five, Nepal in four, and Burma in one; but by 1894 Burma was ruled by the British, Vietnam was under French control, and Korea was increasingly exposed to Japanese pressure while also being a matter of interest to Western powers: the British had a consul in Seoul from 1883. Thus the foreign forces present in the concession areas within China around the treaty ports were not alone in overthrowing the old Chinese diplomatic system. The new diplomatic order was represented by the imposing new embassy buildings and substantial embassy compounds in Beijing and Tokyo. The British compound in Tokyo was acquired in 1872.[35]

Diplomacy for China and Japan was not just a case of responding to Western pressure in the region, but also of sending envoys to the West in order to represent their interests. The Iwakura embassy sent by Japan to the USA and Europe provided important information on economic matters that contributed to Japanese modernization,[36] while by 1873 there were nine Japanese legations. By 1878 China, which actively competed with Japan, had envoys in London, Washington, St Petersburg and Tokyo, legations following in Berlin, Paris and Madrid the following year. The appointment of these Chinese envoys reflected a significant shift in the official mind. Diplomacy had been seen as a type of banishment and as entailing a dishonorable association with barbarians; but these attitudes were overcome, and by the 1870s and '80s 'barbarian affairs' had become 'Western affairs'.

Training was provided by the T'ung-wen kuan (Interpreters' College) established in Beijing in 1862, which taught English, French, German, Russian and, by 1879, international law. Japanese diplomats also reflected the development of Western-style education. Many were graduates of the Law Faculty of Tokyo Imperial University. They were dressed in the Western-style splendour that had become the uniform of diplomats, not least the wearing of gold braid, medals and swords.[37]

The earliest resident Chinese legation was that of Kuo Sung-tao, the first Chinese minister to Britain, who opened his legation in London in 1877. Kuo advanced two priorities for Chinese diplomats, first understanding aspects of their host country that might benefit China, in other words not just information-gathering but the diffusion of best practice, and secondly maintaining peaceful relations.

There were major gaps in Japanese and Chinese representation, while other Asian states were far worse provided; but the change from the situation in the 1840s was striking. Korea, where the Taehan Empire was declared in 1897 as part of an assertion of nationalism, enjoyed a brief diplomatic episode before Japan extinguished its independence. In 1896 Min Yông-Hwan served as Korean envoy to the coronation of Nicholas II of Russia, following this up in 1897 with using Queen Victoria's Diamond Jubilee as an opportunity for a mission to London.[38]

The entry of these states into the Western-dominated international system was a key development for the latter, and one that looked toward the adjustments made in the twentieth century as new states received independence with the collapse of the Western imperial system. Each of these processes was difficult, albeit with the difficulties often concealed by compliance with the conventions of Western diplomatic behaviour. Moreover, looking toward the current situation for the former Western colonies, the entry of East Asia into the global diplomatic order was not to be a change that was reversed. Once Japan and China were fully fledged members of the international system, alliances followed. In particular, the Anglo-Japanese alliance of 1902 marked a major effort to incorporate Japan into equations of international strength and the algebra of great power calculations. A Ministry of Foreign Affairs was established in China in 1901, and both Japan (in 1914) and China (1917) declared war on Germany in the First World War. As a result, they were able to participate in the post-war peace conference among the victors.

States that failed to develop diplomatic networks such as those of China and Japan were more dependent on the role of Western representatives and, without a diplomatic apparatus, appeared more primitive. These representatives, moreover, were as likely to be colonial governors as diplomats habituated to an idea of the integrity and mutuality of sovereign states. It would be going too far to trace the contrasting fates of Morocco (partitioned between France and Spain before the First World War) and Japan to their different diplomatic trajectories, while Turkey, which had lost most of its European empire by 1914, had long-lasting diplomatic relations with the West which did not provide protection,[39] but this element is worthy of note.

So also were the consequences of treating foreign and colonial policies as different, even if overlapping. Once a Western state decided that a particular area was a matter of colonial policy then its states were handled in a very different type of diplomacy to those designated as a matter for formal diplomatic relations. Instead, diplomacy in the former case became a process of keeping other Western powers at bay and of negotiating frontiers.

China and Japan represented contrasting diplomatic worlds, and relations with them posed challenges for Western powers, but it is all too easy to see these challenges as more troublesome than those arising from changes within the Western diplomatic world. Instead, it is appropriate to think in terms of a range in each category. As far as the Orient was concerned, there were, for example, major contrasts between the Western response to Japanese expansionism at the expense of China in 1894–5, and that to the Boxer Uprising in China in 1900.

The former, an episode that made Chinese affairs a matter of deep concern to European foreign ministries,[40] led to the conventional response of international pressure by a stronger diplomatic combination, the Triple Intervention by Russia, Germany and France in 1895. This pressure obliged Japan to back down, so that it gained none of the Chinese province of Manchuria and only limited influence in Korea. This episode was an instance of the standard methods of Western diplomacy, one seen, for example, in 1878 when Britain successfully put pressure on Russia to limit the gains of its protégé Bulgaria from the defeated Turkish empire.

In contrast, the Boxer Uprising appeared to be a far more dramatic challenge to the norms of international order, and one, moreover, appropriately represented in the siege of the embassies in Beijing. This attack made their relief, in which forces from eight foreign states took part, a totem of Western civilized values; and thus helped underline the degree to which, in the Western mind, the norms of diplomacy were apparently those of civilization. The prominent role played by Japan in defeating the Boxers indicated its full membership in the international system, and looked toward later Japanese expansionism in China.

There was also a marked range in behaviour in the Western world. The 1850s witnessed armed diplomacy leading to warfare not only in the case of China, but between Russia and Turkey, resulting in 1853 in the outbreak of the Crimean War. Yet armed diplomacy did not always have these results, while the armaments could also be secondary to the diplomacy. Moreover, the situation was rarely one in which the European powers alone had the initiative. For example, Latin America posed challenges to outside powers, notably as a result of long periods of civil war, as in Argentina and Mexico, with all the difficulties these resulted in when considering how best to respond to political instability. Diplomats also had to worry about their personal safety.[41]

This issue was not restricted to Latin America. The declaration of independence by the Confederacy in 1861 created acute problems, not least because the Confederates wanted to lead Britain and France into war with the Union. The Union's attempt to prevent diplomatic (and other) relations with the Confederacy was notably difficult for Britain after Confederate envoys en route to Britain were seized on 8 November 1861 from the British mail steamer *Trent* en route from Havana to Nassau, two neutral ports. The British envoy was given instructions to leave if no apology was provided. In 1863 there was talk of war because of the building of warships for the Confederacy in British shipyards.

Again, however, it would be misleading to see such issues as occurring only outside Europe. Instead, repeated revolutions there created serious issues, notably in Spain. These episodes were compounded by foreign intervention. Britons fighting for the Carlists in the Carlist (civil) Wars in Spain were examples of a widespread tendency to become involved in the great causes on the Continent, such as Greek independence in the 1820s and Italian freedom and unification in the 1840s and '50s; and the same was seen elsewhere, as in French interest in the cause of Polish freedom from Russian rule, a cause that led to serious rebellions in the 1830s and '60s.

Focus on the diplomatic world of courts and cabinets, which responded to these causes in terms of power politics as well as the exigencies of domestic politics,[42] is apt to underplay, if not overlook, popular interests and drives, but the latter were very important to the linkage between diplomacy and the public politics of the era. The latter can seem like the Middle Class, always on the rise yet rarely arriving, but, by the late nineteenth century, these politics were an important factor across the West, whatever the formal constitutional nature of the state. Structural changes played a key role, notably the marked rise in literacy stemming from the provision of mass education, the development of a large cheap press, and the politicization of foreign policy as adversarial politics came to play a greater role in the public sphere.[43] The role of public appeal was shown when Henry, 3rd Viscount Palmerston, as British Foreign Secretary from 1846 to 1851, deliberately aligned himself with public opinion as a means to advance and defend foreign policy. He was subsequently to do the same as Prime Minister. The press came to play a role alongside the diplomats.[44]

These changes encouraged calls to action, whether for (or against) imperial expansion, for example by the Society for German Colonisation founded in 1884, or for (or against) foreign powers. Thus in 1898 there was considerable pressure within France for a firm stance against Britain, after a French military expedition had been faced down at Fashoda in Sudan in a confrontation with a more powerful British force under General Kitchener.[45] French lobbies pressing for a robust imperialism, notably the *parti colonial* in the Chambre des Deputés, played a key role in this and other crises, but there was also an informed public to consider.

Moreover, from 1886 the French Foreign Ministry included a section responsible for reporting on the foreign press. The British only did the same in 1906, when a circular dispatch was sent out to embassies in Europe, but it was not followed up and nor did discussions of the foreign press appear in more than the occasional Annual Report from the embassies. Instead, it was Lewis Benjamin, first of the wartime MI7, which was responsible for propaganda in military zones, and then of the Department of Information, who began such reports in 1917 as an individual effort. This function was taken over by the Political Intelligence Department of the Foreign Office in 1919, but that department was closed down in 1920, ending the production of guides to the foreign press by British government agencies.[46]

Although hesitant, interest in foreign newspapers, in Britain and elsewhere, can be seen as looking toward a more modern form of foreign affairs in which diplomats had to pay greater attention to the public lobbying and politics that affected foreign policy, and had to frame at least part of their advocacy accordingly. Such an emphasis was to be called for by critics of the foreign ministries of the 1910s and 1920s, and it may be asked whether such criticisms should not have already been expressed forcefully in the late nineteenth century.

In part, however, such a need appeared less apparent because the diplomatic world delivered many of the outcomes desired by liberal opinion, including the unification of Italy and Germany, the end of slavery, a marked reduction in the size of the Turkish empire, notably in Europe, the spread of free trade, and a series of only short wars. Other war panics, for example between Britain and Russia over Turkey in 1877–8, and in 1885 over Afghanistan, and between Germany and France in 1905–6 and 1911 over Morocco, were settled short of conflict.

Yet each crisis threatened the possibility of world war, while the Crimean War (1853–6), between Russia and an alliance of, eventually,

Turkey, Britain, France and Sardinia, showed how Russian expansionism, and the countervailing diplomacy of confrontation, nearly led to a world war. Austria considered whether to intervene against Russia, while the British sought to win support from Persia and Sweden, which would have increased British commitments, and also contemplated the prospect that a blockade of Russia would bring the USA into the war against Britain.

The Crimean War moreover indicated the often parlous state of coalitions, with Anglo-French rivalry playing a major role in both its politics and strategy. Moreover, the conflict provided a classic instance of the degree to which major powers could have their options limited by their protégés, in this case Turkey. This point serves as a reminder of the need to avoid seeing the policies of non-Western states through the perspective of Western diplomacy. Moreover, the Turks could prove unresponsive to their allies, as when William Williams, the British Commissioner with the Turkish army in Asia Minor failed in 1854–5 to obtain the supplies he sought for the fortress of Kars to forestall a successful Russian attack which, in the event, came in 1855.[47]

For publics that took national strength, imperial expansion and military preparedness for granted as key goals, the extent to which diplomacy generally helped ensure all three without debilitating conflict was valuable. Reciprocal gains in territory or influence for the major states were epitomized in the successful arbitration of the Scramble for Africa, and there were comparable successes in the Pacific, Morocco and Persia. The Madrid Convention of 1880 guaranteed a Moroccan independence that was to be overturned with difficulties but without war, at least between the European powers. The Berlin Congress of 1884–5 delimited future colonies in Africa and underlined the notion of effective occupation, a notion which helped settle what might otherwise have been serious problems. Like other congresses, that at Berlin demonstrated the value of rail travel and telegraph traffic in speeding up diplomacy, as most such meetings took less time than their counterparts in the pre-rail and telegraph age.

Although communications were greatly speeded up and became more predictable (a process that was in part overseen by the International Postal Union), that process did not mean that they approached those of the modern world. Nor did the means of surveillance. Thus, for example, in 1884 it took two weeks for the news of the surrender of Russia of Merv, a key territory in Central Asia and one of great concern to British commentators worried about a Russian advance towards India, to reach Sir Edward Thornton, the British envoy in St Petersburg.[48]

The normative character of imperial expansion, the sheer range of opportunity, and the willingness to accept notions such as equivalent gains or to share in open access, the latter the key to policy toward China, enabled the major powers to cope not only with the aspirations of each other, but also with both new entrants (Germany, Italy, Japan, USA), and minor powers (Portugal, Netherlands). This process extended to North America where a series of agreements settled Anglo-American differences notably over the Canadian border and neutral rights in the American Civil War. The Treaty of Washington in 1871 enabled the British to reduce their garrisons in Canada.[49]

Furthermore, the diplomacy of the period proved dynamic, responding to both new and anticipated problems, as in 1898, when the grave Portuguese financial crisis led to a secret Anglo-German treaty allocating Angola and Mozambique, the major Portuguese colonies in Africa, in the event that Portugal wished to sell them, which in fact she was not to do. Indeed, British success in obtaining Portugal to abandon its claims to the territory between Angola and Mozambique compromised the popularity of the Portuguese government. In 1906 Britain, France and Italy signed an agreement defining their interests in Ethiopia and also promising non-intervention. More generally, the ability to control 'men on the spot', governors and agents on the colonial periphery, was important to the diplomacy of imperial restraint; it also meant that states sought to use professionalism and technology to direct both diplomats and colonial officials.

The peaceful (to Western publics) management of the expansion of rival empires was an important instance of a more general process by which the Concert of Europe adapted to a range of challenges and changes. These were significant in both extent and range, encompassing major changes in population, technology, economic activity, social structures, constitutions and military capability. Ideologies also played a role, especially the rise of nationalism. Yet, what was striking was the ability to manage change. France's drive to regain position after the Napoleonic Wars was accommodated, notably in the 1850s, while Prussia's creation of a German empire led only to a series of short wars (1864, 1866, 1870–71) and, crucially, did not cause the collapse of the Austrian empire when Austria was defeated in 1866.[50] As another instance of the ability to manage change, agreement over the Balkans between Austria and Russia in 1897 was intended to manage the decline of the Turkish empire and, in particular, the question of the future of Macedonia.

The contrast with the inability in 1914–45 to satisfy realist goals and ideological rivalries short of large-scale conflict is instructive and suggests that the nineteenth-century international system was more effective, a conclusion that casts a positive light on the diplomacy of the period. Such a comparative judgement, however, is not without serious problems, not least as it is not the case of comparing like with like. For example, the disruptive millenarian ideological drives of 1917–45 were attached to powerful states. Moreover, the state nationalism and great power rivalry that led to the First World War had many roots in the late nineteenth century.

At the time, periodic crises and war panics led to anxiety about the international system, anxiety that included an element of criticism of contemporary diplomacy. Yet, the avoidance of major war after 1871 helped ensure that it is not surprising that insufficient attention was devoted to some of the troubling aspects of the international relations of the period. Moreover, the degree to which alliances were not necessarily going to lead to restraint was to become increasingly apparent in the early twentieth century. There was of course a long background of a failure to ensure such restraint, as with the Anglo-Prussian treaty of 1756 or the Anglo-Turkish alignment in 1853. Instead of restraint, alliances led to a commitment to the more determined member of any pact (Frederick II of Prussia in 1756 or Austria, rather than Germany, in the Balkan crisis of 1914), and thus served to underline their determination.

Moreover, in judging foreign states, there could be a serious failure by diplomats and other commentators to appreciate the extent to which political contention, and indeed politics in general, made geopolitical and other considerations a matter and means of debate, rather than being constant. This point underlined an unwelcome contingency that challenged the consistency of policies, and thus of international alignments and strategic cultures.

In helping negotiate and sustain alliances, diplomats fulfilled the expectations of the political élites of which they were members. It may well be anachronistic to assume that they should have done otherwise, but already there were commentators, such as Field Marshal Count Helmuth von Moltke the Elder (1800–91), earlier, in 1864–71, Chief of the General Staff, the planner of German unification, who in his last years warned about the risks posed by large-scale conflict. Instead, there was an aggressive furtherance of national interest by many diplomats, and notably in areas seen as particularly volatile, such as the Balkans. Thus, after its victory over the Turks in 1826–9, Russia exercised a protectorate over Moldavia and Wallachia (parts of modern Romania) until the Treaty of Paris of 1856 at the close of the Crimean War replaced this by the collective guarantee of the great powers.

In turn, a more assertive Russia in the 1870s cajoled Romania into providing support in war against the Turks in 1877–8. Romania's declaration of independence from the Turks in 1877 underlined the dependence of the country's diplomatic position on international power-politics. This dependence was further demonstrated with Russia's gain of southern Bessarabia from Romania and, at the Congress of Berlin in 1878, with recognition of Romanian independence (and thus full membership in the diplomatic order) made to follow agreement on the extension of civil rights to the large community of Romanian Jews;[51] although in practice most of these Jews were excluded while there was no mechanism to ensure compliance.

Diplomacy also involved subversion. The Russian envoy to Constantinople, Count Nikolaï Ignatiev, established in 1867 the secret Central Bulgarian Committee which, in turn, that year sent partisan bands into Turkish-ruled Bulgaria. Ignatiev wished to overturn the view that Bulgarians would not take up arms against the Turks, and thus that rule by the latter was both stable and legitimate.[52] In turn, once Bulgaria became independent, Russian envoys there frequently appeared patronizing and overbearing, operating in an imperial fashion that scarcely implied mutuality. Indeed, in 1885 the Russian representative in Sofia suggested that it would be best if Bulgaria was brought under a Russian Governor General and Russian laws.[53]

As far as Anglo-Russian relations over Central Asia were concerned, there are suggestions that Russian diplomats surreptitiously supported the forward policy of Russian army officers and provided them with cover by offering excuses, obfuscation, and a misleading distancing from the military. In contrast, as far as British policy was concerned, there were significant differences between London and Calcutta, army and government, and foreign service and both army and the Viceroy in India. These differences seriously handicapped British policy.[54]

A different furtherance of national interest was provided by the development of the roles of military and naval attachés. These attachés were the legitimate end of information-gathering processes that became increasingly systematic, in part because of the possibility that other states could alter their relative international position. The pace of technological change was an important topic for reports. In 1909 Colonel Frederick Trench, the British military attaché in Berlin, reported that the Germans were proposing to introduce power traction vehicles 'of a type suitable for military use' and in 1910 that they were aiming to build 'large airships of great speed, endurance and gas-retaining capacity'.[55] Attachés also proposed policies, as when Colonel Chenevix Trench, the British military attaché in St Petersburg in 1885, suggested putting Herat in Afghanistan into a state of defence in order to thwart Russian expansion.[56] There was also a development in Intelligence gathering behind diplomatic cover, for example with the British appointment of Military Vice-Consuls in the Turkish Empire.[57]

Another aspect of diplomacy was provided by the use of commercial agreements, notably lower tariffs, in order to strengthen international links and for state-building. This tendency was notably seen in the Prussian-dominated *Zollverein* or German Customs Union founded in 1834. Much bilateral diplomacy involved trade, for example between Britain and France leading to their trade treaty of 1860. Nevertheless, protectionist pressures that owed much to the economic problems of the 'Great Depression' adversely affected attempts in the late 1870 to 1880s to lower tariffs.[58]

The growing prominence of commercial issues led to the development of the post of commercial attaché, of which the first prominent one was Joseph Crowe, British commercial attaché in Paris from 1880. Yet progress was slow, not least in the arms trade, in which there was limited coordination with diplomacy.[59] Crowe was initially expected to cover the whole of Europe, and France only appointed its first commercial attaché, in London, in 1904. Germany also only followed suit in the 1900s. However, by 1913 France was appointing to its embassies technical counsellors, seconded from the Ministry of Public Works and designed to help in gaining contracts.

Returning to international crises, the ultimate excuse for the diplomats was that their power was limited. Policy was set by governments; and diplomats, despite their claims and their culture, had relatively little success in altering the parameters. In part, this limited success reflected the major professionalization of diplomacy, one that replaced the family embassies, in which envoys chose their own subordinates by processes of official appointment and supervision. To an extent, this shift was a product of the broadening out of the nineteenth-century élites, one also seen for example in the military.

This broadening-out provides an opportunity to consider the argument of the radical and committed pacifist John Bright who, in 1858, while MP for Birmingham, claimed that 'foreign policy . . . is neither more nor less than a gigantic system of outdoor relief for the aristocracy'.[60] Bright was certainly correct about the aristocratic bias of British diplomacy; while this was even more pronounced in the case of Germany. All its ambassadors in 1871–1914 were aristocrats, as were 84 per cent of all its diplomatic representatives. The percentage fell only in the case of minor German missions to non-European states, notably Peru. Parliamentary pressure in Germany for more bourgeois diplomats had scant impact.[61]

A similar emphasis can be seen with Austria, both in the foreign service and in the ministry in Vienna. When in a junior capacity, Austrian aristocrats gained rapid promotion while living on a private income.[62] Indeed, it has been argued that there was a tendency towards greater social exclusivity in the Austrian diplomatic service at the end of the century.[63]

Élite background and connections were also crucial to the Russian diplomatic service, not least with senior envoys coming from prominent social backgrounds.

Political changes in France made the situation more complex, with the aristocratic dominance seen in 1852–70 under Napoleon III, as well as in the early years of the Third Republic, qualified after the 1877 elections, which strengthened republicanism and led to the departure of anti-republican envoys. The percentage of aristocrats then declined, and in 1903–14 only 7 per cent of French diplomats were aristocrats. Instead, the higher bourgeoisie became far more influential. As representatives of a republic from 1870, French diplomats had to adjust some of their forms and style, but there was an emphasis on continuity rather than a repetition of the radical republican episode of the 1790s.

The general social bias in European diplomacy was scarcely accidental. The recruitment strategies were not spelled out in formal edicts, but there were usually financial qualifications for new recruits. That, however, did not mean that diplomats were always wealthy. Some were far from it, but social background was a key element. However, in a contrast with the situation in the eighteenth century, entrance examinations were now necessary, being introduced, for example, in Prussia in 1827, in Britain in 1856, and in France in 1877 and, again, 1880.

The emphasis on entry by examination encouraged professionalism, but very much in the context of the existing social system, and not least because the leading educational institutions that provided many diplomats were dominated by the social élite, for example Eton College in Britain or the Imperial Alexander Lycée at St Petersburg. Moreover, the processes or results of examinations could be bypassed or manipulated in order to ensure that members of the élite were not inconvenienced. This process was readily apparent, for example in Prussia, where a full or partial exemption could be had and assistance provided by experienced diplomats; while in France, although exams were introduced, they were without much success in altering the entry.

Professionalism was in part expressed in a particular personal character, which was developed, it was believed, through education in its broadest sense. This character combined behavioural and moral characteristics thought necessary both in representing the state and to the discharge of business. Yet these characteristics were very much constructed in terms of the social élite or, more particularly, of a traditional conception of how this élite was supposed to behave. Concepts of honour, such as those of the German student fraternities, were particularly important. Those from outside the exalted lists of rank who entered diplomacy were expected to absorb these cultural values.

This process happened not only in diplomatic services where the number of non-aristocrats was small, such as Germany, but also in those with a large tranche from a different background, notably France. There, the members of the *haute bourgeoisie* who were recruited had similar values to the affluent aristocracy whom they increasingly supplanted. In particular, they took the Catholic and anti-republican side in the divide that was so important to French political culture in the 1890s and 1900s. Captain Dreyfus, the victim in a *cause célèbre* of anti-republican obloquy, had few supporters in the French diplomatic corps.

The fictional account of diplomacy was very much that of aristocratic pretension, as in the character of the Duke of Plaza Toro, a Spanish grandee in Gilbert and Sullivan's comic operetta *The Gondoliers* (1889), and aristocratic ease, as in Franz Lehár's comic operetta *The Merry Widow* (1905). The latter depicted a fictional Balkan embassy in Paris, with the nightclub Maxims providing a key locale for action.

Such activity contributed to criticism. Indeed, the Prince of Ligne had written of the Congress of Vienna, 'le Congrès danse et ne marche pas', but his contrast was mistaken. Social activity was not incompatible with progress in negotiations, but instead, as diplomatic correspondence amply illustrated, provided opportunities for discussions that matched those offered at royal courts. Talleyrand noted that 'les bons dîners font la bonne diplomatie'.

Diplomatic services were scarcely cross-sections of society, but their social composition, while still taking on lustre from diplomats' roles as representatives of the sovereign, also reflected a self-conscious professionalism[64] based on different criteria to that of the *ancien régime*. Foreign ministry bureaucracies were a source of diplomats, with Sir Julian Pauncefote, the Permanent Under-Secretary at the British Foreign Office, going on to serve as envoy in Washington from 1889 until 1902, a choice that reflected the importance attached to the post. Bureaucratic systems of control and direction developed through emulation between foreign ministries and reflected a stress on the need to control the diplomatic process that arose from a strong belief in its importance, and also of its dangers if uncontrolled. Diplomacy, both as a means to understand developments abroad, and as an attempt to influence them, was encouraged by a sense of unpredictability and competitiveness in international developments and relations. In turn, an emphasis on action in order to influence both encouraged a matching response by others.

One aspect of the shift towards professionalism was a deliberate distancing of many diplomatic appointments from the political arena, especially junior ranks, although, again, this process was more apparent in some states, for example Britain, than others. In the USA senior appointments continued to be regarded as a form of political patronage, a situation that has persisted to the present, as with Louis Susman, a former banker and major supporter of President Obama, who was appointed Ambassador in London in 2009. In the 1890s most appointments in the American Diplomatic and Consular Services and the Department of State were the product of political patronage, with the East Coast establishment dominating the system.[65]

Variety in European diplomatic services was largely provided by the extent to which the royal court was still a major centre of political power. Where it was, then it was difficult to think of senior diplomats as separated from the political process, and professionalism constructed in these terms was of limited value. Overlapping as it did both government and court, the location of diplomacy indeed was largely responsible for its character, not least with the stress on the strict formality involved in the observance (and observation) of diplomatic protocol, which were an aspect of the representation of the sovereign. Social distinctions played an important part in this culture, and notably, but not only, in highly status-conscious courts such as Vienna, where protocol served as a way to reconcile the pretensions of the aristocracies of the different Habsburg lands, notably Austria and Hungary.

Thus the social shift of resident-diplomacy in the seventeenth and eighteenth centuries, away from the non-aristocratic envoys who had predominated earlier, had consequences that remained highly important to the diplomatic world of the late nineteenth century, a period, nevertheless, in which the mass male franchise was becoming the key political mode of legitimation. The central point was that of exalted residential representation, as it ensured that the particular rituals of court display that had earlier been exemplified in the diplomacy of special missions were maintained, albeit in a different, more practical and diurnal form. In turn, these rituals encouraged the emphasis on aristocrats as they appeared the necessary counterpart that would validate this world. Whether policed or not by aristocrats, aristocratic norms prevailed.

Meanwhile, the settings for diplomatic activity changed. Monarchs remained important, but foreign ministries rather than royal courts became the key setting for meetings between ministers and diplomats; although the courts continued to be significant for social occasions. However, more business and diplomatic socializing was handled at embassies, the nature of which changed. Permanent embassy buildings became common. In 1814 Britain purchased the imposing Paris house of Princess Pauline Borghese, formerly Pauline Bonaparte, and it became the first permanent British embassy building.

Such an embassy building, however, remained unusual until the 1860s, when embassies shared in a more general differentiation of function, emphasis on continuity, and need to house larger staffs, that characterized government buildings as a whole. The same development was seen in foreign offices, as in the British, French and German ones on Whitehall, the Quai d'Orsay and the Wilhelmstrasse, respectively. The sense of coherent national diplomatic traditions was linked to the development of schools of diplomatic history and to the publication of guides and archival material, such as the *Recueil des Instructions données aux Ambassadeurs et Ministres de France depuis les Traités de Westphalie jusqu'à la Révolution Française* from 1884. Such works encouraged a sense of continuity and of diplomats as furthering the particular long-term interests of specific countries.

Professionalism could ensure that diplomats lost touch with domestic politics, parliamentary pressures, public opinion and, more generally, the compromises that underlay domestic decision-making. This was a particular problem with long-serving envoys, and with those who became attached to specific alliances. Moreover, a careful reading of diplomatic correspondence, both public and, more clearly, private, suggests that many envoys lacked sympathy with the nature and consequences of public debate in their home countries. In part, this critique was an aspect of what was more generally true of diplomats, a sense that they were misunderstood at home, and that the policymakers were insufficiently sensitive to events abroad.

In addition, there was a specific disquiet about the public debate that reflected a disdain for the character of popular politics. Again, aristocratic norms played a role, notably hostility to the supposed consequences of democracy. Social disdain was also directed at the middle class, let alone the bulk of the populace, as well as against Jews. At the same time, there were signs of engagement with public opinion, notably for envoys in states where it was seen as important, such as the USA, and also with the creation of the new role of the press attaché.

The chance of losing touch with home society was alleviated by membership of a common aristocratic culture and a supra-national caste; and, anyway, was lessened by the improvement in communications for people, messages and goods. This improvement also counteracted one of the major problems with the profession, that of isolation, a problem compounded when postings seemed dull, as George Bosanquet found Madrid in 1824.[66] Distance from family, friends and connections became less serious as a consequence of steamship and rail travel, and of the use of telegraphs. The loneliness notable among earlier diplomats, a loneliness linked to the isolation of a profession that frequently complained of neglect, was thus transformed as part of a major shift in its means of operation. For long-serving diplomats, such as consuls, this loneliness was often alleviated by friendship and intermarriage within the consular community, while the increase in embassy staffs meant that a diplomatic world became more fully formed at most capital cities. The presence of wives was important to this process.

Speedier travel also meant safer travel. Among the advantages was an ability to cope with the often deleterious consequences for health of diplomatic service in the Tropics by withdrawing and replacing sick envoys. Postings to Brazil, for example, claimed the health of several diplomats.

Steamships and railways also allowed rulers and ministers to travel far more easily than had been the case in the age of the sailing ship and the carriage. Some eighteenth-century rulers, notably Peter the Great of Russia, the Emperor Joseph II and Gustavus III of Sweden, had travelled extensively abroad; but such activity was relatively uncommon, for reasons of time, convenience, preference and protocol. Numerous rulers, for example George III of Britain (r. 1760–1820) and Louis XVI of France (r. 1774–92), never left their countries.

The opportunities for personal diplomacy by monarchs dramatically changed with the nineteenth century. In part, this was a matter of the extensive coalition diplomacy that led to and accompanied the defeat of Napoleon, and notably the willingness of Tsar Alexander I of Russia (r. 1801–25) to travel west. This willingness represented a return to the practice of Peter the Great after a period largely dominated by female tsarinas who, as rulers, had not left Russia. In turn, competitive emulation led other rulers to travel, and meetings provided an opportunity for monarchs and ministers to evaluate each other. This process was maintained during the post-war diplomacy of the Holy Alliance, and the frequent congresses of the period, such as those at Aix-la-Chapelle in 1818 and Verona in 1822.

Yet the easing of transport was also important, not least to the travels of the British royal family. George IV (r. 1820–30) visited Hanover in 1821, the first visit of the King of Hanover to his realm: Hanover had been acknowledged as a kingdom at the Congress of Vienna. However, he did not subsequently leave Britain. His visit to Hanover, accompanied by the Foreign Secretary, Castlereagh, provided an opportunity for the latter to meet his Austrian counterpart, Metternich, who, significantly, came to Hanover to meet minister, and not monarch. Nor did William IV (r. 1830–37) travel abroad as monarch.

Victoria (r. 1837–1901), in contrast, used railways and steamships, not only to travel within the British Isles, but also to the Continent where she played an active role in pursuing good international relations. In the 1830s and 1840s she often met her uncle, Leopold I of Belgium, to whom she turned for advice. Marital alliances were a key element of Victoria's diplomacy, one designed to link major dynasties; but more was involved in her activity. She also eased relations with France, not least in 1843 when, accompanied by Aberdeen, the Foreign Secretary, she visited King Louis-Philippe.

Other monarchs visited Britain, both European, for example Pedro V of Portugal, and non-European, for example Nasir-ud-Din of Persia in 1889 and Rama V of Siam (Thailand) in 1897. The tours of the latter two included visits to Cragside, the Northumbrian seat of William Armstrong, the armaments king, as arms deals were important to their diplomacy. As a result of a tour around the world in 1881, King Kalākaua of Hawaii built up his military on European models.

The importance of royal diplomacy was maintained by Victoria's son and heir, Edward VII (r. 1901–10). He played a notable role in improving Anglo-French relations, leading to the Entente of 1904, while his visits to Continental spas provided opportunities for negotiations. He also served to further relations with other royal families, such as that of Portugal.

Yet royal diplomacy of this period was most influential when in accord with ministerial, political and public opinion. The room for independent operation comparable to the eighteenth-century *Secret du Roi* was limited as far as the major states were concerned; although the situation was different for states such as Bulgaria with a less dispersed concentration of power. However, royal influence in the major powers, such as Britain, Germany and Russia, could be exercised in the appointment of envoys, while the animosity of Edward VII and his nephew, Wilhelm II of Germany, and notably the aggressive and ambitious views of the latter, were important to the serious deterioration in Anglo-German relations.[67]

While diplomats were, increasingly, dignified officials of bureaucratic states, albeit highly privileged in background, connections and ambience, the international system itself was far from static, not only in content but also in form. In particular, towards the close of the period and extending into the twentieth century, both prior to the First World War (1914–18) and then with the post-war creation of the League of Nations, there was an attempt to create a system of international rules that would forestall the recourse to war. Binding arbitration, neutrality laws, the Hague Peace Conferences and the World Court were all key aspects of a legalistic approach to international affairs, one that provided diplomats with new opportunities, methods and challenges. Arbitration had played a major role in settling Anglo-American differences, notably over the Canadian border, and in 1871 over the British building, during the American Civil War (1861–5), of commerce raiders for the Confederacy. This success encouraged the systematization of arbitration, especially with the 1872 Tribunal of Arbitration in Geneva and the 1899 and 1907 Hague Peace conferences.[68]

Diplomats were expected to encourage international arbitration and become practitioners of what was seen as the science of public international law, a cause advanced by influential bodies such as the American Society of International Law, which was established in 1906.[69] In 1905 President Theodore Roosevelt of the USA negotiated a settlement to the Russo-Japanese War, a key sign of America's newfound influence, for which he was honoured with the Nobel Peace Prize the following year. Yet internationalism appeared to clash with the defence of national interests, a theme that was to be repeated to the present day, albeit to a different tune and with different players. Moreover, as a radical strand, alongside peace campaigners opposed to particular conflicts came a rise in a pacifism that called for a new diplomacy.[70]

Ideas and practices of binding international law were presented by some commentators as crucial to the successful operation of collective security. They were not to prevail in the test of the European crisis of 1914, but, like the post-1814 resumption of pre-1792 ideas of European international order, they looked forward to later attempts to align legalism, moralism and realism, combining national interests in an international order. However, the problem of lack of consent by states, strong or weaker, in such an order, remained (and remains) a key problem.[71]

SIX
1900–1970

Two very different accounts set the parameters for this chapter. That they are both British signifies the role of the British in framing arguments about diplomatic activity, as well as the continuity in diplomatic service that they represented: Britain was not occupied, and did not face revolution. However, similar accounts can be found for other countries. In 1956 Sir Nevile Bland set out to write a preface to the fourth edition of Sir Ernest Satow's *A Guide to Diplomatic Practice*, which had first appeared in 1917 and which had become the classic text on the subject, not only for Britain but also more generally. A second edition appeared in 1922 and a third in 1932. Satow himself linked to a key theme of the last chapter, that of the broadening of the Western diplomatic world. After many years in consular service in Japan, Siam (Thailand), Peru and Morocco, he was appointed Minister to Tokyo in 1895, moving on to Beijing in 1900.

Born in 1886, Bland was very much a figure of the old diplomatic order and saw himself in that light. He came from a classic establishment background. Bland had been a scholar and Captain of Boats at Eton, the source of many British diplomats. Indeed, the 1914 report of the Royal Commission on the Civil Service noted that 25 out of the 37 attachés recruited to the diplomatic service in 1908–13 were from Eton.

Bland had moved on to be a scholar at King's College, Cambridge, where he had gained a First at Classics, a non-utilitarian degree that was prized as a sign of intellectual quality. Entering the Foreign Office in 1911, Bland was head of the Treaty Department from 1935 to 1938 and was also concerned in this Department with the Foreign Office's part in jubilees, coronations and funerals. From 1938 to 1948, he had been Minister and, later, Ambassador to the Netherlands, a country with a royal court. Bland's distinctions included being a KCMG (Knight Commander of the Order of St Michael and St George) and a KCVO (Knight Commander of the Royal Victorian Order).

In 1932 Bland had written the preface to the third edition of Satow, and it lacked the anger and regret that was to be seen in his preface published in the fourth edition in 1957, which remained the verdict of an old order on change, for new impressions of this edition appeared in 1958 and 1962, and another, with corrections, in 1964. Bland wrote in 1956:

> with the advent of Hitler [1933] the usually accepted 'practice of diplomacy' received some rude blows from which, in some respects, it has never recovered. The present editor is not qualified to assess the extent to which the parentage of some of the habits observable today should rightly be attributed to the diplomatic brutalities of the Hitler regime, but undoubtedly there has been a growing tendency, since 1933, to supersede the professional diplomat by the creature of the local ideology and to substitute for the discreet exchange of notes, tendentious press conferences and abuse over the air. Whatever the disadvantages of so-called secret diplomacy may have been, can it be claimed that the airing of national dislikes and prejudices in uncontrolled language, whether at the UN [United Nations] or over the radio, is less likely to lead to international friction? . . . can those practices rightly be called 'diplomacy'? To these there can surely be only one answer. At any rate, for the purposes of this volume, I am assuming that it is negative: those who are contemplating, or have already embarked upon a diplomatic career can see all too clearly from the daily press with what, in those respects, they will have to contend, and in any case 'guidance' as to the methods of dealing with this type of non-diplomacy, if I may coin a word, cannot be prescribed· the response can only be framed in the light of the circumstances and the authority dealing with them . . . a 'Guide to Diplomatic Practice' today, so quickly do new diplomatic situations develop, could really only be kept up to date if it were possible to bring out a monthly, if not a weekly, supplement. What are left of the old canons of diplomacy, are continuously subject to change, both deliberate and unconscious. Increasing questioning and criticism in parliament and press; a growing tendency for ministers dealing with foreign affairs to travel about the world and take into their own hands consultations which a few decades back could, and would, have been conducted by the heads of the diplomatic missions concerned; the vastly increased speed and facility of communication between the Foreign Office and Her Majesty's Missions abroad; the growing habit of parliamentary and other groups of paying visits to foreign countries – all these

tend to undermine the confidence and independence of members of the Foreign Service and in some cases to usurp, in favour of the activities of an amateur hotel and travel agency, time and money formerly, and more usefully, devoted by members of Her Majesty's Embassies, Legations and Consulates to the cultivation of local contacts.[1]

The challenges to the established system were not only those discussed by Bland. In *Democracy and Diplomacy: A Plea for Popular Control of Foreign Policy* (1915), Arthur Ponsonby, a radical MP, argued that the telegraph had transformed international relations, resulting in centralization in the shape of greater government control. According to Ponsonby, this development led to a need for reform, especially 'the concentration and the simplification of negotiations, if possible, by the immediate formation of a European Council of representatives, to whom matters of dispute should be submitted and the sole conduct of negotiation should be entrusted'. To Ponsonby, there were serious problems with the practice and society of diplomacy:

In this sort of atmosphere nations become inanimate chessmen, diplomacy becomes a highly specialized game, and, while secrecy and intrigue are prevalent, guiding principles are obscured or lost sight of. The exclusive and surreptitious character of our intercourse with foreign nations, due to the unrestricted powers of the Foreign Secretary, is further accentuated by the aristocratic and unrepresentative nature of the instrument through which he works, and the medium through which all communications reach him. . . . A small number of men, associating only with others of their own class, and carrying on their intercourse in whispers, cannot fail to have a distorted perspective, a narrow vision, and a false sense of proportion. A tradition of intrigue has been carried down from the Middle Ages, but it is not only out of place, but positively dangerous, in the twentieth century.

Instead, Ponsonby pressed for diplomats who had 'a constant sense that they are the servants of a people, not the puppets of a court, or even the tools of a government'.[2]

These two publications can be cited to suggest a fundamental division in diplomacy, one between two very different cultures; and a division that provided both contrast and chronology as the movement from one type to another helps ensure the drive of change. There is a measure of truth in this approach, but it is also overly simplistic. Instead, as suggested in the previous chapter, the drive for radical reform had already been present in the nineteenth century. To a certain extent, indeed, features of the old order in 1900, in turn, reflected earlier pressures for change and, in particular, professionalism.

The different languages employed by Bland and Ponsonby, to press for continuity or change are instructive, but they also capture a continuing division over the nature of professionalism and the relationships between diplomatic representation and peoples. Ponsonby might appear a dangerous radical, but the Royal Commission on the Civil Service that reported in 1914 pressed for improvements in both knowledge and breadth of outlook on the part of British diplomats, and argued that:

> wider opportunities and greater encouragement can be given to junior members of the Diplomatic Corps to examine and report upon the institutions and political conditions of the country in which they are serving and to improve their knowledge of similar questions at home, as well as of such special and important subjects as international law.

Again, while such remarks might appear novel, they reflected calls heard for centuries for a wider range of information from diplomats. Similarly, in 1914, three months before the outbreak of war, the Reichstag Budget Commission argued for a transformation of the German diplomatic service. In the USA the Progressive Movement's emphasis on good government and civil service reform took a while to feed through to the Foreign Service, and they did not become priorities until the Second World War and the Cold War. Thus, prior to the First World War, established practices were under attack in many states, as well as affected by domestic political and governmental changes,[3] but with mixed results.

The call for reform continued in Britain during the First World War. In December 1914, soon after the war had broken out, Austen Chamberlain, a leading figure in the Conservative opposition and later British Foreign Secretary (1924–9), pressed on F. D. Acland, the Parliamentary Under Secretary for Foreign Affairs, the need to publish material showing that Britain had struggled to keep the peace with Germany:

> I am deeply impressed by our undeserved good fortune in carrying our people so unanimously with us. There had been nothing beforehand in official publications to make known to them the danger that we ran or to prepare them for the discharge of our responsibilities and the defence of our interests. Those who knew most were silent. . . . Now is the time . . . to form an enlightened public opinion

which will support the Government through whatever sacrifices are needed in the weary months of war and will uphold them in insisting upon stable terms of peace. Now is our opportunity to lay the foundations in the minds of the public of a wise, responsible, and consistent foreign policy after the war is finished.

Nothing was done in the short term, but such ideas contributed to the large-scale publication of official documents from 1926.[4]

A degree of reluctance, however, on the part of the British Foreign Office to accept reform can be readily glimpsed, not least an opposition to any dilution of the sense of diplomacy as a distinct vocation with particular requirements, which tended to be those of the commentator in question. In his defence of what he saw as a coherent 'old diplomacy', with long traditions, against new approaches, in both goals and practice, to the conduct of international relations, Harold Nicolson praised Callières' *De la manière de négocier avec les souverains* as 'the best manual of diplomatic method ever written'. In Britain, although some reforms, postponed by the war, were subsequently introduced, with the Diplomatic Service joining with the Foreign Office in 1918–19, there was particular opposition to interchangeability with the Home Office until 1943.

Moreover, the social attitudes seen in the diplomatic service were scarcely those of an advanced society, although they were certainly typical of the age. Theo Russell, the Diplomatic Secretary, was worried in 1918 that men who had not been to public school might become diplomats, let alone 'Jews, coloured men and infidels who are British subjects'.[5] Similarly, American diplomats had social and racial views that reflected the social group from which most were drawn: the East Coast WASP establishment. These views, and the associated appointment policies, facilitated a club-like atmosphere.[6]

A lack of novelty in calls for a wider range of information from diplomats does not mean that there was not a major shift of emphasis in diplomatic activity. Many diplomats accepted the need to engage with wider audiences. Philip, 11th Marquis of Lothian, British Ambassador in Washington in 1939–41, was described as having 'talked to the press and faced the cameras'. Lothian himself declared 'it is part of the duty of a British Ambassador to explain to the American public, so far as he judiciously can, what his own countrymen think about matters of common interest'.[7]

Moreover, by 1970 there was a greater stress on economic information than there had been at the beginning of the century. The period in which this stress became more apparent varied, but from about the start of the century diplomats were increasingly expected to provide advice on economic matters alongside their support of commercial issues and individual merchants. Consuls proved a key source of information. For example, the British Consul in Shanghai, the leading figure in the International Settlement there, provided a series of regular reports to the British envoy to China. Alongside trade returns, there was a series of quarterly political reports and six-monthly intelligence summaries from 1920 until the Japanese occupation of the city in 1937.[8] Other sources and forms of information became more common during the century, not least as a result of the thickening of international links.

There were significant changes in diplomatic activity during the century aside from a greater stress on particular types of information. The revival of ideological diplomacy was important, although the earlier episodes of such diplomacy, notably those arising from the Protestant Reformation and the French Revolution, were not identical with the nature of ideological diplomacy in the twentieth century, even if they captured some of the themes also seen then. The theme of continuity was captured by the British embassy in Moscow on 14 March 1946 when it suggested the 'danger of the modern equivalent of the religious wars of the sixteenth century' in the shape of a struggle between Communism and an alliance of American capitalism and Western social democracy.

In the twentieth century there was certainly a challenge from ideological diplomacy to the liberal diplomatic order dominant at the start of the century. The standard narrative would be to look at the problems posed by Communism and Fascism, but that does not capture the range of the challenge. For example, it is possible to chart a challenge to the liberal diplomatic order that is more clearly linked to the opposition to Western dominance, notably in China, starting with the Boxer Rising in 1900 and ending with the Cultural Revolution of the 1960s. If the emphasis is on East Asia, then the chronology can be thickened by discussing a series of changes in the period 1900–11, including the Anglo-Japanese treaty of 1902, the Russo-Japanese War of 1904–5 and the Chinese Revolution of 1911–12, which overthrew the imperial monarchy. Major episodes in the intervening years included the Japanese invasion of Manchuria in 1931, with the Japanese view that China was not capable of being a state with equal sovereignty playing an important role in encouraging intervention, even among Japanese internationalists.[9] At the other end of the period, the Cultural Revolution can be complemented by President Richard Nixon's visit to Beijing in 1972 and the Japanese–Chinese peace treaty of 1978. Each was highly important to the diplomacy of the region and to wider developments, both short and long term.

This point serves as a reminder that the coverage, and indeed periodization, of the history of diplomacy are far from fixed, and this point can further be seen in the thematic treatment in this chapter. Ideological challenges are treated before international co-operation, but first there is mention of the First World War (1914–18).

There is an understandable stress on the shared culture of late-nineteenth century and pre-war diplomacy, but the states that fought in the war displayed major differences in strategic cultures and in the political context of policymaking. Élite ethos were far from identical, with the republicanism of the French and Americans leading to a different pattern of cohesion and obedience to that of autocratic imperial monarchies. There was also a contrast between élites, notably (but not only) in Austria, Germany, Russia and Japan,[10] that were willing to see war as a tool of policy, and other élites, such as those of Britain and the USA, that did not want to fight major wars against other great powers if at all possible, although they were happy to use war as a tool of imperial expansion, such as the Spanish–American War of 1898.

Alliances, the traditional remedy of the diplomat seeking to strengthen the national position, but ironically also a restraint on action because they brought together states with differing interests, appeared inadequate as insurance policies in the 1900s and early 1910s, as anxieties grew about shifts in international geopolitics and national politics. Moreover, specific crises, notably the First Moroccan crisis of 1905–6 and the Bosnian crisis of 1908–9, encouraged brinkmanship and led to an accumulation of distrust. Diplomats, however, only played a secondary role in the mounting international crisis, as the prospect of war led military considerations to come to the fore, while the ruler and his advisers took the key role in arbitrating or, as in the case of Russia prior to its war with Japan in 1904–5, failing to arbitrate between contrasting attitudes and policies, a longstanding problem for rulers, both Russian and others.[11]

Germany was concerned about the problems of its Austrian ally and the problem of having Austria as an ally. Neither power was to restrain the other sufficiently in July 1914 and instead, in the crisis that led to the First World War, the geopolitical logic of alliances drew powers into actions that were highly damaging and in the end destroyed the logic of the alliances. Although diplomats only played a secondary role in the crisis, they did not always help the cause of peace. Aside from the conversion of Leopold Berchtold, the Austrian Foreign Minister, in July 1914 to a military solution to the challenge posed by Serbia to Austrian rule over other South Slavs, notably in Bosnia, the aristocratic culture of the Austrian diplomatic corps did not favour compromise. Instead, the South Slavs were generally viewed with contempt, and there was a strong cultural preference supporting the alliance with Germany. At the same time, military decision-makers, not diplomats, played the key role in pushing for conflict with Serbia.[12]

Once the war had begun, diplomacy again served the ends of geopolitical goals. The entry of Bulgaria (1915), Italy (1915) and Romania (1916) into the conflict reflected not a depth of commitment, but the continued determination and perceived need for second-rank powers to make assessments of opportunity. Far from the perceived ideology of either alliance playing a role, the crucial element was the gain of territories – small in themselves, but made important as a result of nationalist public myths; and their acquisition seen as a sign of success. In a diplomacy of bribes, Italy was offered (and accepted by the Pact of London of 1915) gains at the expense of Austria, while the Bulgarians were promised Macedonia and most of Thrace by Germany, and Romania sought (and eventually gained) Transylvania from joining the Allies.[13] The USA, in contrast, constructed national interest in terms of the freedom of international trade from the unrestricted submarine warfare declared by Germany, which ensured that the declaration of such warfare in 1917 led the USA into the war.

Other powers stayed neutral, finding that the pressures of what was seen as the total clash of industrialized societies pressed hard on their trade, not least as a consequence of the Allied blockade of Germany and of German submarine warfare. States such as the Netherlands and Denmark found themselves under contrary pressures, and their use of diplomacy had to be accompanied by careful consideration of the military situation, for example the possibility of invasion, and also of economic interests.[14]

The eventual peace settlement, a number of treaties generally referred to as the Paris Peace Settlement, most famously the Treaty of Versailles with Germany, was to be criticized. One strand of criticism came from disappointed states, angry that their goals had not been achieved, a group including not only the defeated but also some of the victors, notably Italy.

Another strand of criticism came from liberal commentators, as an aspect of the more general critique of diplomacy and international relations that had been seen during the war.[15] It was widely argued by such commentators that the peoples involved in the war were fundamentally benign, but had been led astray by their governments, including the foreign ministries and diplomatic services. In October 1917 Sir John Simon, the former Liberal Home Secretary, who had resigned from the British government in opposition to the introduction of conscription and then enlisted in the army, wrote to his father:

> The schemes of German conquest, which most undoubtedly inspired the German government, are being knocked on the head, and all that remains is that the German people should realise that they have been worshipping the wrong god. When that happens

... the war must be ended of course by negotiations. All the blather about unconditional surrender is ... nonsensical.[16]

The critique of diplomacy gathered pace after the war's close. The boost that the war gave pacifism contributed to opposition to diplomacy, at least as constructed by its critics. The attack on secret diplomacy came from President Woodrow Wilson of the USA, who also pressed for self-determination (within Europe). In the Fourteen Points he declared in January 1918, there was a call for a new international order. The first Point pressed for 'Open covenants of peace, openly arrived at, after which there shall be no private international understandings of any kind but diplomacy shall proceed always frankly and in the public view'. The following month, he delivered his 'Four Principles' speech to the American Congress, calling for no more secret diplomacy of the sort that had led Europe into calculating deals, rash promises and entangling alliances. In the event, journalists were thwarted in the Paris Peace Conference when they tried to attend meetings of the Supreme Council.[17]

The critique of secret diplomacy came more pointedly from the Communists, who seized power in Russia in 1917 and revealed the details of various secret treaties entered into by Russia. Some historians concurred with the critics. In *The Origins of the World War* (New York, 1928), Sidney Fay had 'the system of secret alliances' as the first of his five underlying causes of the war. Ramsay MacDonald, Leader of the British Parliamentary Labour Party in 1911–14 and Labour Prime Minister in 1924 and 1929–31, was also opposed to 'secret diplomacy' and blamed it for the outbreak of the First World War.

Diplomacy suffered from a number of critiques, some of which looked back to earlier criticisms, for example of diplomacy in the early modern period (see p. 46) and of that at the time of the French Revolution (see p. 131). There were also some more distinctively modern slants to the reaction, notably widespread populist/nativist hostility to professional diplomats as suspiciously cosmopolitan, too sympathetic to foreigners, smooth-talking and sly. The supposed combination of cosmopolitanism and secrecy appeared to demonstrate malice. There was a parallel to the attack on armaments firms as 'merchants of death' who had supposedly helped cause and sustain the war and who were a continuing force for instability.

Focus on the reparations (payments) demanded from post-war Germany, as an aspect of its war guilt, proved a particular source of liberal (and German) criticism in the 1920s and 1930s, encouraging the view that the peace had been mainly retributive. In short, it was argued that a mishandled, if not misguided, total war had led to a harsh peace, the latter a consequence of the former.

This verdict, which contributed to the critique of diplomacy as dishonest, selfish and short-sighted, was an inappropriate judgement of peace terms that were certainly far less severe than those of 1945. Germany lost territory in 1919, but talk in France of a different future for the Rhineland led nowhere. Diplomacy adapted to practicalities, as well as to ideological concerns; Germany had not been overrun by the Western powers, while, as a result of her earlier defeat of Russia, she was still in occupation of large territories in Eastern Europe when the war ended. Moreover, the victorious powers were determined to try to prevent the spread of Communist revolution from Russia to Germany.

The terms of the 1919 peace were designed to prevent Germany from launching fresh aggression, and thus to serve as a form of collective security. This was true of the serious limitations on the German military, of the occupied area along the French and Belgian frontiers, and of the demilitarized zone that Germany had to accept. The first, which the Anglo-French dominated Inter-Allied Military Control Commission sought to enforce, was an important development in the field of arms control.[18]

As an aspect of the self-interest and compromise disliked by critics, the victors, however, maintained very different logics of territorial legitimacy outside and within Europe. Whereas local consent, in the form of plebiscites, was used to determine some European frontiers, for example those between Germany and both Poland in East Prussia and Denmark, such consent-frontiers were not granted outside Europe. The Treaty of Sèvres (1920) established particularly harsh terms on the Turks, but, in the event, diplomacy followed the drums: the Turks defeated the Italians and French in 1921 and, even more decisively, the Greeks in 1921-2, and faced down the British in 1922, and as a result were able to force the acceptance of far more lenient terms by the Treaty of Lausanne in 1923.

While the war led to the search by the combatants for assistance from groups that were not yet sovereign, notably opponents of the great empires, such as Czech, Irish and Polish nationalists, as well as Zionists; the post-war world took this process forward as would-be states and regimes were contested internally and their alliance pursued by foreign bodies. Throughout, these processes entailed a broadening out of the range of diplomacy, although most of this activity did not involve accredited diplomats.

In turn, the new states that were acknowledged established or formalized diplomatic representation in order to put their point of view and to advance their interests. It was not always easy to find envoys. For example, John Chartres, a former British civil servant of Irish parentage, became second secretary in the Irish delegation that negotiated the treaty establishing the Irish Free State. He had studied in Germany and had an

Irish-German wife, which helped him secure a posting to Berlin, but his lack of experience and, crucially, his failure to associate himself closely with the politics of the new Irish government, led to his recall.[19] The primacy of political considerations reflected a more general reluctance to adopt notions of an impartial foreign service.

The peace settlement after the First World War included the establishment of the League of Nations, founded in 1919 (see p. 178), and was followed by a series of international agreements designed to prevent conflict. These agreements included the Locarno Agreement of 1925, which provided for a mutual security guarantee of Western Europe, the multilateral Kellogg–Briand Pact of 1928, which outlawed war as a means of settling disputes between them, and the Pact of Non-Aggression and Conciliation signed at Rio de Janeiro five years later. This Pact condemned wars of aggression and the territorial gains stemming from them, and imposed on the Pact's signatories the obligation to settle their differences by peaceful means.

It was not only would-be states that found themselves using agents who were not acknowledged. In May 1921 the French government sent an unofficial mission to the Turkish Nationalists at Ankara who were (successfully) seeking to replace the Ottoman government. The mission's head, Henri Franklin-Bouillon, was an ambitious politician who had expertise as a former President of the Senate Foreign Relations Committee. Travelling in the guise of a war reporter, he went on to Ankara, once assured of a favourable reception, and was able to negotiate first a compromise and then, after he returned with full powers, an agreement settling differences between the two powers.[20] A similar pattern can be seen in many other cases where states were able to win recognition, a process represented by the acceptance of formal diplomatic relations. There was a break in Turkish representation in Britain from 1914, when the two powers went to war, but in 1924, a year after Turkey was established as a democratic republic, the embassy in London was activated and Yusuf Kemal Tengirçenk was appointed as the first envoy to London.

Reparations diplomacy, such as that which led to the Dawes plan in 1926, the Young Plan in 1929 and the Hoover Moratorium in 1931, was another branch of the search for security through compromise. An important role was taken by the Reparation Commission established under the Peace Settlement but the major states proved the key players. International naval agreements, notably the Washington (1922) and, less successfully, London (1930) treaties, sought to end the possibility of any resumption of the pre-war naval races. Responsible *realpolitik* entailed compromise and benefited from the idealistic currents of 1920s' international relations, notably in the person of Gustav Stresemann, German

Foreign Minister from 1923 to 1929, and an influential and active figure in European diplomacy.[21]

Such concepts and agreements, however, were anathema to the ideologically driven powers of the period which deplored compromise as weakness and saw peace as only a stage en route to fresh conflict. Soviet activity, which focused on Europe, rested on the belief that Communism was a global need and a worldwide movement, and that the legitimacy of the Russian Revolution lay in Russia transforming the world, which was seen as a necessary result of the historical process. Institutionally, this belief was expressed in the Comintern, or Communist International, created in 1919; and, in the situation of great flux that followed the First World War and accompanied the Russian Civil War, major efforts were made to spread the revolution and to encourage revolutionary movements elsewhere, notably in Germany, which was seen as particularly susceptible to revolution. There were also high hopes of parts of Eastern Europe, especially Bulgaria.

Attempts to spread revolution, however, failed and it became necessary for the Russian revolutionaries both to accept a new international order[22] and to consolidate their position in the state that was to become the Soviet Union. As a result, in 1921 the People's Commissariat for Foreign Affairs (*Narkomindel*) became more important, and that year talented individuals were moved to it from the Comintern. Diplomatic links were also developed with capitalist states. In March 1921 an Anglo-Soviet trade agreement was used by the Communists to affirm Russia's legitimate role as a state. An indignant Winston Churchill, who was a fervent anti-Communist, complained that David Lloyd George, the Prime Minister, had grasped the 'hairy hand of the baboon' in welcoming the Soviet representative, Leonid Krassin, to No. 10. As Secretary for War in 1918–20, Churchill had sought to strengthen the war effort against the Communists during the Russian Civil War, and this effort had entailed commitments to the new states of the area, such as Finland, commitments that were not acceptable to the Cabinet. In the end, the Communists defeated their opponents in Russia.

The hope of the British government that trade would prove a way to dissolve Communism in Russia proved fruitless, in the face of the coercive nature of the authoritarian Communist state and Lenin's mastery of *realpolitik*. The latter was seen in 1922 when the Treaty of Rapallo with Germany brought two states of very different political alignment into alliance, serving each as a way to try to overcome their diplomatic weakness. In particular, Germany was able to use Russia for military training that was forbidden under the Paris Peace Settlement, thus evading the Inter-Allied Military Control Commission.

Diplomacy served the Soviets in different ways. Thus in 1923, when the Soviets planned war with Germany, in support of a hoped-for Communist revolution there, diplomatic efforts were used to support this policy through attempted arrangements with Poland and the Baltic Republics whose territory separated Germany from the Soviet Union. In that crisis, there was no division between the realists of the People's Commissariat for Foreign Affairs and the 'bomb-throwers' – revolutionaries – of the Comintern; but instead there was excessive optimism at the prospects of revolution.[23] In the event, there was no revolution in Germany. The Soviet envoy, Viktor Kopp, had also failed to win Polish support for any Soviet intervention.

The pressure in the Soviet Union for a *realpolitik* in international relations that represented the normalization of relations with other states was linked not to the abandonment of the Communist cause, but to the pursuit of Socialism (i.e. Communism) in one state, a course presented as leading to the strengthening of the cause. This emphasis, associated with Joseph Stalin who dominated the state after Lenin's death in 1924, was opposed by Leon Trotsky's demand for permanent revolution and, at a meeting of the Politburo in 1926, he accused Stalin of becoming 'the gravedigger of the revolution'. Trotsky was to be forced into exile by Stalin, and in 1940 was murdered in Mexico in a plot by Soviet Intelligence, the NKVD.[24]

Politics did not only play a role in the Soviet Union. In 1924 Britain's Labour government recognised the Soviet Union and negotiated a trade treaty, only for its Conservative successor, alleging Soviet support for subversion, to end the trade agreement and to break off diplomatic relations in 1927. The pro-Conservative press had made the same claim at the time of the 1924 general election, claiming that a letter, supposedly by Zinoviev, one of the Soviet leaders, demonstrated that the Soviet government sought Labour's re-election.

Ideological commitment leads to a downplaying of negotiation and also treats value-free representation and information-gathering as impossible. The resulting tensions can be seen not only with the Soviet Union but also in the case of Nazi Germany (1933–45), and the problems it posed for diplomatic relations, both for individual states and for the principles and practices of international co-operation.

The attitudes of the Fascist powers, notably Italy and Germany, provided a key demonstration of a discourse that longed to get rid of temporizing diplomats and to reassert the primacy of raw force wielded by someone prepared to break the rules to get their way. Futurism and primitivism contributed to this discourse, which was seen in the seizure of the town of Fiume in 1919–20 by Gabriele d'Annunzio, an Italian novelist and super-charged patriot inspired by Nietzsche. This attempt to settle the fate of the town, disputed by Italy and Yugoslavia, through force was eventually brought to an end, but d'Annuzio influenced the Italian Fascist dictator Benito Mussolini, who seized power in 1922. There were to be echoes of some of the emphasis on unilateral justice and might in several of the arguments advanced by American neo-conservatives in the 1990s and 2000s, albeit in a very different context.

The problems posed to other states in the 1920s and 1930s were not solely a matter of the ideological direction of Soviet, Italian, German or other policies and attitudes, for in many senses the problems were those of the response that should be pursued. Thus, aside from differing over the nature and severity of the challenge posed by Nazi Germany (or the Soviet Union), diplomats could not agree how to respond, both personally and as far as policy was concerned.

Some diplomats found the regimes to which they were accredited so atrocious that they tried to have only limited links. William Dodd, American Ambassador in Berlin from 1933 to 1937, sought to avoid meeting Hitler from 1934 and also refused to attend Nazi rallies in Nuremberg on the grounds that they were Party events, and not therefore related to the executive machinery of the state to which he was accredited. In contrast, Sir Nevile Henderson, the far less critical British envoy, attended the rallies in 1937 and 1938.

Yet in trying to distinguish between the German government and the Nazi Party, Dodd was deliberately ignoring the dynamic of German politics. In part, this choice reflected his hope that Germans would reject the regime, just as he also pressed Roosevelt on the threat from Germany. However, the unwillingness of the American government and public to abandon isolationism left him depressed and without any real role. Responding to German criticism, Dodd was relieved by Roosevelt in December 1937; the critical Sir Eric Phipps, British envoy in Berlin since 1933, was moved to Paris the same year, while Edward, Viscount Halifax, the Foreign Secretary, made apologetic excuses for hostile coverage of Hitler in the British press.

Dodd's successor, Hugh Wilson, was a career Foreign Service officer who sought to improve relations, praising Hitler and avoiding criticism of German internal affairs. Indeed, Wilson applauded the *Anschluss* (enforced union with Austria in 1938) and the extorted absorption of the Sudetenland from Czechoslovakia in 1938 as likely to satisfy Germany and to ensure peace. In the event, Hitler went too far for American domestic opinion: the American, and then German, ambassadors were recalled after the *Kristallnacht* assault on German Jews on 9 November 1938; an assault for which the excuse was the murder of a member of the German embassy.

The tension between Dodd and Wilson (and indeed, for Britain, between Phipps and his successor, Henderson)[25] captured different attitudes to diplomacy, as well as to American policy. In this case, neither policy proved effective. Wilson's stance did not lessen Nazi hostility, which owed much to contempt for America as a deracinated society with a consumerist politics and culture. In addition, neither Dodd nor Wilson were able to support Germans who wanted a peaceful resolution of issues. Moreover, even Wilson's recall had no impact. It was seen in Berlin as a concession to Jewish activists that would not affect American attitudes. Indeed, in 1939 Congress failed to relax restrictions on the immigration of Jewish children from Germany.[26]

Nazi Germany is correctly seen as peculiarly vicious and deadly, and as a result there is a tendency to treat the very maintenance of diplomatic relations with Berlin as deeply flawed. This view interacts with that outlined earlier in the chapter, with such relations presented as an aspect of the undesirable old diplomatic order. Yet in practice the challenge from Nazi attitudes and practices was such that there is a sense of conventional diplomatic practices and views as under pressure when considering what happened to the diplomats who were posted to Berlin.

The same was true for the German diplomats. Alongside 'old school' professionals came committed ideologues, but the common issue in both cases was that of ideological direction by a government that had no lasting interest in compromise with other powers. Only one high-ranking diplomat, the envoy in Washington, Count Friedrich von Prittwitz und Gaffron, resigned in protest against Hitler's rise to power.

Similarly, Mussolini's Italy employed a mixture of professionals and Fascist Party figures as envoys. Only very occasionally did Mussolini use military figures as diplomatic go-betweens, although he employed such figures to open up weapons deals. Diplomats were expected to conform to Mussolini's anti-liberal ideology and to his contempt for Britain and France, and the use of Fascist diplomats who held these views, such as Dino Grandi, envoy in London from 1932, led to a failure to note British strengths or to probe the possibilities for co-operation. Similarly, there was an unwillingness on Mussolini's part to appreciate warnings from Italian diplomats about the risks of co-operation with Hitler,[27] warnings that were to be borne out by the increasingly troubled fate of the Fascist regime from June 1940, when Mussolini declared war on Britain and France, to its fall in 1943.

Japan was governed by an authoritarian regime dominated by the military, and this affected its diplomatic service. The key envoy, Lieutenant-General Hiroshi Ōshima, who came from a military background, was envoy in Berlin from 1938 to 1939 and from 1941 to 1945, negotiating the

Anti-Comintern and Tripartite Pacts. His messages, intercepted by the USA as part of the MAGIC system, were an extremely useful source of Allied Intelligence. Ōshima was sentenced to life imprisonment at the Far East War Crimes Trials, but was given parole in 1955. In contrast, Shigeru Yoshida, who had entered the diplomatic service in 1906, having studied at Tokyo Imperial University and who had been envoy in Rome (1930–32) and London (1936–8), was out of favour because of his support for conciliation. Having unsuccessfully tried to persuade the government to surrender in early 1945, he became Foreign Minister in the post-war government that October and served as Prime Minister for most of the period from 1946 to 1954.

The attempted Nationalist coup in 1936 that launched the Spanish Civil War divided the Spanish diplomatic service. Some embassies continued to support the Republicans, and in many states there were representatives from both sides: in Britain the embassy backed the Republic but the Duke of Alba, who was well linked into the British élite, represented the Nationalists until Britain formally recognized them in late 1938, when he became Ambassador. Obtaining arms supplies was a major goal of the diplomats from both sides. Ideological factors played an important role in Spanish diplomatic relations after the Nationalist triumph in 1939. For example, those with Peronist Argentina were strong.

Ideological suppositions about the weakness of liberal democracy and the inherent necessity of the triumph of its more apparently more purposeful alternative played a key role for the totalitarian regimes. Reports from abroad were understood in this light, and diplomacy was certainly not grasped as an opportunity to find a commonality of interest; or, at least, other than in terms of short-term interests. The dominance of ideological suppositions was linked to the neglect of professional perspectives, and of professionalism as a separate sphere.

Thus in the early 1930s the Soviet government saw the rise of Hitler as a way to advance its interests, distracting France and radicalizing Germany en route towards a proletarian revolution.[28] This approach was at complete variance with the idea of collective security, which should have encouraged opposition to Germany, while the approach also rested on a misunderstanding of the situation within Germany and of the serious challenge posed by Hitler's opposition to Communism and to the Soviet Union.

Despite the rejection of Trotsky and the focus on the development of the Soviet Union, the pursuit of Soviet foreign policy by Stalin was still characterized by a willingness to expand Communist interests worldwide, while subversive means also played a role. Stalin also did not trust decision-making to the foreign ministry, and instead used multiple sources of information as well as a number of agents and institutions to implement policy.[29] The challenge posed to other states helped lead Britain and China to cut off relations with the Soviet Union in 1927, while two years later relations with France were affected by the Soviet attempt to recruit French Communists to spy on French military and logistical capabilities.[30] The USA did not grant the Soviet Union recognition until 1933, when a Democratic Presidency succeeded a longstanding period of Republican Presidents.[31]

Distrust also played a central role when the Soviet Union did ally with other powers. This distrust was particularly directed at the Western powers, notably Britain, which was regarded as especially anti-Communist. Thus when, in May 1941, Rudolf Hess, Hitler's deputy, flew to Britain on an unauthorized and unsuccessful attempt to settle Anglo-German differences, this mission was seen by Stalin as a possible means of negotiation designed to isolate the Soviet Union. Moreover, while allies during the war from later in 1941 to 1945, the Soviets mounted a major Intelligence offensive against Britain and the USA, one that laid the basis for the acquisition of American nuclear secrets.[32]

At the same time, it is pertinent to note that the problem of conventional practices and views under challenge was not solely posed by the Fascist and Communist powers. Nor, over the longer term of the entire twentieth century, was it simply a matter of the ideological newcomers on the block who were at issue. Instead, there was a general situation in which many new regimes posed a challenge because they sought not to conform to existing patterns, but rather to propose new demands, even methods. Again, it is necessary to be cautious before regarding this as an aspect of novelty, for many of the same themes can be seen in previous centuries, not least as existing hierarchies of significance and customs of deference were challenged.

However, in the twentieth century there was a more conscious rejection of the established diplomatic order, and this process helped create the sense of flux noted by Bland. Part of this rejection can be traced to the typecasting of an old diplomacy as anachronistic and linked to a redundant liberal democracy, a theme seen on both Left and Right, and notably, but not only, from populists and activists who pressed for a commitment, for example to the sides in the Spanish Civil War (1936–9), that the 'respectable' liberal democratic powers did not display.[33] Thus the hostile social characterization of diplomacy, in terms of class interest and behaviour, was related to a critique of the established form of states and their practice of international relations, and therefore to a question of the relevance of diplomacy as conventionally understood.

In part, the departure from conventional diplomacy was linked to a greater reliance on unofficial agents, not least as efforts were made to link with sympathetic groups abroad. Thus representation was related to propaganda. In turn, there were responses including the focusing of Intelligence operations on supposed foreign subversion, with, in particular, an attempt to spy on unofficial agents. Moreover, in the USA the Foreign Agents Registration Act of 1938 sought to monitor those who lobbied for foreign causes.

Much of this may seem very different to the world of pre-1914 diplomacy, but it is necessary to be cautious in treating the latter in terms simply of bureaucratic professionalism and an absence of ideology. Instead, diplomatic systems produced information that was important to political struggles within, as well as between, states. Information was not separate from opinion. Indeed, opinion about the policies of other powers was central to the search for information, and its evaluation was generally linked to the needs of the ministry. This point underlines the interconnectedness of the key issues. The partisan nature and/or consequences of information flows accentuated the need to choose diplomats carefully, and emphasized the issue of control. This partisan nature also made the subsequent task of accurate assessment more difficult, and this issue cuts to the heart of the problem of judging the formulation and execution of foreign policy.

There was also an additional dynamic at play in the twentieth century to that of tensions within Europe, and again one that was a continuation from the previous century, namely the dynamic of new states. In the nineteenth century the established European diplomatic system had had to adapt to the new states of the New World, to the consequences of nationalism within Europe, and to the need to bring non-Western powers into the ambit of the Western worldview. In the twentieth century these processes continued, but they became more difficult as nationalism and ideology helped lead Europe to the funeral pyre between 1914 and 1945, and as the assertiveness of non-Western powers was often expressed not, as in the late nineteenth century, in terms of a desire to accommodate to Western norms, but, rather, as a matter of rejection or only partial accommodation.

This process of rejection was facilitated by the extent to which ideological divisions provided a new vocabulary of dissent, and these divisions also exacerbated the pressures coming from nationalism. Indeed, many diplomats found their careers compromised or ended, and some had to live in exile, because they opposed the degree to which the furthering of national interests was pushed in terms of extravagant nationalist policies that owed much of their impetus to populism, ideology and an unwillingness to compromise. Temperament played a particular role with diplomats who were aristocratic by inclination and habit, if not always birth, lacking populist instincts and seeking to mould nationalist policies in light of their understanding of the views of the states to which they were accredited, as well as of the interrelationships of issues, and the inherent value of peace and the balance of power. There was thus a systemic clash between professionalism and the realistic and informed diplomacy to which it generally gave rise, and the dynamic of growing state power, its populist themes, and the clarity of the ideologies embraced by major governments.

The appeal to non-Western powers of Western concepts and models of dissent has to be set alongside indigenous patterns of identity and expression. It is also too easy to group the diplomatic attitudes of non-Western states in terms of tensions within the West. Nevertheless, authoritarian right-wing regimes of the 1930s and early 1940s, for example in Argentina, Spain or Persia (Iran), can be linked to Italy or Germany, while the Soviet Communists sought to sponsor left-wing activity elsewhere. Similar points can be made about the Cold War.

From the outset, Soviet interests were not restricted to Europe. Sun Yat-sen, the leader of the Chinese nationalists, was sent a message declaring all unequal treaties null and void, a call that challenged the basis of the foreign presence in China and that was intended to hit Britain's commercial position there. Mongolia was also an area of Soviet activity. In 1920 the Soviet Union held a Congress of Peoples of the East at Baku. However, the initial attempts to exploit anti-imperialism in the 1920s were of limited success, for example in the Dutch East Indies (later Indonesia) and in Inner Mongolia (against Chinese rule). These attempts became far more important from the late 1940s, as the Soviet Union, and later also China and Cuba, backed what could be defined as national liberation struggles. Once independent, the resulting governments had limited purchase in the world of conventional diplomacy and, instead, potent links to the Communist powers.[34]

The questions of ideology and new states were therefore intertwined, they had been from the sixteenth century in Europe. The multiple relationships that resulted provided the key theme and context for the pursuit of negotiation, representation and information-gathering. They were more significant than shifts in process arising from technology, notably, for this period, the growth of air transport to move diplomats and ministers, and of improved communications for the more speedy movement of messages, both diplomatic and those relating to foreign policy. Telegrams were succeeded by radio, and then by satellite-based systems.

Air transport was to be important to trans-oceanic diplomacy, opening up a dimension hitherto not generally taken by leaders because of the length of time required to sail across the world. For the Paris Peace

Conference of 1919, President Woodrow Wilson sailed to France taking a very large delegation with him, such that the voyage permitted the furtherance of American preparations. Similarly, the heavy cruiser *Augusta* took President Harry Truman to and from Europe for the Potsdam conference in 1945. Meanwhile, within Europe, although some, notably Stalin, did not wish to fly, air transport was significant in speeding up diplomacy, notably for those, such as the leaders of Britain and Scandinavia, otherwise in part dependent on ships. However, for many leaders, air transport essentially took forward the possibilities already presented by the nineteenth-century development of a train network across Europe.

As a result, ministers were able to take initiatives and to negotiate, and over a wide geographical span, whereas otherwise they might have entrusted all or part of their mission to diplomats. Thus, when, in 1933, Mussolini proposed a 'European Directorate', based on a Pact of Four of Britain, France, Germany and Italy that could agree on a revision of the Paris Peace treaties of 1919, Nicolae Titulescu, the Romanian Foreign Minister, on behalf of the Permanent Council of the Entente of Romania, Czechoslovakia and Yugoslavia, went on a mission to Britain and France to persuade them to oppose the plan. France had already decided to reject it, but the mission reflected the interaction of diplomacy with international structures. The architecture of the latter tended to demand representation by ministers rather than (more junior) diplomats. Diplomats, however, could be critical, the Italian Daniele Varè writing of a visit to Berlin in 1932:

> If professional diplomats cannot settle them in unhurried, unadvertised 'conversations', the world's international problems cannot be solved merely by getting a few politicians to meet round a green table. . . . Yet the illusion that 'a conference' is a panacea for all the world's troubles still persisted in 1932. And meanwhile, in Germany and elsewhere, young men of university education had to beg from foreigners in the Unter den Linden.[35]

Attitudes toward the governance of the international system were important, just as they were dynamic. The most pertinent issues were those of permanent institutions for international links and, secondly, the creation of new relations within imperial systems. The latter have been overshadowed by the former, but these new relations were important as they testify to the sense of flux.

Changes in the British Empire were particularly significant, as it was the largest empire in the world and because these changes were an important counterpart to the development of permanent institutions for international links. The development of the notion of a Commonwealth, unity in independence, proved significant in maintaining the support of most of the Dominions for the Empire. An imperial conference in 1926 defined the Commonwealth as 'the group of self-governing communities composed of Great Britain and the Dominions'. This definition formed the basis for the Statute of Westminster (1931), which determined that Commonwealth countries could now amend or repeal 'any existing or future act of the United Kingdom Parliament . . . in so far as the same is part of the law of this Dominion'. Economic diplomacy within the Commonwealth led to Imperial Preference, established in agreements reached at Ottawa in 1932. The diplomacy of the Dominions' links was maintained by the Dominions Office in London, a body that managed relations with High Commissioners in Dominion capitals and with the Dominions' High Commissioners in London.[36] British politicians considered the Commonwealth a key force for influencing international relations, with Harold Wilson devoting great attention to it in the mid-1960s while Prime Minister.

Yet there were also serious problems. The unwillingness of the Dominions to back Britain in the Chanak Crisis with Turkey in 1922 was significant, while their reluctance to fight Germany in 1938 had an impact on British policy at the time of the Munich Crisis, although in part in each case, this unwillingness reinforced an existing policy preference on the part of at least part of the British government.

Imperial negotiations also served as a way to settle specific concerns, as in 1923 when the imperial conference addressed the grievances of the Indian community in the colony of Kenya. Tensions, however, arose within the Empire as a result of differences over colonial policy. For example, in the 1930s, Britain encountered major difficulties in negotiations over the future of India with the Indian princely states, for example at the round-table conference of 1930-32. Later, the white-dominated Central African Federation (now Zambia, Zimbabwe and Malawi) actively supported the white cause in Congo from the Belgian pull-out in 1960, leading to international policies at variance with those of Britain, including separate negotiations with Portugal, the neighbouring colonial power (in Angola), as well as military support for secessionism in the Katanga Province of Congo. The British government, in contrast, was opposed to the break-up of Congo, and also backed independence for Nyasaland (now Malawi) and Northern Rhodesia (Zambia), measures rejected by the Federation government.

The role of mercenaries in the conflict in Katanga indicated the limited control wielded by formal governmental processes. In 1965 Southern Rhodesia was to issue its unilateral declaration of independence from

Britain. This attempt to maintain white rule lasted until 1980, and led to a covert diplomacy on the part of the new government as it struggled for recognition and support.[37]

Returning to the 1920s and 1930s, the British Empire had in effect become a sphere for diplomacy, one that lacked formal processes akin to those of international state-to-state diplomacy but, nevertheless, that looked more to the type of diplomacy characteristic of the late twentieth century: one of multiple links, many of which were only imperfectly grasped by the formal diplomatic mechanisms. Aid was to be a classic instance of such links. The same was to be true of the French Empire.

More ambitious and challenging tasks awaited diplomacy within international bodies that were not grounded on a common experience of imperial rule, not least because of the view, expressed in a lecture in 1920 by Lord Hankey, the British Cabinet Secretary, that the best hope lay 'in the judicious development of diplomacy by conference',[38] a view strongly shared by much of the British public. After each world war, institutional aspirations towards a moral world order were expressed in the foundation of a new body for representation, negotiation and arbitration: the League of Nations and the United Nations respectively. Each, however, failed to live up to expectations.

The League, established in 1919, was weakened because its key founder, America's President Woodrow Wilson, who won the Nobel Peace Prize that year for his efforts, could not persuade the Senate to ratify the treaty. The Senate sought to limit the commitments that would come from a promise to preserve the territory and independence of member states and, instead, to maintain Congress's role in deciding on war. The British failed to persuade Wilson to accept changes to the League's covenant pressed for by his congressional opponents. Indeed, the USA was never a member of the League, and also refused to join the permanent Court of International Justice. Nor did the Soviet Union join the League until the mid-1930s. Moreover, as another deficiency of the post-war international settlement, the Anglo-American unwillingness to make security promises to assist France if attacked strengthened the latter's reluctance to ease Germany's re-entry into power politics.

The League, however, had value as a forum for international debate, and notably as a platform for the weaker powers, and also provided a means by which to explain and manage the division of German and Turkish colonies and territories among the victorious powers after the First World War. The new colonies were League of Nations' mandates, a status of trusteeship seen as an alternative to colonialism, both because the mandatory powers were subject to inspection by the League's permanent Mandates Commission and because the status was presented as a preparation for independence, as indeed happened with Iraq. The search for independence on the part of the mandated territories, a search that involved lobbying outside the confines of imperial control as well as within them, expanded the number of bodies seeking to pursue diplomatic options, as with the Jewish Agency for Palestine, which was a British mandate. In turn, the mandates and the Commission became a new focus for international diplomacy.[39]

The League also looked toward more modern international diplomacy in seeking international agreement on a range of issues including disarmament, drug control, and the (illegal) slave trade. Ethiopia was only allowed to join in 1923 when it agreed to ban slavery and the slave trade. There were major agreements on the control of drugs in 1925 and 1931 and the establishment of the International Opium Commission in Shanghai.[40] Furthermore, the Minorities Section was assigned responsibility for their care, while the International Labour Office sought to regulate migration. The League's Finance Committee, however, proved less successful in managing international financial issues.

Germany joined the League in 1926 as part of its reintegration into the new diplomatic order linked to the Locarno Agreement. Moreover, a sense of the League as part of a new and better diplomatic order was reflected in Jules Cambon's *The Diplomatist* (1931), a work that saw a change in diplomacy: 'We are living in an age of publicity. The diplomatists of today only faintly resemble their forerunners who took part in the Congress of Vienna.'[41] The large number of inter-governmental organizations in this period looked toward the situation after the Second World War.

The savage global recession that spread from 1929, the Slump and the subsequent Depression, however, increased domestic and international pressures. These exposed tensions in the international order, not least between the collective security offered by the League and the attempt, especially by France, to create a separate alliance system, as well as the failure of policymakers to take advantage of the peace in the late 1920s in order to establish ways to co-operate. Economic and political competition was accentuated by the Depression, and co-operation did not seem the way to overcome differences.[42]

The League encountered fatal problems in the 1930s, as it proved unable to respond to the aggression of the Axis powers, notably the successful Japanese invasion of Manchuria in 1931 and the triumphant Italian invasion of Abyssinia (Ethiopia) in 1935. Under article 10 of the League's covenant, member states agreed 'to respect and preserve ... the territorial integrity and existing political independence of all members', while article 16 provided for immediate economic and social, and possible military, sanctions against any aggressive power.

Reality, however, proved otherwise. The League's Council found Italy an aggressor in October 1935, but France thwarted any serious consequences. The League was weakened by its failure to act, a failure that reflected the limitations of both the leading powers in it and of collective security, in part as a result of American isolationism. The powers put their individual concerns first, although, looked at differently, they were anxious, in a hostile world, not to derail the main planks of policy by a focus on issues – such as Abyssinia or, indeed, the Spanish Civil War – that appeared of lesser consequence. In addition, diplomats warned of the dangerous consequences of firm action, Sir Francis Lindley, the British Ambassador in Tokyo, and his embassy staff, pressing against Britain backing League action over Manchuria, especially sanctions.[43]

The League was also weakened by the extent to which states left it without consequence, Japan and Germany doing so in 1933 and 1934. Five years later, the Soviet Union, which had entered the League in 1934, was expelled for invading Finland, but this expulsion had no consequence. In the mean time, the League had played scant role in the crisis caused by the Spanish Civil War. The Republic had pledged support for the League as a major aspect of its foreign policy, but its requests for League support proved fruitless.

The Soviet attack on Finland was a product of the Molotov-Ribbentrop Pact with Germany of 23 August 1939 which had allocated spheres of expansion between the two states. Such bilateral diplomacy, named significantly after the two foreign ministers, was very much the antithesis of the League. The failure of collective security had also been seen in the earlier inability, of both the League and the major powers, to prevent expansionism by Germany, Italy and Japan. 1935, for example, saw a Franco-Soviet defensive alliance, followed by the Stresa Front of Britain, France and Italy, aimed against German rearmament, but neither brought stability. Nor, in 1935, did the Hoare-Laval Pact, an attempt by the British and French foreign ministers to produce a negotiated end to the Abyssinian war at the cost of major Abyssinian cessions of territory. Looking back to pre-1914 attempts to reconcile colonial expansionism with stability among the European powers, such diplomacy was now judged unacceptable by the British public and was anyway insufficient to stop Italian expansionism that owed much of its character to Mussolini's ideological commitment to a different, anti-liberal world order.[44]

The number of 'revisionist' powers, keen to further their own expansionism and to justify it in terms of the overthrow of an 'unfair' Paris Peace settlement, posed a particular problem, as they could co-operate at the expense of others. Moreover, Italy, Germany and Japan were not alone. For example, Poland, which had seized Vilnius from Lithuania in

1920, forced it to acknowledge this loss in 1938, and also seized territory from Czechoslovakia the same year. Comparisons can be made with the powers that partitioned Poland out of existence in 1772–95, but the situation in the 1930s was more flagrant as it defied the norms and processes presented by, and in, the League. A similar point can be made about the Japanese attempt to justify expansionism on the grounds that it was emulating earlier Western conduct.

The failure of the League was followed by the wartime disruption of much conventional diplomatic activity. Conflict resulted in the breach of diplomatic relations, but air attack and (unlike in the First World War, from the very outbreak of the war), unrestricted submarine warfare led to considerable damage to diplomatic infrastructure and personnel. Embassies, consulates and residences were bombed and diplomats were killed, each to a degree not seen in any previous war. Already, prior to the outbreak of large-scale conflict in Europe in 1939, the Japanese full-scale invasion of China in 1937 led to the strafing of a car carrying Sir Hughe Knatchbull-Hugessen, the British Ambassador, who was seriously injured, and to the movement of embassies to Nanjing. Its fall to Japan ensured, in turn, that they moved to the temporary Nationalist capitals of Hankou and Chongqing.

A disillusioned V. K. Wellington Koo (Vi Kynin Koo), who had represented China at the League, forlornly calling for action against Japanese aggression, was clear that a stronger international replacement was required, and, in January 1942, he pressed for 'a central authority with adequate means to enforce peace and prevent international gangsterism . . . prescribing for observance everywhere the uniform rule of law and the same standard of conduct'.[45] Thus diplomacy was to serve a global order dedicated to the enforcement of systemic rules; the world could not afford the use of diplomacy to forward disparate national interests opposed to these rules.

In the meanwhile, the summit diplomacy of the Second World War was an abrupt demonstration of the change from established diplomatic practices, and one that, in part, represented an adoption by the Allies (Britain, the Soviet Union and the USA) of a practice made more common by the Axis dictators. Hitler, in particular, had scant time for conventional diplomacy. With his belief in the potency of his will, his fascination with power-politics and his disdain for diplomats, Hitler was convinced of the value of personal meetings. They served to demonstrate his centrality to both domestic and foreign opinion, and provided stage-managed occasions for the display of German power and Nazi ceremonial.

Once the German empire and alliance system was established, these meetings provided opportunities to plan closer links and the pursuit of

German-directed policies. Meetings such as those of Hitler and Francisco Franco, the Spanish dictator, at Hendaye in 1940 were key occasions in the definition of relations, while more pliant leaders were expected to travel to Berlin, for example Marshal Antonescu of Romania in 1941.

The treatment of Germany's allies was scarcely on the basis of mutual respect and equality of position. Hitler, for example, was totally unimpressed when he met Franco, who very much wished to co-operate with Germany, although this drive was greatly underplayed after the war. Instead of mutual respect, there was on the part of Hitler an expectation of compliance, notably over the provision of troops and other resources, with the imposition of anti-Semitic policies in some cases, and with assumptions that Allied territory could be used for operations and be reallocated to suit German diplomatic goals. Thus in 1940 Transylvania was transferred from Romania to Hungary (of which it had been part until the Paris Peace Settlement), and the southern Dobrudja from Romania to Bulgaria.

Among Germany's allies, however, there were serious tensions exacerbated by such territorial changes, as well as hostility or opposition to German requirements.[46] Tensions in the German alliance system would have existed anyway: those between German allies, as well as their particular goals, looked back to pre-war issues, notably with Romania and Hungary. These issues were exploited by the Germans, but could also restrict their options. Germany's allies also sought to manoeuvre to their own advantage, and successfully so in the case of Finland. The Finns were helped by their separate sphere of military operations against the Soviet Union, as well as their control of raw materials, which made it possible to bargain with Germany from a position of some strength. The Finns were also able to ignore German pressure to hand over Jews. The situation was similar in relations between Japan and Thailand. The management of relations in the latter case owed much to a liaison conference which sought to advance Japanese interests.

The Allies could also be coercive towards neutrals, as with the British against Vichy France in 1940–42 and in Iraq in 1941, and the British and Soviets in Persia (Iran) the same year. The USA, however, did not need to use force as their allies did, and American influence was such that most of the world's remaining neutrals followed suit after it declared war on Germany on 11 December 1941. Cuba, the Dominican Republic, Guatemala, Nicaragua and Haiti also declared war that day. Honduras and El Salvador followed the next day, and Panama, Mexico and Brazil in 1942, the last being influenced by German attacks on Brazilian shipping as well as by American pressure.

These entries marked a major blow to German diplomatic and espionage attempts to build up support in Latin America. In part, these hopes reflected the desire to exploit opportunities, not least those presented by local German populations and by authoritarian governments, such as the Peron dictatorship in Argentina. The hopes were partly a product of the global aspirations of key elements in the German government. As in the case of Mexico in the First World War, there was also a desire to weaken the USA by causing problems in its backyard. Thus there was a strategic intention underlying Germany's Latin American policy.

This policy had many flaws, not least encouraging American hostility and the inability of Germany to give teeth to its hopes, an inability which in part reflected British naval strength as well as the German focus on operations in Europe. Yet despite the flaws of Germany's Latin American policy, there was a potential for causing trouble. This potential was one of the victims of Hitler's decision to declare war on the USA.

America's success in Latin America, nevertheless, had limitations, which in part reflected the appeal of the German authoritarian model as well as indicating what diplomacy alone could achieve. Many Latin American states delayed entry into the war: Bolivia and Colombia until 1943, and Ecuador, Paraguay, Peru, Venezuela, Chile and Argentina (in which there was much sympathy for Germany) until 1945. Although once they joined the war, none of the Latin American states played a major, let alone crucial, role in the conflict, their experience as combatants and neutrals reflected the global impact and nature of the struggle, at once military, political, ideological and economic. The state that played the leading military role was Brazil.[47] Other late entrants into the war were Liberia in 1944, and Saudi Arabia, Egypt and Turkey in 1945.

Moreover, the war became more truly global because the alliance between Britain, the USA and the Soviet Union from December 1941 led these three powers to declare war on those who were already at war with their allies. Thus Britain and the USA went to war with Hitler's allies that had attacked the Soviet Union, while the latter went to war with Japan at the close of the war. The need to win Soviet military support against Japan provided a key instance of the extent to which the diplomacy of the war was both subordinate to the campaigning, and yet also shaped it as the powers looked to the post-war world. The British, whose role in the formulation of Allied policy was eroded by the greater economic strength and military power of their allies, as well as by Soviet successes in Eastern Europe and American advances in the Pacific, were determined not only to keep the Soviet Union in the war, but also to ensure that the USA sustained the peace settlement, unlike after the First World War. In turn, President Franklin Delano Roosevelt wanted to make certain that Stalin was committed in the short term to conflict with Japan, and in the long term to the eventual peace settlement.[48]

The reality of the Soviet advance vitiated subsequent claims that Roosevelt and Churchill had 'sold out' Eastern Europe to Stalin in February 1945 at the Yalta conference. In practice, Poland was already occupied and eastern Germany soon would be.[49] At Yalta, it was also agreed that the Soviets would have an important presence in Manchuria including the naval base of Port Arthur. China, one of the Allies, was not consulted. As in 1814–15, when the future of the European world was negotiated at the Congress of Vienna in the aftermath of Napoleon's defeat, Russian/Soviet power and success were key factors that could not be wished away from the negotiating table. Indeed, in some respects the diplomatic position in 1944–5 was similar to that in 1814–15, albeit with the significant difference that the role of the victorious oceanic power was now played by the USA, or by an uneasy Anglo-American condominium dominated by the USA and not, as in 1814–15, by Britain alone.

In 1814–15 there was a de facto delimitation of spheres of influence, with Russia dominant in Eastern Europe. Crucially, this meant Russian rule over most of Poland. The Russian gain of Bessarabia and Finland in recent wars with the Turks and Sweden were also part of the post-Napoleonic order, just as the Soviet gain of Bessarabia and Karelia and control over key aspects of Finnish policy were part of the post-Hitlerian order. Russia in 1814–15 also played a central role in determining the fate of the defeated kingdom of Saxony, and in the face of opposition from Austria, Britain and France; and this role also looked toward the situation in 1944–5.

In many respects, what was unusual was the assumption, in 1944–5, as in 1790–91 during the Ochakov Crisis, that Britain could play a key role in determining the fate of Eastern Europe. This assumption, however, reflected the sense that the war could and must lead to a new and more benign international order: if there was to be a United Nations, there should also be self-determination for the peoples conquered by Germany, notably the Poles.

For the Allies, the post-war world was a key issue throughout and not only in the closing stages of the war. This concern with the future linked public with politicians. In October 1943 *Life* declared 'Of one thing we are sure. Americans are not fighting to protect the British Empire'; something the USA would later regret in some areas as it faced difficulties with nationalist movements and states that resisted or replaced the European empires. At the Tehran conference of Allied leaders that December, there were bitter differences over the fate of European colonial empires. Roosevelt was opposed to colonial rule (although not by the USA in the Pacific) and instead in favour of a system of 'trusteeship' as a prelude to independence. Under the Tydings-McDuffie Act of 1934, the Americans had already promised to give the Philippines, a 'Commonwealth', its independence from 1934 after a ten-year transitional period; delayed by the war, it fulfilled this promise in 1946. The USA was still imperial, but argued that it was using a different model, a point taken further by its informal empire in Latin America.

Willing to satisfy Stalin at the expense of Eastern Europe and over Manchuria, Roosevelt pressed Churchill on the status of both Hong Kong (which he wanted returned to China) and India, and British officials were made aware of a fundamental contradiction in attitudes. Britain's attempt to increase its influence in Ethiopia after the Italians were driven out in 1941 was resisted by the USA, and indeed, the State Department arranged a meeting for Emperor Haile Selassie with Roosevelt in Egypt in February 1945. Roosevelt told Churchill that Britain had to adjust to a 'new period' in global history and to turn their back on '400 years of acquisitive blood in your veins',[50] although he did not press the point for India. Roosevelt's opposition to French and Dutch imperialism in Asia was also very strong.

Britain and the USA competed over Middle Eastern oil, with America successfully developing links with Saudi Arabia,[51] and over economic interests elsewhere,[52] while there was also strong American support for a Jewish state in Palestine, a policy opposed by Anthony Eden, the British Foreign Secretary. Roosevelt's opposition to key aspects of British policy was shared by significant advisers such as Sumner Welles.[53] Highly conscious of his Irish antecedents as well as an isolationist, Joseph Kennedy, ambassador to Britain from 1938 to 1940, and a politician and rival of Roosevelt with ambitions to lead the Democratic Party, had scarcely been supportive to Britain and was criticized by George VI for defeatism in 1939.[54] More serious in the long term was American opposition to imperial preference, the commercial adhesive of the British empire. Article seven of the Lend Lease agreement of 1942 stipulated the eventual end to such preference.

There is a balance to be struck here. Roosevelt's critical treatment of Churchill at the Tehran conference on 2–7 December 1943, and his refusal to have any truck with re-establishing Britain's empire, have to be set alongside his open-handed support of Britain in very problematic circumstances in the USA in 1940 and his Germany-first military strategy.

Nevertheless, Churchill's determination to save the empire in what in one respect was a War of the British Succession was directed at the USA, the Soviet Union and China, as well as Germany and Japan. The decline in British power he felt so keenly made him clear on the need to retain the empire as well as imperial preference in trade, although in 1943 Britain and the USA signed treaties with China ending the extra-territorial rights they had acquired with the Treaty Ports system of the nineteenth century.

Alongside ignoring pressures for decolonization and trying to save their empires, Britain and France indeed had territorial ambitions on the Italian colony of Libya, while Churchill was also interested in the Kra isthmus in southern Thailand, which would provide a continuous land route between the neighbouring British colonies of Burma and Malaya. In the event, the British, French and Dutch colonial empires were largely to be gone within two decades. Instead, a prime result of the war was the spread of American influence, not only military and power, but also potent economic and cultural models underpinned by financial strength. This process affected not only Europe's empires, but also Europe itself.[55]

As with the diplomacies of other conflicts, neutrals had registered the changing politics of the war. Thus, Afghanistan maintained its links with Germany despite British opposition, but ended them under pressure after Germany attacked the Soviet Union in 1941. This left Afghanistan between Allied powers, a process completed when British and Soviet forces occupied Iran. Spain, where Germany had its largest embassy as well as thirty consulates, provided Germany with a degree of assistance that was to be overlooked subsequently.[56] The neutrals also provided channels for real or attempted communication between the combatants. Thus in 1944 the British asked the Swiss diplomat Alfred Escher to negotiate the surrender of Athens with the Germans, so as to ensure that it was kept out of Communist hands; while in 1945 Japan made limited approaches to the USA via Switzerland.[57]

The Allies did not follow the imperial theme seen with Hitler's use of personal meetings. Factors of distance, time, politics and ideology ensured that the 'Big Three' (Roosevelt, Stalin and Churchill) did not meet in Washington, while Yalta in 1945 was the closest they all got to Moscow. Allied conferences at Casablanca (1943), Cairo (1943), Tehran (1943) and Potsdam (1945) reflected the importance of intermediary locations. At the same time, there was an emphasis on personal agreement among the leaders rather than on formal diplomatic processes, an emphasis that reflected the conviction on the part of the leaders that they could change the world by personal diplomacy. This conviction proved misplaced, although this diplomacy helped to manage the issues at stake, including the transition of great-power status from Britain to the USA,[58] a transition that was further recorded in post-war summitry, notably the shift from the four-power Paris summit of 1960 to the American–Soviet summit of 1961.

Summit diplomacy represented a continuation of pre-war practices including of special diplomatic missions,[59] as well as an attempt to maintain alliances and provide forums for negotiation to cope with the failure or deficiencies of international agencies such as the League of Nations and, later, the United Nations. The term came from Churchill's frequent calls in the 1950s for meetings at the highest levels of government in order to resolve international differences.⁶⁰ Such diplomacy also stemmed from the determination of leaders to control the diplomatic process. As such, summit diplomacy was a product of problems posed by international developments, but also of the wish of leaders to circumvent the limitations and constraints of bureaucratic systems. Thus diplomacy was reconceptualized as what in some respects was a departure from conventional methods. This, however, was not an anti-diplomacy in the sense of an explicit rejection of the established system comparable to the revolutionary diplomacy advocated by ideologues.

Moreover, summit diplomacy was in part prepared by conventional diplomats and, indeed, provided them with a greatly expanded sphere for activities, not least because jet travel made it easier to recall envoys in order to seek their advice on policy.⁶¹ In addition, summit diplomacy did not bring to an end the significance of the regular efforts of the diplomats. For example, Lords Lothian and Halifax proved effective British wartime envoys in Washington during the Second World War.⁶² Nevertheless, summit diplomacy was a major change from conventional practices in that it saw a power-broking to which these conventional practices were at best subordinate and, more commonly, irrelevant.

Thus the diplomat as an intermediary who played a key role in shaping the development of relations was less central than in the nineteenth century, and this factor looked toward the present situation. In pursuing their policies, leaders received diplomatic advice on the views of others and on how best to pursue interests, but this advice was but part of a wide range of such material. In particular, it was increasingly complemented by Intelligence advice, as well as constrained by the need to accord with ideological and political assumptions. Thus summit diplomacy in part represented an attempt to advance the domestic perspective more directly, if not forcefully, and was a rejection of the idea of diplomacy as a means of compromise grounded in a professional understanding of (and often sympathy for) other points of view.

It is unclear how far this rejection of the ethos of compromise was related to the failures of individual summits. Nor is it apparent that Stalin's paranoid dictatorship left room for any alternative for Soviet diplomacy to that of personal direction by the leader. Maxim Litvinov (1876–1951), who had headed the Commissariat for Foreign Affairs in the 1930s before being dismissed in 1939 as an aspect of the *rapprochement* with Germany, was in part reinstated in 1941, becoming envoy to the USA that December. However, his replacement as Foreign Minister, Molotov, was a pliant vehicle for Stalin's views, which were focused on a distrust of the West. The net result was a hostility that helped create, and then entrench, the Cold

War that lasted until the collapse of the Warsaw Pact in 1989.

As with the conclusion at the end of the previous chapter, it is clear that diplomacy as the activity of diplomats should not take the blame for failings in international relations that were at once systemic, political and ideological. For both the Soviet Union and the USA, habits respectively strengthened and developed during the Second World War were extrapolated into the antagonisms of the Cold War. The traditional diplomats' goal of finding common understanding meant little in terms of the clarities of ideological confrontation. Joseph E. Davies, who had served as American envoy to Moscow, producing a sympathetic book, *Mission to Moscow* (1943), that was turned, at the behest of the Office of War Information, into a propaganda film designed to promote American–Soviet relations, *Mission to Moscow* (1943), was now rejected in the USA as a dupe. Several of those involved in making the film were in trouble during the post-war McCarthyite attack on real or supposed Communists.[63]

In the winter of 1941–2 Allied negotiators, taking forward the Atlantic Charter agreed by Churchill and Roosevelt in August 1941, had drawn up a statement of war aims called the United Nations Declaration. This agreement for joint-support was the first official use of the term United Nations. The Declaration was signed by the leading Allied powers and in due course by other Allied nations. The United Nations Conference on International Organisation, held in San Francisco in April-June 1945, was the inaugural meeting of the United Nations (UN). Attended by delegates from fifty Allied states, the conference agreed a United Nations Security Charter. The Security Council, the executive of the UN, was to consist of five permanent (USA, Soviet Union, Britain, France and China) and six temporary members: its first meeting was held in London on 17 January 1946. The San Francisco conference, however, also indicated serious tensions within the alliance, notably between the USA and the Soviet Union.

Representation proved a serious problem, with the USA unwilling to accept the Soviet claim that the Moscow-supported Polish government was independent. The Polish seat was left vacant. There was also controversy over the membership of Franco's Spain. Most Latin American states wanted Spain expelled, as did the Communist states, but the USA proved a support, particularly as the Cold War gathered pace. As UN membership increased, the USA was able to find more support for its case. Spain was excluded from most other international bodies, including the Council of Europe, NATO and the European Economic Community, until after democracy was re-established there.

Such problems were to occur throughout the post-war Cold War, and they helped ensure a series of failures for the United Nations: while, moreover, the idea that the International Court of Justice could use international law to ensure harmonious international relations was not realized. Hopes of an end to the traditional politics of aggression, and the customary deterrence through competing alliance system, proved abortive. In practice, however, there were successes, not least in the development and use of economic sanctions and arms-control diplomacy, as well as failures, although the UN's critics have tended to ignore the former.

Furthermore, the UN did no worse in preventing conflict than older systems of collective security. Such systems have hitherto worked, if at all, largely as short-term palliatives, serving the ends of particular leaders and states and only proving effective as far as they could do so. In the 1810s Viscount Castlereagh, the British Foreign Secretary, and Alexander I of Russia had both been aware of the limits of collective action, and this was also true of Woodrow Wilson at the Versailles peace talks in 1919. He argued that it was likely to be a long time before the League of Nations could begin to make much difference. The UN, like the League, moreover, proved a way for the integration of newly independent states into the international system; indeed offering an important alternative to the standard process of recognition and relevance via bilateral representation.

The UN was not alone as part of the architecture of a new post-war international order in which agreements and institutions were to manage interests and issues. Thus, providing institutional cohesion to earlier ad hoc attempts to manage international financial relations, the General Agreement on Tariffs and Trade (GATT) and the World Bank, both launched in 1944, were intended to revive and sustain a global economy and financial system that was seen as the underpinning of peace.[64] From the outset, however, this process failed to fulfil hopes, with, for example, the projected permanent International Trade Organization failing at the political hurdle, although the World Trade Organization was to be a sequel.[65]

As part of the replacement of the old international order, there were moves against Western imperialism. In 1943 Britain and the USA ended the system of extra-territorial treaty ports in China, while the principle of national self-determination was pushed to the fore in discussion of the colonial future, albeit with the general assumption that individual colonies equated with distinct nations, and should thus become states without territorial changes and the consent that might be necessary to legitimate such a process.

The UN as an alternative to the standard process of diplomatic recognition and relevance also entailed the willingness of international bodies to take an interest in national liberation struggles, in short in the process of dissolution of empire. Indeed, anti-colonial movements, such as the Indonesians opposing the return of Dutch colonial rule in the late 1940s, deliberately sought to win the support of the UN in order to collapse the distinction between international and internal conflicts and law. Self-determination was a key goal as far as both the rebels and the UN were concerned. This process of winning UN support was opposed by the colonial powers, although it became more pronounced as the General Assembly became larger and less dominated by the Security Council.

A major departure in scale for the diplomatic efforts of anti-colonial movements was the achievement of the Algerian National Liberation Front (FLN), which secured much international support. Founded in 1952, the FLN created a foreign service, with bureaus in Cairo, Damascus, Tunis, Beirut, Baghdad, Karachi, Djakarta and New York; from the last, the FLN pursued links with the UN, the media and the State Department. Other delegations moved between capital cities and international bodies such as UNESCO. Pressure was put on the UN by the recognition of the FLN provisional government by states including China, Czechoslovakia and East Germany. Such recognition was linked to the 'hard diplomacy' through which the FLN obtained money, arms and other assistance from sympathetic states. Involving terrorism, counter-insurgency warfare, and the complex interplay between events in Algeria and wider international developments, the struggle also offered a template for many of the issues seen during de-colonization. Within Algeria, an autonomous role was taken by the FLN's military leadership, which underlines the problems of thinking of international actors in terms of homogenous units.

The internationalization of the Algerian conflict had a major impact on France, the colonial power. The ability of the FLN to keep itself in the forefront of attention ensured that France could not define the war, and this contributed to the important move of the American government toward an acceptance that Algeria would become independent, and thus a determination to ensure that it did so with minimum disruption as the latter was seen as likely to provide opportunities for the Soviet Union. Ironically, looking toward the diplomacy of the 2000s, and the French reluctance to accept American views in the 'War on Terror', France's allies were unconvinced that her struggle against the FLN was a key defence of the West. The Americans had also been influenced in their response to the Indonesian question in 1948 by UN attitudes, although other factors, including the Dutch failure to suppress opposition, played a role. The FLN eventually became a negotiating partner of France. Initially, there was little dialogue, but high-level talks began in 1960 leading to a definitive cease-fire in 1962. Algeria became independent that year.

The FLN led the way for other movements, notably setting a model for the Palestinian Liberation Organization (founded in 1964) in its challenge to Israel.[66] National liberation movements, however, did not need to look to the FLN for a model, not least as their diplomatic requirements were relatively clear. Thus in the Vietnam War the Communist National Liberation Front (NLF) sought to present itself as the true and therefore legitimate representative of the South Vietnamese people and to maintain the backing of both China and the Soviet Union despite the growing rift between them. The NLF also manoeuvred to weaken its opponents, not least by exploiting tension between the USA and South Vietnam. Thus diplomacy was an aspect of the revolution, which was unsurprising given the military context as well as the belief that revolutionary struggle was a constant in history.[67]

These notions, which continued Soviet and Chinese ideas of foreign policy and diplomacy, took forward the ideological approach seen with the French Revolution, rather as the idea of a revolutionary 'people in arms' took forward another aspect of that legacy. Compromise clearly was only to be on the agenda as a means to forward the goal of victory, which indeed turned out to be the case in 1972–5 as American disengagement, and the assumptions and terms on which it had been obtained, was transformed instead into the overthrow of South Vietnam.

At the same time as the international system responded to national liberation movements and new states, it was placed under significant challenge from the increase in the growing number of independent states, and their willingness to pursue their interests through conflict. In addition, the growing number of independent states meant the need for outside powers to appoint more envoys. Thus, whereas in Africa Britain had had missions in Egypt, Abyssinia and South Africa in the early years of the twentieth century, as well as a consulate in Monrovia, the capital of Liberia, from 1902, in the 1960s the Foreign Office established a West and General Africa Department. By 1993 there were British missions in more than fifty African states under the specialist area desks in the Africa Department (Equatorial), the Central and Southern Africa Department, and the Near East and North Africa Department. Careers were transformed with more fundamental changes in the institutional structure, notably as the Colonial Office was merged with the Commonwealth Relations Office, leading to a Commonwealth Office that merged with, and in effect was subsumed into, the Foreign Office. In some cases, political agents became envoys. Thus with Kuwait's independence in 1961, Sir John Richmond became envoy. Moreover, men with a background in the Indian Civil Service, such as Ian Scott, became diplomats.[68]

While diplomatic systems spread, representation also reflected existing social and ethnic norms. Thus in the USA, despite the civil rights movement and interest by African Americans in international affairs,[69] few were accepted into the Foreign Service, and those who were tended to receive lower-level positions.[70] This situation may have affected the governmental ability to understand the nature and consequences of American policy in Africa. In contrast, African Americans played a more conspicuous role in the Foreign Service from the late 1970s with Andrew Young, a congressman, serving as representative to the UN from 1977 to 1979, when he was obliged to resign after it became known that he had met secretly with members of the PLO. The following decade Edward Perkins, a career Foreign Service officer, became the first African American to be American envoy to South Africa and the first to become Director General of the Foreign Service. He played an important role in helping to exert American pressure for a peaceful end to apartheid.[71] Anti-apartheid activists in the USA, notably TransAfrica and the Free South Africa Movement, also played an important part; and they helped mobilize support for the Comprehensive Anti-Apartheid Act of 1986, which introduced a serious sanctions regime.[72]

The major transition in the international system after the Second World War was from empires to numerous independent states, although the Soviet empire did not collapse until the early 1990s. As in Latin America after the collapse of the Spanish empire, there were attempts to create larger entities, notably those resting on the idea of Pan-Arabism, for example the United Arab Republic of Egypt and Syria in 1958–61,[73] but these proved unsuccessful. This failure rested on incompatibilities that led to a subsequent need for diplomacy as, following their failures, alliances were pursued in a competitive context, or at best as relations were redefined. In contrast, greater success in supra-national integration was to be achieved in both Western and Eastern Europe. Other failures included those of ideas for an Indo-China Federation among former French colonies, and for a Central African Federation and for Caribbean integration, also among former British colonies, while in addition Singapore left the newly established federal state of Malaysia.[74]

Just as earlier in Latin America, the end of imperial rule was followed by clashes between former territories, for example between Morocco and Algeria on their frontier in 1962–3, or between Tanzania and Uganda in the 1970s, or arising from the absence of a hegemonic power. Moreover, issues that could have been handled by empires without war were the cause of conflict, as in 1977 when Egypt mounted an attack on Libya in order to indicate its anger with Libyan pretensions and policies under its quixotic and interventionist dictator Colonel Muammar al-Gaddafi: such an attack would not have occurred when Egypt was within the British system and Libya an Italian colony unless, as with the Italian attack in 1940, in pursuit of more general imperial issues.

This greater propensity to conflict created serious problems for diplomacy, both the diplomacy of the states in question and that of allies and would-be mediators, including former imperial powers.[75] Thus, for example, the process by which the colony of British Honduras eventually became the independent state of Belize in 1981 was complicated and delayed by the major territorial claim from Guatemala, which in turn brought up other international complications.[76] Moreover, these problems were accentuated by the general absence of practices of accommodation and of detailed knowledge of the views of both sides on particular issues in dispute.

There was also the problem posed by the limited extent to which new states had well-grounded practices of diplomatic activity. In particular, the sense that contentious issues of foreign policy should be handled by diplomats as part of a distinct, not to say autonomous, process of diplomacy had scant traction in many states. Thus the situation deplored by Bland at the outset of this chapter was matched across much of the world in a context of new-build. The architecture of foreign policy could be as much military as diplomatic, and direction by the ruler was generally paramount.

If these characteristics of a move from diplomats affected representation and negotiation, they also played a role in the acquisition of information. Here diplomats were affected by shifts in technology, notably enhanced surveillance from the air, by aircraft and even satellites, as well as through SIGNIT or signals interception. Such information was fed directly to governments, rather than coming through agents in foreign countries.

Yet of equal significance in representation, negotiation and information-acquisition was the extent to which diplomats were no longer the prime members of national communities abroad. Instead, large – or compared to earlier circumstances, relatively large – numbers of individuals travelled, notably for business, and were able to provide information and press for specific policies. This was a two-way process, as foreign states could also obtain information by these methods.

All diplomatic systems are in flux. Indeed, as they register shifts in power, interest and policy, their task is to understand and respond to flux. Nevertheless, the situation in 1900–70 was particularly in flux and was seen as such by the diplomats of the period. The focus was on global conflict and confrontation, and notably on the challenge posed by those who believed that these were normative. Yet in the long term it was the marked rise in the number of states that constituted the greatest problem, not least as it was accompanied by the failure of international and regional agencies to provide binding forums for the settlement of disputes.

This rise had a range of consequences, not least that of making agreement difficult in agencies that greatly expanded in size. As the European Union, the successor of the European Economic Community, swelled to 27 members by 2009 with the prospect of more accessions, notably Iceland, so the ratification of the Treaty of Lisbon by all the members opened the way for the new jobs of EU President and EU Foreign Minister, as well as for a Foreign Office for the EU with embassies around the world. Such a system seemed necessary not only to federalists but also to commentators concerned about the need for coherent representation.

Returning to the 1950–80s, if the co-operative mechanisms of the Council for Mutual Economic Assistance (COMECON) and the European Economic Community suggested that the situation was less bleak in post-1945 Europe than earlier, the stability of Eastern and Western Europe during the Cold War owed much not to diplomacy, but rather to the military hegemony of the Soviet Union and the USA respectively. Thus diplomacy adapted to power, although this context did not prevent lesser states from operating with considerable autonomy. In part, their success was a product of diplomatic skill, although this skill was not simply a matter of the formal processes of foreign policy. France and Romania were states that proved particularly adept in pursuing national strategies within supra-national contexts, in Western and Eastern Europe respectively.[77]

At the same time, the unresolved 'German Question' ensured that West and East Germany proved classic instances of the degree to which the Cold War for a long time limited diplomatic representation. Under the Hallstein Doctrine of 1955, West Germany claimed to represent all Germans, which was a challenge to the legitimacy of East Germany, and diplomatic relations were broken off with states that established them with East Germany.

The same limitation was true outside Europe. Due to the American recognition of the claims of the Taiwan-based Nationalist government of Jiang Jieshi (Chiang Kai-shek) to be the rightful government of China, there was no American recognition of the Communist regime of Beijing. In August 1949 the USA rejected Mao Zedong's terms for diplomatic recognition. Australia also did not recognize the Communist government. In contrast, Britain recognized the new regime in January 1950, although Chinese obduracy ensured that no envoys were exchanged for over four years.

There was no American representative in mainland China from the Communist seizure of power in 1949 to the establishment in 1973 of a Liaison Office. The Office was headed by David Bruce, an experienced senior diplomat who had been envoy in London from 1961 to 1969, a choice that reflected both the importance the Americans placed on the new mission and the symbolic message to that end that they wished to send.[78] This mission was to be headed by George H.W. Bush from 1974 to 1976, as part of a career that took him from a congressman in Texas (1966–70) to representative to the United Nations (1971–3) and Chairman of the Republican National Committee (1973–4), both under his fellow Republican colleague Nixon, and then, after Beijing, to Director of the CIA (1976–7), Vice-President (1981–9) and President (1989–93).

This career trajectory placed diplomatic office in a very different pattern to that in most European states. Although becoming President was scarcely typical, the role of presidential appointment to diplomatic posts was such that many American ambassadors were appointed from a non-diplomatic background. Thus William Donovan (1893–1959), a veteran of the First World War, became Assistant to the Attorney General (1925–9), served as an unofficial foreign observer for the government, ran the Office of Strategic Services (1942–5), the forerunner of the CIA, and served as Ambassador in Bangkok (1953–4). Donovan's career had included providing reports on the situation in Britain in 1940 that contradicted the defeatist dispatches sent by the isolationist Ambassador, Joseph Kennedy, a Boston businessman and politician who had become Ambassador in 1938.

Both Donovan and Bush served in the CIA, which was created under the National Security Act of 1947, and the role of Intelligence services in Cold War activity serves as a reminder of the problems of writing international history without devoting due attention to their activities and the perceptions that they inculcated. The KGB under both Beria (1938–53) and Andropov (1967–83) played a particularly important role in influencing Soviet foreign policy.

The major expansion of Intelligence services from the Second World War on underlined the importance of the information they provided; although just as it is mistaken to write of the State Department without considering the CIA,[79] so it is also important to consider other Intelligence services. For example, the Army Counter-Intelligence Corps was an important source of information and policy suggestions for the USA and the GRU for the Soviet Union.

Another militarized branch of diplomacy was provided by arms sales. These provided an incentive for relations, but were also a field in which other considerations could play a role, as in July 2009 when Britain blocked the sale of spare parts for Israel's Saar 4.5 gunships because they had been used in the recent military campaign against the Hamas presence in Gaza.

Confrontations, both those of the Cold War and subsequent others, encouraged a distrust of the diplomats of opposing powers. They were seen as hostile and as actively seeking to propagate subversion. Thus in 1948 Mao Zedong was distrustful of Angus War, the American Consul General.

Alongside the animosity between rivals that had to be managed, the Cold War also encouraged diplomacy as there was an active search for allies among the 'non-aligned' powers, as well as attempts to strengthen international blocs. Each policy posed problems, notably those of aligning the search for co-operation with the ideological suppositions of the particular bloc. Yet at the same time, the combination of the unprecedented number of sovereign states resulting from decolonization and the greater ease of communications stemming from the spread of jet aircraft ensured that this search was pressed forward with great vigour. Indeed, in terms of the extent of activity and the money spent on it, the Cold War was good for diplomacy. Diplomatic representation was increased. Many new embassies were opened and diplomacy became a much larger profession. This expansion posed organizational challenges, notably but not only for the new states. Sir Francis Rundall, the Chief Clerk at the British Foreign Office, wrote to John Addis, then Ambassador to Laos, telling him he would have to stay there for longer than he wanted, adding:

> Vientiane is, I agree, a post with an unpleasant climate, few amenities and a limited social life. But there are unfortunately many such places – some even more unpleasant and restricted – in places like the Persian Gulf and West Africa. . . . Nowadays reputations are made in the back-of-beyond and no longer in the comfortable but unimportant posts of Western Europe (with a few obvious exceptions). However, I wish that we did not keep having to open up Missions on the Equator.[80]

The ease of communications ensured that the spread of the diplomatic network was not the sole response. Instead there were plentiful visits by heads of state and ministers. These included the Third World, as when Crown Prince Faisal of Saudi Arabia visited the USA in 1953, having two meetings with President Eisenhower,[81] or when Eisenhower's Vice President, Richard Nixon, toured Latin America in 1958, a visit that also provided an opportunity for anti-American protests. This increase in activity by heads of state and ministers created problems in ensuring consistency, both within the representation of individual states and between allies.

It was not only the Western powers that faced problems in adjusting to the major changes in the international system. Under Stalin there was a reluctance to see other Communist powers as more than clients, and notably in the case of Asian states. Mao's China was a key recipient of this patronage and attempted direction, notably at the time of the Korean War (1950–53) which was ironic as Stalin's attitude represented a new version of the hegemonic culture of international relations (with its diplomacy of deference) earlier associated with Imperial China. There was also a disdain for Third World movements unless they corresponded with Soviet suppositions. Instead, their leaders were seen as bourgeois nationalists.

This tendency remained after Stalin's death in 1953, but it was challenged in 1955. The establishment that year, with the Bandung Conference held in Indonesia, of the Non-Aligned Movement was seen by the Soviets as providing an opportunity to break free of what they regarded as encirclement by the West. Specific opportunities were also grasped.

In 1956, moreover, Stalin's Foreign Minister, Molotov, was replaced by Dmitrii Shepilov: he was sent to be envoy in Mongolia, an instance of diplomacy as a form of political exile. Shepilov had played a key role in the opening up toward Egypt in 1955 and symbolized the increased Soviet interest in the Third World. However, in 1957 Shepilov was replaced by Andrey Gromyko, who was to hold the post until 1985, when he became President. Gromyko was an expert on relations with the USA where he served at Washington from 1939, before becoming delegate to the United Nations from 1946 to 1949.

Under Gromyko, Soviet diplomacy was nearly as rigid as he was unsmiling. Certainly, there was no bold initiative comparable to the American approach to China under President Nixon, which itself was a product of the degree to which the Soviet geopolitical and diplomatic position had been compromised by the Sino-Soviet split. The latter was not the responsibility of the Soviet diplomatic system, and it revealed how far foreign policy was scarcely under the control of the latter. Instead, diplomats were expected to respond to policies determined from a wider spectrum of office-holders. Party unity reinforced institutional conformity, with the General Secretary of the Communist Party determining policy on what were presented as Party lines. Conformity and cohesion as prime values ensured that information as prepared, presented and analysed accordingly.

There were alternative sources of information, notably regional institutes associated with the Soviet Academy of Sciences that were established for Latin America (1961), Africa (1962), Asia (1966), and North America (1967). However, although they had access to information about the outside world, their ability to influence the decision-making process was limited.[82] There was no equivalent in the Soviet Union to the often politicized and frequently open debate about policy options seen in the USA, nor to the alternation of power between the political parties. Alongside the hypocrisies in American approaches to international affairs,[83] the Cold War thus saw a significant qualitative difference between the diplomatic systems in the two states, and one very much in favour of the USA.

The Cold War placed considerable strain on diplomatic relations between the powers, while also leading to diplomatic activity in order to strengthen the respective blocs. The latter, for example, entailed collaborative military planning that was not limited to the formal multinational structures such as NATO. Thus the USA and Canada developed their security arrangements as the USA sought defensive depth against Soviet attacks across the North Pole.

Relations between the competing blocs also encouraged a search for solutions that was not without value. In part there was a reaffirmation of diplomatic procedures, with international codification in the Vienna Convention on Diplomatic Relations in 1961 and the Vienna Convention on Consular Relations two years later. There was also the diplomacy of summitry.

Alongside summitry, there was a reliance on other, more characteristic, diplomatic solutions. The choice of envoys was seen as sending particular signals. Thus the appointment in 1968 by Harold Wilson's Labour government of Christopher Soames, a prominent pro-European Conservative, as British Ambassador to Paris was designed to show that there was now a consensus, at least among the political leadership, in favour of joining the European Economic Community.

Diplomatic services adapted from the exigencies of the Second World War to those of the Cold War. For the neutrals in the former, such as Spain and the Vatican, the process of transition was not always easy, although anti-Communism provided an opportunity to integrate into a potent alignment. Some states, for example Ireland and Sweden, maintained a neutral position, while others, notably Austria and Finland, found new neutral roles forced on them by the post-war peace settlement, at the same time that they manoeuvred to increase their practical independence.[84]

Such manoeuvring was also seen in the competing blocs of the Cold War because the allies of both the USA and the Soviet Union were able to play independent or autonomous roles. These roles, moreover, affected the overall struggle, while also leaving considerable room for diplomacy as a means both to strengthen the blocs and also to try to direct their policies.[85]

Consideration of the neutrals serves as a reminder of the large number of different players involved in international diplomacy. This number could be increased if due weight is given to the determination of other groups to play a role not only within or alongside sovereign states and international bodies, but also in a deliberate contrast to them. The anti-colonial national liberation movements already referred to offered an instance that could be fitted into a tradition of such activity looking back to the American Revolution.

The development of transnational radicalism in the West in the 1960s drew on a different strand of activity, although these radicals sought a presence with non-Western states, notably Cuba, and movements, particularly the Palestine Liberation Organization, which was founded in 1964. Radicals in different countries attempted to ensure links in what they saw as a common struggle against capitalism and American imperialism.

If this attempt possibly pushed definitions of diplomacy too far, the diplomats of Communist China during the Great Proletarian Cultural Revolution, with their abrupt and striking attack on diplomatic norms, an attack matched in the treatment of Western diplomats and embassies in China, amply indicated the range of diplomatic conduct. Chinese envoys were recalled from across the world, while the British compound in Beijing was broken into in August 1967 and the embassy burned and looted. Earlier, the Soviet, Czech and East German embassies had been attacked, a blunt product of the Sino-Soviet split.[86]

Less prominently, there were parallel actions by Third World States hostile to the West. Under Gamal Abd al-Nasser, the dictatorial President of Egypt from 1954 until his death in 1970, pan-Arabism, the patronage of anti-Western liberation movements, notably in Algeria, and links with the Soviet Union, were matched to hostility to Britain, the former colonial power, and the USA. Diplomatic relations with both were broken off in 1967, on the basis of the false claim that they had joined Israel in attacking Egypt, Nasser's way of explaining defeat at the hands of Israel; while in a symbolic step that focused on the importance of cultural relations, the American Library in Cairo was burned in 1964.

To adopt a very different approach, the range of conduct in the field of diplomacy was taken further in the field of fiction, especially in the treatment of relations with aliens in terms other than those of automatic conflict. Television series and films such as *Star Trek* and *Star Wars* offered a number of different alien societies with their own goals and practices as well as a variety of co-operative international organizations at the stellar level, notably the Federation, which was the key organization in *Star Trek*. Both space for agreement and opportunities for conflict were portrayed.

In the American film *Mars Attacks* (1997), the presidential science adviser explained, on more than one occasion, that the approaching Martians were bound to be peaceful because no advanced culture would wage war. This view was in keeping with a progressive account of diplomacy, one that presented it as an aspect of the improvability of society, if not mankind. The latter had led to calls for the rationalism of the balance of power in the eighteenth century, for open diplomacy in the 1790s, and for international law and institutions, disarmament and human rights from the early twentieth.

Yet the notion that advanced civilizations of great potency might dispense with war was not one that frequently engaged the imaginative attention of humans in the twentieth century. In H. G. Wells' novel *The War of the Worlds* (1897) the Martians destroy London and overcome resistance until they are destroyed by bacteria. Orson Welles' radio adaptation of 1938 caused panic when he transposed the story to the USA. In many Hollywood films, including *Mars Attacks*, the bellicosity of advanced aliens was different to those of rampaging Tyrannosaurs Rexes only in their cold deliberation and planned determination.

However pessimistic this visual account, ideas of the most appropriate treatment of other human societies were much less bleak. Planning for nuclear war, with all the possibilities this suggested of the destruction of human society, represented not a goal, but a deterrent to aggression. Indeed, concern about the nuclearization of West Germany by the USA was a major factor in Soviet thought in the 1950s, while the Soviet refusal to fulfil promises to make China a nuclear power, or to make its own nuclear weapons available to serve Chinese goals, helped provoke the Sino-Soviet rift at the end of the decade. Moreover, anxiety about the possibility of MAD (Mutually Assured Destruction), of nuclear destruction as a result of war, helped encourage a major increase in the pace of great-power diplomacy in the 1970s and 1980s; and this diplomacy played a key role in the end of the Cold War.

It is striking how far this diplomacy was not necessarily pursued through foreign ministries and their diplomats, and this point needs underlining when considering the extent to which aspects of public politics, including NGOs, challenged the established pattern of diplomacy after the Cold War (see p. 211). While that view is not without merit, it needs to be stressed that this pattern was already one in which foreign ministries were frequently circumvented.

Thus during the Nixon presidency (1969–74), the State Department, under William Rogers, found itself undercut by the White House combination of Nixon and his talented, ambitious and influential Assistant for National Security Affairs, Henry Kissinger. Both men favoured 'back-channel' communications, not least with Anatoly Dobrynin, the Soviet envoy, who held regular meetings with Kissinger. The latter also had special communication channels to Egon Bahr, the West German State Secretary, as well as to the American envoys to Pakistan, South Vietnam, and to the Vietnam peace negotiations. Moreover, in 1971 the arrangements for Kissinger's first visit to China were made independently of the State Department.[87]

Such activity serves as a reminder of the problems of treating diplomacy in terms of bureaucratic forms, and this point underlines the continuing extent to which diplomacy represented a tension between form and substance. The form of established mechanisms had, and has, value, but it has never been the complete story, and any attempt to discuss diplomacy in terms of the development of resident diplomats administered through a foreign ministry is necessarily limited. As a consequence, it is inappropriate to treat such a system as the perfect type of diplomatic activity.

SEVEN
1970 to the Present

Any account of recent decades is particularly shot through with the problem of anachronism. A trend that appears readily apparent at one moment seems less secure a year later, while it is not always clear how best to distinguish between competing interpretations. A propensity to offer slogans is another challenge, while it cannot be said that contributions by political scientists has necessarily been helpful other than in providing theses, such as Francis Fukuyama's 'End of History' and Samuel Huntington's 'Clash of Civilisations', that require qualification.[1] Neither concept in fact was new, that of the clash of civilizations being employed frequently: as, for example, by both sides during the Algerian independence struggle against French rule in 1954–62.

The basis pattern for this period appears to be that of *détente* between the USA and first China and then the Soviet Union, followed, after a short-lived American–Soviet Second Cold War in the early 1980s, by the collapse of the Soviet bloc in 1989–91. This collapse led to the diplomatic version of globalization, a global homogeneity of diplomatic order and method. However, this system was confronted by the rise of NGOs (non-governmental organizations), whether international charities, financial and economic conglomerates, or terrorist groups.

The diplomatic situation had been eased by the gradual winding down of Cold War tensions, a crucial development in international relations, albeit one that looks less secure in terms of the issues of the late 2000s. Diplomacy was a central means in this winding down, but the key impetus was political, namely the coming to power in West Germany in 1969 of a Social Democrat-Free Democrat coalition under Willy Brandt. In its *Ostpolitik*, the new government sought a more benign relationship with Eastern Europe, one that would bring stability and also enable West Germany to take a more central role in Europe. Under the previous Christian Democratic Party-dominated governments of the 1950s and 1960s, there had been a refusal to consider *détente* with the East until both the division of Germany and frontier disputes with Poland had been addressed; but this policy had failed to deliver results.

Ostpolitik instead reflected a degree of assertion based on West German economic recovery and political stability, as well as a rejection of the nostrums of the previous generation. *Ostpolitik* was also a key instance of a recurring, but not invariable, European preference for diplomacy, possibly as the means of influence for weaker powers, diplomacy, moreover, serving as a political alternative to the military logic of the arms race. This strategy reached its height with *détente* and the Helsinki Accords, while in the final stages of the Cold War the Americans took the strategy over. This process invites the question whether a similar transition will eventually be seen in other disputes.

American attitudes were also very important over *Ostpolitik*, which serves as a reminder that those states not formally conducting the diplomatic process could nevertheless play a key role. Concerned about East Asia, and forced by its weakened circumstances to accept change, the American government at the time of the Vietnam War was unwilling to focus on its former goal of German reunification. In contrast, President Nixon was willing to accept *Ostpolitik* as a means for stabilization in Europe, while, as a key aspect of diplomacy within the alliance, the West German government took pains to ensure that American support was retained during the negotiations.

In part, this end was ensured by limiting the consequences of *Ostpolitik*. Whereas in 1970 West Germany signed treaties with the Soviet Union and Poland, recognising the existing borders, the attempt by some West German commentators to suggest a shift in alignments and the rediscovery of an 'Eastern vocation' for West Germany got nowhere. West Germany, crucially, was not to be neutralized like Austria and Finland.

The diplomatic context in the Soviet Union was evidence of the extent to which *détente* appealed to different constituencies. Stability in Europe was seen by the Soviet government as helping ensure a stronger position from which to confront China, while there was interest in cutting defence costs and importing Western technology. Interest in stability was shown in 1971 in Leonid Brezhnev's speech to the Party Congress when he called for international security and devoted scant space to the cause of 'national liberation', the argument used to justify support for anti-Western struggles in the Third World. West German recognition of East Germany led to a sober, measured *rapprochement* and a resumption of relations between the two states.

The entire issue indicated some of the ambiguities of foreign relations, ambiguities frequently misapplied by critics to diplomats and their methods. For example, as part of the new German–German community of responsibility, concern within West Germany about the plight of East Germans, let alone backing for reunification, markedly declined, and, partly as a consequence, there was no real West German support for the citizens' rights movements in East Germany. Instead, stabilization was more significant as a goal.

The easing of relations as a result of successful diplomacy thus entailed an acceptance of the governing system in Eastern Europe, for example of the suppression of Czech liberal Communism, the Czech Spring of 1968, by the military of the Soviet Union and its allies, including East Germany. East Germany, recognized for the first time as a state by much of the world in 1973, was admitted to the United Nations and other international bodies. 'Normalization' also meant recognizing the legality of a totalitarian state that treated its citizens harshly, while an aspect of the secret diplomacy of the period was payments by the West German government in return for people being allowed to leave East Germany, many for family reunification.

The West Germans were not alone in compromising. The Papacy had had terrible relations with the atheistically and anti-clerical Communist governments, but it also pursued an *Ostpolitik*, notably, in 1966, the dispatch of an apostolic delegate and envoy to Yugoslavia, a post later upgraded to a nunciate, the first to any Communist government.

The easing of relations was also an aspect of a growing conservatism in the Soviet bloc, which underlined the particular centrality of political considerations in the diplomacy of totalitarian states, notably because the institutional autonomy of foreign policy and diplomacy was especially limited in such a context. There was a rejection of the adventurism associated with Nikita Khrushchev, who had fallen from power in the Soviet Union in 1964. His replacement as General Secretary of the Communist Party by the more complacent Brezhnev was significant. 'Peaceful co-existence' with the West was declared a form of class struggle, which was certainly squaring the circle, and anti-Western propaganda was reduced. The West German ambition of 'change by closer relations' proved more successful than this goal, but only in the long term; while in the short term the Western aid provided under *Ostpolitik* stabilized the Communist regimes without bringing much liberalization.

The Helsinki Accords of 1975 were a key episode. Produced by the Conference on Security and Co-operation in Europe, they represented a success for the European-wide process of stabilization that also owed much to American support for *détente*. The text of the Accords reflected the issues confronting diplomacy as well as the difficulties of reconciling liberalism and totalitarianism. Existing borders were accepted (Principle III), as was non-intervention in the internal affairs of other states (Principle

VI), thus meeting Soviet objectives. Although linked, in Principle VII, to remarks about human rights and fundamental liberties, the Soviet Union was sufficiently adept in preaching rights while practicing autocracy for this to appear to pose no problem. There were also agreements to cooperate in trade, industry, science, the environment, and cultural and educational matters.

Yet *détente* scarcely described the situation in large parts of the Third World in the 1970s, notably much of Africa, which is a reminder of the complexity and intensity of the Cold War, of the interaction of local and global tensions, and of the extent to which chronologies did not coincide. For example, the Soviet willingness to overlook the reign of terror of Haile Mengistu, the dictator of Ethiopia from 1977 to 1991, indicated the degree to which the attitudes associated with Stalinism continued thereafter. As a reminder of the longstanding tendency for diplomats (and others) to interpret developments in terms of the history of their own countries, the Soviet envoy, Anatolii Ratanov, saw a similarity between the brutal activities of Mengistu's supporters within the Derg and the early revolutionary experience in Russia. Moreover, from the mid-1960s it was clear to Moscow and Washington that the focus for Cold War competition in Africa was shifting to southern Africa, in part because of the Marxist orientation of many of the liberation movements. Far from being marginal, success in Africa in the 1970s gave many Soviets a renewed sense of pride in their own achievements, and a conviction that the Soviet Union could contribute decisively to breakthroughs for Communism elsewhere.

In practice, however, Africa was to disappoint the Soviets, as were Iran and Afghanistan. The Soviets did not win the anticipated benefits, and opposition to the USA did not necessarily extend to support for the Soviet Union. Two days after the Soviet invasion of Afghanistan in December 1979, the Soviet envoy in Iran promised Ayatollah Khomeini, the leader of the Islamic Revolution there, assistance in any conflict with the USA, only to be told that there could be no mutual understanding between a Muslim nation and a non-Muslim government.[2]

The Soviet military intervention in Afghanistan in 1979 was a key episode in the hotting up of the Cold War,[3] as was the Soviet-backed suppression of the liberal Solidarity movement in Poland in 1981. In turn, the Soviets were convinced that they were subject to American plans for attack. Information to that end was carefully collated, while contradictory material was ignored. The KGB played a key role in the supply of information, and the influence of Yurij Andropov, its head from 1967 until he succeeded Brezhnev as General Secretary of the Communist Party in 1982, was such that KGB views were highly influential. In contrast, the Foreign Ministry was very much a secondary source for information and policy ideas. The relative weight of the KGB and the Foreign Ministry was more generally true of totalitarian states, and encouraged the systematic feed of information on foreign states from the international network of KGB agents.

The sickly Andropov died in 1984, to be replaced by the elderly Konstantin Chernenko, who himself died in 1985. His replacement, the far younger Mikhail Gorbachev, sought to reform the Soviet Union and to that end transformed foreign policy, again indicating the subordination of diplomacy to politics. Although a one-time protégé of Andropov, Gorbachev was also willing to challenge the confrontational world-view outlined in KGB reports, as well as the vested interests of the military-industrial complex. For example, Gorbachev was convinced that American policy on arms control was not motivated by a hidden agenda of weakening the Soviet Union, and this view encouraged him to negotiate.

The architecture of the Cold War was steadily dismantled with agreements, from 1987, on arms control. There was also a new context for diplomacy in the Communist bloc. Visiting Prague in 1987, Gorbachev repudiated the Brezhnev Doctrine of intervention in order to uphold Communism, claiming instead that 'fraternal parties determine their political line with a view to national conditions'. In 1988 he announced, significantly at the United Nations, that Eastern European states should be free to choose their own political path.

The subsequent collapse of Communism in Eastern Europe, followed by that of the Soviet Union, created new contexts for diplomacy. Thus in December 1991 a Commonwealth of Independent States (CIS) replaced the Soviet Union, although several republics refused to join the latter, while the hope of Russia's Boris Yeltsin, President from 1991 to the close of 1999, that the CIS would become a truly federal system proved abortive.

The fall of Communism encouraged debate within Russia about diplomacy, as well as the liberalism of the new Ministry of Foreign Affairs. However, in a reminder of the habitual pressures affecting diplomacy, there was pressure from other agencies interested in foreign policy, notably the Ministry of Defence, the Presidential Security Council, the Intelligence Agencies, and the Defence and International Relations Committees of Parliament. Authoritarianism and intransigence as characteristics of Russian foreign policy became more pronounced with the Putin years. A former KGB operative, Putin was President from 2000 until 2008.

The Putin years also led to a revival in realist discussion of international relations at the same time that much of the debate in the West was about idealist concepts, 'soft power', international law, and international non-governmental organizations or INGOs, bodies frequently referred to as NGOs. The use of 'soft power' was not restricted to the West, but there was a long-term tension between what was allowed by liberal Western states and the more controlling attitudes of many non-Western powers, including Russia and China. It was indicative of general attitudes that in 1949, as part of an extension of its control in Eastern Europe, the Soviet Union had pressed for the closure of all Western culture and information centres. In the 2000s the tendency to treat such bodies as hostile, for example the BBC and the British Council, a tendency shown by states as varied as Iran, Russia and Zimbabwe, reflected a continuing sense that all foreign institutions were directly under state control, and that NGOs were indeed important, as well as threatening. This issue was a prime instance of the degree to which the nature and conduct of diplomacy remained vexed.

As an instance of the nature of the diplomatic presence within not a NGO, but a related agency, it is instructive to look at the Board of Directors of the United States Institute of Peace which was created by Congress in 1984 as an independent, non-partisan, federal institution to strengthen the nation's capacity to promote the peaceful resolution of international conflict by expanding knowledge about ways to achieve a more peaceful world. The Board of Directors included eleven presidential appointees, mostly academics, and four ex officio members from government, of whom, in 1991, one was an Assistant Secretary of State: for Human Rights and Humanitarian Affairs. In 2009 the Board had three former members of the State Department, one a career diplomat and two Assistant Secretaries, and thus political appointments.

In the context of assertive NGOs, it was not surprising that realist interpretations of national interest and international due-process were challenged by the development of new or newly powerful idealistic codes, notably on environmental matters and human rights. Each illustrated the resilience of the aspiration for international law that had been so strong in the 1900s, but more generally of cultural and ideological approaches to international relations.

At the same time, much of the thrust behind this development came from international lawyers encouraged by human rights groups such as the London-based Amnesty International and the New York-based Human Rights Watch; and there was less of an integration with the foreign policy establishments than there had been in the 1900s and 1920s. Violations against human rights were pursued through the European Court of Human Rights or with regard to the Declaration of Human Rights passed by the UN General Assembly in 1948 and complemented in 1976 by an international covenant on social, economic cultural rights and also by one on civil and political rights. In 2005 a gathering of world leaders at a UN summit agreed that there was a general 'responsibility to protect' humans from genocide, ethnic cleansing, war crimes, and crimes against humanity: a concept known as R2P that, however, has subsequently been criticized as constraining the sovereignty of states at the behest of a Western world-order.[4]

As the agenda of international relations changed, at least in part under the pressure from the new idealistic codes, diplomacy struggled to keep up, with diplomats obliged to learn more of particular issues and their related 'languages'. The changes could be radical, as when Anglo-Chilean relations were greatly affected in 1998 by the presentation, on behalf of Baltasar Garzón, a Spanish magistrate, of a writ for the arrest and extradition for trial on human rights offences of a former Chilean head of state, General Augusto Pinochet, then visiting Britain for health reasons. Pinochet was arrested and put under house arrest for sixteen months, although he was not extradited to Spain.

As I know from personal conversations, such practices horrified diplomats used to realist concepts of international relations and to diplomacy as a means not only for the pursuit of state interests but also for the reconciliation of different national views. For them, the profession has changed dramatically in their time and is still evolving.

In part, there is the question of the psychology of diplomacy. Diplomats tend to develop distinctive psychological relationships with an identity of their state, both taking on a 'selfhood' accordingly and acting as a psychological agent of the state. This process, however, makes their 'selfhood' vulnerable not only to fate or their mission, but also to the changing place of diplomacy.[5]

Aside from that psychological dimension, there is the question of the stress caused by the disruption of established systems of diplomatic communication and symbolic interaction. A mutual understanding of these systems is important to communication and analysis,[6] but this understanding is challenged by changes in the content and significance of gestures and language; and frequently deliberately so. In part, this process represents a disruption of existing hierarchies of prestige, hierarchies that are sustained by the creation of an image of pre-eminence, competence and success.[7]

Yet it would be foolish to overplay the challenge from the NGOs because that risks implying that 'government' otherwise offers a coherence that has the answers, or, alternatively, poses the problems. The reality, instead, is that government involves serious contention between often contradictory interests. Far from foreign policy and diplomacy being in some respect protected from this contention, the inability of the official foreign policy mechanisms to control representation and negotiations with foreign states is far more apparent today than was the case a century ago, and the situation has become more pronounced in recent decades.

The issue is one of control as well as representation. The Senate's rejection of membership of the League of Nations shows that this factor is scarcely new for the world's leading state, and the continuing need to seek Congressional authority for appropriations and treaties is a key element affecting American diplomacy. Thus in 1974 American support for *détente* with the Soviet Union was affected by pressure on behalf of Jews seeking to leave the latter, notably with the Jackson-Vanik amendment to the trade act, an amendment which prevented the extension of Most Favoured status to Communist countries that restricted the emigration of their citizens. The Helms-Burton Act passed by Congress in 1996 reflected Congressional opposition to Cuba that was particularly associated with Jesse Helms, the Chairman of the Senate Foreign Affairs Committee.

Moreover, different government agencies play a role. To take American-Swiss relations, not a key issue in American diplomacy, the State Department tends to pursue an emollient line, not least because Switzerland serves a valuable role in providing the USA with a means to pursue relations with Iran, with which it has no diplomatic links; rather as the EU has done with Palestinian bodies. However, the Internal Revenue Service (IRS) adopted a far harsher stance in 2009 in pursuit both of the implementation of a new bilateral tax treaty with Switzerland and of a legal case against Switzerland's biggest bank, UBS. Whereas the Swiss government proved willing to accept a degree of dilution of the practice of bank secrecy that had proved so unwelcome to the IRS, and indeed to the G20, it was unwilling to surrender client privacy and confidentiality, for example to accept fishing expeditions into accounts designed to gain evidence of possible tax evasion.

The issue brought up the range of bodies involved in diplomacy, not only, in this case, the IRS but also the Swiss Parliament, which has to ratify any new treaty, and indeed the public, which has a chance of overturning it in a referendum. As an instance of the range of diplomacy, tax avoidance regimes are also at issue in the relations of Germany with states such as Luxembourg and Liechtenstein, while in the late 1990s a British tax exile resident in Belize, Lord Ashcroft, was both Belize's ambassador to the United Nations and the Party Treasurer of, and prime donor to, the Conservative Party in Britain.

It is easy to forget bodies such as the IRS when concentrating on the challenge to conventional means of foreign policy presented by heads of government. Yet they are significant not only because they can complicate relations, but also because the institutional continuity they represent provides coherence for alternative views and memories. Moreover, these views direct attention to the arbitrating role of leading ministers, and thus to the subordination of the diplomatic system to them. This is even more the case for powerful constituencies of interest such as Ministries of Defence.[8]

In some respects, the current situation represents a continuation of the wartime development of diplomatic representation, as the needs of pursuing total war led to the representation of a host of government agencies. Isaiah Berlin, who was responsible for the weekly political reports from the British embassy in Washington during the Second World War, noted:

> New missions were established to represent the Treasury, the Ministries of Supply, Food, Aircraft Production, Political and Economic Warfare, Information, and other departments; almost every Ministry in London had its representatives, in one form or another, in Washington or New York. . . . The result was the creation in the American capital, at the beginning of the 'forties, of what was, in effect, a short-lived microcosm of Whitehall.[9]

The major role of leading ministers in giving shape to diplomacy reflects the complexity of modern government, both in terms of internal structures and with reference to representation and negotiation. Other issues that play a role, aside from the ease of transport, include the extent to which the presence of leaders calls forth that of others. The entire process can be located with reference to globalization, but specific factors also play a role, for example the part of meetings of heads of state in such international bodies as the EU and NATO.

The pertinence of recent international developments for the future is unclear and reflects questions about the likely character of future crises. For example, an impression of rapidly deteriorating environmental circumstances may well throw the emphasis onto idealist, or indeed realist, concepts of environmental diplomacy. Conversely, if the stress is on great-power competition, possibly between China and the USA, or on regional stability, notably in the Far East, South Asia, the Persian Gulf and the Middle East, then more conventional notions of diplomacy may come into play, albeit with a powerful military dimension.

The place of conventional issues can be seen with the continued importance of representation as an issue. For example, Turkey rejects diplomatic relations with Armenia, in part as a result of opposition to Armenian control of the region of Nagorno-Karabakh, which it occupied in its 1993 war with Azerbaijan, and also in response to Armenia's campaign for international recognition of what it presents as a genocide, the Armenian Massacres during the First World War, a charge Turkey rejects.

In part, the Turkish government is punishing Armenia for making it feel guilty, although the Turks do not appreciate part of their country being called Western Armenia. The border has been closed since 1993. In April

2009 Turkey revealed a draft agreement to establish diplomatic ties and to reopen its border, but the threat that Azerbaijan, in response, would turn to Russia led an anxious Turkey to insist anew that Armenia withdraw from Nagorno-Karabakh, thus ending the draft agreement.

The nature of diplomatic relations was at issue elsewhere in 2009. Ecuador broke off relations with Colombia in March when Columbian forces crossed the border to attack a base of FARC, Columbia's largest guerrilla group. Again, this issue serves as a reminder of the extent to which diplomatic relations are closely intertwined with support (explicit, implicit, or by the omission of opposition) for rebellious movements in other states. Also in 2009 the Honduran coup threw up issues of recognition as coups always do, underlining the continued role of diplomacy as a form of legitimation.

On the whole, power is accepted, diplomacy helping to manage the transition. In 2008 a military junta successfully staged a coup in Mauritania, leading to a degree of international isolation, including suspension from the African Union and threats of sanctions from both it and the European Union. In turn, international diplomacy, in the shape of mediation by Abdoulaye Wade, President of neighbouring Senegal, arranged a settlement of the domestic impasse that prepared the way for an election process in which the head of the junta resigned and then became President.

As a reminder of the extent to which membership in international bodies is a key aspect of modern diplomacy, the election was attended by observers from the African League, the Arab League and the International Francophone Organisation, all of which endorsed the result, and was seen as the prelude to the improvement of relations with the World Bank, the International Monetary Fund, the European Union and the African Union.

There was also a coup in Guinea in 2008, and again recognition in return for the holding of elections was an issue. Moreover, the slaughter of pro-democracy demonstrators in September 2009 led to pressure from the African Union and the European Union, the latter prompted by the former colonial power, France.

Turning to other types and aspects of diplomacy, the financial institutions played a key role in a financial diplomacy that was an important aspect of international relations.[10] At the same time, trade in key goods, notably oil and grain, was commonly affected by government intervention, as in the supply of grain to China in the 1960s and 1990s.[11]

The significant military dimension in diplomacy in part reflects the extent to which some militaries have developed their own systems for acquiring information about foreign countries, and for fostering and forwarding interests there. A prominent instance is the Pakistani ISI (Inter-Services

Intelligence Agency), but the Pentagon's development of a system of strategic reviews of other states is also noteworthy. In particular, the need for the Pentagon to turn to the State Department or the CIA for information is apparently lessened. Moreover, the Pentagon's area commands offer a spatial infrastructure that structures a different form of presence and diplomacy to that of the State Department.

Insurrectionary movements continued to provide an occasion for a diplomacy focused on violence, as with the Pakistani, Saudi Arabian and American support for the Afghan resistance to the Soviet-backed Kabul regime of the 1980s. Diplomats also appear to have played a role in terrorism, as in 1988 when, alongside reports of Libyan direction that led to successful legal action, there are others suggesting that the Iranian envoy to Syria provided the Damascus-based Popular Front for the Liberation of Palestine General Command with money that was used to fund the blowing up of Pan Am Flight 103 over Lockerbie.[12] The 'War on Terror' led to an increase in the Intelligence dimension of American foreign policy, with embassies expanded accordingly. Thus Addis Ababa became a major centre of American representation because of the strength of Islamic activism in neighbouring Somalia. The same was true of Dijbouti.

The role of Intelligence agencies serves as a powerful reminder of the extent to which the place of diplomacy as a privileged source of information has been superseded in part. More seriously, the ability of these agencies to direct, as well as analyse, the gathering of information is a powerful qualification of the position of diplomats, not least as Foreign Ministry systems are often less well attuned to such direction and analysis.

In a situation with many historical antecedents, the established structure of embassies has been supplemented if not supplanted by more confidential envoys. Thus, in 2009, the new Obama administration appointed special envoys to the Middle East (George Mitchell) and to Afghanistan and Pakistan (Richard Holbrooke), while the Chairman of the Senate Foreign Relations Committee, John Kerry, acted as an intermediary with Syria, reportedly keeping in touch with the President of Syria, Bashar al-Assad, by telephone. The last was necessary in the absence of diplomatic representation. The Obama administration's attempts to improve relations led in March 2009 to the visit of a high-level delegation (the acting Assistant Secretary of State for the Near East as well as a representative of the National Security Council), followed by talk of reopening the embassy in Damascus.

In July 2009 the administration's determination to move forward the Middle East peace process was shown in the dispatch of a series of prominent figures to the region including not only George Mitchell, but also Robert Gates, the Secretary of Defence, James Jones, the National

Security Adviser, and Dennis Ross, a special adviser on foreign policy. Their presence was seen as necessary in order to provide the security guarantees, particularly against Iran, that might encourage Israel to be accommodating over settlements on the West Bank, but their role, like that of Holbrooke, was also seen as circumventing the position of Hillary Clinton, the Secretary of State.

At the same time, the traditional issue of representation remains very important in the Middle East. This issue focuses on Israel and Palestine, with the Islamist Hamas movement, which won the 2006 election in Gaza, isolated because it refused to recognize Israel or disavow violence. The Quartet of countries and organizations that had been instructed to foster negotiations – the USA, Russia, the UN and the European Union – laid down three conditions for Hamas to join negotiations. Hamas had to honour all previous agreements of the Palestine Liberation Organization (the basis of the Palestinian Authority, the previous government) with Israel, to recognize Israel, and definitively to disavow violence. Hamas, in turn, rejected the idea of preconditions and claimed that Israel had repeatedly flouted UN resolutions, and that the rival Fatah movement had gained nothing from the formal recognition of Israel.

The challenge to diplomatic history proved an instructive parallel with that to diplomacy from other negotiators. A strong bias against diplomatic history came to the fore in the mid-twentieth century, with the subject often being disparaged, in the words of G. M. Young, 'as the record of what one clerk said to another clerk'.[13] The techniques employed were considered outdated, and the discipline as archaic, as well as irrelevant to contemporary issues and concerns. Bridging the gap between political science and the humanities, diplomatic history came in for criticism from both directions. For the former, diplomatic history lacked the theoretical sophistication that was required.[14] Within the humanities, diplomatic history provoked antagonism from the post-modernist, post-structuralist schools of thought.

Indeed, the pervasive proliferation of relativism – the socially determined character of human action and identities – has fostered a marginalization of diplomatic history. With the value of historical documents disputed, diplomatic history – relying on such documents to recreate the past – was commensurately divested of meaning and significance. Given the linguistic preoccupation of much Western historiography with discourse, many scholars came to reject empirical criteria, and shifted away from diplomacy, to narrowly conceived social, cultural, anthropologically inspired or gender-related themes.

Moreover, the reaction against Eurocentrism – which was crudely equated with intellectual imperialism in historical writing – generated a parallel aversion to the formation of the Western State System and the rise of the Great Powers: the staples of conventional diplomatic history. Instead, Europe's declining importance in the world ensured that the classic themes of diplomatic history seemed less relevant. World tendencies gathering force since 1945, problems seemingly resistant (if not impervious) to diplomatic solutions, further contributed to the discrediting of the norms and principles of traditional diplomacy, as did relentless technological growth. Ideological issues were also significant, notably the discrediting of diplomatic (and military) historians by ideologies favouring peace studies and institutions.[15] Indeed, traditional diplomacy was critically associated with war in a theme that can be traced back to the 1790s, and that lay behind the first of President Wilson's Fourteen Points in 1918. In the USA the proportion of university history departments employing at least one diplomatic historian fell from three-quarters in 1975 to less than half in 2005, and that in a period of major expansion in the profession.[16] A similar trend could be seen in Britain.

Ironically, this period also saw a marked improvement in the scope and sophistication of studies in foreign policy. From the 1970s, diplomatic historians not only progressively expanded the range of sources consulted – from the private papers of ministers, officials and diplomats to documents illuminating the public discussions of policy; they also increasingly adopted a self-consciously multi-dimensional approach,[17] and embraced more general questions, such as the moral and intellectual assumptions of national policy, the military/naval dimensions of diplomatic action, the importance of systemic influences, and the extent to which foreign affairs were conditioned by the considerations and restraints of personal, domestic and court politics.[18] The last can be extended to include the individuals and institutions that vied for influence in modern court systems, such as the American presidency.[19]

The fate of diplomatic history is instructive, but far from unique. The same trajectory can be traced in military history,[20] as well as in constitutional and legal history. This point does not minimize the importance and resonances of the changes in diplomatic history, as the factors involved are similar, but there is clearly a need to place them in context.

There were clearer indications of the plight of diplomacy than the state of diplomatic history. In particular, the rise in the number of independent states led to an embrace of diplomatic activity as an assertion of sovereignty and significance, only for many states to find that they could not sustain their representation. The serious recession of the early 1970s triggered by the sharp rise in the price of oil following the Yom Kippur War caused a general crisis in government finances, not least as it brought to a close the 'Long Boom' that had followed the Second World War; and there were recurrent problems linked to recessions in the early 1980s, early 1990s and late 2000s.

Difficulties were accentuated by the collapse of particular states and regimes, such as Mobutu's Zaire in the mid-1990s. As a consequence, Zairean envoys were not paid and representation collapsed. The public nature of much diplomacy was such that this was no secret. In 1993–5 there were numerous newspaper reports of Zairean diplomatic personnel in Bonn (Germany) living without electricity and telephones, the unpaid *chargé d'affaires* in Warsaw sleeping in the railway station, and the embassy in Harare (Zimbabwe) closed because of the non-payment of rent. The last was important as the Mugabe regime played an important role in Zaire.

A different aspect of the plight of diplomacy was provided by the breakdown of ideas of immunity. Neither diplomats nor their embassies were safe from attack. These attacks were mounted not only by terrorists and populist crowds, but also by radical regimes deliberately seeking a prominent symbol of both the old order and external control for attack. Thus embassies, notably that of Britain, proved real and symbolic targets during China's Great Proletarian Cultural Revolution. Moreover, mob attacks were mounted on the American and British embassies in Tripoli (Libya) in 1967, in response to inaccurate claims that these powers had supported Israel in the Six Days' War.

The storming of the American embassy in Tehran in 1979 and the holding of the staff as hostages for over 400 days helped entrench the Islamic Revolution as an anti-American force and also provided a key issue in American–Iranian relations. When told that international law was being violated, Ayatollah Khomeini, the leader of the revolution, claimed that the observance of such principles should always be secondary to Islam and asked what international law had ever done for the people of Iran. Moreover, the fate of the 52 hostages became significant in American domestic politics, with the failure of President Carter's attempt to rescue them in 1980 serving as a symbol of his weakness, which contributed to his failure to win re-election. The attack on the embassy was both symbolic and an attempt to close down what was seen as a rallying-point for those opposed to the Islamic Revolution.

The USA still does not have diplomatic relations with Iran. Instead, Switzerland represents American interests in Iran, both providing consular services to Americans living in Iran and also acting as a diplomatic channel of communication. Thus in June 2009 the Iranian government summoned the Swiss envoy to protest at what they saw as interventionist statements by President Obama about the recent Iranian election. Britain and Iran also broke off diplomatic relations in 1979, renewing them in

1988, although they have remained troubled. Comparisons between the state of American and British relations with Iran raise questions about the value of the 'constructive engagement' offered by the presence of an embassy; although the embassy also fulfils other functions. Moreover, representation is not only offered to an unsympathetic regime but also, in the form of the encouragement provided by its presence, to its opponents: the presence is a testimony to the extent that the country's people have not been forgotten. A refusal to send envoys is regularly used in order to display anger, as in August 2009 when Russia refused to send an ambassador to Ukraine.

Embassies are deeply symbolic sites, and are understood in these terms. Thus their location can affirm political commitments, as in 1995 when the American Israel Public Affairs Committee persuaded Congress to vote for the movement of the American embassy from Tel Aviv to Jerusalem, a move unwelcome to the two governments. The sensitivity of the location of embassies in Israel was shown furthermore in 2009 when Britain abandoned plans to move its Tel Aviv embassy into a new tower block owned by a London-based Israeli billionaire criticized for investing in Israeli settlements on the West Bank.

Israel is not the sole issue. China maintained its embassy in Belgrade during the Milosevic years, which left it a target to American air attack in 1999: the Americans claimed that the cruise missile that hit it was not aimed at the embassy, but some commentators suggested that the attack was intended to send a message to China about the need to keep its distance from Serbia. Saudi Arabia was one of only three states to recognize the Taliban government of Afghanistan in the 1990s: it had provided funding for fundamentalist activism in Afghanistan from the opposition to Soviet rule in the 1980s on. Conversely, Saudi Arabia was very reluctant in heeding American requests to reopen its embassy in Baghdad after the Second Gulf War, a step that was seen as accepting the replacement of Saddam Hussein's government.

Western publics tend to imagine that their embassies and diplomats are most commonly assaulted. Indeed, the IRA attacked British diplomats while al-Qaeda assaulted the American embassies in Nairobi (Kenya) and Dar es Salaam (Tanzania) with truck bombs in 1998, causing heavy casualties (mostly to the local population), which in part captured attention for these attacks. The British consulate in Istanbul was bombed in 2003.

However, the embassies and diplomats of other states have also been targets. Turkish diplomats were attacked by the Secret Army for the Liberation of Armenia from the 1970s. In 1980 the Iranian Embassy in London was seized by terrorists leading to its storming after a siege. In May 2008 Hezbollah militia sought to kill Saudi diplomats in Beirut because of Saudi support for rival militias. In October 2009 a suicide bomb attack was mounted outside the Indian embassy in Kabul: India has long been seen by both Pakistan and Muslim fundamentalists as intervening in Afghanistan in order to pursue geopolitical interests.

Events such as embassy sieges grabbed the headlines, but, in practice, the plight of diplomacy was more a matter of the growing role of other actors and intermediaries in foreign policy and international relations, even though there were also classic failures of reporting and representation by diplomats. Thus in 1982 Anthony Williams, the British envoy in Buenos Aires, failed to appreciate the likelihood of an Argentinean attack on the Falkland Isles, while in July 1990 April Glaspie, the American envoy in Baghdad, a Arabic-speaking career diplomat, appears to have left Saddam Hussein with the impression that the USA would not respond to action against Kuwait. She certainly underestimated the severity of the crisis. Yet Saddam Hussein was quite able to misunderstand what was said to him in pursuit of the bombastic wishful thinking that underlay his aggression.[21]

The Falklands war of 1982 indicated both the value of diplomatic skill and the number of agencies involved in formulating foreign policy. In Argentina, a dictatorship, the military determined policy, while in Britain the major roles were taken by the Prime Minister, Margaret Thatcher, the War Cabinet and the Chief of Defence Staff, and the Foreign Secretary, Francis Pym, was sidelined by a critical Prime Minister. Yet British diplomats, notably Sir Nicholas Henderson (Washington) and Sir Anthony Parsons (UN), played a key role in limiting attempts at international mediation and thus in providing the British military with an opportunity to attack and win. Henderson replied to American pressure for restraint by asking how much British neutrality might be appreciated if Puerto Rico was under attack. In the USA the President, Ronald Reagan, the Secretary of State, Alexander Haig, the Secretary for Defence, Caspar Weinberger, and the UN envoy, Jeanne Kirkpatrick, all took different positions. The American response was a reminder of the conditional nature of alliances and the need, therefore, to rely on resolution and to benefit from the divisions among the policymakers of allied states.[22]

Meanwhile, the creation from the 1940s of new institutions in foreign policy provided both occasion for diplomacy and also opportunities for diplomats. Their expertise proved a key element in the staffing and operation of the proliferating world of international institutions and of national bodies established to deal with these institutions and with the range of activities now understood as foreign policy. Membership of international bodies, such as the Security Council of the United Nations, the World Trade Organization, and the G7, now G8, became a key objective of diplomacy.

States such as Brazil, Germany, India and South Africa pursued membership of the Security Council as a sign of their own significance, while claims were also made about the role of specific states as representing regional constituencies. This diplomacy of assertion reflected the extent to which the Security Council represented a very public breach with any principle of equivalence between sovereign bodies. Lesser bodies, such as the UN Conference on Trade and Development or the Latin American Economic Secretariat, also provided opportunities for individual and national activity and assertion, as did the location of the Olympics.

Although in theory offering equality for all powers involved, multilateral diplomacy in practice is inherently hierarchical, which leads to an emphasis on membership and position in relevant inter-governmental organizations, an emphasis that is not simply symbolic in its origins.[23] For lesser powers, such membership provides an opportunity for a diplomacy of significance.[24] China or the USA may not have much time to think about Poland, let alone Slovenia, but the latter can play a role as a member of the European Union.

The importance of membership in international bodies is such that it can be ended as a sign of disfavour. Apartheid led to South Africa losing its presence in international forums, and this pariah status complicated diplomacy as the state remained important. Alternatively, meetings can be suspended. Thus in 2008 the NATO–Russia Council, the formal body for talks at ministerial and ambassadorial level was suspended after Russia's conflict with Georgia. In turn, the Council was re-opened in the spring of 2009 as President Obama sought to improve relations with Russia.

Within Europe the number of relevant organizations for international co-operation included not only the EU and NATO, but also the Western European Union, the Council of Europe, and the Organization for Security and Co-operation in Europe. They were charitably seen as interlocking institutions, but the attempt to provide coherence entailed considerable diplomatic effort within Europe with the multiplication of negotiation to try to alleviate difficulties. The number of institutions also complicated the process of, and issues involved in, international representation, as well as providing numerous posts for diplomats.

At the same time, this multiplication of institutions helped ensure that a variety of bodies did exist to confront particular challenges. In particular, a European alternative to NATO was now possible, and although it lacked the latter's military weight, it was not dependent on the USA politically. The Kosovo Crisis of 1999 proved a major catalyst for the development of the EU's international role, and in turn encouraged the EU to take a more active stance in Balkan diplomacy and in crisis management.[25] The variety of bodies with diplomatic representation also reflected the specialization of international diplomacy, as with the International Atomic Energy Agency, which has played a greater role with the rise of proliferation as a major issue.

Trade is a particularly significant source, and goal, of international co-operation and thus of intergovernmental organizations that require diplomacy. The European course, from European Economic Community to European Union and currency union, within just over four decades, has not been followed elsewhere, but in the Americas much diplomacy has been involved in the creation and maintenance of NAFTA, ANDEAN (Acuerdo de Cartagena/Grupo Ardino, 1969) and MERCOSUR (Mercado Común del Cono Sur, Common Market for the Southern Part of America, 1990), as well as in discussion about their extension.

It has proved far more difficult to obtain co-operation at this level over the issues of immigration and drugs. Instead, bilateral diplomacy play a major role in these fields. This diplomacy is also an important correlate to multilateral structures. Bilateral attempts to improve relations between the USA and China led to the Senior Dialogue, which began in 2005 and focused on diplomacy, the Strategic Economic Dialogue, established in 2006, and the Strategic and Economic Dialogue, first held in July 2009. The last is designed to widen the political nature of this diplomatic forum, and thus was attended by the Secretary of State, Hillary Clinton, as well as the Treasury Secretary.

Thus alongside new and expanded bodies for multilateral diplomacy came a greater range in bilateral bodies, not least as states sought to use the soft power of cultural and other links to ease relations. This goal was pursued most strongly between allies who felt that their alliance lacked sufficient grounding in public attitudes. In 1975 the Ford administration established the Japan–US Friendship Commission, a federal agency that exists to this day and is pledged to develop educational and cultural ties. There was no Japanese equivalent, but the Japan Foundation, established by the government in 1972, devoted much attention to comparable relations with the USA. However, television, cinema and trade proved far more important than diplomatic links in the creation of perceptions and ties.

Across its broad range of activity, diplomacy drew explicitly on realist and idealist concepts, a pattern that can be traced back, and one for which there was particular continuity in the case of the Papacy. Issues such as famine, disease and poverty were seen to affect not only the countries where they occurred but also others, with refugee flows or the movements of infections linking often very distant states. International co-operation as the medium of addressing such issues provided the occasion for diplomacy, not least in the creation and implementation of norms and responses.

Natural and political environments also proved key areas for co-operation as transnational action was seen as crucial. Environmentalism was pushed forward as an attempt to create international norms, and, in particular, to locate them in agreements that did not rest on bilateral agreements as the latter were seen as insufficient, if not self-interested and dictated by the powerful. Human rights issues served as another basis for diplomacy, with, again, an overlap between the formal processes of diplomacy and those discharged by non-diplomats, notably lawyers.

The need for co-operation against unwanted political threats provided an additional foundation for diplomacy. These threats included terrorism and the movement of weaponry. Thus, the apparent breakdown of earlier restraints, especially in the trade of nuclear technology, led to international non-proliferation becoming a major issue in the 2000s, leading to new structures and practices. Notably, in May 2003 the USA launched the Proliferation Security Initiative, an attempt to take shared action against the transfer of weapons of mass destruction. By 2009 there were over ninety states involved in the PSI, and the latter is instructive as an organization in that it lacks a structure, having no headquarters or secretariat. In 2006 the Global Initiative to Combat Nuclear Terrorism followed: by 2009 it had 75 participants.

The importance of proliferation was such that Libya's willingness, in 2003, to abandon its nuclear weapons programme (as well as to pay compensation for those killed in the bombing of Pan Am Flight 103 over Lockerbie in 1988) was followed by the UN Security Council agreeing to lift sanctions. This improvement in relations was linked to the restoration in diplomatic ties: with Britain (after 17 years) in 2001 and with the USA (after 24 years) in 2006.

Alongside the arguments of, and for, human rights, entitlement is another form of international rhetoric and a would-be driver of international agreement. The language of entitlement, whether to co-operation or to assent, can be seen across a range of attempts to create coalitions against what are presented as outrages, notably terrorism, environmental degradation or the world economic system. Moreover, the language of entitlement is employed across the political spectrum.

At the same time as the stress on multilateral organizations, conventional diplomacy remains important. Thus the American–Saudi relationship in the early 2000s focused on the Saudi envoy in Washington, Prince Bandar bin Sultan. In addition, if national leaders travel more than ever before, that represents at one level another strand in conventional diplomacy as much as a belittling of professional diplomats.

The pace of such travel certainly greatly increased in the second half of the twentieth century, while ironically, landing rights for airlines frequently became a matter of contention and negotiation. Born in 1869, Neville Chamberlain first went abroad only in 1938. He went three times to try to arrange a peaceful settlement of the Czech crisis, and then to Rome in January 1939. The Cold War was to affect the scope of travel by later Prime Ministers, but in 1959 Harold Macmillan visited Moscow in order to try to ease the Berlin Crisis. This was the first visit to Moscow by a senior Western leader since 1941 and it was intended to take forward summit diplomacy. A foreign ministers' conference followed that year at Geneva.[26]

By the 1980s the situation was very different to that a half-century earlier. Margaret Thatcher, according to her former Cabinet colleague and supporter, Nicholas Ridley, 'never attempted to speak in a foreign language',[27] but she frequently travelled abroad, particularly to Washington and to European Union summits. Public diplomacy involving national leaders had become a major part of international relations, notably with Richard Nixon's trip to Beijing in 1972, Anwar Sadat's role in settling bitter Egyptian–Israeli tensions in the 1970s, notably his trip to Jerusalem in November 1977,[28] and Mikhael Gorbachev's part in ending the Cold War in the 1980s, especially his 1986 Reykjavik summit with President Ronald Reagan. Jet travel had become more comfortable. John Addis, the British Ambassador in Beijing, noted in 1972, 'The 1st class cabin of a 747 [Jumbo-Jet] is more like the saloon of a ship and altogether avoids the cramped feeling of travelling in a tube or a pipe.'[29]

The pace for British leaders became more frenetic under Tony Blair, Prime Minister from 1997 to 2007. These visits were used for economic as well as political diplomacy, as in 2007 when his visit to Tripoli, the capital of Libya, served as an opportunity to announce a deal involving BP for investment in Libyan oil and gas production worth about $900 million. He had already visited Libya in 2004, the first trip there by a British Prime Minister since 1948. Blair also extended his institutional control over foreign policy, notably with the creation of the Overseas and Defence Secretariat inside Number 10 Downing Street in 2001. The importance of high-level links was also shown in 2008, when President George W. Bush spoke to Colonel Gaddafi of Libya by telephone, while in July 2009 President Obama shook hands with Gaddafi.

National leaders, however, had neither the time, interest nor aptitude to negotiate detailed agreements, while they could scarcely go everywhere. Most of the field was therefore left to diplomats, although many were greatly constrained by the need to respond to political exigencies, notably the policy, and thus ideological, commitments of their governments. Professionalism, in the service of a broader definition of the national interest, was generally insufficient. Commitment was expected from diplomats, and, in democracies, was probed in public legislative committees.

When, therefore, President George W. Bush called for a 'diplomacy of freedom', in other words a foreign policy focused on spreading democracy, diplomats were expected to comply. This process was more significant than the political travels of national leaders in constraining diplomacy.

Bush's policy was scarcely a novelty. Aside from the long-standing American preference for dealing with democratic governments when the choice presented itself, there had also been attempts to mould such choices, as with the encouragement (eventually strong encouragement) of democracy in Latin America, the Philippines and South Africa. More generally, diplomats thus had to manoeuvre in relation to the strategic culture of their own states. In doing so, they needed to understand that of the states to which they were accredited, but this process could create a tension with their instructions.

Alongside a discussion of Western powers and views, including the role of NGOs, the flavour of much current international diplomacy was represented by a meeting in Yekaterinburg, Russia in June 2009. The presidents of Brazil, China and Russia, and the Prime Minister of India, the BRIC states, met and called for 'a greater voice and representation in international financial institutions'. As they represent 42 per cent of the world's population and 15 per cent of the GDP and hold about 40 per cent of the gold and hard currency reserves, this diplomacy was significant, not least because the growth rates of China and India are considerably higher than those of the USA and Europe; although the BRIC states also have different views on many topics, both political and economic.

Such summitry qualified the role of resident diplomats, while the range of government (and non-government) agencies involved in the formulation and implementation of foreign policy also reflected the range of the state. With governments concerned about the international aspects of such domestic challenges as drug consumption, criminal syndicates, terrorism, human trafficking and public health issues, it is scarcely surprising that many ministries and agencies devoted to domestic policy maintain agents and information sources abroad, and seek to influence foreign policy. The terrorist challenge of the 2000s has pushed this diplomacy of policing to the fore, not least by emphasizing the role of the Intelligence services, but this challenge overlaps with other issues, such as the drug trade, criminality and the illegal movement of individuals.

In turn, terrorism can affect the diplomatic terrain by exacerbating relations between states, especially those seen as bases and victims. A notable instance is provided by the impact of Pakistani terrorists on relations between India and Pakistan. Thus the attack on Mumbai in November 2008 led India to end a four-year attempt to normalize relations, the 'composite dialogue' launched in 2004. Similarly, the attack on the Indian parliament in 2001 had badly damaged relations for a while. Pakistan-based terrorism not only affects the chronology of relations with India, but also becomes a major issue in negotiations.

The drug trade plays a major role in diplomatic relations with several Caribbean and Latin American states. The USA, in particular, seeks to curtail both drug production and illegal drug exports to the USA. This activity leads to a new level of diplomacy, only part of which is within the conventional diplomatic structure. In particular, the implementation of American policy involves the presence of American drug-enforcement agents as well as troops. When relations are friendly, as with Colombia, drugs plays a major role, but conversely, American policy can also cause problems. The linkage of a preferential trade agreement to Bolivia's performance in combating the drug trade was unwelcome to Evo Morales, the populist elected as President in 2005. A representative of the coca farmers and a keen ally of other left-wing Latin American populists, notably Fidel Castro and Hugo Chávez, Morales expelled American diplomats and drug-enforcement agents, and criticized the American refusal to renew the agreement. Political differences over relations with the USA have helped divide the Brazilian-inspired UNASUL, the Union of South American Nations.

A separate strand of concern relates to environmentalism. That in turn involves a range of topics and a number of different diplomatic formats, from bilateral diplomacy to global-level agreements based on summitry, such as the Kyoto Accord and the UN-sponsored climate-change summit in Copenhagen in December 2009. Whaling, carbon emissions and water supplies[30] are very different topics to those familiar a half-millennium ago.

At the same time, conventional roles and obligations continue to play a part. The role of diplomats in protecting the image of their country, or at least the governmental view of it, was amply demonstrated in 2009. The Austrian envoy in London complained about the depiction of his country in the satirical film *Brüno*, but a more political note was struck that October when the acting Turkish Ambassador was summoned by the Israeli Foreign Minister to hear a protest about *Farewell*, a fictional television series falsely showing Israeli soldiers as killing Palestinian children. The Foreign Minister declared that the series was inappropriate for broadcast 'in a state which maintains diplomatic relations with Israel'.[31]

China deployed its diplomats in protest at what it saw as critical views of the treatment of the Uighurs, who rioted in July 2009 in the Xinjiang region. Chunmei Chen, the cultural attaché in the consulate in Melbourne, pressed the organizers of the Film Festival there to drop *10 Conditions of Love*, a documentary about Rebiya Kadeer, the leader of the World

Uighur Congress. Chen also criticized the decision to invite Kadeer as a guest and accused her of crimes, including being a terrorist. Subsequently, hackers broke into the festival's website and posted a Chinese flag and demands for an apology. In London Fu Ying, the Ambassador, took to the press, arguing in the *Guardian* that the violence was not an ethnic conflict and pressing *The Times* to let her reply to Kadeer.[32]

Such action was part of a longstanding process. Thus the London publisher Dorling Kindersley, when preparing its flagship DK *World Atlas* in 1996, received unsuccessful representations from the Chinese embassy presenting the case for not showing Taiwan as a separate entity. On another occasion, after the Chinese Ambassador had been presented with a selection of Penguin and DK products as part of Pearson's attempt to enter the Chinese education market, the embassy complained about the 'misrepresentation' of China in the FT *World Desk Reference*, produced by DK. The lengthy list of criticisms focused on Chinese territorial claims on land and sea, including almost all of the South China Sea and most of the Indian province of Arunachal Pradesh: all of which they wanted shown as lying within their state borders.[33]

Western criticism of Chinese action in Xinjiang in 2009 was largely motivated by Human Rights concerns, but elsewhere other contexts played the leading role, notably religious and ethnic considerations. A sense of Islam under attack led al-Qaeda affiliates to threaten reprisals against Chinese workers in the Moslem world in 2009, while ethnic fellow-feeling affected relations with Turkey, whose refuge and support for the Uighur cause had affected diplomatic relations with China in the 1990s.

The 2009 dispute indicated how far diplomats played a secondary role in such relations. Attempts during the 2000s to improve relations reflected Turkey's concern to benefit from China's rise, and in 2009 Abdullah Gal, the former Foreign Minister of Turkey, and then the President, after visiting China, spoke of 'a new page' in relations. The riots, however, led the Turkish Prime Minister, Recep Tayyip, who was on the Islamicist wing of Turkish politics, to see 'genocide' as at work at the expense of the Uighurs and to suggest a discussion at the UN Security Council, while the Trade Minister proposed a consumer boycott of China.

The role of envoys as representatives of their countries to wide audiences reflected the range and contentiousness of public engagement with foreign policy in many countries. Another development, one that can be seen more in terms of realist accounts of international relations, was that of the move towards a more multipolar world, notably with a relative decline in American power. As with all discussion of the future, there is a problematic element there, but evidence of such a decline can be seen not only in terms of American military over-commitment and grave fiscal problems, but also with reference to far higher economic growth rates in China and India.

These changes can be conceptualized in terms of a transition in great-power status from America to China, or the end of 'Chimerica', or by proposing a shift to a multipolar system in which China and the USA both play major roles.[34] Each of these scenarios suggest a major need for diplomacy, not least in managing the processes of transition. Furthermore, even if China becomes the great power of the twenty-first century, that does not mean a return to earlier diplomatic cultures, for example the myth of universal kingship or the classical Chinese sense of spatiality and geopolitics.[35] China will be very different to the empire of the eighteenth century (and earlier), and will be engaging in a very different world. China is again extending its influence into Central Asia, but the means are different.[36]

Offering credit to shore up economies (and thus win support), and securing energy and resource supplies, represent an engagement with the outer world on the part of China not seen in the earlier period. The construction of big embassies can be noted in parts of the world not known to Classical China, for example at Malabo, the capital of oil-rich (and dictatorial) Equatorial Guinea. This is a different diplomacy to the earlier support for African nationalism, a support, notably in the 1970s, that had blended military action and ideological affinity.[37] The transformation in Chinese diplomacy indicated the different demands placed upon the latter over the last half-century, but also its flexibility.

To end on China may appear inappropriate given the extent to which, whatever the possible course of future developments, the leading power at present is the USA, while the agenda is as much to do with multilateral structures and diplomacy as with classical great-power activity. At the same time, a focus on China underlines the extent to which established patterns of diplomatic activity have to adapt, and not least in terms of a changing engagement with the non-Western world. Such adaptation can be moulded in rhetoric and/or with hindsight into a progressive, indeed teleological, account, but to do so underplays not only the strains and stresses involved in any adaptation, but also the multiple narratives and analyses that are possible when diplomacy is considered at the global level.

Conclusions: The Future

Is conventional diplomacy redundant? The question has frequently been asked, and not simply from an abstract viewpoint. Competing for resources, foreign ministries and diplomats face pressure for cuts, notably reduced networks of representation as well as the sale of embassy buildings and cuts in expenditure. Aside from this, there are repeated and longstanding calls for relevance, modernity and the 'joined-up' representation of states by a more multi-agency process.[1] Thus the *Review of Overseas Representation* (1977) by the British Central Policy Review Staff recommended a severe reduction in the diplomatic service. Instead, diplomacy was to be carried out from London, with civil servants sent out to fulfil tasks.

In part, this report reflected a situation in which the use of Home civil servants drafted into British diplomacy arose from the apparent inadequacy of the Diplomatic Service when dealing with foreign officials negotiating specialized non-political matters.[2] Thus the changing nature of international relations led to questions about the adequacy of diplomats, questions given fictional resonance by the tendency to present diplomats as smooth to the point of duplicity and as representatives of dated social views, as with the incompetent Carlton-Browne of the Boulting Brothers 1959 film, who would rather be at the socially prestigious races at Ascot.[3]

The far more complex reality was seen in the correspondence and diaries of diplomats. John Addis (the son of Sir Charles Addis and a product of Rugby and Christ Church, Oxford), while Counsellor and Consul General in Britain's Beijing embassy, wrote to his sister in 1955 'Our social whirl continues at the same intensity. Last week I had one lunch by myself but otherwise it was lunch and dinner parties every day. To give you an extreme example, my day on Monday of this week' included '1–3pm lunch at the Pakistan Ambassador's . . . 5–6.30 one cocktail party out of duty, 6.30–8.00 second cocktail party . . . on duty, introducing people all the time. 8–10.30 at a dinner party'. Yet selective quotation is useful for journalists, not academics. Addis, a bachelor, was also putting in the other hours at the office or learning Chinese, as this letter made clear. Ambassador at Beijing in 1972, he noted his office hours as 9.15am–1.00pm and 2.30pm–5.00pm daily, with Wednesday afternoon off, but not Saturday morning.[4]

A process of contraction in the diplomatic service was particularly apparent in the case of Britain in the late twentieth century. This change arose in part from the end of its once-hegemonic position, but also reflected and represented the developing world of diplomacy. Power-relationships were to the fore. In the early 1990s the British decided to close, or at least scale down, ten missions in Africa and Central America in order to respond to the collapse of the Soviet Union, which had led to a series of new states. There was only a consul, and no embassy, in Honduras to protect British interests there at the time of the 2009 coup. British concern about Commonwealth ties ensured that envoys were still sent to small countries such as Gambia, Lesotho, Seychelles and Swaziland. However, non-resident envoys were used in francophone Africa, with, in the 1990s, the High Commissioner in Nigeria also representing British interests in Benin or Chad, and that in Ghana doing the same for Togo, while the envoy to the Ivory Coast was also envoy to Mali and Burkina Faso, and that to Morocco fulfilled the same function for Mauritania. In 1991 W. E. Quantrill in Cameroon was also envoy to Chad, Gabon, the Central African Republic and Equatorial Guinea.[5] There were parallels with the representation of major powers in *ancien régime* Europe, notably with envoys being accredited to several German or Italian principalities. Closures by Britain in 1991 included the embassies in Gabon, Liberia and the republic of Congo, while for much of the 1990s the Ambassador to Chad was in fact Head of the West African Department, and thus was based in London.

In contrast, Brazil, led since 2003 by Luiz Inácio Lula da Silva, has tried to develop links in the Third World, and by 2009 had doubled the number of its embassies in Africa to thirty. Embassies clearly served as a centre of influence. In 2009 the Brazilian embassy in Honduras played an important role in the struggle for power there after the overthrow of the President. As an instance of the opening of embassies in pursuit of influence, Iran under President Mahmoud Ahmadinejad since 2005 has regarded diplomatic representation in Latin America as an important tool of policy. Iran opened embassies in Chile, Colombia, Ecuador, Nicaragua and Uruguay, while the President has visited Bolivia, Ecuador, Nicaragua and Venezuela, in part in pursuit of the creation of an international anti-American alignment.

Alongside changes in the diplomatic network has come the privatization of diplomacy, expressed by the growing reliance on lobbyists to advance national interests abroad. By 2009 nearly one hundred countries relied on lobbyists in Washington, and this group included major states such as Australia, Japan and Norway. These lobbyists have been found more effective than embassies in lobbying on Capitol Hill, while the use of insiders is seen as a way to help navigate the structure of the American government. The overlap can be striking, as with Randy Scheunemann, a lobbyist for Georgia, Latvia, Macedonia and Romania, and a key adviser to John McCain, not least in favouring NATO's eastward expansion. Had McCain won the presidential election in 2008, then it is likely that such individuals and practices would have played a major role in American foreign policy. Indeed, the controversial role of McCain, or at least his advisers, in encouraging Georgia in its crisis with Russia in 2008 served as a reminder of the varied nature of foreign policy links and of the difficulty of monopolizing representation.

Lobbyists were also important in obtaining American support for Kosovo's independence, which was achieved in February 2008. Hybrid law and lobbying firms, such as Patton Boggs and the BGR Group, play a major role in representing foreign states, in particular helping mid-size and small embassies that lack the manpower to cover government or to compete with lobbyists. Some lobbyists represent international business interests, such as Airbus and Gazprom, which do not wish to be reliant on national governments, but whose activities affect these governments.

There are also domestic groups with an importance in foreign policy,[6] such as the American Israel Public Affairs Committee, although the extent to which, as alleged by domestic and international critics, this Committee and related American groups and 'interests' affects American policy is controversial. This controversy, which became acute in 2006–9,[7] relates centrally to the process of foreign policy formulation, rather than its implementation. Moreover, it is unclear how far American lobbies, however influential, should be seen in terms of a parallel diplomacy as their foreign linkage is generally less important than their domestic base. The point about lobbying and domestic interests can also be applied to other states.

As far as the USA is concerned, there is also room for a major emphasis on regional interests, an emphasis that lessens the formal role of the diplomatic system, or at least diminishes its part in policymaking. The longstanding juxtaposition of competing American regions in part seeking to define the national interest in order to respond to their different economic interaction with the global economy, a situation abundantly seen in episodes such as the War of 1812 with Britain, as well as during America's rise to great-power status,[8] has to be addressed alongside an awareness of the varied and often contradictory definition of regions.[9] In the 1950s there was a major geographical shift in the USA with the rise of the West and the New South.

Culturally, this shift challenged the influence of the East Coast establishment in the USA, and there were consequences for American foreign policy and diplomacy, not least greater concern with the Far East (of Asia) and a degree of militarization of policy, or at least a lessening of the role of traditional élites. The American Foreign Service had to take note of this shift, a process facilitated by the explicitly political character of its direction and senior ranks.

Despite the standard presentation of diplomacy in terms of serving the national interest, a language that drew on both the conventions of the profession and on the idea of an apolitical civil service, this political direction of diplomacy was true of most states, with diplomacy seen as the means to implement political concepts of foreign policy. This situation represents more continuity from earlier, pre-bureaucratic ages than discussion of diplomacy in terms of professionalism often allows. Looked at differently, here is another instance of the clash in international relations between realism and idealism.

Alongside lobbying and the role of other domestic groups, there are transnational networks seeking to advance particular agendas. These networks both provide a system that mirrors some aspects of diplomacy, in leading to an effective international means of linkage and representation, and also offer a means of seeking to influence foreign policy. Thus transnational networks of arms control supporters and peace activists played a role during the Cold War, notably during the Gorbachev years of the late 1980s.[10]

Such transnational networks, however, had less influence than international organizations, and notably so in regions and countries where political expression by citizens was limited. Thus in the Middle East a key role was taken by OPEC, the Organization of Petroleum Exporting Countries, founded in 1960, which drew together the major Middle Eastern oil producers, as well as Indonesia, Nigeria and Venezuela. OPEC pursued a foreign policy of its own when in 1973 it banned all oil exports to the USA and the Netherlands in protest at their support for Israel. The Gulf Co-Operation Council was a more explicitly regional body. Such organizations owed little to the popular will, and were criticized on this head by radicals. There are also regional groupings in Africa, such as ECOWAS, the Economic Community of West Africa States and SADC, the Southern African Development Community.

Alongside the ideological demands of radical reformers, there have also been calls for sweeping changes in diplomacy from commentators drawing on functional criteria of how best diplomacy should operate. Thus Richard Langhorne, the former Director, first of the Centre of International Studies at Cambridge and then of the British Foreign Office's conference centre, discerned crisis in 2000:

an international system consisting only of states or organisations which are the creatures of states cannot cope with developments and pressures which, because of the effects of the global communications revolution, extend horizontally across state boundaries and evade the controlling policies of their governments.[11]

The declining power of the state is a key theme in some of the literature,[12] and this argument extends to conventional means of state activity. Diplomacy, for example, is challenged by international aid as an institutional form of problem-solving and national representation. This aid is provided both by government agencies and by NGOs, and the latter tend to dominate attention. Moreover, such aid appears to satisfy domestic political and popular constituencies with greater success than that provided by government; although it also causes (and reflects) international disputes, as with the Brothers to the Rescue and American–Cuban relations in the 1990s.

As another instance of the range of state activity, the crisis in Anglo-Iranian relations in 2009 in part arose from Iranian governmental concern about the influence of the BBC within Iran. Furthermore, although Iran expelled two British diplomats and detained Iranian employees of the embassy, the main charge of its rhetoric was against a supposed subversion provided not only by the BBC but, allegedly, by droves of secret service agents. In reality, it was the Iranian government that had subverted the situation by manipulating the election results.

In part, the current emphasis on international aid is an instance of the calls for relevance and soft power, with conventional diplomacy presented as having deficiencies under both heads. Such an account of diplomacy is mistaken. The roles of diplomatic representation and negotiation are still crucial, and notably so as the volatility of international relations have increased. New states, such as East Timor (Timor Leste) which gained independence from Indonesia in 2002, hastened to establish embassies, for example in Lisbon, the capital of Portugal, the colonial power until 1975, in order to assert a presence and win support.

Moreover, the adroit diplomat still opens doors and gains favoured access for particular views.[13] The approach advocated by Sir Ronald Lindsay, the British envoy in Washington from 1930 to 1939, is valid not only for Anglo-American relations but also more generally. Lindsay argued that British envoys should never be seen to be practising propaganda or influencing American politics, should give honest and open answers when that was possible, and say nothing otherwise, and should press home on Whitehall the point that the USA was not a cousin but a distinct nation with its own agendas.[14]

CONCLUSIONS: THE FUTURE

The last point needs underlining given the continuing British tendency to exaggerate the American commitment to an Anglo-American 'Special Relationship'. This tendency reflects the important role in public discussion of longstanding props designed to aid thought and argument, but also the extent to which these props are generally shaped without an understanding of the more complex nature of international relations. In particular, there is a tendency to underplay the extent to which alliances entail tension, and, notably, struggles for leadership and the negotiation of trade-offs; to neglect the extent to which these problems are smoothed out in hindsight; and thus to underplay the importance of diplomatic skills in managing alliances. The Anglo-American alliance is no exception, as was made clear when Louis Susman, the new American Ambassador, discussed relations and lauded the 'Special Relationship' in September 2009.[15]

As a further defence of diplomacy, there also remains a need for privileged information-gathering in the midst of the mass of material that is available, some of which is discussed in the next chapter. Moreover, accumulated wisdom and experience, not least an understanding of relevant languages,[16] makes it easier to appreciate the world-views and negotiating codes of others,[17] and thus to facilitate information acquisition and negotiations. This point is true both for policy at the level of states and also for the efforts of international bodies, such as UN peacekeeping missions.

The value of experience is also seen with interventions by heads of state. Thus Oscar Arias Sánchez, President of Costa Rica from 1986 to 1990 and from 2006, was a plausible mediator in 2009 for the internal rift in Honduras that had led to the overthrow of the President, a political struggle that attracted international attention, because in 1987 he had won the Nobel Peace Prize for his plan to settle regional conflicts in Central America. Bill Clinton, the former President of the USA, was able to conduct discussions with Kim Jong Il, the dictator of North Korea, in August 2009 in a fashion that would not have been possible for a diplomat. Jimmy Carter played a similar role after he ceased to be President in 1981, serving on peace missions, for example to Nicaragua in 1990, and being awarded the Nobel Peace Prize in 2002. Carter's activity, however, was not always welcome to the American government, not least as it could take an ambivalent, if not hostile, attitude to discussions with states and movements judged anti-American, as with Carter's role in Palestine.

Yet Carter's missions, like that of Clinton, served not to deny value for the diplomatic service but rather to underline the extent to which diplomacy entails more than one means of representation and negotiation. Thus, far from summitry overturning the achievement represented by the creation of permanent or residential diplomacy, they should both be seen as aspects of an activity that has lasting value but where the relevance of differing forms varies greatly. This point is underlined by the practice of appointing close confidants of the head of government to key embassies, as when James Callaghan, British Prime Minister from 1976 to 1979 and a keen Atlanticist, appointed his son-in-law, Peter Jay, envoy in Washington.

The range of diplomatic activity in the case of America today was shown in August 2009 when Jim Webb, the head of the Senate's Foreign Relations Sub-Committee on East Asia, travelled to Naypyidaw, the capital of Burma (Myanmar), in pursuit of his policy of engagement with that country. This, the first meeting of a senior American official with General Than Shwe, the head of the Burmese junta, was intended to pursue a constructive engagement, although the need to assuage concerns about human rights was such that the spokesman of the US National Security Council declaed that this trip would permit Burma 'to hear of the strong views of American political leaders about the path it should take toward democracy, good governance, and genuine national reconciliation'.[18] Soon after this meeting, the American government explicitly moved towards constructive engagement with Burma.

Again returning to the values of residential diplomatic service, an evaluation of the domestic position of other states remains highly important to the decision of how much, and how best, to respond to them at the international level. This facet links the contemporary consideration of policy towards Iran with many episodes in the past. For example, domestic instability under the later Stuarts weakened English diplomacy, leading to comment and complaint by diplomats, such as from the loyalist Charles, 2nd Earl of Middleton, in Vienna in 1680.[19] At the same time, this position was scarcely a value-free stance, as English envoys opposed to the situation at home could use its real or alleged consequences on their position to argue for a change, while foreign diplomats were always going to frame their reports on English politics in accordance with their views. Philippe-Johan Hoffmann, the Imperial (Austrian) envoy in 1688, who was unsympathetic to James II, presented his policies as unpopular in order to encourage Emperor Leopold I not to provide backing for his fellow Catholic.[20]

With regard to the changing world today, far from globalization making diplomacy redundant or at best marginal, it has made more of abroad relevant to both people and governments, has increased the complexity of international relations, not least by sharpening issues of legitimacy and expanding the number and range of interests that have to be considered; and thus has resulted in greater need for mediation by diplomats.[21] The relevant globalization includes the exposure of diplomatic acts to wider audiences by the spread of radio and television, for example in the Arab world from the 1950s.[22]

The greater need for mediation by diplomats is not the same, however, as arguing for a continuation of the Satow/Bland tradition, while the idea of diplomacy as necessarily 'devoid of subjective elements'[23] is a conceit. Indeed, the role of political considerations makes any assessment of diplomatic effectiveness in terms of administrative criteria somewhat limited. An understanding of its explicit or inherent politicality is central to any assessment of foreign policy, and thus of diplomacy.

Nevertheless, as with Intelligence agencies, the need for flexibility in the conduct of foreign policy puts a premium on traditional diplomatic skills, notably the in-depth study of other powers' culture and history, and especially of the historical relationship between nations. The value of such skills appears particularly appropriate in inter-cultural relations, especially in adapting strategy to opponents' cultural needs and in resisting the temptation for haste,[24] a temptation that is central in certain political cultures, notably that of the USA. Thus the 'how' of diplomacy remains important to its content and effectiveness. The changing nature of international relations from the early 1990s is highlighted in the Postscript, but it would be a misleading form of presentism to neglect or discard the key skills that are still required.

Postscript

There is a tendency among British historians to treat history as a subject where the scholar can and should offer not only impartiality and objectivity, but also a disjuncture or gap between their own work and changing political concerns. I am unconvinced by this argument; and I think it relevant to discuss this book in terms of current issues. There are important questions at present about the practicality and effectiveness of diplomacy in particular contexts, and also in general. The former, for example, relate to issues such as the value of negotiating with radical Islamic movements, notably Hamas, Hezbollah and the Taliban, as part of a settlement to conflict in the Middle East, Afghanistan and Pakistan, while in August 2009 there was controversy over the degree of representation at the ceremony in which President Ahmadinejad's contentious re-election in Iran was officially endorsed by the Supreme Leader of that country.

The issue of the more general effectiveness of diplomacy includes discussion of the use of the United Nations. The UN has many failings, but it is notable that international bodies are more numerous today than ever before, and that they serve as a key means to advance co-operation. Diplomacy thus appears, in this context, as the successor to imperial power, and as a more effective means of incorporation, both regionally and globally. Indeed, it is the versatility and durability of forms of association that are based on co-operation that deserve attention, and these should be seen not as a stage on the progress towards a stronger 'state', whether international or domestic, but as valuable and capable in their own right. Such a view of diplomacy reflects an explicit critical engagement with the apparent value of strong state forms, and notably if their power is linked to an international ambition that can be seen as disruptive.

Diplomacy, therefore, can be located in terms of pressing domestic as well as international political issues, issues which relate not only to specific concerns but also to the culture of international relations. The same was true for the past.

At the present moment, a key concern is the value of diplomacy, both functionally and as a result of 'contradictory notions of legitimacy'.[1] Diplomacy as a form of conventional governmental activity faces criticisms from those advocating different, more liberal, if not radical, forms of international engagement.

Secondly, there are criticisms of diplomatic practice from exponents of the value of 'hard power'. The latter criticism saw a peak during the Bush presidency of 2001–9, with unilateral American action at variance with calls for multilateral compliance with a rule-based international system; but although convenient, this presidency alone does not deserve blame for such unilateral action. Indeed, the Putin presidency in Russia, offered as clear, if not more clear, a demonstration of the same tendency, not least in its treatment of Georgia, its supply of nuclear technology to Iran, and the use of energy supplies as a means to apply diplomatic pressure.

A location of diplomacy in terms of 'soft power', and therefore at variance with 'hard power', is also convenient but not completely correct. For example, the Area Commands of the American military have a diplomatic role alongside their more martial conceptions, objectives and capabilities. Nevertheless, past military planning generally failed to understand the political character of the domestic circumstances of other states: a result of, and also producing, strategy unilluminated by diplomacy.[2] This tendency remains a ever-present characteristic.

Diplomacy is more commonly located today as a means of 'soft power'. In place of the classic traditions of foreign policy and strategy, there is, from that perspective, the messy, untidy, media-mediated world of external relations. This is a world that greatly challenges earlier assumptions. Diplomats have moved on from traditional inter-state relations, and related research and analysis. They are now projecting and seeking to influence across a broad front, although this is more true of the USA and other major Western countries than of the smaller European Union states. Cultural diplomacy conducted by an Ambassador today will cover football diplomacy and working with domestic fan organizations to prevent hooliganism in overseas matches as well as preparations for the next European summit. Such hooliganism, and the response, are seen as highly significant for popular perceptions of other states. Officials dealing with the European Union, who may be diplomats or civil servants, will deal with any part of the EU *acquis* from the size of plugs, to carbon emissions, to the single farm payment.

Furthermore, the target now for embassies will not be the government of accreditation, but as much public opinion, whether in the mosque or university or streets. Hence Ambassadors spend a lot of time in television studios or on air, or even taking part in television game shows. Most

British Ambassadors found themselves interacting with the 'street' at the time of Princess Diana's death in 1997. In an explicit quest for accessibility, diplomats have to be open to domestic as well as foreign audiences, and to adapt to changing media. Thus on 26 August 2009 Mark Sedwill, the British Ambassador in Kabul, who had already been much in evidence on the television screens, answered e-mail questions from the British public in a press conference live from Kabul by video link. The website of the British Foreign Office now has links to blogs, Facebook and Twitter. The Israeli Ambassador in London is often on Radio 4's *Today* programme.

More specifically, the British Foreign Office conducts a major programme of outreach to overseas Islam, and even to domestic Islam. In turn, the Moslem 'street' took anger against the appearance in 2005 in a Danish newspaper of cartoons of the Prophet Muhammad so far as to attack Danish embassies. Al-Qaeda operatives were responsible for attacking the embassy in Pakistan. Outreach was also the theme of Louis Susman, the new American envoy to London, in the interview with the *Financial Times* published on 22 September 2009: 'I want to be the best salesman I can for our strategic interests. I want to become part of the fabric of the UK community . . . I have a definite commitment to public policy outreach. We need to reach out to a lot of groups, including the Muslim community, in a way that isn't superficial and that is real. I intend to talk to people in the mosques and the academic community and the student community.'

The perceived role of public attitudes and actions in international relations reflects, and is reflected in, the important part played by the news media in the making of policy. Ministers and politicians now play more to the global media than to the quiet back channel. During the First Gulf War (1990–91) CNN was used by Saddam Hussein to convey his messages to the West and became compulsory viewing in Western foreign ministries. Now, politicians spend much time trying to devise messages for players in the Middle East through the Al Jazeera television network and other channels. President Obama's Cairo speech of 2009 is a fair instance of diplomacy in the media age, targeting all Muslim countries in a way that traditional diplomacy cannot hope to reach, although it is unclear how far this attempt will succeed. Obama insisted that members of the Muslim Brotherhood be located prominently in the audience, which considerably angered President Mubarak of Egypt, an opponent of the Brotherhood.

Moreover, the 24-hour news cycle has totally transformed relationships between political leaders and their officials and staff. The time available for research, strategic analysis and recommendation has been brutally foreshortened. Politicians need to be on air around the clock. They do not have the time to wait for major policy papers and recommendations. Instead, politicians need bullet points and instant facts to enable a swift appearance on the White House Lawn, the BBC's *Today* programme, or the equivalents.

In addition, because of the sheer volume of open-source information, traditional practitioners are at a disadvantage, and, in terms of analysis, face serious competition from open-source agencies, such as the International Crisis Group, Janes, private security companies, for example Control Risks, and even international banks. The fiscal stability and importance of creditworthiness underlines the significance of the latter. The online BBC is now a global resource, and therefore an asset for British cultural diplomacy. Furthermore, because of shrinking resources for diplomacy, smaller overseas networks, and the expanded range of concerns, many foreign ministries will necessarily use the private sector, a process encouraged by their resort to management consultants who tend to press for this policy. Some countries even outsource their lobbying and media campaigns to well-established lobbying groups, such as the Sawyer Miller Group, which has been described as 'spin doctors to the world'.

Such activity in part reflects the pressure created by the role of NGOs. Amnesty and Human Rights Watch are global players. In the Human Rights sphere (the capitalization reflecting the extent to which more than description is involved), the late 1990s was of great importance, notably with the detention of General Pinochet in 1998, Tony Blair's speech to the Chicago Economic Club on 24 April 1999 on interventionism, and being 'a force for good', and the 1999 NATO campaign against Serbia as a result of its policy of ethnic violence in Kosovo. Both Amnesty and Human Rights Watch played a significant role in the Pinochet hearings before the Law Lords in London. Now Human Rights, responses to disasters, climate change and environmental considerations, are all major drivers in the conduct of international relations, with the UN's Human Rights Council playing a role in the former as with the 2009 controversy over the nature of conflict in Gaza earlier that year.

Another aspect of the changing world of diplomacy is demonstrated by the extent to which consular activities, notably protecting the interests of citizens abroad, have risen very far up the diplomatic agenda. This change owes much to the 24-hour media, which ensures that the fate of one missing child can dominate the media, and thus have a great impact on politicians. The case of Madeleine McCann (which greatly affected Anglo-Portuguese relations in 2007) was exceptional, but for the last decade any envoy will now be told instantly of an unusual or dramatic consular case. In the event of any air or bus crash, explosion or natural disaster around the world, diplomats will be on the way to the site, as there is the expectation that they should be there and able to brief ministers and the media.

As another instance of the responsiveness to a domestic agenda, foreign offices have become a platform for a variety of different interests. Thus there are questions about there being the requisite number of disabled, gay and ethnic minority diplomats. Embassies are expected to report on how green they are, and what savings they are making in carbon emissions; and so on. In 2009 British embassies were encouraged to fund equal-rights activities in countries with homophobic governments, for example Jamaica and Nigeria, such as gay pride marches and legal challenges from local campaigners. Robin Barnett, the envoy to Romania, attended a gay pride march in Bucharest.

Concern with 'soft power' is not simply a question of Western views. Aspects of 'soft power' are pursued at present by most states, including for example China, particularly in Africa.[3] China recognized the impact of the new global world in allowing astonishing coverage of its response to the recent huge earthquake. In the case of the domestic and international responses to the fraudulent Iranian elections of 2009, there was a movement to more informal networks, notably Facebook and Twitter.

'Soft power' has its critics as well as its advocates, and not only in terms of the approach of 'How many divisions has the Pope?'. This remark of Stalin's, however, appeared far less apposite after the collapse of Communism in Eastern Europe and, eventually, the Soviet Union in part thanks to the activities of Pope John Paul II (r. 1978–2005), notably in supporting opposition to Communist rule in Poland.

Yet the argument that hard facts of national strength and international coercion, or, in these cases, its absence, are central, seems appropriate from the perspective of contemporary Sudan and Zimbabwe, in each of which authoritarian governments are able to govern in a tyrannical fashion, largely heedless of international condemnation and diplomatic action. Indeed, as also after the establishment of the League of Nations, the weaknesses of diplomacy appear to have become more obvious with the humanitarian and other pretensions of international norms that have been energetically advanced since the end of the Cold War.

The challenge to international diplomacy from state power is matched by that from political and religious forces that reject the practice as well as the conventions of compromise, and thus weaken political management through diplomacy. Indeed, when that situation occurs, and the negotiation for influence is rejected by one or more sides, then the ceremonies and institutions of diplomacy can appear like a façade.

In practice, however, these ceremonies and institutions are required to help secure and consolidate any eventual settlement. Indeed, from this perspective, activity since the end of the Cold War is a reflection of the need for diplomacy as the means of reconciling international issues (and, in some cases, domestic ones also), and as the culture that appears most appropriate for such resolution. Diplomacy here does not entail idealism as opposed to realism, but instead is an aspect of both currents of international analysis and activity. Realism demands an understanding of the complex pluralism of international relations, and this understanding has become more important as grand narratives of human development have been qualified, forcing an understanding of global order in terms of pluralism and of globalization as a product of compromise.

This process of qualification of grand narratives has been particularly apparent over the last century. The liberal, free-trading optimism of the nineteenth century, and the related attempts in the 1890s and 1900s to advance a rule-based co-operative international order, were both derailed by the First World War. The internationalist, democratic sequel to that conflict, offered by ideas of self-determination and by the League of Nations and the diplomacy of the 1920s, was overthrown in the 1930s by opposition from totalitarian states. Fascist solutions to questions of international order were subsequently discredited by the nature and fate of the Axis powers in 1943–5, while Communism, in turn, was discredited at the international level by the Sino-Soviet split that became public in the 1960s, and also by its association with totalitarianism and imperialism, before it was overthrown in 1989–91 as a governing system in much of the world as a consequence of multiple and serious political and economic failures. Moreover, powerful signs in the 1990s and 2000s of the resilience of religion and ethnicity as forms of identity and forces for action not only created problems for diplomatic culture and practice in particular junctions, as well as specific issues for activity, but also led to a querying of the parabolic, teleological account of change. Instead, this resilience led to renewed interest in more pessimistic theories, including cyclical ones.

While the political agenda in many states became more cautious in the 1980s and 1990s, notably about the domestic capability of government, nevertheless, a conviction that international order could, and should, be created and enforced was expressed by liberal interventionists, motivated by humanitarian and environmental considerations, notably in the 1990s, and, in response to the terrorist al-Qaeda attacks in the USA, by American neo-conservatives from 2001. This disjuncture between cautious views on domestic and bold view on international politics and governance is problematic, however, not least if solutions for international problems are assumed to have domestic consequences, as is indeed the case. Indeed this linkage poses a serious challenge to First World consumers and Third World populists alike.

Nevertheless, diplomacy represents a crucial cultural context, as well as being a key tool as we look beyond ideologies of facile optimism to the real and necessary complexities and compromises of power and authority. Diplomatic activity can result in differences of perception, but, more commonly, it is designed to help highlight them as part of a process of resolution; although the latter is far from easy. In part, this difficulty arises because a coherent policy is desirable for any process of effective bargaining, but such coherence requires a domestic stability that is difficult to secure or maintain.[4] Cordell Hull, a long-serving American Congressman before becoming the longest serving Secretary of State (1933–44), declared in 1948,

> Partisan considerations have no place in foreign policy . . . it is inadmissible to inject advantages of party or of person into foreign policy. Attempts to do so weaken the influence of our government abroad by presenting to foreign and possibly hostile governments a picture of divided councils, confusion, and lack of popular support of this government's position toward the world.[5]

Diplomats, like Secretaries of State, were frequently critical of the very different reality. George Kennan, Director of Policy Planning in the State Department and Ambassador to the Soviet Union (1952–3) and Yugoslavia (1961–3), offered reflections that are true for so many states that they cast doubts on the standard account of diplomacy:

> the function of American career diplomacy is marked by a certain tragic contradiction. The Foreign Service Officer is taught and encouraged to believe that he is serving the *national* interest – the interest, that is, of the country as a whole – in its external relations. He finds himself working, nevertheless, for people to whom this is not the main concern. Their main concern is domestic politics; and the interests they find themselves pursuing in this field of activity are not often but usually in conflict with the requirements of a sensible national diplomacy. Such is the degree of egocentricity of the participants in the American domestic-political struggle that the possibility of taking action – or, more commonly, making statements – in the field of external relations presents itself to them primarily as a means of producing this or that effect on the political scene.[6]

Looked at differently, the cerebral Kennan was unwilling to adapt to the domestic political dimension of diplomacy.[7] The same point can be made about the criticisms of the character and conduct of the Blairite foreign policy made by Sir Christopher Meyer, Ambassador in Washington under Blair, although his argument that 'New Labour' lacked a sense of national interest and that this led to misguided policies executed in an incoherent fashion has considerable force.

The need for diplomacy does not necessarily mean a reliance on conventional diplomatic channels, or indeed diplomats; but their value and experience are such that they will remain important, at the same time that they are frequently decried. Such has been the context for, and conduct of, diplomacy for over a century, and the criticisms, in part warranted but often unrealistic, will continue.

This book closes therefore with an observation of change and continuity. Such a conclusion might seem to be a cliché, but it captures a truth of the human condition, whether individual or collective. At the same time, the emphasis here on change and continuity is not the customary one in historical discussions of diplomacy, with their stress on a trajectory from Ancient Greece to the Italian Renaissance and on, via the Peace of Westphalia of 1648, to a European diplomatic old regime that survived the French Revolution only to be transformed by successive challenges from 1914.

Instead, the theme has been one of a less coherent development, not least because of the need to give due weight to non-Western patterns of diplomacy. The key issues are as much as the relationship between Western and non-Western practices as challenges within the West. This relationship has changed significantly over the last two centuries, and there are no signs that this situation of continued change will cease. Given the shift in relative power within the world, the extent to which the diplomatic practice of India, China, and other prominent non-Western states will conform to established conventions will probably be the most important question over the next few decades. The resulting changes in diplomatic activity may well make the customary account of diplomatic history seem even more limited, if not redundant, than it does at present.

References

Preface

1 P. G. Wodehouse, *Hot Water* (London, 2008 edn), pp. 15–16, 27.
2 P. Wells, 'Comments, Custard Pies and Comic Cuts: The Boulting Brothers at Play, 1955–65', in *The Family Way: The Boulting Brothers and Postwar British Film Culture*, ed. A. Burton, T. O'Sullivan and P. Wells (Trowbridge, 2000), p. 59.
3 A. P. Calhamer, 'Diplomacy', in *The Games and Puzzles Book of Modern Board Games* (London, 1975), pp. 26–44; R. Sharp, *The Game of Diplomacy* (London, 1979).
4 J. Black, *British Diplomats and Diplomacy, 1688–1800* (Exeter, 2001), *European International Relations, 1648–1815* (Basingstoke, 2002), *Rethinking Military History* (Abingdon, 2004), and *Great Powers and the Quest for Hegemony: The World Order since 1500* (Abingdon, 2008).
5 J. Black, *Kings, Nobles and Commoners: States and Societies in Early Modern Europe, a Revisionist History* (London, 2004).

Introduction

1 A-M. Juvaini, *Genghis Khan: The History of the World-Conqueror*, ed. J. A. Boyle (2nd edn, Manchester, 1997), p. 80.
2 E. Satow, *A Guide to Diplomatic Practice* (London, 1917), p. 1.
3 H. Nicolson, *Diplomacy* (Oxford, 1963), pp. 3–4.
4 P. Barber, *Diplomacy* (London, 1979), p. 6.
5 J. Der Derian, 'Mediating Estrangement: A Theory for Diplomacy', *Review of International Studies*, 13 (1987), p. 9.
6 J.C.E. Gienow-Hecht, *Transmission Impossible: American Journalism as Cultural Diplomacy in Postwar Germany, 1945–1955* (Baton Rouge, LA, 1999); R. T. Arndt, *The First Resort of Kings: American Cultural Diplomacy in the Twentieth Century* (Dulles, VA, 2005). This section was written soon after walking past 'The Texas Embassy' in London, a restaurant.
7 T. W. Zeiler, *Ambassadors in Pinstripes: The Spalding World Baseball Tour and the Birth of the American Empire* (Lanham, MD, 2006). See also B. J. Keys, *Globalizing Sport: National Rivalry and International Community in the 1930s* (Cambridge, MA, 2006).
8 L. B. Fritzinger, *Diplomat without Portfolio: Valentine Chirol, His Life, and 'The Times'* (London, 2006).

9   *The Times*, 24 July 2009, p. 18.
10 *Ten O'Clock News*, BBC 1, 15 October 2009.
11 F. Lidz, 'Biblical Adversity in a '60s Suburb', *New York Times*, 27 September 2009, p. 9.
12 F. Adams, *Dollar Diplomacy: United States Economic Assistance to Latin America* (Aldershot, 2000).
13 P. Y. Beaurepaire, *Le mythe de l'Europe française au XVIIIe siècle: Diplomatie, culture et sociabilités au temps des Lumières* (Paris, 2007).
14 For diplomats as negotiators, intelligence sources and cultural contacts, M. J. Levin, *Agents of Empire: Spanish Ambassadors in Sixteenth-Century Italy* (Ithaca, NY, 2005); P. M. Drover, 'Letters, Notes and Whispers: Diplomacy, Ambassadors and Information in the Italian Renaissance Princely State', PhD thesis, Yale, 2002.
15 Reporting Cardinal Fleury, French first minister, John Burnaby, private secretary to James, Earl Waldegrave, British envoy in Paris, to Horatio Walpole, envoy in the Hague, 1 February 1735, NA. SP. 84/341 fols 56–7.
16 P. Jackson, *France and the Nazi Menace: Intelligence and Policy Making, 1933–1939* (Oxford, 2000).
17 E. W. Nelson, 'The Origins of Modern Balance of Power Politics', *Medievalia et Humanistica*, I (1943), pp. 124–42.
18 Herodotus, *The Histories*, Book VII, 131–2. Trans. for the Loeb edition by A. D. Godley (1922).
19 R. Cohen and R. Westbrook, eds, *Amarna Diplomacy: The Beginnings of International Relations* (Baltimore, MD, 2000), p. 173.
20 R. A. Roland, *Interpreters as Diplomats: A Diplomatic History of the Role of Interpreters in World Politics* (Ottawa, 1999).
21 F. Adcock and D. J. Mosley, *Diplomacy in Ancient Greece* (London, 1975); P. Low, *Interstate Relations in Classical Greece: Morality and Power* (Cambridge, 2007).
22 A. Eckstein, *Mediterranean Anarchy, Interstate War, and the Rise of Rome* (Berkeley, CA, 2006) is the key work, esp. pp. 58–65.
23 Translation of word sometimes given as the Barbarians.
24 Plutarch, *Life of Sulla*, 5, 4–5; from *Six Lives by Plutarch* trans. R. Warner, *Fall of the Roman Republic* (London, 1958), p. 61.
25 W. Treadgold, 'The Diplomatic Career and Historical Work of Olympiodorus of Thebes', *International History Review*, XXVI (2004), p. 714.
26 F. A. Wright, ed., *Liudprand of Cremona: The Embassy to Constantinople and Other Writings* (London, 1930).
27 B.K.U. Weiler, 'The *Negotium Terrae Sanctae* in the Political Discourse of Latin Christendom, 1215–1311', *International History Review*, XXV (2003), p. 35.
28 G. Post, *Studies in Medieval Legal Thought* (Princeton, NJ, 1964); D. E. Queller, 'Thirteenth-century Diplomatic Envoys: *Nuncii* and *Procuratores*', *Speculum*, XXXV (1960), pp. 196–213.
29 For a flavour from the Renaissance, M. J. Haren, ed., *Calendar of Entries in the Papal Registers Relating to Great Britain and Ireland. Papal Letters*, XVIII: *Pius III and Julius II: Vatican Registers, 1503–13, Lateran Registers, 1503–1508* (Dublin, 1989).
30 A. D. Beihammer, M. G. Parani and C. D. Schabel, eds, *Diplomatics in the Eastern Mediterranean: Aspects of Cross-cultural Communication* (Leiden, 2008).

31 D. Berg, M. Kintzinger and P. Monnet, eds, *Auswärtige Politik und internationale Beziehungen im Mittelalter* (Bochum, 2002).

32 J. P. Huffman, *The Social Politics of Medieval Diplomacy: Anglo-German Relations, 1066–1307* (Ann Arbor, MI, 2000).

33 J. Sumption, *The Hundred Years War. III. Divided Houses* (London, 2009), p. 784.

34 P. Chaplais, *English Diplomatic Practice in the Middle Ages* (London, 2002).

35 C. R. Cheney, *Pope Innocent III and England* (Stuttgart, 1976).

36 B. Bombi, 'Andrea Sapiti: His Origins and His Register as a Curial Proctor', *English Historical Review*, CXXIII (2008), pp. 132–6.

37 B. Behrens, 'Origins of the Office of English Resident Ambassador in Rome', *English Historical Review*, XLIX (1934), pp. 640–56.

38 J. Sayers, *Innocent III: Leader of Europe, 1198–1216* (London, 1994); L. Shepard, *Courting Power: Persuasion and Politics in the Early Thirteenth Century* (New York, 1999)); P. Zutshi, 'Innocent III and the Reform of the Papal Chancery', in A. Sommerlechner, ed., *Innocenzo III. Urbs et Orbis. I* (Rome, 2003), pp. 84–101; R. P. Blet, *Histoire de la représentation diplomatique du Saint-Siege, des origines à l'aube du XIXe siècle* (Rome, 1982).

39 C. Smith, ed., *Christians and Moors in Spain*, I: *711–1100* (Warminster, 1988), pp. 62–75.

40 A. A. Hajjī, *Andalusian Diplomatic Relations with Western Europe during the Umayyad Period: An Historical Survey* (Beirut, 1970); Y. Istanbuli, *Diplomacy and Diplomatic Practice in the Early Islamic Era* (Karachi, 2001); M. Vaiou, 'Diplomatic Relations between the Abbasid Caliphate and the Byzantine Empire: Methods and Procedures', DPhil, Oxford University, 2002; N. M. El Cheikh, *Byzantium Viewed by the Arabs* (Cambridge, MA, 2004); B. Lewis, *The Muslim Discovery of Europe* (London, 1982); M. P. Proncaglia, *Essai Bibliographique de Diplomatique Islamique*, I (Beirut, 1979). I have benefited greatly from the advice of Paul Auchterlonie.

41 D. Abulafia, *Frederick II: A Medieval Emperor* (London, 1988).

42 P. Jackson, *The Mongols and the Latin West, 1221–1410* (Harlow, 2005); R. Amitai-Preiss, *Mongols and Mamluks: the Mamluk-Īlkhānid War, 1260–1281* (Cambridge, 1995); N. McLean, 'An Eastern Embassy to Europe in the Years 1287–8', *English Historical Review*, XIV (1899), pp. 299–318; M. Prestwich, *Edward I* (London, 1988), pp. 313–14, 330–31.

43 R. Matthee, 'Iran's Ottoman Diplomacy During the Reign of Shah Sulayman I (1077–1105/1666–94)', in *Iran and Iranian Studies*, ed. K. Eslami (Princeton, NJ, 1998), pp. 152–9.

44 R. G. de Clavijo, *Embassy to Tamerlane, 1403–1406* (London, 1928).

45 N. R. Zacour and H. W. Hazard, eds, *A History of the Crusades. V. The Impact of the Crusades on the Near East* (Madison, WI, 1985).

46 N. Housley, *The Later Crusades, 1274–1580 from Lyons to Alcazar* (Oxford, 1992).

47 R. I. Burns, 'Societies in Symbiosis: The Mudejar-Crusader Experiment in Thirteenth-Century Mediterranean Spain', *International History Review*, II (1980), pp. 349–85.

48 S. Barton '"Do Not Touch Me, for You are a Pagan": A Case of Interfaith Marriage from Eleventh-century Iberia', unpublished paper; J. Pitt-Rivers, *The Fate of Shechem, or the Politics of Sex: Six Essays in the Anthropology of the*

Mediterranean (Cambridge, 1977).
49 W. Cook, *The Hundred Years War for Morocco: Gunpowder and the Military Revolution in the Early Modern Muslim World* (Boulder, CO, 1994).
50 A. Wang, *Ambassadors from the Islands of Immortals: China–Japan Relations in the Han-Tang Period* (Honolulu, HI, 2005).
51 G. Wang, 'Early Ming Relations with Southeast Asia: A Background Essay', in *The Chinese World Order: Traditional China's Foreign Relations*, ed. J. K. Fairbank (Cambridge, MA, 1968), pp. 34–62.
52 M. McGrath, 'The Reigns of Jen-tsung and Ying-tsung', in *The Cambridge History of China V, pt 1. The Sung Dynasty and Its Predecessors, 907–1279*, ed. D. Twitchett and P. J. Smith (Cambridge, 2009), pp. 302–15.
53 M. Lower, 'Tunis in 1270: A Case Study of Interfaith Relations in the Late Thirteenth Century', *International History Review*, XXVIII (2006), p. 511.
54 T. A. Breslin, *Beyond Pain: The Role of Pleasure and Culture in the Making of Foreign Affairs* (Westport, CT, 2002).
55 D. Ostrowski, 'The Growth of Muscovy, 1462–1533', in M. Perrie, *The Cambridge History of Russia*, I: *From Early Rus' to 1689* (Cambridge, 2006), p. 233.
56 T. A. Allsen, *The Royal Hunt in Eurasian History* (Philadelphia, PA, 2006).
57 D. Obolensky, *The Byzantine Commonwealth* (London, 1971).
58 M. Rossabi, ed., *China among Equals: The Middle Kingdom and its Neighbors, 10th–14th Centuries* (Berkeley, CA, 1983).
59 N-Y. Lau, 'Waging War for Peace? The Peace Accord Between the Song and the Liao in AD 1005', in *Warfare in Chinese History*, ed. H. van de Ven (Brill, 2000), p. 215.
60 D. C. Wright, *From War to Diplomatic Parity in Eleventh-Century China: Sung Foreign Relations with Kitan Liao* (Brill, 2005).
61 M. Khodarkovsky, 'The Non-Christian Peoples on the Muscovite Frontiers', *Cambridge History of Russia*, I: *From Early Rus' to 1689*, p. 333.
62 I.C.Y. Hsü, 'Modern Chinese Diplomatic History: A Guide to Research', *International History Review*, I (1979), pp. 102–3.
63 Jing-shen Tao, *Two Sons of Heaven: Studies in Sung-Liao Relations* (Tucson, AZ, 1988); P. Lorge, *War, Politics, and Society in Early Modern China, 900–1795* (Abingdon, 2005).
64 H. G. Marcus, *A History of Ethiopia* (Berkeley, CA, 1994), pp. 20–21, 26, 73–6, 106.
65 R. Islam, *Indo-Persian Relations: A Study of the Political and Diplomatic Relations between the Mughul Empire and Iran* (Tehran, 1970).
66 P. Barber, *Diplomacy* (London, 1979), pp. 51–2.
67 N. Standen, *Unbounded Loyalty: Frontier Crossings in Liao China* (Honolulu, HI, 2007); *Battlefronts Real and Imagined: War, Border, and Identity in the Chinese Middle Period*, ed. D. J. Wyatt (New York, 2008).
68 J. Gommans, *Mughal Warfare: Imperial Frontiers and Highroads to Empire, 1500–1700* (London, 2002).
69 J. Black, 'Frontiers and Military History', *Journal of Military History*, LXXII (2008), pp. 1047–59.
70 For France from 1285 to 1314, see J. Strayer, *The Reign of Philip the Fair* (Princeton, NJ, 1980), pp. 314–16.
71 L.V.D. Martín, 'Castilla 1280–1360: Politica exterior o relaciones accidentals?',

in *Genesis medieval del Estado Moderno: Castilla y Navarra, 1250–1370*, ed. A. Ruquoi (Valladolid, 1988), pp. 125 47.
72 R. Bireley, *The Jesuits and the Thirty Years War* (Cambridge, 2003).
73 J. Black, *Great Powers and the Quest for Hegemony: The World Order since 1500* (Abingdon, 2008).
74 H. H. Rowen, *The King's State: Proprietary Dynasticism in Early Modern France* (New Brunswick, NJ, 1980).
75 For a critique of the latter see R. E. Clayton, 'Diplomats and Diplomacy in London, 1667–1672', DPhil, Oxford University, 1995, pp. 290–91.
76 W. R. Childs, 'England in Europe in the Reign of Edward II', in *The Reign of Edward II: New Perspectives*, ed. G. Dodd and A. Musson (York, 2006), pp. 116–17.
77 M. Prestwich, *Edward I* (London, 1988), p. 312.
78 B.K.U. Weiler, *Henry III of England and the Staufen Empire, 1216–1272* (Woodbridge, 2006).
79 J. Smith, 'The Diplomatic Mirror: Views of British and United States Diplomats on Brazil, 1889–1930', unpublished paper, pp. 8–9. I would like to thank Joe Smith for letting me cite from this paper.
80 *Sunday Times*, 12 July 2009, pp. 1–2. See also C. Meyer, *Getting Our Way: 500 Years of Adventure and Intrigue: The Inside Story of British Diplomacy* (London, 2009), e.g. pp. 262–4.
81 Gansinot to Ferdinand, Count Plettenberg, First Minister of the Elector of Cologne, 9 October 1728, Münster, Staatsarchiv, Deposit Nordkirchen, Plettenberg papers, NB 25 fol. 21.
82 C. Windler, 'Diplomatic History as a Field for Cultural Analysis: Muslim-Christian Relations in Tunis, 1700–1840', *Historical Journal*, XLIV (2001), p. 81.

ONE: 1450–1600

1 M. S. Anderson, *The Origins of the Modern European State System, 1494–1618* (Harlow, 1998), pp. 52–3; G. Mattingly, *Renaissance Diplomacy* (London, 1955); O. Krauske, *Die Entwickelung der ständigen Diplomatie* (Leipzig, 1885).
2 P. Zutshi, 'Proctors Acting for English Petitioners in the Chancery of the Avignon Popes (1305–1378)', *Journal of Ecclesiastical History*, XXXV (1984), p. 27.
3 J. Sumption, *The Hundred Years War. III. Divided Houses* (London, 2009), p. 785.
4 M. E. James, *English Politics and the Concept of Honour, 1485–1642* (Oxford, 1978).
5 G. Mattingly, 'The First Resident Embassies: Medieval Italian Origins of Modern Diplomacy', *Speculum*, XII (1937), pp. 423–39.
6 R. A. Griffiths and J. Law, eds, *Rawdon Brown and the Anglo-Venetian Relationship* (Stroud, 2005).
7 B. Behrens, 'Treatises on the Ambassador Written in the Fifteenth and Early Sixteenth Centuries', *English Historical Review*, LI (1936), pp. 616–27.
8 L. Bély, *La Société des Princes: XVIe–XVIIIe siècle* (Paris, 1999).
9 As is done, for example, in K. Hamilton and R. Langhorne, *The Practice of Diplomacy: Its Evolution, Theory and Administration* (Abingdon, 1995).

10 R. Fubini, 'Diplomacy and Government in the Italian City-States of the Fifteenth Century (Florence and Venice)', in *Politics and Diplomacy in Early Modern Italy: The Structure of Diplomatic Practice, 1450–1800*, ed. D. Frigo (Cambridge, 2000), p. 48.
11 M. C. Wright, 'The Adaptability of Ch'ing Diplomacy: The Case of Korea', *Journal of Asian Studies*, XVII (1958), pp. 363–81.
12 H. M. Scott, 'Diplomatic Culture in Old Regime Europe', in *Cultures of Power in Europe during the Long Eighteenth Century*, ed. H. M. Scott and B. Simms (Cambridge, 2007), pp. 58–9.
13 Act IV, scene 3.
14 G. M. Bell, 'Elizabethan Diplomatic Compensation: Its Nature and Variety', *Journal of British Studies*, XX/2 (1981), pp. 1–25.
15 F. Braudel, *The Mediterranean and the Mediterranean World in the Age of Philip II* (New York, 1973), pp. 355, 365. See also E.J.B. Allen, *Post and Courier Service in the Diplomacy of Early Modern Europe* (The Hague, 1972).
16 I am most grateful to Robert Finlay for this information.
17 K. Lowe, 'Representing Africa: Ambassadors and Princes from Christian Africa to Renaissance Italy and Portugal, 1402–1608', *Transactions of the Royal Historical Society*, 6th ser., XVII (2007), pp. 101–28.
18 M. Strachan, *Sir Thomas Roe* (London, 1989).
19 N. Matar, *Islam in Britain, 1558–1685* (Cambridge, 1998); *Turks, Moors, and Englishmen in the Age of Discovery* (New York, 1999); *Britain and Barbary 1589–1689* (Gainesville, FL, 2005); and *Europe through Arab Eyes, 1578–1727* (New York, 2008). For the Algerine envoy visiting a magic-show in London, *Craftsman*, XX February 1731.
20 D. Goffman, *Britons in the Ottoman Empire, 1642–1660* (London, 1998).
21 F. J. Baumgartner, *Louis XII* (Stroud, 1994).
22 X. Le Person, 'A Moment of "Resverie": Charles V and Francis I's Encounter at Aigues-Mortes (July 1538)', *French History*, XIX (2005), pp. 1–27.
23 S. Gunn and A. Janse, eds, *The Court as a Stage: England and the Low Countries in the Later Middle Ages* (Woodbridge, 2006).
24 R. Finlay, *Venice Besieged: Politics and Diplomacy in the Italian Wars, 1494–1534* (Farnham, 2008).
25 P. Brummett, *Ottoman Seapower and Levantine Diplomacy in the Age of Discovery* (Albany, NY, 1994).
26 N.R.K. Keddie and R. Matthee, eds, *Iran and the Surrounding World: Interactions in Culture and Cultural Politics* (Seattle, WA, 2002); M. Mazzaoui, ed., *Safavid Iran and Her Neighbors* (Salt Lake City, UT, 2003).
27 H. Fürtig, *Iran's Rivalry with Saudi Arabia between the Gulf Wars* (Reading, 2002).
28 R. W. Olson, *The Siege of Mosul* (Bloomington, IN, 1975), p. 64.
29 G. David and P. Fodor, eds, *Hungarian-Ottoman Military and Diplomatic Relations in the Age of Suleyman the Magnificent* (Budapest, 1994).
30 S. Carroll, *Noble Power during the French Wars of Religion: The Guise Affinity and the Catholic Cause in Normandy* (Cambridge, 1998); D. Parrott, 'The Mantuan Succession, 1627–1631: A Sovereignty Dispute in Early Modern Europe', *English Historical Review*, CXII (1997), pp. 20–65, and 'A *Prince souverain* and the French Crown: Charles de Nevers, 1580–1637', in *Royal and Republican Sovereignty in Early Modern Europe*, ed. R. Oresko, G. C. Gibbs

and H. M. Scott (Cambridge, 1997), pp. 149–87; H. H. Rowen, *The Prince of Orange* (Cambridge, 1988).

31 J. Dewald, *Aristocratic Experience and the Origins of Modern Culture: France, 1570–1715* (Berkeley, CA, 1993), p. 207.

32 T. Osborne, *Dynasty and Diplomacy in the Court of Savoy: Politics, Culture and the Thirty Years' War* (Cambridge, 2002).

33 G. M. Bell, ed., *A Handlist of British Diplomatic Representatives, 1509–1688* (London, 1990).

34 G. Parker, *The Grand Strategy of Philip II* (New Haven, CT, 2000). I have benefited from hearing a paper by Edward Tenace, 'Messianic Strategy of Philip II and the Spanish Failure in the Wars of the 1590s'.

TWO: 1600–1690

1 B. T. Whitehead, *Braggs and Boasts: Propaganda in the Year of the Armada* (Stroud, 1994).

2 D. Biow, *Doctors, Ambassadors, Secretaries: Humanism and Professions in Renaissance Italy* (Chicago, 2002); J. R. Snyder, *Dissimulation and the Culture of Secrecy in Early Modern Europe* (Berkeley, CA, 2009).

3 S. Brigden, '"The Shadow That You Know": Sir Thomas Wyatt and Sir Francis Bryan at Court and in Embassy', *Historical Journal*, XXXIX (1996), pp. 9–27.

4 Rochefort to the Council of the Marine, 13 Sept. 1717, Paris, Archives Nationales, Archives de la Marine, B7 272.

5 R. Hutton, 'The Making of the Secret Treaty of Dover 1668–1670', *Historical Journal* (1986), 29, pp. 297–318.

6 For reports from the English agent in Brussels, see O. G. Dyfnallt and S. P. Anderson, *Report on the Manuscripts of the Most Honourable The Marquess of Downshire VI: Papers of William Trumbull the Elder, 1616–1618* (London, 1995).

7 E. McCabe, 'England's Foreign Policy in 1619: Lord Doncaster's Embassy to the Princes of Germany', *Mitteilungen des Instituts für Österreichische Geschichtsforschung*, LVIII (1950), pp. 457–77.

8 W. B. Patterson, *King James VI and I and the Reunion of Christendom* (Cambridge, 1997).

9 A. Milton, *The British Delegation and the Synod of Dort, 1618–1619* (Woodbridge, 2005).

10 J. Dunindam, *Myths of Power. Norbert Elias and the Early Modern European Court* (Amsterdam, 1995); J. Adamson, ed., *The Princely Courts of Europe. Ritual, Politics and Culture under the Ancien Régime, 1500–1750* (London, 1999); H. Watanabe-O'Kelly, *Court Culture in Dresden: From Renaissance to Baroque* (Basingstoke, 2002).

11 Charles Delafaye, Under Secretary, to Charles, 2nd Viscount Townshend, Secretary of State for the Northern Department, 22 June 1725, London, National Archives, State Papers (hereafter NA. SP.) 43/74.

12 I have benefited from hearing a lecture by Denice Fett on 'Information, Gossip and Rumor: The Limits of Intelligence at the Early Modern Court, 1558–1585'. See also E. Opitz, 'Diplomacy and Secret Communications in the Seventeenth Century: Some Remarks on the Method of Gaining News in the Age of Absolutism', in *Clio Goes Spying. Eight Essays on the History of Diplomacy*,

ed. B. Huldt and W. Agrell (Solna, 1983).
13 D. Croxton, '"The Prosperity of Arms Is Never Continual": Military Intelligence, Surprise, and Diplomacy in 1640s Germany', *Journal of Military History*, LXIV (2000), pp. 981–1004, esp. pp. 991, 1001.
14 For an English abridgement of the terms, G. Symcox, ed., *War, Diplomacy and Imperialism, 1618–1763* (London, 1974), pp. 39–62. Recent work can be approached through K. Bussmann and H. Schilling, eds, *1648: War and Peace in Europe* (3 vols, Münster, 1998), and H. J. Duchhardt, ed., *Der Westfälische Friede* (Munich, 1998), pp. 369–91.
15 K. J. Holsti, *Peace and War: Armed Conflicts and International Order, 1648–1989* (Cambridge, 1991), p. 39; L. Bély, ed., *L'Europe des Traités de Westphalie: Esprit de la Diplomatie et Diplomatie de l'Esprit* (Paris, 2000); R. Lesaffer, ed., *Peace Treaties and International Law in European History* (Cambridge, 2004). For a recent example of the widespread application of the term, see F. H. Lawson, 'Westphalian Sovereignty and the Emergence of the Arab States System: The Case of Syria', *International History Review*, XXII (2000), pp. 529–56 and *Constructing International Relations in the Arab World* (Stanford, CA, 2006).
16 D. Croxton, 'The Peace of Westphalia and the Origins of Sovereignty', *International History Review*, XXI (1999), pp. 569–91.
17 P. H. Wilson, *German Armies: War and German Politics, 1648–1806* (London, 1998).
18 Count Törring, Bavarian foreign minister, to Plettenberg, 29 February 1727, Münster, Staatsarchiv, Plettenberg papers, NA. 148 fol. 76.
19 M. Roberts, ed., *Swedish Diplomats at Cromwell's Court, 1655–1656* (London, 1988), p. 301.
20 T. Venning, *Cromwellian Foreign Policy* (Basingstoke, 1995).
21 D. Croxton, *Peacemaking in Early-Modern Europe: Cardinal Mazarin and the Congress of Westphalia, 1643–1648* (Selinsgrove, PA, 1999).
22 R. E. Clayton, 'Diplomats and Diplomacy in London, 1667–1672', DPhil, Oxford University, 1995, p. 16.
23 M. Haehl, *Les Affaires étrangères au temps de Richelieu: Le Secrétariat d'États les Agents Diplomatiques, 1624–1642* (Brussels, 2006).
24 L. Bély, 'Méthodes et perspectives dans l'étude des négociations internationales à l'époque moderne', in *Frankreich im europäischen Staatensystem der Frühen Neuzeit*, ed. R. Babel (Paris, 1995), pp. 219–34.
25 S. C. Neff, *War and the Law of Nations: A General History* (Cambridge, 2005).
26 O. Asbach, ed., *War, the State and International Law in Seventeenth-Century Europe* (Farnham, 2010).
27 Re Congress of Cambrai, BL. Stowe Mss fol. 73.
28 K. R. Robinson, 'Centering the King of Chosŏn: Aspects of Korean Maritime Diplomacy, 1392–1592', *Journal of Asian Studies*, LIX (2000), pp. 109–25; K. M. Swope, 'Deceit, Disguise, and Dependence: China, Japan, and the Future of the Tributary System, 1592–1596', *International History Review*, XXIV (2002), p. 763; H. G. Marcus, *A History of Ethiopia* (Berkeley, CA, 1994), pp. 89–90.
29 R. P. Toby, *State and Diplomacy in Early Modern Japan: Asia in the Development of Tokugawa Bakufu* (Stanford, CA, 1991; E. H. Kang, *Diplomacy and Ideology in Japanese-Korean Relations from the Fifteenth to the Eighteenth Century* (New York, 1997).

REFERENCES

30 C. J. Heywood, 'English Diplomatic Relations with Turkey, 1689–1698', in *Four Centuries of Turco-British Relations*, ed. W. Hale and A. I. Bağiş (Walkington, 1984), p. 29; I. Parev, *Habsburgs and Ottomans between Vienna and Belgrade, 1683–1739* (Boulder, CO, 1995). For a later special embassy, N. Itzkowitz and M. Mote, eds, *Mubadele: An Ottoman/Russian Exchange of Ambassadors* (Chicago, IL, 1970).

31 Sir Everard Fawkener, British envoy in Constantinople, to Thomas Robinson, envoy in Vienna, 20 Oct. 1736, NA. SP. 80/123.

32 Russia was allowed to retain control of this position, contested since the 1690s, as long as it was unfortified.

33 P. C. Hartmann, *Geld als Instrument europäischer Machtpolitik im Zeitalter des Merkantilismus: Studien zu den finanziellen und politischen Beziehungen der Wittelsbacher Territorien Kurbayern, Kurpfalz und Kurköln mit Frankreich und dem Kaiser von 1715 bis 1740* (Munich, 1978).

34 E. Edwards, 'The Personal Archive of the Grand Pensionary, Gaspar Fagel, 1672–1688', *Archives*, XXVIII (2003), p. 17; Baron Ritter to Baron Beckers, 18 Feb. 1764, Munich, Haupstaatsarchiv, Bayr. Gesandtschaft, Wien 676. For hunting dogs for Saxony, Ernst Manteuffel, Saxon minister, to Zamboni, Saxon agent in London, 15 June, 28 Oct. 1729, Oxford, Bodleian Library, Rawlinson Letters 118(1) fols 305–6. For turnips from Poland, Sir Charles Hanbury-Williams to Henry Fox, 17 Dec. 1750, BL. Add. 51393 fol. 125.

35 S. Dixon, *Catherine the Great* (London, 2009), p. 261.

36 T. Osborne, *Dynasty and Diplomacy in the Court of Savoy: Political Culture and the Thirty Years' War* (Cambridge, 2002).

37 Boehmer to Landgrave of Hesse-Darmstadt, 2, 9 May 1735, Darmstadt, Staatsarchiv, EI M14/2.

38 Martine, Hesse-Cassel envoy in Paris, to Landgrave Karl of Hesse-Cassel, 1 Nov. 1723, Marburg, Staatsarchiv, Series 4f, France 1586 fols 215–16.

39 M. Mancall, *Russia and China: Their Diplomatic Relations to 1728* (Cambridge, 1971), pp. 30–31.

40 E. J. Markel, *Die Entwicklung der diplomatischen Rangstufer* (Erlangen, 1951).

41 Baron Wachtendonck to Elector Palatine, 13 Feb. 1733, Munich, Bayerisches Haupstaatsarchiv, Kasten Blau 84/40.

42 K. Müller, *Das Kaiserliche Gesandtschaftswesen im Jahrhundert nach dem Westfälischen Frieden, 1648–1740* (Bonn, 1976), p. 249.

43 Barrillon, French envoy in London, to Louis XIV, 8, 12 Ap., Louis XIV to Lusignan, envoy in Vienna, 2 June, Lusignan to Louis, 29 July 1688, Paris, Ministères des Relations Extérieures, Correspondance Politique (hereafter AE. CP.) Angleterre 165 fols 224, 234–5, Autriche 63 fols 120, 202–3.

44 V. Larminie, 'The Jacobean Diplomatic Fraternity and the Protestant Cause: Sir Isaac Wake and the View from Savoy', *English Historical Review*, CXXI (2006), p. 1326.

45 D. J. Taylor, 'Russian Foreign Policy 1725–39', PhD thesis, University of East Anglia, 1983, p. 17.

46 BL. Add. 72578–84, for copies in the papers of William Trumbull, envoy in Paris (1685–6) and Constantinople (1687–91). See also Earl of Hyndford to Onslow Burrish, 27 Feb. (OS) 1752, NA.SP. 110/6 and W. C. Ford, ed., *Writings of John Quincy Adams* (2 vols, New York, 1913), I, 192.

47 Skelton to the Lord President, 24 March 1688, NA.SP. 78/151 fol. 160.

48 W. J. Roosen, 'The True Ambassador: Occupational and Personal Characteristics of French Ambassadors under Louis XIV', *European Studies Review*, III (1973), pp. 121–39.

49 S. Jettot, 'Diplomacy, Religion and Political Stability: The Views of Three English Diplomats', in *War and Religion after Westphalia, 1648–1713*, ed. D. Onnekink (Farnham, 2009), pp. 89–102.

50 Baron Ritter to Baron Beckers, Palatine Foreign Minister, 2 Feb. 1774, Munich, Bayr. Ges. Wien 702.

51 G. Braun, 'Une tour de Babel? Les Langues de la négociation et les problèmes de traduction au congrès de la Paix de Westphalie', in *Le Diplomatie au travail. Entscheidungsprozesse, Information und Kommunikation im Umkreis des Westfälischen Friedenskongresses*, ed. R. Babel (Munich, 2004), pp. 139–72.

52 K.H.D. Haley, *An English Diplomat in the Low Countries: Sir William Temple and John de Witt, 1665–1672* (Oxford, 1986), p. 57.

53 G. Signorotto and M. A. Visceglia, eds, *Court and Politics in Papal Rome, 1492–1700* (Cambridge, 2002).

54 E. Serra, 'The Treaty of the Pyrenees, 350 Years Later', *Catalan Historical Review*, I (2008), p. 82. See also L. Williams, ed., *Letters from the Pyrenees: Don Luis Méndez de Haro's Correspondence to Philip IV of Spain, July to November 1659* (Exeter, 2000).

55 Augustus II of Saxony to Count Watzdorf, 12 October 1730, Dresden, Hauptstaatsarchiv, Geheimes Kabinett, Gesandschaften 2676 I fol. 12.

56 H. Kugeler, '"Le Parfait Ambassadeur": The Theory and Practice of Diplomacy in the Century following the Peace of Westphalia', DPhil, Oxford, 2006, p. 262.

57 D. Van der Cruyse, *Louis XIV et le Siam* (Paris, 1991); M. Jacq-Hergoulach, 'La France et le Siam de 1680 à 1685: Histoire d'un échec', *Revue française d'histoire d'Outre-Mer* (1995), pp. 257–75; R. S. Love, 'Monarchs, Merchants, and Missionaries in Early Modern Asia: The Missions Étrangères in Siam, 1662–1684', *International History Review*, XXI (1999), pp. 1–27.

58 C. Pincemaille, 'La guerre de Hollande dans le programme iconographique de la grande galleries de Versailles', *Histoire, Economie et Société*, IV (1985), pp. 313–33; C. Mukerji, *Territorial Ambitions and the Gardens of Versailles* (Cambridge, 1997).

59 James Howell, *A Discourse* . . . , p. 195 (London, 1664).

60 L. Lemaire, 'L'Ambassade du Comte d'Estrades à Londres en 1661', *Annuaire-bulletin de la Société de l'Histoire de France*, LXXI (1934), pp. 181–226.

61 O. N. Gisselquist, 'The French Ambassador, Jean Antoine De Mesmes, Comte d'Avaux, and French Diplomacy at The Hague, 1678–1684', PhD thesis, University of Minnesota, 1968; J. R. Jones, 'French Intervention in English and Dutch Politics, 1677–88', *Knights Errant and True Englishmen: British Foreign Policy, 1660–1800*, ed. J. Black (Edinburgh, 1989), pp. 1–23.

62 C. Boutant, *L'Europe au Grand Tournant des Années 1680: La Succession palatine* (Paris, 1985).

63 AE. CP. Espagne 75 fol. 84, Saxe 14 fols 100–105.

64 P. Sonnino, *Louis XIV and the Origins of the Dutch War* (Cambridge, 1988).

65 K.H.D. Haley, *William of Orange and the English Opposition, 1672–4* (Oxford, 1953).

66 Edward Finch, British envoy in Stockholm, to William, Lord Harrington, Secretary of State for the Northern Department, 20 Feb. 1739, NA. SP. 95/84

fol. 233; H. M. Scott, 'Prussia's Royal Foreign Minister: Frederick the Great and the Administration of Prussian Diplomacy', in *Royal and Republican Sovereignty*, ed. Scott, R. Oresko and G. C. Gibbs (Cambridge, 1997), pp. 500–26.
67 Villars to Louis, 20, 30 October 1688, AE. CP. Bavière 41 fols 61, 86.
68 Serra, 'The Treaty of the Pyrenees, 350 Years Later', p. 89.
69 P. Wilson, *Europe's Tragedy: A History of the Thirty Years War* (London, 2009), p. 747.
70 R. Porter and M. Teich, eds, *The Scientific Revolution in National Context* (Cambridge, 1992); L. Stewart, *The Rise of Public Science: Rhetoric, Technology and Natural Philosophy in Newtonian Britain, 1660–1750* (Cambridge, 1992); M. Jacob, *Scientific Culture and the Making of the Industrial West* (Oxford, 1997); P. Dear, *Revolutionizing the Sciences: European Knowledge and Its Ambitions, 1500–1700* (Basingstoke, 2001).
71 J. A. Downie, 'How Useful to Eighteenth-century English Studies is the Paradigm of the "Bourgeois Public Sphere"?', *Literature Compass*, I (2003), pp. 1–18, and 'Public and Private: The Myth of the Bourgeois Public Sphere', in *A Concise Companion to the Restoration and Eighteenth Century*, ed. C. Wall (Oxford, 2005), pp. 58–79.
72 Louis XIV to Villars, 2, 11 November, Louis to Rebenac, envoy in Spain, 3 November 1688, AE. CP. Bavière 41 fols 76, 90, Espagne 75 fol. 158.
73 J. Black, 'The Theory of the Balance of Power in the First Half of the Eighteenth Century: A Note on Sources', *Review of International Studies*, IX (1983).
74 Hop to Fagel, 11 Aug. 1739, NA. SP. 107/31.
75 Thomas Bruce, 2nd Earl of Ailesbury, *Memoirs* (London, 1890), II, 573.
76 For example, on Franco-Spanish relations, A. Baudrillart, *Philippe V et la cour de France* (5 vols, Paris, 1890–1901).

THREE: 1690–1775

1 G. Livet, *L'Equilibre européen de la fin du XVe à la fin du XVIIIe siècle* (Paris, 1976), p. 137.
2 H. K. Kleinschmidt, *The Nemesis of Power* (London, 2000), esp. pp. 114–70, and 'Systeme und Ordnungen in der Geschicht der internationalen Beziehungen', *Archiv für kulturgeschichte*, LXXXII (2000), pp. 433–54; A. Osiander, *The States System of Europe, 1640–1990: Peacemaking and the Conditions of International Stability* (Oxford, 1994).
3 Hyndford to Thomas, Duke of Newcastle, Secretary of State for the Northern Department, 11 April 1752, NA. SP. 80/190.
4 E. Dziembowski, *Un Nouveau Patriotisme français, 1750–1770. La France face à la puissance anglaise à l'époque de la guerre de Sept Ans* (Paris, 1998).
5 M. Schlenke, *England und das friderizianische Preussen, 1740–1763* (Munich, 1963), pp. 171–225.
6 G. Yagi Jr, 'A Study of Britain's Military Failure during the Initial Stages of the Seven Years' War in North America, 1754–1758', PhD thesis, University of Exeter, 2007.
7 W. Robertson, *The History of the Reign of the Emperor Charles V* (London, 1769; 1782 edn), I, 134–5.

8 Villeneuve, French envoy, 1735, Paris, Bibliothèque Nationale, Nouvelles Acquisitions Françaises 6834 fol. 58.
9 E. Gibbon, *The History of the Decline and Fall of the Roman Empire*, ed. J. B. Bury (London, 1896–1900), IV, pp. 163–6.
10 D. Headrick, *When Information Came of Age: Technologies of Knowledge in the Age of Reason and Revolution, 1700–1850* (New York, 2000).
11 R. White, *Middle Ground: Indians, Empires and Republics in the Great Lakes Region, 1650-1815* (Cambridge, 1991); I. K. Steele, *Fort William Henry and the 'Massacre'* (Oxford, 1990).
12 J. A. Sweet, *Negotiating for Georgia: British–Creek Relations in the Trustee Era, 1733–1752* (Athens, GA, 2005).
13 T. J. Shannon, *Indians and Colonists at the Crossroads of Empire: The Albany Congress of 1754* (Ithaca, NY, 2000).
14 R. Law, '"Here is No Resisting the Country": The Realities of Power in Afro-European relations on the West African "Slave Coast"', *Itinerario*, XVIII (1994), pp. 50–64.
15 Ritter to Beckers, 14 Sept. 1774, Munich, Bayr. Ges. Wien 702.
16 S. Subrahmanyam, *Penumbral Visions: Making Polities in Early Modern South India* (Ann Arbor, MI, 2001).
17 M. Fisher, *Indirect Rule in India: Residents and the Residency System, 1764–1858* (Delhi, 1991).
18 J. Sebes, *The Jesuits and the Sino-Russian Treaty of Nerchinsk (1681): The Diary of Thomas Pereira, S.J.* (Rome, 1961).
19 L. M. Brockey, *Journey to the East: The Jesuit Mission to China, 1579–1724* (Cambridge, MA, 2007).
20 S. Anderson, *An English Consul in Turkey: Paul Rycaut in Smyrna, 1667–1678* (Oxford, 1989).
21 J. L. Stevenson, *A Journey from St Petersburg to Peking, 1719–1722*, ed. J. Bell (Edinburgh, 1965).
22 Fawkener to Newcastle, then Secretary of State for the Southern Department, 20 Jan. 1739, Cambridge, University Library, Cholmondeley Houghton papers, correspondence no. 2830.
23 Haslang, Bavarian envoy in London, to Count Preysing, Bavarian foreign minister, 20 January 1758, Munich, Bayr. Ges. London 234.
24 Thomas Robinson, British envoy in Vienna, to William, Lord Harrington, Secretary of State for the Northern Department, 27 July 1733, NA. SP. 80/97.
25 Paris, Bibliothèque Nationale, Manuscrits Francais, 7186 fol. 302, Nouvelles Acquisitions Français, 14914 fol. 83, 14196 fols 138, 218–19.
26 Irvine, Vice-Consul in Ostend, to James Wallace, Under Secretary, 17 July 1757, NA. SP. 110/6.
27 Rennel de Lescut, Lorraine envoy at the Congress of Cambrai, to Duke Leopold of Lorraine, 5 Ap. 1725, Nancy, Archives de Meurthe-et-Moselle, Fonds de Vienne, series 3F, vol. XXXII, no. 132.
28 J. P. Mackey, *The Saxon Post* (Blackrock, Ireland, 1978); M. C. Lowe, 'The Development of the Portuguese Postal Service', *Stamp Lover*, LXXXIV (1992), p. 136; W. Behringer, *Im Zeichen des Merkur. Reichspost und Kommunikationsrevolution in der Frühen Neuzeit* (Gottingen, 2003).
29 John Ward's journal, BL. Add. 6235 fol. 49.
30 *Sbornik Imperatorskago Istoricheskago obshcestva* (St Petersburg), 64, 365.

31 Chesterfield to William, Lord Harrington, Secretary of State for the Northern Department, 20 January 1745, NA. SP. 84/408 fol. 64.
32 Robert, 4th Earl of Holdernesse, Secretary of State for the Northern Department, to Hanbury Williams, 11 April 1755, Newport, Public Library, Hanbury Williams papers.
33 D. Altbauer, 'The Diplomats of Peter the Great', *Jahrbücher für Geschichte Osteuropas*, XXVIII (1980), pp. 14–16. See also A. Bohlen, 'Changes in Russian Diplomacy under Peter the Great', *Cahiers du Monde russe et soviétique*, VII (1966), pp. 341–58.
34 A. G. Cross, *'By the Banks of the Thames': Russians in Eighteenth Century Britain* (Newtonville, MA, 1980), p. 10.
35 Kaunitz to Joseph II, 11 May 1781, *Joseph II, Leopold II und Kaunitz. Ihr Briefwechsel*, ed. A. Beer (Vienna, 1873), p. 52.
36 Zamboni to Count Lagnasc, Saxon minister, 15 Feb. 1732, Dresden, Haupstaatsarchiv, Geheimes Kabinett, Gesandtschaften 637 fols 180–83.
37 Joseph Yorke to Newcastle, 1 May 1753, Earl of Bristol to Earl of Holdernesse, 8 Nov. 1755, NA. SP. 84/463, 92/63 fol. 180; Praslin, French foreign minister, to Chatelet, envoy in Vienna, 7, 16 July 1763, AE. CP. Autriche 295 fols 36, 48–50. See also *Centinel*, 24 Nov. 1757.
38 François de Saint-Contest, Foreign Minister, to Marquis de Bonnac, envoy in The Hague, 18, 27 May 1753, Paris, Archives Nationales KK. 1400, pp. 189–90, 212.
39 Hautefort, French envoy in Vienna to St Contest, 12, 22 Ap. 1752 and reply, 7 May, AE. CP. Autriche 251 fols 101, 110–22, 135.
40 Reporting the complaints of Alleyne Fitzherbert: Richard Grenville to Sir Robert Murray Keith, envoy in Vienna, 23 Dec. 1783, BL. Add. 35530 fol. 269.
41 J. M. Hartley, *Charles Whitworth: Diplomat in the Age of Peter the Great* (Aldershot, 2002).
42 J. Burkhardt, *Abschied vom Religionskrieg: Der Siebenjährigen Krieg und die päpstliche Diplomatie* (Tübingen, 1985).
43 L. Wolff, *The Vatican and Poland in the Age of Partitions: Diplomatic and Cultural Encounters at the Warsaw Nunciature* (New York, 1988).
44 H. M. Scott, 'Religion and Realpolitik: The Duc of Choiseul, the Bourbon Family Compact, and the Attack on the Society of Jesus, 1758–1775', *International History Review*, XXV (2003), pp. 37–62.
45 Dubois, French foreign minister, to Philippe Destouches, envoy in London, 8 Mar. 1719, AE. CP. Ang. 322 fol. 264; G. Thuillier, 'L'Académie Politique de Torcy, 1712-1719', *Revue d'Histoire Diplomatique*, XCVII/1–2 (1983), pp. 54–74.
46 For the Austrians doing the same, Baron Halberg, Bavarian envoy in Vienna, to Baron Vieregg, 4 Feb. 1786, Munich, Bayerisches Hauptstaatsarchiv, Bayr. Ges, Vienna 727.
47 J. Voss, 'L'Ecole diplomatique de Strasbourg: L'ENA de l'Ancien Régime?', and E. Buddruss, 'Les Élèves de Schoepflin au Ministère des Affaires Etrangères à Versailles', in *Strasbourg, Schoepflin et l'Europe au XVIIIe siècle*, ed. B. Vogler and J. Voss (Bonn, 1996), pp. 207–24.
48 Viry to Charles Emmanuel III, 18 December 1761, Turin, Archivio di Stato, Lettere Ministri Inghilterra 66.
49 Harrington to Horatio Walpole, envoy in The Hague, 8 Nov., 1737, NA. SP. 84/368 fol. 136.

50 Instructions to Marquis de Valory, French envoy to George II on his trip to Hanover, 3 May 1750, AE. CP. Brunswick-Hanovre 50 fol. 202.
51 Joseph, Count Wackerbarth, Saxon envoy in Vienna, to Ernst Manteuffel, Saxon minister, 19 May 1728, Dresden, Hauptstaatsarchiv, Geheimes Kabinett, Gesandtschaften 3331.
52 Paris, Archives Nationales KK 1393.
53 C. Storrs, 'Savoyard Diplomacy in the Eighteenth Century', in D. Frigo, *Politics and Diplomacy in Early-Modern Italy* (Cambridge, 2000), p. 246.
54 D. Starkey, 'Representation through Intimacy: A Study of the Symbolism of Monarchy and Court Office in Early-Modern England', in *Symbols and Sentiments*, ed. I. Lewis (London, 1977), pp. 201–3.
55 Chavigny to Chauvelin, 9 October 1731, AE. CP. Allemagne 379.
56 Sparre to Count Horn, Sweden's first minister, 28 November 1735, Cambridge, University Library, Cholmondeley Houghton papers, correspondence, no. 2517. On intolerable pay arrears, Joseph, Count Haslang, long-standing Bavarian envoy in London, to Baron Preysing, Bavarian foreign minister, 25 May, 3 September 1745, Munich, Bayerisches Hauptstaatsarchiv, Gesandtschaft London 213.
57 NA. SP. 94/135 fol. 302. He had already made this point in 1737, Keene to Newcastle, 22 July 1737, NA. SP. 94/128.
58 AE. CP. Angleterre 438 fol. 305, 439 fol. 169.
59 R. Oresko, G. C. Gibbs and H. M. Scott, eds, *Royal and Republican Sovereignty in Early Modern Europe* (Cambridge, 1997).
60 AE. CP. Espagne 517 fols 26–8, 192–3, 281–5; A. Bourquet, *Le Duc de Choiseul et l'Alliance Espagnole* (Paris, 1906), pp. 6–7, 25.
61 H. Kamen, *Philip V of Spain* (New Haven, CT, 2001), pp. 152–7.
62 AE. CP. Angleterre 364 fols 395–406.
63 Robinson to Horatio Walpole, 7 Jan. 1736, BL. Add. 23852 fol. 17.
64 M. Lindemann, *'Liaisons dangereuses': Sex, Law, and Diplomacy in the Age of Frederick the Great* (Baltimore, MD, 2006).
65 James, Earl Waldegrave, British envoy in Paris, to Newcastle, 1 Aug. 1739, London, British Library, Department of Manuscripts, vol. 32801.
66 Abbé Strickland to Bartenstein, 16 Nov. 1734, Vienna, Haus-, Hof-, und Staatsarchiv, Staatenabteilung, England Varia 8.
67 AE. CP. Autriche 263 fol. 54.
68 F. Boutaric, ed., *Correspondance secrète inédite de Louis XV sur la politique étrangère* (2 vols, Paris, 1886); M. Antoine and D. Ozanam, eds, *Correspondance secrète du Comte de Broglie avec Louis XV, 1756–1774* (Paris, 1956–61), and 'Le Secret du Roi et la Russie jusqu'à la mort de la Czarine Elizabeth en 1762', *Annuaire Bulletin de la Société de l'Histoire* (1954–5), pp. 80–81.
69 T. E. Kaiser, 'Who's Afraid of Marie-Antoinette? Diplomacy, Austrophobia and the Queen', *French History*, XIV (2000), pp. 241–71; M. Price, *Preserving the Monarchy: the Comte de Vergennes, 1774-1787* (Cambridge, 1995); J. Hardman and Price, eds, *Louis XVI and the Comte de Vergennes: Correspondence, 1774–1787* (Oxford, 1998).
70 R. Butler, 'The Secret Compact of 1753 between the Kings of France and of Naples', in *Royal and Republican Sovereignty in Early Modern Europe*, ed. R. Oresko, G. C. Gibbs and H. M. Scott (Cambridge, 1997), pp. 551–79, e.g. p. 561.
71 For his intercepted correspondence with envoys in London, Hull, University

Library, Hotham papers 3/3, and in Dresden, Sauveterre, French envoy in Berlin, to Chauvelin, 27 Mar. 1728, AE. CP. Prusse 87 fol. 104.
72 Sinzendorf to Fonseca, 31 March 1729, Diemar to Eugene, 15 January 1734, Vienna, Haus-, Hof-, und Staatsarchiv, Staatenabteilung Nachlass Fonseca 13, Grosse Korrespondenz 85a; Kinsky to Eugene, [late August 1729], Vienna, Palais Kinsky, Correspondence of Count Philip Kinsky, vol. 3a; M. Braubach, *Die Geheimdiplomatie des Prinzen Eugen von Savoyen* (Cologne, 1962).
73 L. Schilling, *Kaunitz und das Renversement des Alliances* (Berlin, 1994).
74 S. Dixon, *Catherine the Great* (Harlow, 2001), pp. 155–60.
75 K. de Leeuw, 'The Black Chamber in the Dutch Republic during the War of the Spanish Succession and its Aftermath, 1707–1715', *Historical Journal*, XLII (1999), pp. 133–56 and 'Cryptology in the Dutch Republic: A Case-Study', in *The History of Information Security*, ed. K. de Leeuw and J. Bergstra (Amsterdam, 2007), pp. 327–67.
76 Papers of Charles, 2nd Viscount Townshend, Secretary of State for the Northern Department, Canberra, National Library of Australia, MS 1458, 9/1-20, 10/-4; J. Black, 'British Intelligence and the Mid-eighteenth-century Crisis', *Intelligence and National Security*, II (1987), pp. 209–16, and 'Eighteenth-century Intercepted Dispatches', *Journal of the Society of Archivists*, XI (1990), pp. 138–43.
77 Regarding those of Prussia, Harrington to Guy Dickens, envoy in Berlin, 17 Feb. (os) 1739, NA. SP. 90/45.
78 J. Israel, *The Dutch Republic: Its Rise, Greatness, and Fall, 1477–1806* (Oxford, 1995), p. 990.
79 Cyril Wych, envoy in Hamburg, to Townshend, 18 July 1725, NA. SP. 82/42 fol. 195.
80 Cotterell to Harrington, NA. SP. 36/42 fol. 218.
81 Instructions to Count Utterodt, 21 Feb. 1739, Dresden, Haupstaatsarchiv, Geheimes Kabinett, Gesandschaften 2677 I fol. 12.
82 Dickens to Harrington, 14 Feb. 1739, NA. SP. 90/45.
83 Complaining about Seckendorf's conduct at Dresden, Count Karl Hoym, Saxon minister, to Prince Eugene, 27 Feb. 1730, Palais Kinsky, papers of Count Philip Kinsky, box 4i; for problems of avoiding commitments, Saint-Severin to Amelot, 29 July 1738, A. Vandal, *Une Ambassade Française en Orient sous Louis XV* (Paris, 1887), p. 377; I. de Madariaga, *Britain, Russia and the Armed Neutrality of 1780* (London, 1962); R. M. Hatton, 'Gratifications and Foreign Policy: Anglo-French Rivalry in Sweden during the Nine Years War', in *William III and Louis XIV*, ed. Hatton and J. S. Bromley (Liverpool, 1968), pp. 68-94; D. A. Miller, *Sir Joseph Yorke and Anglo-Dutch Relations, 1774–1780* (The Hague, 1970); M. F. Metcalf, *Russia, England and Swedish Party Politics, 1762–1766: The Interplay between Great Power Diplomacy and Domestic Politics during Sweden's Age of Liberty* (Stockholm, 1977); M. Roberts, *British Diplomacy and Swedish Politics, 1758–1773* (London, 1980).
84 D. Ozanam, *Les Diplomates Espagnols du XVIIIe siècle* (Madrid, 1998).
85 Woodward to Charles, Viscount Townshend, Secretary of State for the Northern Department, 5 April 1727, NA. SP. 80/60 fol. 388.
86 G. Braun, 'Frédéric-Charles Moser et les langues de la diplomatie européene (1648–1750)', *Revue d'histoire diplomatique* (1999, part 3), pp. 261–78; A. Ostrower, *Language, Law and Diplomacy: A Study of Linguistic Diversity in Official International Relations and International Law* (Philadelphia, 1965).

87 Edward Weston, Under Secretary, to Onslow Burrish, 10 Feb. 1744, NA. SP. 110/6.
88 Baron Schroff to Antoine-Louis Rouillé, French Foreign Minister, 1 Feb. 1755, Munich, Bayr. Ges. Paris 13.
89 M. Keens-Soper, 'Callières', in G. R. Berridge, M. Keens-Soper and T. G. Otte, *Diplomatic Theory from Machiavelli to Kissinger* (Basingstoke, 2001), p. 122.
90 For the manual of Fernán Núñez, Bernard Quaritch, catalogue 1039, p. 47.
91 J.-C. Waquet, *François de Callières: L'art de négocier en France sous Louis XIV* (Paris, 2005).
92 Schleinitz to Charles, Count of Morville, French foreign minister, 4 July 1727, AE. CP. Brunswick-Wolfenbüttel 46 fol. 157.
93 J. C. Rule, 'Colbert de Torcy, an Emergent Bureaucracy, and the Formulation of French Foreign Policy, 1698–1715', in *Louis XIV and Europe*, ed. R. Hatton (London, 1976), pp. 261–88.
94 D. Frigo, *Principe, Ambasciatore e 'Jus Gentium': L'Amministrazione della Politica Estera nel Piemonte del Settecento* (Rome, 1991).
95 L. Wiesener, *Le Régent, l'Abbé Dubois et les Anglais*, 3 vols (Paris, 1891–9); E. Bourgeois, *Le Secret du Regent et la politique de l'Abbé Dubois* (Paris, 1907).
96 Harrington to Woodward, 14 July 1730, NA. SP. 88/37, Newcastle to Kenne, 27 July 1730, BL. Add. 32769 fol. 55, re. getting Saxony and Spain to send envoys.
97 Abbé Bignon to Bertin du Rocheret, 2 Ap. 1735, A. Nicaise, ed., *Oeuvres choisies de Bertin du Rocheret* (Paris, 1865), p. 182.
98 Instructions to Feraty de Valette, 17 April 1725, Dresden, Hauptstaatsarchiv, Geheimes Kabinett, Gesandschaften 2797.
99 Frederick William I to Count Degenfeld, Prussian envoy in London, 31 Jan. 1733, NA. SP. 107/8.
100 Instructions to Count Watzdorf, 12 October 1730, ibid., 2627 I, fols 12–13.
101 Mémoire justificatif by Montaigu, no. d., Paris, Bibliothèque Nationale, Nouvelles Acquisitions Françaises, 14906, fols 118–19.
102 A. Mézin, *Les Consuls de France au Siècle des Lumières, 1715–1792* (Paris, 1997).
103 Princeton, University Library, CO 689.
104 Stepney to Charles, 1st Earl of Halifax, 26 September 1704, BL. Eg. 929 fol. 63.
105 A. Thompson, *Britain, Hanover and the Protestant Interest, 1688–1756* (Woodbridge, 2006).
106 T. Claydon, *Europe and the Making of England 1660–1760* (Cambridge, 2007); C. G. Pestana, *Protestant Empire: Religion and the Making of the British Atlantic World* (Philadelphia, 2009).
107 Choiseul, French envoy in Vienna, to Richelieu, commander of French army in Germany, 24 Aug. 1757, Paris, Bibliothèque Victor Cousin, Fonds Richelieu, vol. LVIII, fols 20–21.
108 D. Szechi, *The Jacobites: Britain and Europe, 1688–1788* (Manchester, 1994).
109 L. H. Boles, *The Huguenots, the Protestant Interest, and the War of the Spanish Succession, 1702–1714* (New York, 1997).
110 For a critical account of an envoy, from a military background, and at a minor post, L. de Laigue 'Le Comte de Froullay, ambassadeur à Venise, 1733–1743', *Revue d'Histoire Diplomatique* (1913), p. 70.
111 For a similar view on the late seventeenth century, W. J. Roosen, *The Age of Louis XIV* (Cambridge, MA, 1976), p. 189.
112 Robinson to Stone, 14 July 1736, NA. SP. 80/227.

FOUR: 1775–1815

1. P. L. Ford, ed., *The Autobiography of Thomas Jefferson, 1743–1790* (New York, 1914), p. 94; C. R. Ritcheson, 'The Fragile Memory: Thomas Jefferson at the Court of George III', *Eighteenth-Century Life*, VI/2–3 (1981), pp. 1–16.
2. Adams to John Jay, 2 June 1785, C. F. Adams, ed., *The Works of John Adams* (Boston, 1853), VIII, 255–7; Adams to Jefferson, 3 June 1785, L. J. Cappon, ed., *The Adams-Jefferson Letters* (Chapel Hill, NC, 1988), p. 27.
3. AE. CP. Ang. 582 fol. 9.
4. AE. CP. Ang. 582 fols 80, 111, 586 fol. 343.
5. A. Mezin, 'Le consul Charles Flüry: de l'ambassade de Choiseul-Gouffier à la Restauration', *Revue d'Histoire Diplomatique*, CXI/3 (1997), pp. 273–90.
6. AE. CP. Turquie 175.
7. AE. CP. Russie 121.
8. J. Kington, *The Weather of the 1780s over Europe* (Cambridge, 1988).
9. Eden to Lord Grenville, Foreign Secretary, 18 Dec. 1794, NA. Foreign Office 245/4, p. 423.
10. BL. Add. 58938 fols 3–4.
11. E. H. Pritchard, *The Crucial Years of Early Anglo-Chinese Relations, 1750–1800* (Pullman, WA, 1936), pp. 236–311; J. L. Cranmer-Byng, 'Lord Macartney's Embassy to Peking in 1793, from Official Chinese Documents', *Journal of Oriental Studies*, IV (1957–8), pp. 117–87; P. Roebuck, ed., *Macartney of Lisanoure* (Belfast, 1983), pp. 216–43; A. Singer, *The Lion and the Dragon: The Story of the First British Embassy to the Court of the Emperor Qianlong in Peking, 1792–94* (London, 1992); A. Peyrefitte, *The Collision of Two Civilisations: The British Expedition to China, 1792–4* (London, 1993).
12. Staunton to Burges, 12 Nov. 1793, Oxford, Bodleian Library, Bland Burges papers, vol. 46 fol. 30.
13. E. Ingram, 'An Aspiring Buffer-State: Anglo-Persian Relations in the Third Coalition, 1804-1807', *Historical Journal*, XVI (1973), pp. 509-33.
14. His letter books form part of the Kentchurch Court Collection in the Herefordshire Record Office. In 1826 he assumed the additional name of Brydges.
15. M. M. Cloake, ed., *A Persian at the Court of King George, 1809–10: The Journal of Mirza Abul Hassan Khan* (London, 1988), pp. 144–5. For his 'minder', see H. M. Johnston, *Ottoman and Persian Odysseys: James Morier . . . and his Brothers* (London, 1998).
16. Thomas Trigge to Henry Addington, 1 February 1804, Exeter, Devon Record Office 152M OC 10.
17. A. H. DeGroot, 'Ottoman North Africa and the Dutch Republic in the Seventeenth and Eighteenth Centuries', *Revue de l'Occident Musulman et de la Méditerranée*, XXXIX (1985), pp. 131–47; C. Windler, *La Diplomatie comme expérience de l'autre. Consuls français au Maghreb, 1700–1840* (Geneva, 2002).
18. T. B. Lam, 'Intervention versus Tribute in Sino-Vietnamese Relations, 1788–1790', in *The Chinese World Order: Traditional China's Foreign Relations*, ed. J. K. Fairbank (Cambridge, MA, 1968), pp. 165–79.
19. B. Oberg, ed., *The Papers of Benjamin Franklin*, XXIX: *March 1–June 20 1779* (New Haven, CT, 1992).
20. Ibid., XXVIII (1991).

21 J. H. Hutson, *John Adams and the Diplomacy of the American Revolution* (Lexington, KT, 1980); J. R. Dull, 'Benjamin Franklin and the Nature of American Diplomacy', *International History Review*, V (1983), pp. 351–5, and *A Diplomatic History of the American Revolution* (New Haven, CT, 1985).
22 Elliot to William Eden, 11 July 1776, BL. Add. 34413.
23 Mason to Burges, 16 August 1789, Oxford, Bodleian Library, Bland Burges papers, vol. XVIII.
24 John Quincy Adams to John Adams, 27 July 1794, *Writings of John Quincy Adams*, ed. W.C. Ford (2 vols, New York, 1913), I, p. 196.
25 P. and N. Onuf, *Federal Union, Modern World: The Law of Nations in an Age of Revolutions 1776–1814* (Madison, WI, 1993); D. Hendrickson, *Peace Pact: The Lost World of the American Founding* (Lawrence, KS, 2003).
26 J. M. Banner, *To the Hartford Convention* (New York, 1970).
27 F. Merk, *Slavery and the Annexation of Texas* (New York, 1972), pp. 21–2.
28 E. L. Pierce, ed., *Memoirs and Letters of Charles Sumner: 1860 to Death* (London, 1893), pp. 68–9.
29 G. S. Rowe and A. W. Knott, 'The Longchamps Affair (1784–1786), The Law of Nations, and the Shaping of Early American Foreign Policy', *Diplomatic History*, X (1986), pp. 199–220.
30 J.Q. Adams to John Adams, *John Quincy Adams*, I, 19.
31 A. DeConde, *Entangling Alliance: Politics and Diplomacy under George Washington* (Durham, NC, 1958).
32 AE. CP. Ang. 583 fols 171–2.
33 BL. Add. 58920 fol. 105.
34 AE. CP. Ang. 583 fols 211–12, 302, 361–3, 586 fol. 79.
35 AE. CP. Ang. 582 fols 51, 167.
36 AE. CP. Ang. 578 fol. 216, 581 fol. 49.
37 AE. CP. Ang. 580 fol. 267.
38 AE. CP. Ang. 581 fols 89, 280, 341; AE. CP. Hollande 583 fol. 298.
39 AE. CP. Ang. 581 fol. 233.
40 BL. Add. 59021 fol. 16; Broomhall, Fife, Elgin papers 60/1/184. I would like to thank the Earl of Elgin for permission to use these papers.
41 M. Price, *The Road from Versailles: Louis XVI, Marie Antoinette, and the Fall of the French Monarchy* (New York, 2002).
42 G. Savage, 'Favier's Heirs: The French Revolution and the Secret du Roi', *Historical Journal*, XLI (1998), pp. 225–58.
43 M. Belissa, *Fraternité universelle et intérêt national (1713–1795): Les cosmopolitiques du droit des gens* (Paris, 1998).
44 AE. CP. Ang. 582 fols. 113, 256, 583 fol. 172; L. Frey and M. Frey, '"The Reign of the Charlatans is Over". The French Revolutionary Attack on Diplomatic Practice', *Journal of Modern History*, LXV (1993), pp. 706–44.
45 F. Attar, *La Revolution française déclare la guerre à l'Europe* (Brussels, 1992).
46 M. Degos, 'Les Consulats de France sous la Révolution des États Barbaresques ... en Italie ... en Espagne et au Portugal', *Revue d'Histoire Diplomatique*, CV (1991), pp. 102–33, CVII (1993), pp. 243–77, CVIII (1994), pp. 151–80.
47 Vieregg, Bavarian foreign minister, to Hallberg, Bavarian envoy in Vienna, 6, 9 November, 4, 14 December 1787, 15 January 1788, Munich, Bayerisches Hauptstaatsarchiv, Gesandtschaften, Wien 730–1.
48 M. S. Anderson, *The Discovery of Russia, 1553–1815* (London, 1958), pp.

143–85; A. Cunningham, 'The Oczakow Debate', *Middle Eastern Studies*, I (1964), pp. 209–37.
49 A. Cunningham, 'Robert Adair's Mission to St Petersburg', in *Anglo-Ottoman Encounters in the Age of Revolution* (London, 1993), pp. 32–50.
50 Lindsay to William, Lord Grenville, Foreign Secretary, 31 August 1791, Oxford, Bodleian Library, Bland Burges papers, vol. LVIII, p. 1.
51 D. Bell, *First Total War: Napoleon's Europe and the Birth of Warfare as We Know It* (Boston, 2007).
52 J. Black, *War in the Nineteenth Century, 1800–1914* (Cambridge, 2009), pp. 7–10.
53 D. Armstrong, *Revolution and World Order: The Revolutionary State in International Society* (Oxford, 1993).
54 For intelligence reports from French and Spanish ports sent by British diplomats in Nice and Genoa in 1779–83 to John, Viscount Mountstuart, envoy in Turin, Manchester, John Rylands Library, English MS 1146–7.
55 H. Ammon, *The Genet Mission* (New York, 1973).
56 E. R. Sheridan, 'The Recall of Edmund Charles Genet: A Study in Transatlantic Politics and Diplomacy', *Diplomatic History*, XVIII (1994), pp. 463–88.
57 J. C. Herold, *Bonaparte in Egypt* (London, 1962), pp. 3–4.
58 Frey and Frey, '"Reign of the Charlatans"', p. 740; M. Belissa, *Repenser l'ordre européen (1795–1802): De la société des rois aux droits des nations* (Paris, 2006).
59 N. Thompson, 'The Continental System as a Sieve: The Disappearance of Benjamin Bathurst in 1809', *International History Review*, XXIV (2002), pp. 528–57.
60 E. A. Whitcomb, *Napoleon's Diplomatic Service* (Durham, NC, 1979); M. S. Chrisawn, 'A Military Bull in a Diplomatic China Shop: General Jean Lanne's Mission to Lisbon, 1802–1804', *Portuguese Studies Review*, III (1993–4), pp. 46–67.
61 For the latter, see P. Schroeder, *The Transformation of European Politics, 1763–1848* (Oxford, 2002) and P. Krüger and P. Schroeder, eds, *'The Transformation of European Politics, 1763–1848': Episode or Model in Modern History?* (Münster, 2002).
62 E. Kurz, *The Kissinger Saga: Walter and Henry Kissinger – Two Brothers from Germany* (London, 2009); J. Suri, *Henry Kissinger and the American Century* (Cambridge, MA, 2007); A. Horne, *Kissinger's Year* (London, 2009).
63 H. M. Scott, 'Diplomatic Culture in Old Regime Europe', in *Cultures of Power in Europe during the Long Eighteenth Century*, ed. H. M. Scott and B. Simms (Cambridge, 2007), pp. 58–60.
64 J. L. Cranmer-Byng, ed., *An Embassy to China: Being the Journal Kept by Lord Macartney* (London, 2004), p. 166.

FIVE: 1815–1900

1 C. N. Parkinson, *Edward Pellew, Viscount Exmouth, Admiral of the Red* (London, 1924), pp. 419–72.
2 H. Ellis, *Journal of the Proceedings of the Late Embassy to China* (London, 1817); Chia Ch'ing Emperor to George, Prince Regent, 11 September 1816, NA. FO. 93/23/10, printed, in part, in P. Barber, *Diplomacy* (London, 1979), pp. 138–9.
3 *The Dictionary of National Biography* (London, 1885–1900), I, 360.

4 Abraham Stanyan to Charles, 3rd Earl of Sunderland, Secretary of State, 2 Oct. 1717, BL. Add. 61537 fol. 127.
5 V. Viaene, 'King Leopold's Imperialism and the Origins of the Belgian Colonial Party, 1860–1905', *Journal of Modern History*, LXXX (2008), p. 759.
6 Brathwaite to Burges, 28 July 1792, Oxford, Bodleian Library, Bland Burges papers vol. 31 fol. 106; R.E. May, *Manifest Destiny's Underworld: Filibustering in Antebellum America* (Chapel Hill, NC, 2002).
7 S. W. Murray, *Liberal Diplomacy and German Unification: The Early Career of Robert Morier* (Westport, CT, 2000).
8 D. M. Smith, *Mazzini* (New Haven, CT, 1994).
9 Earl of Orford to Charles Vaughan, 12 Jan. 1826, All Souls College, Oxford, Vaughan papers C77 no. 2.
10 R. Franklin, *Lord Stuart de Rothesay* (Brighton, 2008).
11 D. M. Pletcher, *The Diplomacy of Involvement: American Economic Expansion across the Pacific, 1784–1900* (Columbia, MO, 2001).
12 J. Belich, *Replenishing the Earth: The Settler Revolution and the Rise of the Anglo-world* (Oxford, 2009).
13 P. Marshall, *Bengal: The British Bridgehead. Eastern India, 1740–1828* (Cambridge, 1987), pp. 96–7; C. A. Bayly, 'The British Military-Fiscal State and Indigenous Resistance. India, 1750–1820', in *An Imperial State at War: Britain from 1689 to 1815*, ed. L. Stone (London, 1994), pp. 322–54.
14 C. Windler, 'Diplomatic History as a Field for Cultural Analysis: Muslim-Christian Relations in Tunis, 1700–1840', *Historical Journal*, XLIV (2001), pp. 107–34.
15 J. F. Rippy, *Rivalry of the United States and Great Britain over Latin America, 1808–1830* (Baltimore, MD, 1929); Guillaume-Tell Poussin, French envoy in USA, to Alexis de Tocqueville, French Foreign Minister, 17 Oct. 1849, *Tocqueville on America after 1840*, ed. A. Craiutu and J. Jennings (Cambridge, 2009), p. 445.
16 J. P. Daughton, 'When Argentina Was "French": Rethinking Colonial Politics and European Imperialism in Belle-Époque Buenos Aires', *Journal of Modern History*, LXXX (2008), p. 862.
17 M. P. Coesteloe, *Bonds and Bondholders: British Investors and Mexico's Foreign Debt, 1824–1888* (Westport, CT, 2003).
18 S. Roberts, *Charles Hotham: A Biography* (Melbourne, 1985).
19 T. L. Whigham, *The Paraguyan War*, I: *Causes and Early Conduct* (Lincoln, NB, 2002).
20 C. Bergquist, *Coffee and Conflict in Colombia, 1886–1910* (Durham, NC, 1978); M. A. Centano, *Blood and Debt: War and the Nation-State in Latin America* (University Park, PA, 2002).
21 D. A. Low, *Fabrication of Empire: The British and the Uganda Kingdoms, 1890–1902* (Cambridge, 2009).
22 T. Winichakul, *Siam Mapped: A History of the Geo-Body of a Nation* (Honolulu, HI, 1994).
23 S. Smith, ed., *The Red Sea Region: Sovereignty, Boundaries and Conflict, 1839–1967* (Cambridge, 2008).
24 T. G. Otte and K. Neilson, eds, *Railways and International Politics: Paths of Empire, 1848–1945* (London, 2004).
25 S. Freitag and P. Wende, eds, *British Envoys to Germany, 1816–1866*, I: *1816–1829* (London, 2001).

26 R. J. Blyth, 'Redrawing the Boundary between India and Britain: The Succession Crisis at Zanzibar, 1870–1873', *International History Review*, XXII (2000), pp. 785–805; J. Onley, *The Arabian Frontier of the British Raj: Merchants, Rulers, and the British in the Nineteenth-Century Gulf* (Oxford, 2007).
27 K. A. Hamilton and P. Salmon, eds, *Slavery, Diplomacy and Empire: Britain and the Suppression of the Slave Trade, 1807–1975* (Brighton, 2009).
28 A. F. Corwin, *Spain and the Abolition of Slavery in Cuba, 1817–1886* (Austin, TX, 1967).
29 G. S. Graham, *Great Britain and the Indian Ocean: A Study of Maritime Enterprise, 1810–1850* (Oxford, 1967), pp. 106–7.
30 R. J. Gavin, 'The Bartle Frere Mission to Zanzibar, 1873', *Historical Journal*, V (1962), pp. 122–48.
31 G. Melancon, *Britain's China Policy and the Opium Crisis: Balancing Drugs, Violence, and National Honour, 1833–1840* (Aldershot, 2003).
32 T. F. Tsiang, 'New Light on Chinese Diplomacy, 1836–1849', *Journal of Modern History*, III (1931), pp. 578–91.
33 J. Y. Wong, *Deadly Dreams: Opium and the Arrow War (1856–60) in China* (Cambridge, 1998).
34 P. B. Wiley, *Yankees in the Land of the Gods: Commodore Perry and the Opening of Japan* (New York, 1990).
35 J. E. Hoare, *Embassies in the East: The Story of the British and their Embassies in China, Japan, and Korea from 1859 to the Present* (London, 1999).
36 C. Tsuzuki and R. J. Young, eds, *Japan Rising: The Iwakura Embassy to the USA and Europe* (Cambridge, 2009).
37 I.C.Y. Hsu, *China's Entrance into the Family of Nations: The Diplomatic Phase, 1858–1880* (Cambridge, MA, 1960).
38 M. Finch, *Min Yông-Hwan: A Political Biography* (Honolulu, HI, 2002).
39 F.A.K. Yasamee, *Ottoman Diplomacy: Abdülhamid II and the Great Powers, 1878–1888* (Istanbul, 1996).
40 P. Joseph, *Foreign Diplomacy in China 1894–1900* (London, 1928), p. 416.
41 Richard Pakenham, Secretary to the Legation in Mexico, to Vaughan, 18 Oct. 1827, All Souls, Vaughan papers c81 no. 2.
42 S. Matsumoto-Best, *Britain and the Papacy in the Age of Revolution, 1846–51* (Woodbridge, 2003).
43 M. R. Gordon, 'Domestic Conflict and the Origins of the First World War: The British and German Cases', *Journal of Modern History*, XLVI (1974), pp. 191–226.
44 D. Brown, *Palmerston and the Politics of Foreign Policy, 1846–55* (Manchester, 2002).
45 T. G. Otte, 'From "War-in-Sight" to Nearly War: Anglo-French Relations in the Age of High Imperialism, 1875–1898', *Diplomacy and Statecraft*, XVII (2006), pp. 693–714.
46 K. Wilson, 'Foreign Office Reports on the Foreign Press, 1906 and 1917–19', *Archives*, XIX (1991), pp. 308–14.
47 W. Baumgart, *The Crimean War, 1853–1856* (London, 1999).
48 R. A. Johnson, 'The Penjdeh Incident, 1885', *Archives*, XXIV (1999), p. 35.
49 D. A. Campbell, *Unlikely Allies: Britain, America and the Origin of the Special Relationship* (London, 2007); P. E. Myers, *Caution and Cooperation: The*

American Civil War in British-American Relations (Kent, OH, 2008).
50 W. Baumgart, *Europäisches Konzert und nationale Bewegung: Internationale Beziehungen, 1830–1878* (Paderborn, 1999).
51 N. Constantinesco, *Romania on the European Stage, 1875–1880: The Quest for National Sovereignty and Independence* (New York, 1998); C. Fink, *Defending the Rights to Others: The Great Powers, the Jews, and International Minority Protection, 1878–1938* (Cambridge, 2004).
52 R. J. Crampton, *Bulgaria* (Oxford, 2007), p. 87.
53 Ibid., p. 131.
54 Johnson, 'The Penjdeh Incident, 1885', pp. 28–48.
55 M. S. Seligmann, 'A View from Berlin: Colonel Frederick Trench and the Development of British Perceptions of German Aggressive Intent, 1906–1910', *Journal of Strategic Studies*, XXIII (2000), p. 131.
56 Johnson, 'The Penjdeh Incident, 1885', p. 31
57 J. Fisher, 'On the Baghdad Road: On the Trail of W. J. Childs. A Study in British Near Eastern Intelligence and Historical Analysis, c. 1900–1930', *Archives*, XXIV (1999), pp. 55–8.
58 A. Howe, *Free Trade and Liberal England, 1846–1946* (Oxford, 1997); P. T. Marsh, *Bargaining on Europe: Britain and the First Common Market, 1860–1892* (New Haven, CT, 2000).
59 J. A. Grant, *Rulers, Guns, and Money: The Global Arms Trade in the Age of Imperialism* (Cambridge, MA, 2007).
60 E. T. Rogers, ed., *Speeches on Questions of Public Policy by . . . John Bright* (London, 1898), p. 470.
61 L. Cecil, *The German Diplomatic Service, 1871–1914* (Princeton, NJ, 1976).
62 W. D. Godsey, *Aristocratic Redoubt: The Austro-Hungarian Foreign Office on the Eve of the First World War* (West Lafayette, IN, 1999).
63 T. G. Otte, '"Outdoor Relief for the Aristocracy"? European Nobility and Diplomacy, 1850–1914', in *The Diplomats' World: A Cultural History of Diplomacy, 1815–1914*, ed. M. Mösslang and T. Riotte (Oxford, 2008), p. 38.
64 R. A. Jones, *The British Diplomatic Service, 1815–1914* (Gerrards Cross, 1983), p. 217.
65 H. Werking, *The Master Architects: Building the United States Foreign Service, 1890–1913* (Lexington, KY, 1977).
66 George Bosanquet to Vaughan, 18 Feb. 1824, All Souls Oxford, Vaughan papers C23 no. 1.
67 R. R. McLean, *Royalty and Diplomacy in Europe, 1890–1914* (Cambridge, 2001).
68 F. M. Carroll, *A Good and Wise Measure: The Struggle for the Canadian-American Border, 1783–1842* (Toronto, 2001).
69 F. L. Kirgis, *The American Society of International Law's First Century, 1906–2006* (Leiden, 2006).
70 P. Laity, *The British Peace Movement, 1870–1914* (Oxford, 2001).
71 F. A. Boyle, *Foundations of World Order: The Legalist Approach to International Relations, 1898–1922* (Durham, NC, 1999).

SIX: 1900–1970

1 N. Bland, preface to E. Satow, *A Guide to Diplomatic Practice* (4th edn, London, 1964), pp. v–vii.
2 A. Ponsonby, *Democracy and Diplomacy: A Plea for Popular Control of Foreign Policy* (London, 1915), pp. 61–7.
3 M. Hughes, *Diplomacy before the Russian Revolution: Britain, Russia, and the Old Diplomacy, 1894–1917* (Basingstoke, 2000).
4 K. Wilson, 'In Pursuit of the Editorship of British Documents *On the Origins of the War, 1898–1914*: J. W. Headlam-Morley before Gooch and Temperley', *Archives*, XXII (1995), p. 83.
5 A. Sharp, 'Adapting to a New World? British Foreign Policy in the 1920s', in *The Foreign Office and British Diplomacy in the Twentieth Century*, ed. G. Johnson (Abingdon, 2005), p. 77.
6 M. Weil, *A Pretty Good Club: The Founding Fathers of the U.S. Foreign Service* (New York, 1978).
7 Memoir by Sir Edward Grigg in *The American Speeches of Lord Lothian* (Oxford, 1941), p. xxviii; speech, p. 47.
8 R. Jarman, ed., *Shanghai: Political and Economic Reports, 1842–1943* (Cambridge, 2008).
9 T. W. Burkman, *Japan and the League of Nations: Empire and World Order, 1914–1938* (Honolulu, HI, 2008).
10 F. R. Dickinson, *War and National Reinvention: Japan in the Great War, 1914–1919* (Cambridge, MA, 1999).
11 D. S. van der Oye, *Towards the Rising Sun: Russian Ideologies of Empire and the Path to War with Japan* (DeKalb, IL, 2001).
12 W. D. Godsey, 'Officers vs Diplomats: Bureaucracy and Foreign Policy in Austria-Hungary, 1906–1914', *Mitteilungen des Österreichischen Staatsarchiv*, XLVI (1998), pp. 43–66.
13 W. A. Renzi, *In the Shadow of the Sword: Italy's Neutrality and Entrance into the Great War, 1914–1915* (New York, 1988).
14 M. Frey, 'Trade, Ships, and the Neutrality of the Netherlands in the First World War', *International History Review*, XIX (1997), pp. 541–62; M. M. Abbenhuis, *The Art of Staying Neutral: The Netherlands in the First World War* (Amsterdam, 2006).
15 E. D. Morel, *Truth and the War* (London, 1916); F. Neilson, *How Diplomats Make War* (New York, 1916).
16 D. Dutton, '"Private" Papers: The Case of Sir John Simon', *Archives*, XXXI (2005), p. 79.
17 M. Macmillan, *Paris 1919* (New York, 2002), p. 57. Published in Britain as *Peacemakers: The Paris Conference of 1919 and Its Attempt to End War* (London, 2003).
18 R. J. Shuster, *German Disarmament after World War I: The Diplomacy of International Arms Inspection, 1920–1931* (London, 2006).
19 B. P. Murphy, *John Chartres* (Blackrock, 1995).
20 Y. Güçlü, 'The Struggle for Mastery in Cilicia: Turkey, France, and the Ankara Agreement of 1921', *International History Review*, XXIII (2001), pp. 593–7.
21 J. Wright, *Gustav Stresemann* (Oxford, 2002).
22 J. Borzecki, *The Soviet-Polish Peace of 1921 and the Creation of Interwar*

Europe (New Haven, CT, 2008).

23 D. R. Stone, 'The Prospect of War? Lev Trotskii, the Soviet Army, and the German Revolution in 1923', *International History Review*, XXV (2003), pp. 799–817, esp. pp. 801–2.

24 B. Patenaude, *Stalin's Nemesis: The Exile and Murder of Leon Trotsky* (London, 2009).

25 P. Neville, *Appeasing Hitler: The Diplomacy of Sir Nevile Henderson, 1937–39* (Basingstoke, 2000); G. Johnson, ed., *Our Man in Berlin: The Diary of Sir Eric Phipps, 1933–37* (Basingstoke, 2008).

26 D. Mayers, 'Neither War Nor Peace: FDR's Ambassadors in Nazi Berlin and Policy toward Germany, 1933–1941', *Diplomacy and Statecraft*, XX (2009), pp. 50–68.

27 G. B. Strang, *On the Fiery March: Mussolini Prepares for War* (Westport, CT, 2003).

28 J. Haslam, 'Comintern and Soviet Foreign Policy, 1919–1941', in R. G. Suny, ed., *The Cambridge History of Russia*, III: *The Twentieth Century* (Cambridge, 2006), pp. 648–9.

29 Z. Steiner, 'The Soviet Commissariat of Foreign Affairs and the Czechoslovakian Crisis in 1938: New Material from the Soviet Archives', *Historical Journal*, XLII (1999), pp. 777–9.

30 Haslam, 'Comintern and Soviet Foreign Policy', pp. 637–42.

31 N. E. Saul, *Friends or Foes? The United States and Soviet Russia, 1921–1941* (Lawrence, KS, 2006).

32 J. E. Haynes, H. Klehr and A. Vassiliev, *Spies: The Rise and Fall of the KGB in America* (New Haven, CT, 2009).

33 L. H. Mates, *The Spanish Civil War and the British Left: Political Activism and the Popular Front* (London, 2007).

34 T. J. Ulricks, *Diplomacy and Ideology: The Origins of Soviet Foreign Relations, 1917–1930* (London, 1979).

35 D. Varè, *Laughing Diplomat* (London, 1938), p. 425.

36 A. Stewart, *Empire Lost: Britain, the Dominions, and the Second World War* (London, 2008).

37 M. Hughes, 'Fighting for White Rule in Africa: The Central African Federation, Katanga, and the Congo Crisis, 1958–1965', *International History Review*, XXV (2003), pp. 592–615.

38 Lord Hankey, *Diplomacy by Conference: Studies in Public Affairs, 1920–1946* (London, 1946), p. 39.

39 M. D. Callahan, *Mandates and Empire: The League of Nations and Africa, 1914–1931* (Brighton, 1999).

40 W. B. McAllister, *Drug Diplomacy in the Twentieth Century: An International History* (London, 2000).

41 J. Cambon, *The Diplomatist* (London, 1931), p. 139. He had been French ambassador in Berlin in 1914.

42 Z. Steiner, *The Lights That Failed: European International History, 1919–1933* (Oxford, 2005); P. O. Cohrs, *The Unfinished Peace after World War I: America, Britain and the Stabilisation of Europe, 1919–1932* (Cambridge, 2006).

43 I. Nish, 'Jousting with Authority: The Tokyo Embassy of Sir Francis Lindley, 1931–4', *Proceedings of the Japan Society*, CV (1986), pp. 9–19.

44 R. Mallett, *Mussolini and the Origins of the Second World War, 1933–1940* (Basingstoke, 2003).

45 S. G. Craft, 'Saving the League: V. K. Wellington Koo, the League of Nations and Sino-Japanese Conflict, 1931–39', *Diplomacy and Statecraft*, XI (2000), pp. 107–8.
46 J. L. Cox, 'The Background to the Syrian Campaign, May–June 1941: A Study in Franco-German Wartime Relations', *History*, LXXII (1987), pp. 432–52; J. J. Sadkovich, 'German Military Incompetence through Italian Eyes', *War in History*, I (1994), pp. 39–62.
47 F. D. McCann, *The Brazilian–American Alliance, 1937–1945* (Princeton, NJ, 1973); M. L. Francis, *The Limits of Hegemony: United States Relations with Argentina and Chile during World War II* (Notre Dame, IN, 1977); R. A. Humphreys, *Latin America and the Second World War* (London, 1981–2); S. I. Schwab, 'The Role of the Mexican Expeditionary Air Force in World War II: Late, Limited, but Symbolically Significant', *Journal of Military History*, LXVI (2002), pp. 1115–40.
48 M. E. Glantz, *FDR and the Soviet Union: The President's Battles over Foreign Policy* (Lawrence, KS, 2005).
49 F. J. Harbutt, *Yalta 1945: Europe and America at the Crossroads* (Cambridge, 2009).
50 N. Smith, *American Empire: Roosevelt's Geographer and the Prelude to Globalization* (Berkeley, CA, 2003), p. 360; W. R. Louis, *Imperialism at Bay: The United States and the Decolonisation of the British Empire, 1941–1945* (New York, 1978); A. J. Whitfield, *Hong Kong, Empire, and the Anglo-American Alliance at War, 1941–45* (Basingstoke, 2001).
51 F. Venn, *The Anglo-American Oil War: International Politics and the Struggle for Foreign Petroleum, 1912–1945* (London, 2009); for the situation in 1951–3, see S. Marsh, *Anglo-American Relations and Cold War Oil: Crisis in Iran* (Basingstoke, 2003).
52 T. C. Mills, 'Anglo-American Economic Diplomacy during the Second World War and the Electrification of the Central Brazilian Railway', *Diplomacy and Statecraft*, XX (2009), pp. 69–85.
53 C. D. O'Sullivan, *Sumner Welles, Postwar Planning, and the Quest for a New World Order, 1937–1943* (New York, 2009).
54 F. Prochaska, *The Eagle and the Crown: Americans and the British Monarchy* (New Haven, CT, 2008), p. 154.
55 V. de Grazia, *Irresistible Empire: America's Advance through Twentieth-Century Europe* (Cambridge, MA, 2005).
56 S. G. Payne, *Franco and Hitler: Spain, Germany and World War II* (New Haven, CT, 2008).
57 G. Krebs, 'Operation Super Sunrise? Japanese-United States Peace Feelers in Switzerland, 1945', *Journal of Military History*, LXIX (2005), pp. 1081–120.
58 For an account of this transition from the perspective of an individual diplomat, the British envoy in Washington from 1924 to 1930, B.J.C. McKercher, *Esme Howard: A Diplomatic Biography* (Cambridge, 1989).
59 P. Vyšný, *The Runciman Mission to Czechoslovakia, 1938: Prelude to Munich* (Basingstoke, 2003).
60 D. H. Dunn, 'What is Summitry?', *Diplomacy at the Highest Level: The Evolution of International Summitry*, ed. D. H. Dunn (Basingstoke, 1996), p. 4.
61 C. Roetter, *The Diplomatic Art* (London, 1965), pp. 208–9.

62 D. Reynolds, *Lord Lothian and Anglo-American Relations, 1939–1940* (Philadelphia, PA, 1983).
63 D. Culbert, 'Our Awkward Ally: *Mission to Moscow*', in *American Cinema/American History*, ed. J. E. O'Connor and M. A. Jackson (New York, 1979).
64 For the origins of the General Agreement on Tariffs and Trade (GATT), R. N. Gardner, *Sterling-Dollar Diplomacy in Current Perspective: The Origins and Prospects of our International Order* (New York, 1980); T. W. Zeiler, *Free Trade Free World: The Advent of GATT* (Chapel Hill, NC, 1999); R. Toye, 'The Attlee Government, the Imperial Preference System and the Creation of the Gatt', *English Historical Review*, CXVIII (2003), pp. 912–39.
65 Zeiler, *Free Trade, Free World*.
66 M. Connelly, *A Diplomatic Revolution: Algeria's Fight for Independence and the Origins of the Post-Cold War Era* (Oxford, 2002).
67 R. K. Brigham, *Guerrilla Diplomacy: The NLF's Foreign Relations and the Vietnam War* (Ithaca, NY, 1999).
68 D. Judd, *A British Tale of Indian and Foreign Service: The Memoirs of Sir Ian Scott* (London, 1999).
69 B. G. Plummer, *Rising Wind: Black Americans and U.S. Foreign Affairs, 1935–1960* (Chapel Hill, NC, 1996).
70 M. L. Krenn, *Black Diplomacy: African Americans and the State Department, 1945–1969* (London, 1999).
71 A. DeRoche, *Andrew Young: Civil Rights Ambassador* (Wilmington, DE, 2003); E. J. Perkins, *Mr. Ambassador. Warrior for Peace* (Norman, OK, 2009).
72 D. R. Culverson, *Contesting Apartheid: US Activism, 1960–1987* (Boulder, CO, 1999).
73 E. Podeh, *The Decline of Arab Unity: The Rise and Fall of the United Arab Republic* (Brighton, 1999).
74 E. Podeh, *The Quest for Hegemony in the Arab World* (Leiden, 1995).
75 R. Schofield, ed., *Arabian Boundaries, 1966–1975* (Cambridge, 2009).
76 C. H. Godden, *Trespassers Forgiven: Memoirs of Imperial Service in an Age of Independence* (London, 2009).
77 W. Hitchcock, *France Restored: Cold War Diplomacy and the Quest for Leadership in Europe, 1944–1954* (Chapel Hill, NC, 1998).
78 P. Roberts, ed., *Window on the Forbidden City: The Beijing Diaries of David Bruce, 1973–1974* (Hong Kong, 2001).
79 D. E. Murphy, S. A. Kondrashev and G. Bailey, *Battleground Berlin: CIA via KGB in the Cold War* (New Haven, CT, 1997); B. Woodward, *Veil: The Secret Wars of the CIA, 1981–1987* (New York, 1987).
80 Rundall to Addis, 11 Oct. 1960, London, School of Oriental and African Studies (hereafter SOAS), Archives, PPMS 25, 66.
81 T. T. Petersen, 'How Not to Stand Up to Arabs and Israelis', *International History Review*, XXV (2003), p. 618.
82 T. Hopf, 'Moscow's Foreign Policy, 1945–2000: Identities, Instructions and Interests', *Cambridge History of Russia*, III, pp. 685–7.
83 M. Mayer, *The Diplomats* (New York, 1983), p. 375.
84 G. Bischof, *Austria in the First Cold War, 1945–55: The Leverage of the Weak* (Basingstoke, 1999).
85 S. J. Ball, *The Cold War: An International History, 1947–1991* (London, 1998).
86 P. Ardant, 'Chinese Diplomatic Practice during the Cultural Revolution', in

China's Practice of International Law, ed. J. A. Cohen (Cambridge, MA, 1972), pp. 86–128.
87 M. Jones, 'Between the Bear and the Dragon: Nixon, Kissinger and U.S. Foreign Policy in the Era of Détente', *English Historical Review*, CXXIII (2009), pp. 1277–8.

SEVEN: 1970 to the Present

1 J. Black, *Geopolitics* (London, 2009), pp. 169–73.
2 O. A. Westad, *The Global War* (Cambridge, 2006).
3 S. Kaufman, *Plans Unraveled: The Foreign Policy of the Carter Administration* (DeKalb, IL, 2008).
4 I have benefited from hearing a lecture on the subject by Gareth Evans, delivered to the 10th Asia Pacific Programme for Senior Military Officers in Singapore in August 2008.
5 A. Faizullaev, 'Diplomacy and Self', *Diplomacy and Statecraft*, XVII (2006), p. 517. See also A. Wendt, *Social Theory of International Politics* (Cambridge, 1999) and H. J. Langholtz and C. E. Stout, eds, *The Psychology of Diplomacy* (Westport, CT, 2004).
6 R. Cohen, *Theatre of Power: The Art of Diplomatic Signalling* (London, 1987); C. Jonsson and K. Aggestam, 'Trends in Diplomatic Signalling', in *Innovation in Diplomatic Practice*, ed. J. Melissen (Basingstoke, 1999), pp. 151–70.
7 R. K. Herrmann, 'Image Theory and Strategic Interaction in International Relations', in *The Oxford Handbook of Political Psychology*, ed. D. O. Sears, L. Huddy and R. Jervis (Oxford, 2003), pp. 285–314.
8 R. Langhorne, 'Current Developments in Diplomacy: Who are the Diplomats Now?', *Diplomacy and Statecraft*, VIII (1997), pp. 1–15.
9 I. Berlin, Introduction to H. G. Nicholas, ed., *Washington Despatches, 1941–45* (Chicago, 1981), pp. ix–x.
10 M. D. Harmon, 'The 1976 UK-IMF Crisis: The Markets, The Americans, and the IMF', *Contemporary British History*, XI/3 (1997), pp. 1–17.
11 C. J. Mitcham, *China's Economic Relations with the West and Japan, 1949–79: Grain, Trade, and Diplomacy* (London, 2005).
12 1989 report from American Defence Intelligence Agency, noted in *Sunday Times*, 16 Aug. 2009, p. 9.
13 G. M. Young, *Victorian England: Portrait of an Age* (London, 1953), p. 103.
14 P. G. Lauren, ed., *Diplomacy: New Approaches in History, Theory and Policy* (New York, 1987).
15 K. W. Schweizer, 'The Narrowing of Options: The Transformation of Strategic into Tactical Diplomacy in Europe after World War One', *Reports of the 16th International Congress of the Historical Sciences* (Stuttgart, 1985), vol. II, 537–9.
16 *New York Times*, 11 June 2009, section C, pp. 1, 7.
17 E. C. Hoffmann, 'Diplomatic History and the Meaning of Life: Towards a Global American History', *Diplomatic History*, XXI (1997).
18 J. Black and Schweizer, 'The Value of Diplomatic History: A Case Study in the Historical Thought of Herbert Butterfield', *Diplomacy and Statecraft*, XVII (2006), pp. 617–19.

19 A. Siniver, *Nixon, Kissinger, and U.S. Foreign Policy Making: The Machinery of Crisis* (Cambridge, 2008).
20 J. Lynn, 'The Embattled Future of Academic Military History', *Journal of Military History*, LXI (1997), pp. 775–89; V. Hanson, 'The Dilemma of the Contemporary Military Historian', in *Reconstructing History*, ed. E. Fox-Genovese and E. Lasch-Quinn (London, 1999), pp. 189–201.
21 P. Sluglett, 'The Resilience of a Frontier: Ottoman and Iraqi Claims to Kuwait, 1871–1990', *International History Review*, XXIV (2002), pp. 814–15.
22 L. Freedman, *The Official History of the Falklands Campaign* (London, 2005).
23 A. Iriye, *Global Community: The Role of International Organizations in the Making of the Contemporary World* (Berkeley, CA, 2002).
24 C. Ingebritsen, I. Neumann, S. Gstöhl and J. Beyer, eds, *Small States in International Relations* (Seattle, 2006).
25 A.J.K. Shepherd, '"A Milestone in the History of the EU": Kosovo and the EU's International Role', *International Affairs*, LXXXV (2009), p. 529.
26 K. Newman, *Macmillan, Khruschev, and the Berlin Crisis, 1958–1960* (London, 1960).
27 N. Ridley, *'My Style of Government': The Thatcher Years* (London, 1991), p. 159.
28 K. W. Stein, *Heroic Diplomacy: Sadat, Kissinger, Carter, Begin, and the Quest for Arab–Israeli Peace* (London, 1999).
29 Addis to his sister Robina, 18 Jan. 1972, SOAS, PPMS 25, 82.
30 P. G. Harris, ed., *The Environment, International Relations, and US Foreign Policy* (Washington, DC, 2001).
31 *The Times*, 16 Oct. 2009, p. 49.
32 *The Times*, 16 July 2009, p. 32.
33 Email from Andrew Heritage, former Editor-in-Chief of Dorling Kindersley Cartography, 14 Sept. 2009. The *Economist* (17 Oct. 2009, p. 75) has also been criticized by Chinese, Japanese, South Korean and Russian diplomats over its maps of contested regions in the seas off East Asia.
34 C. D. Walton, *Geopolitics and the Great Powers in the Twenty-First Century* (London, 2007); W. H. Overholt, *Asia, America, and the Transformation of Geopolitics* (Cambridge, 2008).
35 L.S.K. Kwong, 'The Chinese Myth of Universal Kingship and Commissioner Lin Zexu's Anti-Opium Campaign of 1839', *English Historical Review*, CXXIII (2008), pp. 1501–3.
36 J. Walsh, 'China and the New Geopolitics of Central Asia', *Asian Survey*, XXIII (1993), pp. 272–84; A. Banuazzi and M. Weiner, eds, *The New Geopolitics of Central Asia and its Borderlands* (Bloomington, IN, 1994); 'Central Asia and the Caucasus: On the Centenary of Halford Mackinder's Geographical Pivot of History', *Journal of Social and Political Studies*, IV (2005), special issue; H. H. Karrar, *The New Silk Road Diplomacy: China's Central Asian Foreign Policy since the Cold War* (Vancouver, 2009).
37 P. Snow, *The Star Raft: China's Encounter with Africa* (London, 1988).

REFERENCES

Conclusions: The Future

1 B. Hocking, ed., *Foreign Ministries: Change and Adaptation* (London, 1998).
2 G. Moorhouse, *The Diplomats: The Foreign Office Today* (London, 1977), p. 390.
3 P. Wells, 'Comments, Custard Pies and Comic Cuts: The Boulting Brothers at Play, 1955–65', in *The Family Way: The Boulting Brothers and Postwar British Film Culture* ed. A. Burton, T. O'Sullivan and P. Wells (Trowbridge, 2000), p. 59.
4 Addis to his sister Robina, 13 Oct. 1955, 13 Feb. 1972, SOAS, PPMS 25, 41, 82.
5 A.H.M. Kirk-Greene, 'Accredited to Africa: British Diplomatic Representation and African Experience, c. 1960–95', *Diplomacy and Statecraft*, XI (2000), pp. 82–3.
6 J. Newhouse, 'Diplomacy, Inc. The Influence of Lobbies on U.S. Foreign Policy', *Foreign Affairs*, LXXXVIII/3 (May/June 2009), pp. 73–92.
7 S. M. Watt, *The Origins of Alliances* (Ithaca, NY, 1987) and J. J. Mearsheimer and S. M. Watt, *The Israel Lobby and U.S. Foreign Policy* (New York, 2007). For a perceptive critique that also notes much of the other literature, B. Fishman, 'The "Israel Lobby": A Realistic Assessment', *Orbis*, LII (Winter 2008), pp. 159–80.
8 P. Trubowitz, *Defining the National Interest: Conflict and Change in American Foreign Policy* (Chicago, 1998).
9 J. F. Hart, ed., *Regions of the United States* (New York, 1972); W. Zelinsky, *The Cultural Geography of the United States* (Englewood Cliffs, NJ, 1973); E. L. Ayers et al., *All Over the Map: Rethinking American Regions* (Baltimore, MD, 1996).
10 M. Evangelista, *Unarmed Forces: The Transnational Movement to End the Cold War* (Ithaca, NY, 1999).
11 R. Langhorne, 'Full Circle: New Principals and Old Consequences in the Modern Diplomatic System', *Diplomacy and Statecraft*, XI (2000), pp. 34–5.
12 R. Langhorne, *Diplomacy beyond the Primacy of the State* (Leicester, 1998).
13 K. Urbach, *Bismarck's Favourite Englishman: Lord Odo Russell's Mission to Berlin* (London, 1999).
14 G. Kennedy, 'Anglo-American Diplomatic Relations, 1939–1945', in *War and Diplomacy*, ed. A. Dorman and G. Kennedy (Washington, DC, 2008), p. 45.
15 *Financial Times*, 22 Sept. 2009, pp. 1, 3.
16 L. McLoughlin, *In a Sea of Knowledge: British Arabists in the Twentieth Century* (Reading, 2002).
17 J. L. Schecter, *Russian Negotiating Behavior* (Washington, DC, 1998).
18 *Times*, 14 Aug. 2009.
19 Middleton to Sir Leoline Jenkins, Secretary of State for the Northern Department, 17, 24, 31 August, 7, 21 September, 7 October, 2, 16 November 1680, 8, 22 February 1681, NA. SP. 80/16; G. H. Jones, *Charles Middleton* (Chicago, 1967), p. 53.
20 Marquise Campana de Cavelli, *Les Derniers Stuarts à Saint-Germain-en-Laye* (Paris, 1871), II, pp. 160–61.
21 R. Wolfe, '*Still* Lying Abroad? On the Institution of the Resident Ambassador', *Diplomacy and Statecraft*, IX (1998), pp. 49–50.
22 R. Cohen, *Theatre of Power: The Art of Diplomatic Signalling* (London, 1987), p. 6.

23 S. Soyer, 'The Diplomat as a Stranger', *Diplomacy and Statecraft*, VIII (1997), p. 184.
24 R. Cohen, *Negotiating across Cultures* (Washington, DC, 1991), pp. 160–61.

Postscript

1 M. Bukovansky, *Legitimacy and Power Politics. The American and French Revolutions in International Political Culture* (Princeton, NJ, 2002), p. 227.
2 A. Mombauer, *Helmuth von Moltke and the Origins of the First World War* (Cambridge, 2001); S. T. Ross, *American War Plans, 1890–1939* (London, 2002).
3 J. Kurlantzick, *Charm Offensive: How China's Soft Power is Transforming the World* (New Haven, CT, 2007).
4 J. L. Richardson, *Crisis Diplomacy: The Great Powers since the Mid-Nineteenth Century* (Cambridge, 1994). For an example, N. Carter, 'Hudson, Malmesbury and Cavour: British Diplomacy and the Italian Question, February 1858 to June 1859', *Historical Journal*, XL (1997), p. 413.
5 *Memoirs of Cordell Hull* (2 vols, London, 1948), II, 1734.
6 G. Kennan, *Memoirs, 1950–1963* (London, 1973), pp. 319–20.
7 N. Thompson, *The Hawk and the Dove: Paul Nitze, George Kennan, and the History of the Cold War* (New York, 2099).

Selected Further Reading

The relevant literature is extensive and very varied, including as it does diplomatic memoirs and studies in international relations. For reasons of space, the emphasis is on recent works. Earlier literature can be followed up in the footnotes and bibliographies of these works. It is also very useful to look at the key journals, notably the *International History Review*, *Diplomacy and Statecraft* and *Revue d'Histoire Diplomatique*. Websites, such as that of the British Foreign Office (www.fco.gov.uk/en/about-the-fco//publications/historians1/history-notes) and, for the USA, 'Frontline Diplomacy: The Foreign Affairs Oral History Collection of the Association for Diplomatic Studies and Training' (http://memory.loc.gov/ammem/collections/diplomacy) also contain material of value.

General

Adcock, F., and D. J. Mosley, *Diplomacy in Ancient Greece* (London, 1975)
Anderson, M. S., *The Rise of Modern Diplomacy, 1450–1919* (Harlow, 1993)
Baillou, J., ed., *Les Affaires étrangères et le corps diplomatique français* (Paris, 1984)
Barber, P., *Diplomacy* (London, 1979)
Berridge, G. R., M. Keens-Soper and T. G. Otte, *Diplomatic Theory from Machiavelli to Kissinger* (Basingstoke, 2001)
Der Derian, J. D., *On Diplomacy* (Oxford, 1987)
—, *Antidiplomacy: Spies, Terror, Speed, and War* (Oxford, 1992)
Dunn, D., ed., *Diplomacy at the Highest Level: The Evolution of International Summitry* (London, 1996)
Eayrs, J., *Diplomacy and its Discontents* (Toronto, 1971)
Graham, R. A., *Vatican Diplomacy: A Study of Church and State on the International Plane* (Princeton, NJ, 1959)
Hamilton, K., and R. Langhorne, *The Practice of Diplomacy: Its Evolution, Theory and Administration* (London, 1995)
Herman, M., *Intelligence Power in Peace and War* (Cambridge, 1996)
Jones, D. V., *The Thought and Conduct of Diplomacy* (Chicago, 1984)
Jönsson, C., and R. Langhorne, eds, *Diplomacy* (London, 2004)
Lauren, P. G., ed., *Diplomacy* (New York, 1979)
Martin, L.W., ed., *Diplomacy in Modern European History* (New York, 1966)
Mookerjie, G. K., *Diplomacy: Theory and History* (New Delhi, 1973)
Nicolson, H., *Diplomacy*, 3rd edn (Oxford, 1963)
—, *The Evolution of Diplomacy* (1962)

Onuf, N., *World of our Making: Rules and Rule in Social Theory and International Relations* (Columbia, SC, 1989)
Polk, W. R., *Neighbors and Strangers: The Fundamentals of Foreign Affairs* (Chicago, 1997)
Sarkission, A. O., ed., *Studies in Diplomatic History and Historiography* (London, 1961).
Towle, P., *Enforced Disarmament: From the Napoleonic Campaigns to the Gulf War* (Oxford, 1997)
Vagts, A., *The Military Attaché* (Princeton, NJ, 1967)

ONE: 1450–1600

Adair, E. R., *The Exterritoriality of Ambassadors in the Sixteenth and Seventeenth Centuries* (London, 1929)
Bély, L., ed., *L'invention de la diplomatie* (Paris, 1998)
Bély, L., *La Société des Princes: XVIe–XVIIIe siècle* (Paris, 1999)
Frigo, D., ed., *Politics and Diplomacy in Early Modern Italy* (Cambridge, 2000)
Hampton, T., *Fictions of Embassy: Literature and Diplomacy in Early Modern Europe* (Ithaca, NY, 2009)
Mattingly, G., *Renaissance Diplomacy* (London, 1955)
Maude-la-Clavière, M.A.R. de, *La Diplomatie au temps de Machiavel* (Paris, 1892–3)
Queller, D. E., *The Office of the Ambassador in the Middle Ages* (Princeton, NJ, 1967)
Russel, J. G., *Diplomats at Work: Three Renaissance Studies* (Stroud, 1992)
Thorp, M. R., and A. J. Slavin, eds, *Politics, Religion and Diplomacy in Early Modern Europe* (Kirksville, MO, 1994)

TWO: 1600–1690

Bély, L., *Espions et ambassadeurs au temps de Louis XIV* (Paris, 1990)
—, *Les Relations Internationales en Europe, XVIIe–XVIIIe siècles* (Paris, 1991)
Levin, M. J., *Agents of Empire: Spanish Ambassadors in Sixteenth-Century Italy* (Ithaca, NY, 2005)
Roosen, W. J., *The Age of Louis XIV: The Rise of Modern Diplomacy* (Cambridge, MA, 1976).

THREE: 1690–1775

Horn, D. B., *The British Diplomatic Service, 1689–1789* (Oxford, 1961)
Keens-Soper, M., and K. Schweizer, eds, *François de Callières: The Art of Diplomacy* (Leicester, 1983)
Ragsdale, H., ed., *Imperial Russian Foreign Policy* (Cambridge, 1994)

FOUR: 1775–1815

Middleton, C. R., *The Administration of British Foreign Policy, 1782–1846* (Durham, NC, 1977)
Whitcomb, E. A., *Napoleon's Diplomatic Service* (Durham, NC, 1979)

SELECTED FURTHER READING

FIVE: 1815–1900

Cecil, L., *The German Diplomatic Service, 1871–1914* (Princeton, NJ, 1976)
Checkland, S., *The Elgins 1766–1917: A Tale of Aristocrats, Proconsuls and their Wives* (Aberdeen, 1988)
Gladwyn, C., *The Paris Embassy* (London, 1976)
Jones, R., *The Nineteenth-Century Foreign Office: An Administrative History* (London, 1971)
Platt, D.C.M., *Finance, Trade and Politics in British Foreign Policy, 1815–1914* (Oxford, 1968)
Yasamee, F.A.K., *Ottoman Diplomacy: Abdülhamid II and the Great Powers, 1878–1888* (Istanbul, 1996)

SIX: 1900–1970

Bell, P.M.H., *John Bull and the Bear: British Public Opinion, Foreign Policy and the Soviet Union, 1941–1945* (London, 1990)
Craig, G. A., and F. Gilbert, eds, *The Diplomats, 1919–1939* (New York, 1967)
Dockrill, M., and B. McKercher, *Diplomacy and World Power: Studies in British Foreign Policy, 1890–1950* (Cambridge, 1996)
Goldstein, E., *Winning the Peace: British Diplomatic Strategy, Peace Planning, and the Paris Peace Conference, 1916–1920* (Oxford, 1991)
Hopkins, M., S. Kelly and J. Young, eds, *The Washington Embassy: British Ambassadors to the United States, 1939–1977* (Basingstoke, 2009)
Kim, S. Y., *American Diplomacy and Strategy toward Korea and Northeast Asia, 1882–1950 and After* (Basingstoke, 2009)
Kissinger, H. A., *Nuclear Weapons and Foreign Policy* (New York, 1957)
Lauren, P. G., *Diplomats and Bureaucrats: The First Institutional Responses to Twentieth-Century Diplomacy in France and Germany* (Stanford, CA, 1976)
Moussa, F., *Le Service diplomatique des états arabes* (Geneva, 1960)
Riste, O., *Norway's Foreign Relations: A History*, 2nd edn (Oslo, 2005)
Schulze, K. E., *Israel's Covert Diplomacy in Lebanon* (New York, 1998)
Steiner, Z. S., *The Foreign Office and Foreign Policy, 1898–1914* (Cambridge, 1969)
Ulricks, T. J., *Diplomacy and Ideology: The Origins of Soviet Foreign Relations, 1917–1920* (London, 1979)
Young, J., *Twentieth Century Diplomacy: A Case Study of British Practice, 1963–1976* (Cambridge, 2008)
Young, J., and J. Kent, *International Relations since 1945: A Global History* (Oxford, 2004)

SEVEN: 1970 TO THE PRESENT

Buckley, R., *Hong Kong: The Road to 1997* (Cambridge, 1997)
Frankel, M., *High Noon in the Cold War: Kennedy, Khrushchev and the Cuban Missile Crisis* (New York, 2004)
Gaddis, J. L., *We Now Know: Rethinking Cold War History* (Oxford, 1997)
Gotlieb, A., *'I'll be with you in a minute, Mr Ambassador': The Education of a Canadian Diplomat in Washington* (Toronto, 1991)
Kaiser, D. E., *American Tragedy: Kennedy, Johnson and the Origins of the Vietnam War* (Cambridge, MA, 2000)

Kissinger, A., ed., *American Foreign Policy*, 3rd edn (New York, 1977)

CONCLUSIONS: THE FUTURE

Ambrose, S. E., *Rise to Globalism: American Foreign Policy since 1938* (London, 1988)
Bacevich, A. J., *American Empire: The Realities and Consequences of US Diplomacy* (Cambridge, MA, 2002)
Benjamin, D., ed., *America and the World in the Age of Terror* (Washington, DC, 2005)
Bull-Berg, H. J., *American International Oil Policy: Causal Factors and Effects* (London, 1987)
Daalder, I. H., and Lindsay, J. M., *America Unbound: The Bush Revolution in Foreign Policy* (Washington, DC, 2003)
Johnson, C., *Blowback: The Costs and Consequences of American Empire* (New York, 2004)
Melissen, J., ed., *Innovation in Diplomatic Practice* (Basingstoke, 1999)

Index

Abyssinia 153, 155, 159, 202–3
Acland, F. D. 183–4
Adams, John 119
Addis, John 219, 243, 248–9
Afghanistan 16, 167, 171, 209, 227–8, 234, 238, 256, 258
Africa 71, 91–2, 169, 214, 227, 233, 249, 251
  see also individual countries
Al-Qaeda 238, 246, 258, 261
Alba, Duke of 195
Albania 157
Alberoni, Giulio 105
Alexander I of Russia 142, 145, 148, 177, 212
Algeria 213, 215, 222, 224
Alt, Justus 70
America 13, 131, 193, 194, 218, 231
  African Americans 214–15
  American Civil War 169
  American Revolution 127, 128–30
  American Society of International Law 179
  Anglo–American relationship 120, 130, 169, 208, 253
  anti-apartheid activists 215
  Asia, links with (1850s) 155
  China, relationship with 217–18, 241
  CIA 16–17, 218, 234
  Civil War 127, 130
  and Cold War 217, 220–21, 227–8
  Declaration of Independence 120, 127, 166
  détente 224, 226, 231
  diplomatic culture 131, 175, 184, 218, 231, 234, 244, 253, 254, 257
  and domestic interest groups 250
  and drugs trade 245
  embassy attacks 237, 238
  Europe, diplomatic contact with (1800s) 154

and Falklands war 239
federalism and diplomacy 130–31
filibustering, state-only (1800s) 153
First World War 186, 187, 201
Foreign Agents Registration Act 197
Helms–Burton Act 231
influence and imperialism 186, 207, 208, 209, 213, 221
Institute of Peace 229
intelligence gathering (1900s) 195
Jackson–Vanik trade act amendment 231
Japan–US Friendship Commission 241
Jay–Gardoqui negotiations 130
and League of Nations 231
Lend Lease agreement 208
lobbyists 250
Longchamps affair 131
and Middle East peace process 234–5
Monroe Doctrine 156
OPEC ban 251
open diplomacy, call for (1900s) 188
and *Ostpolitik* 225
power transition, future 246–7
Proliferation Security Initiative 242
regional interests, importance of 250–51
reparations diplomacy 190
republicanism as diplomatic ethos 127–8, 131
Russian intelligence offensive (1900s) 196
Second World War 195, 196, 205, 206, 207, 208, 209, 210, 211, 212
and South America 156, 205–6
state visits (1900s) 219
trade and international cooperation (modern) 241
Treaty of Wanghia (China) 162
Treaty of Washington 169

trusteeship system (1900s) 207–8
Tydings–McDuffe Act 207–8
United Nations membership 211
and Vietnam War 214, 225
and War on Terror 234
Western diplomacy and Native American tribes (1700s) 90–91, 95, 104
Amherst, William, Lord 151–2
ancien régime diplomacy 46, 56, 105, 127–9, 131–3, 136–8, 140–41, 143–4, 148, 154, 249
Anderson, Matthew 43
Angola 169, 200
Argentina 154, 156, 157, 166, 195, 198, 206, 239
aristocratic diplomacy 102–3, 106, 111, 114, 116–18, 172–6, 182, 184, 188, 196–8
Armenia 232–3, 238
Armstrong, William 178
Arundel, Thomas, 2nd Earl of 60–61
Ashcroft, Lord 231
Auckland, William, 1st Lord 132
Australia 156, 217, 250
Austria 146, 149, 168, 169, 170, 225
  Alliance of Vienna system 116
  aristocratic diplomacy 172–3, 186
  Brüno (film) and national identity 245
  Cold War neutrality 221
  diplomacy 105, 110–11, 113, 141, 143, 144
  Diplomatic Revolution (1756) 78, 108
  dynastic prestige 142
  First World War 186, 187
  and French Revolution 132, 133, 135–6, 139, 140
  Habsburgs *see* Habsburgs
  Imperial Election Scheme 66
  nationalist diplomacy 141, 144
  personal diplomacies (1700s) 105
  Quadruple Alliance 148
  royal court and protocol (1800s) 175
  Second World War 193
  secret diplomacy 108
  Truce of Leoben 140
  War of Austrian Succession 97, 98, 101, 106
Ayrault, Pierre 18
Azerbaijan 233

Bandar bin Sultan, Prince 242
Barnett, Robin 260
Bathurst, Benjamin 142
Batteville, Baron of 77
Bavaria 98

Becket, Thomas 24
Belgium 133, 139, 146, 152, 157, 200
Belize *see* Honduras (Belize)
Bell, John 94–5
Bembo, Zacharias 44
Benjamin, Lewis 167
Berlin, Isaiah 232
Bernard du Rosier 23
bilateral diplomacy 203, 241–2, 245
Blair, Tony 243, 259, 262–3
Bland, Sir Nevile 180–82, 196, 216, 255
Bolivia 206, 245, 249
Bonde, Christer 65
Bosanquet, George 176
Bosnia 186
Brazil 41, 154, 157, 177, 205, 240, 249
Brezhnev, Leonid 225, 226, 227
Bright, John 172
Britain 65, 101, 152, 155, 167, 168, 238, 259
  Africa, relationship with 71, 169, 214
  Alliance of Hanover system 116–17
  and American Revolution 127, 128–9, 130
  Anglo–American relationship 120, 130, 169, 208, 253
  Anglo–Japanese Alliance (1902) 164, 185
  Anglo–Soviet relationship 99, 191, 192, 196
  anti-Catholicism (1700s) 60, 87
  aristocratic diplomacy 172, 184
  arms sales to Israel 218
  Asia, commercial involvement in (1700s and 1800s) 122–4, 126–7
  Battle of Waterloo 147
  BBC in Iran 252
  Black Chambers and code-breaking 109
  China, relations with 117, 122–3, 126–7, 149–51, 161–5, 185, 222
  commerce and free trade 154, 156, 159–60, 166–7, 172
  and Commonwealth 199–201, 214, 249
  diplomatic culture 41, 45, 48–9, 76–8, 80, 104, 128–9, 171, 173
  Diplomatic Revolution (1756) 78, 108
  diplomatic service contraction (modern) 248, 249
  dynastic status (1800s) 147–8
  economic information, importance of 184–5
  embassy attacks 237, 238
  embassy buildings and foreign offices, permanent (1800s) 175, 176
  Falklands war 239

300

First World War 186, 187, 188, 189, 201
Foreign Office 114, 159, 160, 184, 214, 258
foreign press reporting 167
and French peace treaties (early 1800s) 144
and Gibraltar 137
Glorious Revolution 69
Hoare–Laval Pact 203
Houghton art collection 70
Imperial Election Scheme 66
imperialism 147, 158–65, 167, 208–9, 215, 216, 222
India, relations with 51, 92–3, 121–4, 159–60
literacy and mass education (1800s) 166–7
Lockerbie bombing 234, 242
medieval diplomacy 45, 49
and Mexican loans (1800s) 156
modern criticism of diplomatic standards 41
monarchical authority (1700s) 104
Ochakov Crisis, Russia 137, 207
open diplomacy, call for (1900s) 181–4
and pan-Arab hostility 222
permanent embassies 53–4
Perso–Turkish frontier disputes (1800s) 158
'public sphere' and expression of views 79
Quadruple Alliance 148
Regulating Act (1773) 92, 93
reparations diplomacy 190
Second World War 193, 194, 196, 200, 205, 206, 207, 208, 209, 210, 212
secret diplomacy 110
and slave trade 160
South America, consuls to (1800s) 154, 156
sovereignty and autonomy 57
and Spanish Civil War 195
Spanish diplomacy, fears of 60
Stresa Front 203
and tax avoidance regimes 231
travel improvements 177–8, 243
Treaty of Amiens 136
Turkey, first resident envoy from (1793) 123
United Nations membership 211
Venetian report on 45
Bruce, David 217
Brüno (film) 245
Bulgaria 157, 165, 178, 187, 205
Burma 163, 209, 254
Bush, George H.W. 217–18
Bush, George W. 243, 244, 257
Byzantium 20, 22, 23, 25, 31, 34–5

Callières, François de 110, 112, 184
Cambodia 16
Canada 169, 220–21
Carlingford, Nicholas, 2nd Earl of 72–3
Carlton-Browne of The F.O. (film) 7
Carter, Jimmy 237, 253–4
Castelar, Marquis of 103
Castlereagh, Robert, Viscount 146, 149, 153, 177, 212
Cathcart, Hon. Charles 122
Catherine the Great 70, 108–9, 117, 127, 137
Caulaincourt, Armand de 143, 146
Chamberlain, Austen 183–4
Chamberlain, Neville 243
Charlemagne 25, 30, 45
Chartres, John 189–90
Chauvelin, Francois, Marquis de 136
Chauvelin, Germain-Louis de 102
Chavigny, Anne-Théodore Chavignard de 103, 106
Chernyshev, Ivan 109
Chesterfield, Philip, 4th Earl of 98
Chile 206, 230, 249
China 213, 214, 238
  America, relationship with 217–18, 241
  Beijing Convention 163
  Boxer Uprising 165, 185
  Britain, relationship with 117, 122–3, 126–7, 149–50, 151, 152, 161–4, 185, 222
  Chinese Revolution 185
  communication and travel problems (late 1700s) 126
  Cultural Revolution 185, 222, 237
  détente 224
  and diplomatic 'soft power' 260
  and Dorling Kindersley reference books 246
  East India Company 122
  Europe, relationship with 67, 93, 122–3, 161–4, 165
  financial diplomacy 233, 244, 247
  First Opium War 161
  First World War 164
  free-trade agreements (1800s) 159
  International Opium Commission 202
  Japan, relationship with 165, 185, 204
  Jesuit influence 39, 94
  Ming dynasty replacement 66
  and nuclear power 223
  Pig-tail Committee 159
  power transition, future 246–7

301

Russia, relationship with 93–5, 196, 198, 219, 222, 223, 261
sovereign states and boundaries 95
10 Conditions of Love (film) and national identity 245–6
Treaty of Nanjing 161–2
Treaty Ports system 208, 212
Treaty of Tientsin 162–3
and Treaty of Versailles 126
Treaty of Wanghia 162
tributary system and overlordship 33–4, 35–7, 46, 66–7, 72, 151, 152, 162, 163
United Nations membership 211
Western diplomatic similarities (1600s) 67
Western dominance, challenge to (1900s) 185
Western-style education (1800s) 164
Chinggis Khan 11
Chirol, Valentine 13
Choiseul-Gouffier, Marie, Count of 102, 120–21, 122
Choisy, Abbé François-Tomoléon de 76
Chunmei Chen 245–6
Churchill, Winston 191, 207, 208, 209, 210
Clinton, Bill 253, 254
Clinton, Hillary 235, 241
coalition diplomacy 72, 80, 90, 140, 144, 146, 177
coercive diplomacy 156, 162–3
Cold War 51, 60, 90, 144, 217, 227–8, 243
  diplomatic allies and increased activity 218–19
  diplomatic differences of style 198, 220–21
  and great-power diplomacy 223
  Intelligence operations 16, 218
  neutral states 221
  and *Ostpolitik* 225
  representation problems 210–12
  Second 224
  and transnational networks 251
  and United Nations 210–12
  Vienna Conventions 221
  Warsaw Pact collapse 211, 212
Colombia 157, 206, 233, 245, 249
communication and travel 62, 63, 95–7, 99, 120–21, 126, 182, 198–9, 216, 219
compliance diplomacy 205
confessional diplomacy 60, 81
Congo 152, 200, 249
Crowe, Joseph 172

Créqui, Duke of 78
Cuba 16–17, 160, 198, 205, 221, 231, 252
Czechoslovakia 193, 204, 213, 226, 243

d'Amboise, Clermont 102
d'Annunzio, Gabriele 192–3
Davies, Joseph E. 211
Denmark 57, 63, 187, 189, 258
d'Eon, Chevalier 107
diplomacy
  definitions 12–14
  future of 232, 246–7, 248–55
Diplomacy (board game) 7–8
Diplomatic Revolution (1756) 78, 108
Dobrynin, Anatoly 223
Dodd, William 193, 194
Dominican Republic 205
Doncaster, James, Earl of 60
Donovan, William 218
Dorling Kindersley reference books 246
drugs trade 202, 241, 244, 245
dynamic diplomacy 24–6, 43–4, 47, 48–9, 169–70

ecclesiastical diplomacy 23, 61
Ecuador 41, 157, 206, 233, 249
Eden, Morton 121
Edward VII 178
Efendi, Yusuf Agah 123
Efendi, Zulfikar 68
Egypt 19–20, 140, 159, 206, 215, 222, 243, 258
El Salvador 205
Elgin, James, 8th Earl of 162
Elgin, Thomas, 7th Earl of 135
Elliot, Hugh 129
England *see* Britain
environmentalism 232, 242, 245, 261
Escher, Alfred 209
Essex, Algernon, 3rd Earl of 72
Estrades, Count of 77
Ethiopia 169, 202, 227, 234
Europe, medieval 24–42
  allies, search for 25–6
  ambassadorial protection 24
  Asian and African diplomatic links 32–3
  Byzantine influence of court ritual 34–5
  Christendom, belief in unity of 23, 24–5
  communication issues 49–50
  conflict and diplomacy 44
  continuities and multiple states 38
  crusading period 31–2, 40–41

diplomacy, dynamic aspects of 24–6, 43–4, 47, 48–9
diplomatic culture 24–6, 39–41, 43–4, 46, 47, 48–9
dynasticism 26–7, 32, 39–40
and foreign state reporting 28
Holy League 52
independent political legitimacy and foreign policy 25
Islamic states, diplomatic relations with 30–32, 33, 35
Italian Wars 39, 52–4
Leagues of Cambrai and St Mark 52
Lombard League 20, 24
military success and diplomatic combination 39
oratorical skills 47
papal diplomacy 25, 26–7, 28–30, 31–2, 39, 64
Papal Schism 27
Peace of Venice 24
and permanent embassies 53–4
Roman law, application of 23–4
social prominence and political contractualism 47–9
and status securement 27, 53
succession disputes 52
summit conference origins 24
Treaty of Tordesillas 29
vassalage and overlordship 33–4, 45
Venetian system 29–30, 44, 45
see also individual countries
Europe 1450–1600 43–58
communication, limited improvements in 50–51, 58
conceptual limitations of diplomacy 51
diplomatic criticism 46
dynasticism 46, 48, 53, 55–6
Habsburg partition 55–6, 57–8
inter-state competition 51–2, 53, 55–6, 57
international relations and power 54, 55, 56
monopolization and autonomy 57
non-Western states, lack of understanding of 51
organizational limitations 47
papal diplomacy 52–3, 57
Peace of Augsburg 55
permanent embassies, absence of 47
and Reformation 58
state service and personal honour, security of 44
and state sovereignty 56–7
Wars of Religion 44
Whiggish tendencies 40–41, 43, 47
see also individual countries
Europe 1600–1690 59–84
Ambassadors, limited number of 72
arbitration and international relations 66
capital cities attracting diplomats 69–70
and China, trading privileges with 67
clerics as diplomats 74
commercial posts, merchants in 74
communication problems 62, 63
competitiveness and prestige 69–70
confessional diplomacy 60, 81
correspondence intercepted 62
cultural patronage 70
diplomatic culture 59–60, 62–6, 68–74, 78–9, 81–2, 83, 175
diplomatic grades 72
diplomats as communication and information sources 62, 73–4, 82–4
disputes and conflicts, effects of 68–9
and dynasticism 60, 73
financial problems of diplomats 62–3
Grand Alliance 78
hierarchy of representation 69
and inter-state diplomacy 64
Islamic powers, diplomacy with 68
Japan, curtailment of diplomatic links 67
large embassies as anachronism 60–61
League of Augsburg 78, 80
legal ideas on war, changing 66
linguistic confidence 74–5
Nine Years War 80
papal diplomacy 74, 75
and papal representation restrictions 60
Peace of the Pyrenees 75, 80
Peace of Utrecht 75, 133, 144
Peace of Westphalia 27, 63–6, 69, 80, 88, 89–90, 137
permanent embassies, scarcity of 69
public interest in policies 80–81
resident diplomacy spread 65–6, 175
Scientific Revolution 81
sedition fears 59–60
sovereignty and autonomy 64
Treaty of Nijmegen 75, 144
Treaty of Regensburg 63
and Turkish influence 65
see also individual countries

Europe 1690–1775 85–118
  Africa, diplomatic relations with 91–2
  Alliances of Vienna and Hanover 116–17
  aristocrats as senior diplomats 102, 103, 106, 111, 114, 116, 117–18
  balance-of-power politics 86–9, 104
  Black Chambers and code-breaking 109
  ceremonial, reduction in 111
  collective security 85, 88
  commercial goals and social politics of diplomacy 114–15
  communication and travel problems 95–7, 99
  congress system 88
  consuls, relationship with 115
  diplomatic culture 85–6, 93, 101–4, 108–14, 116—18
  diplomatic grading 72, 113
  diplomatic privileges and protocol 89, 98–9, 102, 103, 106, 111–12
  Diplomatic Revolution 108
  diplomatic training 100, 102–3, 112, 116
  diplomats as communication and information sources 94, 99, 101, 103–4, 105–6, 109, 115, 117
  dynastic diplomacy 105
  foreigners as diplomats 100–1
  French as main diplomatic language 110
  Great Northern War 98
  India, diplomatic relations with 92–3
  information revolution 89
  institutionalization of foreign affairs 113
  intelligence operations 109
  leagues and peace conferences 85
  monarchical authority and intervention 104, 108–9, 114, 117–18
  nation, strong sense of 87
  Native North Americans, diplomatic relations with 90–91, 95, 104
  Papal influence, decline of 100
  personal diplomacies and continuity in foreign policy 105–6
  political policy 89, 106–7, 109, 114
  resident diplomats 103, 175
  Russia, diplomatic relations with 88, 98, 99, 100, 116
  secret diplomacy 107–9, 110, 116
  secular system, move towards 85, 90, 115–16
  Seven Years' War 87, 101, 104
  Treaty of Aix-la-Chapelle 20, 81
  see also individual countries
Europe 1775–1815 119–50
  and American Revolution 127, 128–30
  and *ancien régime* 128, 129, 131, 133, 136, 140, 143, 144, 145
  anti-British alliances 121, 122
  Asia, relationship with 122–7
  coalition diplomacy 140, 144, 146, 177
  communication and travel problems 120–21, 126
  Congress System and collective security 148
  diplomatic culture 125, 128–9, 143, 145
  diplomats as communication and information sources 128, 137
  dynastic prestige 124–5, 141–2, 145, 147–8
  nationalism and diplomacy 141, 142–3, 144, 149, 150
  peace treaties 144–6, 148
  political revolutions 120, 121–2, 127, 131–40
  Quadruple Alliance 148
  republicanism as diplomatic ethos 127
  revolutionary diplomacy 132–40
  secondary powers, changes in 143–4
  Triple Alliance (Britain, France and Austria) 145
  Vienna peace conference 144–7, 148–9, 153, 158, 207
  see also individual countries
Europe 1815–1900 151–79
  ancien régime, end of 154–5
  arbitration procedures 178–9
  aristocratic diplomacy 172–4, 175, 176
  armed diplomacy 165–6
  Asia and Africa, links with 153, 155, 158, 161–3, 168, 169
  change management 169
  colonialism 158–65
  commercial attachés 171–2
  communication and travel improvements 168, 169, 171, 176, 177
  Crimean War 158, 165–6, 167–8, 170
  diplomatic culture 153, 156, 157–8, 160, 162–3, 171–5, 176
  diplomatic history schools and archive material 176
  diplomatic precedence 153
  diplomats as communication and information sources 159, 167, 171

dynamic diplomacy 169–70
embassy buildings and foreign offices, permanent 175–6
foreign press reporting 167
free-trade agreements 159–60
haute bourgeoisie diplomats 173–4
Imperial Rome as diplomatic model 155
imperialism 147, 158–65, 167, 168–9
independence and sovereignty 154, 155–6, 158
international affairs, legalistic approach to 178–9
literacy, mass education and public opinion 166–7
and Mexican international debts 156
military and naval attachés, roles of 171
political contention, lack of appreciation of 170
precise frontiers, adoption of 158
press attachés 176
propaganda 167
protectionism 172
revolutions and foreign intervention 166
royal diplomacy 175, 177–8
slave trade 160
state authority of negotiating rights 152–4
Treaty of Paris 158, 170
war avoidance 167–8, 170
see also individual countries
Europe 1900–1970 180–223
  American influence, spread of 209
  aristocratic diplomacy, criticism of 182, 188, 196, 197–8
  bilateral diplomacy 203
  and British Commonwealth 199–201
  Chinese treatment of Western diplomats 222
  Cold War *see* Cold War
  communications and travel, improved 182, 198–9, 216, 219
  compliance diplomacy 205
  compromise ethos 210–11, 214
  conventional diplomacy, call for end to 196–8, 204–5
  diplomatic culture 181, 183, 185–6, 190–93, 195, 197–8, 202, 216
  diplomats as communication and information sources 183, 184, 195, 197, 216
  economic information, importance of 184–5

European Directorate proposal (1933) 199
European Economic Community 211, 217, 221
European Union 216–17, 233, 235, 241, 257
First World War *see* First World War
and global recession 202
ideological diplomacy and nationalism 185–6, 191, 192–3, 195, 197–8
and international aid 201
international order, call for new 188, 191, 199–200, 202–3, 207, 211, 215–16, 222, 261
and League of Nations 178, 190, 201–4, 209, 231, 260, 261
and national liberation movements 213–14
new regimes, problems posed by 196–204, 207, 214, 215–17
open diplomacy, call for 181–4, 185, 188–9
personal diplomacy 209
political leaders, meetings between 204–5
propaganda 197, 211
reparations diplomacy 190–91
revolutionary movements 191, 192
Second World War *see* Second World War
summit diplomacy 209–10
and transnational radicalism 221
and United Nations 201, 210, 211–12, 211–13
war, hopes of dispensing with 222–3
see also individual countries; modern diplomacy (1970 to present)

Falklands War 239
Farewell (TV series) 245
Fawkener, Sir Everard 96
Fawkener, William 137
Ferrières-Sauveboeuf, Count of 122
financial diplomacy 233, 244, 247
Finland 203, 205, 207, 221, 225
First World War 15, 16, 148, 164, 170
  Armenian Massacres 232
  arms control 189
  consent–frontiers after 189–90
  diplomatic culture 186, 187–9
  geopolitical alliances 186–7
  international order, call for new 186, 261
  and League of Nations 41, 190, 201, 212, 261
  open diplomacy, call for 131, 183–4, 188
  and pacifism 188

Paris Peace Settlement 187, 188, 191,
  198–9, 203
 political neutrality 187
Flüry, Charles 120
Fonseca, Mark, Baron de 108
France 167, 168, 178
 Africa, diplomatic intervention (1800s) 169
 and American Revolution 127, 128
 and *ancien régime* policy 136, 140, 141, 145
 anti-British alliances (1700s) 121–2
 aristocratic diplomacy (1800s) 173, 174
 Asia, political involvement in 122, 126, 127
 Battle of Waterloo 147
 commercial attachés (1800s) 172
 communication and travel problems (1700s) 126
 Congress System and collective security (post-Napoleonic) 148
 diplomacy (1600s) 43–4, 66, 71, 75–80
 diplomacy (1700s) 105, 106–7, 112, 113, 120, 121–2, 124, 126, 132–40
 diplomacy (1800s) 141–2, 143, 156, 172, 173
 diplomatic alliances (1900s) 202
 Diplomatic Revolution (1756) 78, 108
 dynastic prestige 141–2
 Edict of Nantes, revocation of 61
 embassy buildings and foreign offices, permanent (1800s) 175, 176
 First World War 186, 189, 201
 foreign press reporting 167
 Franco–Soviet relations 142, 196, 203
 French as diplomatic language 75, 110–11, 112
 French Revolution 88, 90, 100, 106, 107, 120, 121, 127, 131–40, 214
 Hoare–Laval Pact 203
 Imperial Election Scheme 66
 imperialism 167, 208, 209, 213, 215, 224, 233
 India, diplomatic relations with (late 1700s) 124
 Longchamps affair 131
 medieval diplomacy 43–4
 and Mexican loans (1800s) 156
 National Convention 133
 nationalism and diplomacy 141, 142–3, 217
 Nine Years War 80
 open diplomacy, post-Revolution, call for 131–2

 peace treaties (1700s to 1800s) 136, 139, 144, 145–6, 147, 148
 permanent embassies 53–4, 54
 personal diplomacies (1700s) 105
 'public sphere' expressions against (1600s) 79
 Reformation and religious hostility 61
 revolutionary diplomacy, move away from 140–41
 Russian alliance, failure of (early 1800s) 142
 Russian attempt to recruit spies from (1929) 196
 Second World War 194, 205
 Secret du Roi 107, 116
 Strasbourg diplomatic school 100
 Stresa Front 203
 Treaty of Finkenstein 124
 Treaty of Regensburg 63
 Treaty of Tilsit 142, 143
 Treaty of Versailles 126
 United Nations membership 211
 victim compensation (Napoleon) 140
Franklin, Benjamin 91, 128
Franklin-Bouillon, Henri 190
Frederick II of Prussia 101, 102, 111, 170
Fu Ying 246

Gaddafi, Colonel 215, 243
A Game at Chess (Middleton) 60
Genet, Edmond 139
George II 72, 98, 101, 104, 110
George III 104, 119, 177
George IV 151, 177
Georgia 127, 240, 250, 257
Gerbillon, Jean-François 94
Germany 146, 167, 170, 171, 240
 Africa, diplomatic intervention (1800s) 169
 aristocratic diplomacy (1800s) 172, 173
 commercial attachés (1800s) 172
 compliance diplomacy 205
 détente 224–5
 diplomacy (1900s) 183, 192–4, 198, 205–6
 dynastic prestige 142, 148
 East 213, 217, 225–6
 embassy buildings and foreign offices, permanent (1800s) 176
 First World War 186, 187, 188, 189, 201
 German as diplomatic language (1700s) 110, 111

ideological diplomacy 192–4, 198, 205
Latin American policy (1900s) 205–6
and League of Nations 202, 203
Molotov–Ribbentrop Pact 203
Munich Crisis 200
and nuclear power 223
Ostpolitik 224, 225–8
Peace of Westphalia 27, 63–6, 69, 80, 88, 89–90, 137
political leaders, meetings between (1930s) 204–5
reparations diplomacy 190–91
royal diplomacy (1900s) 178
and Russian revolutionary efforts 192
Second World War 192, 193, 194–5, 200, 205–6, 209
sovereignty and autonomy 64
and tax avoidance regimes 231
territorial changes (1800s) 144
Treaty of Rapallo 191
unification (1800s) 157, 170
and Venezuelan debts (1800s) 156
Ghana 249
Gibraltar 137
Giustinan, Sebastian 45
Glaspie, April 239
globalization 38–9, 224–5, 254–5, 259, 260
Gold Coast 155
The Gondoliers (opera) 174
Gondomar, Diego, Count of 60
Gonzalez de Puebla, Rodrigo 49
Gorbachev, Mikhail 228, 243, 251
Gordievsky, Oleg 16
grading system, diplomatic 72, 113
Grandi, Dino 194
Gravanitz, Count 106
Greece 154, 157, 166, 209
    Ancient 20–22, 54
Gritti, Andrea 45
Gromyko, Andrey 220
Guatemala 205, 216
Guinea 233

Habsburgs 39, 53, 55, 57, 61, 63, 75, 90, 133, 142
Haiti 205
Halifax, Lord 210
Henderson, Sir Nevile 193, 194
Henderson, Sir Nicholas 239
Henry VI, Part Three (Shakespeare) 47–8
Henry VIII 56–7, 59, 102

Hitler, Adolf 106, 140, 181, 193, 194, 195, 204, 205, 207
Hoffmann, Philippe-Johan 254
Holbrooke, Richard 234, 235
Honduras 15, 205, 216, 233, 249, 253
Hong Kong 162, 208
Hot Water (Wodehouse) 7
Hotham, Sir Charles 156
Human Rights Watch 229, 259
Hungary 144, 175, 205
Hyndford, John, 3rd Earl of 86

ideological diplomacy 185–6, 191–8, 205–6, 214
Ides, Isbrants 94
immunity, diplomatic 62, 83, 111
India 50–51, 152, 240
    Britain, relations with 50–51, 92–3, 121–4, 159–60
    and colonialism 200, 208
    East India Companies 92–3, 122, 123–4, 152, 155, 159, 161
    embassy attacks 239
    Europe, diplomatic relations with 92–3, 126
    financial diplomacy 244, 247
    First Maratha War 93
    free-trade agreements (1800s) 159
    Second Mysore War 93
    special envoys' diplomacy 38
    and terrorism 244–5
Indonesia 198, 212–13, 220, 251, 252
Innocent III, Pope 29
international order, call for new 188, 191, 199–200, 202–3, 207, 211, 215–16, 222, 261
Iran 227, 229, 231, 234, 235, 237–8, 249, 252, 254, 256
    see also Persia
Iraq 202, 205, 239
Ireland 189–90, 221
Israel 213, 218, 235, 237, 238, 243, 245, 251, 259
Italy 146, 155
    Africa, relationship with 67, 169, 202–3
    archived material, increase in 45–6
    colonialism 215
    diplomatic protocol (1600s) 78
    Duchy of Milan 45
    dynastic prestige 141
    European Directorate proposal (1933) 199

First World War 187
ideological diplomacy (1900s) 192–3, 194, 198
Italian Wars 52–4, 87
medieval diplomacy 44, 45, 49
nationalist diplomacy (1800s) 144
Peace of Lodi 45
permanent embassies 53–4
Renaissance 18, 20, 21, 26–7, 85
Rome, Ancient 22–3, 23–4, 54, 155
Rome, French occupation (1797) 141
Sacred Congregation 'de Propaganda Fide', Rome 82
Second World War 194
Stresa Front 203
unification (1800s) 157, 166
Vatican *see* Vatican
Venetian system 29–30, 44, 45, 53, 144
and Venezuelan debts (1800s) 156
War of Milanese Succession 44–5
Ivory Coast 249

James I 61
James II 72–3, 74, 81, 254
Japan 13, 165
  alliance system (1900s) 205
  American links with 155, 241
  Anglo–Japanese Alliance (1902) 164, 185
  China, relationship with 165, 185, 204
  diplomatic coercion by Americans (1800s) 163
  diplomatic links, curtailment of 67, 93
  expansionism 165, 204
  First World War 164
  free-trade agreements (1800s) 159
  independence and sovereignty (1800s) 154
  Japanese–Chinese peace treaty (1978) 185
  and League of Nations 203
  lobbyists 250
  Manchuria, invasion of 185, 202
  Russo–Japanese War 179, 185, 186
  Second World War 194–5, 206, 209
  tributary system and overlordship 66–7
  Western-style education (1800s) 164
Jaubert, Pierre-Amédée 126
Jay, Peter 254
Jefferson, Thomas 119, 130
Jones, Sir Harford 125

Keene, Benjamin 103
Kennan, George 262

Kennedy, Joseph 208, 218
Kenya 200, 238
Kerry, John 234
Kinsky, Count Philip 106, 108
Kirkpatrick, William 92–3
Kissinger, Henry 8, 148–9, 223
Knatchbull-Hugessen, Sir Hugh 204
Koo, Vi Kynin 204
Kopp, Viktor 192
Korea 66, 67, 163, 164, 253
Kosovo Crisis 240, 250, 259
Krassin, Leonid 191
Kuo Sung-tao 164
Kuwait 214, 239

La Chétardie, Marquise de 100–1, 106
La Loubère, Simon de 76
Laos 219
Law, Colonel J.-A.-B. 143
League of Nations 41, 178, 190, 201–4, 209, 231, 260, 261
Lebanon 15, 238–9
Lebrun, Pierre 132, 133, 136
Léonard, Frédéric 80–81
Liberia 206, 249
Libya 209, 215, 234, 237, 242, 243
Liechtenstein 231
Lindley, Sir Francis 203
Lindsay, Sir Ronald 252
Lindsay, William 137
Litvinov, Maxim 210
Liudprand, Bishop of Cremona 23
Lothian, Lord 210
Lothian, Philip, 11th Marquis of 184
Louis XIV 75–6, 77–80, 81, 100, 126, 138, 140
Louis XV 101, 104, 107, 108
Louis XVI 107, 121, 127, 132, 135–6, 177
Louis XVIII 145, 146
Lovett, Jonathan 125
Luxembourg 231

Macartney, George, Lord 122–3, 126–7, 149–50, 151
Macedonia 169, 187, 250
Macmillan, Harold 243
Malaya 209
Malcolm, Captain John 124, 125
Manchuria 185, 202, 207, 208
Manesty, Samuel 124–5
Mars Attacks (film) 222, 223
Matveev, Andrei 62

Mauritania 233, 249
Mavrocordato, Alexander 68
Mazzini, Giuseppe 154
Mendoza, Dom Bernardino de 58
Mercy-Argenteau, Count of 135–6
The Merry Widow (opera) 8, 174
Mexico 156, 157, 166, 205, 206
Meyer, Sir Christopher 262–3
Middle East 54–5, 208, 234–5, 251, 256
  see also individual countries
Middleton, Charles, 2nd Earl of 254
military diplomacy 39, 72, 80, 90, 93, 102, 143, 233–4
Mirepoix, Gaston, Duke of 103–4
Mission to Moscow (film) 211
Mitchell, George 234
modern diplomacy (1970 to present) 224–47
  bilateral diplomacy 241–2, 245
  ceremonies and institutions 260–61
  and consular activities 259
  détente 224–7
  diplomatic culture 224–5, 228–9, 230, 233–4, 235–7, 244, 250
  diplomatic history, bias against 235–7
  and domestic interest groups 250
  and drugs trade 241, 244, 245
  Eastern Europe, recognition of states 226
  and economic crises 236–7
  embassy attacks 237, 238–9, 258
  and environmentalism 232, 242, 245, 261
  and globalization 224–5, 254–5, 259, 260
  and heads of state 232, 243, 253–4
  Helsinki Accords 225, 226–7
  and hooliganism 257
  human rights' issues 229–30, 242, 246, 259, 261
  and information gathering 233–4, 239, 253, 258–9
  insurrection and violence 234, 237, 260
  and international aid 252
  international bodies, membership of 239–41, 251
  language of entitlement 242
  and lobbyists 250, 259
  and media participation 257–9, 260
  ministerial role 232
  national image, protection of 245–6, 251, 262–3
  and NGOs 224, 228–9, 230–32, 233, 239–40, 244, 252, 259
  and open-source information 259
  and *Ostpolitik* 225–6
  privatization of diplomacy 250
  and qualification of grand narratives 261
  and radicalism 256, 258, 261
  regimes, collapse of 237
  religious and ethnic considerations 246
  and representation, importance of 211–12, 223, 232–3, 238, 262
  and soft power 228–9, 230–32, 233, 239–40, 244, 252, 257, 260
  state power decline 252
  summit diplomacy 229–30
  and tax avoidance regimes 231
  and terrorism 51, 213, 234, 237, 242, 244–5
  and Third World 227
  trade and international cooperation 241
  and transnational networks 251
  and travel 242–3
  and value of diplomacy 257
  see also Europe *1900–1970*; individual countries
Mongolia 198, 220
Montaigu, Count of 115
Morocco 156, 159, 165, 167, 168, 186, 215, 249
Mozambique 169
Mussolini, Benito 193, 194, 199, 203

Napoleon 127, 140–44, 145–7, 148, 207
nationalism and diplomacy 141, 142–3, 144, 149, 150
NATO 211, 240, 250, 259
Nepal 163
Netherlands 78, 143, 145, 146, 148, 155, 157
  criticism of diplomatic standards (1700s) 41–2
  diplomatic culture 49, 71, 80, 83
  Dutch Crisis (1787) 126
  Dutch East India Company 67
  Dutch Revolt 63
  dynastic prestige 141
  First World War 187
  and French Revolution 133
  imperialism 208, 209, 212–13
  OPEC ban 251
  'public sphere' and expression of views 79
  republicanism as diplomatic ethos 127
  Treaty of Basle 136
NGOS 224, 228–9, 230–32, 233, 239–40, 244, 252, 259

Nicaragua 16, 159, 205, 249, 253
Nicolson, Harold 12, 184
Nigeria 249, 251
Nixon, Richard 185, 218, 219, 223, 225, 243
Norway 157, 250
nuclear facility 223, 241, 242

Obama, Barack 35, 234, 237, 240, 258
Oglethorpe, James 90–91
Olivares, Count of 58
Oman 122
   shima, General Hiroshi 194–5
Otto I 23, 30, 151
Ouseley, Sir Gore 125

Pakistan 233–4, 239, 244–5, 256, 258
Palestine 202, 208, 213–14, 221, 231, 234, 235, 253, 259
Panama 205
Paraguay 41, 156, 157, 206
Parish, Woodbine 154
Parkes, Henry 162, 163
Parsons, Sir Anthony 239
Pauncefote, Sir Julian 174
Pellew, Sir Edward 152
Pereira, Tomé 94
Perkins, Edward 215
Persia 17–18, 168, 178
   European relations with (1700s and 1800s) 122, 124–6, 127
   free-trade agreements (1800s) 159
   ideological diplomacy 198
   Mongol Empire 11, 31–2
   Perso–Turkish frontier disputes (1800s) 158
   Second World War 205
   Treaty of Finkenstein 124
   see also Iran
personal diplomacy 105, 177, 209, 210–11
Peru 206
Peter the Great 88, 98, 99, 100, 113, 138, 177
Philippines 207–8
Phipps, Sir Eric 193, 194
Pinochet, General Augusto 230, 259
Plelo, Count 102
Poincaré, Raymond 15
Poland 166, 192, 203–4, 207
   First World War 189
   nationalist diplomacy (1800s) 144
   and *Ostpolitik* 225
   Partitions (late 1700s) 137, 143, 204

Second Word War 207
Solidarity 227
United Nations membership 211
War of Polish Succession 88, 96, 98
Ponsonby, Arthur 182, 183
Ponsonby, John, Lord 154
Portugal 113, 146, 154, 169, 178, 200, 252, 259
Posnikov, Vasili 63
Prittwitz und Gaffron, Count Friedrich 194
professional diplomacy 172, 173, 174–5, 176, 181, 183
Prussia 139, 145, 146, 148, 169
   Battle of Jena 143
   diplomatic culture 105, 113, 172, 173
   Diplomatic Revolution (1756) 78, 108
   First World War 189
   Quadruple Alliance 148
   Treaty of Basle 136
Putin, Vladimir 228, 257

Ratanov, Anatoli 227
reparations diplomacy 190–91
revolutionary diplomacy 132–9
Rhodesia *see* Zimbabwe (Rhodesia)
Richelieu, Louis, Duke of 102, 106
Richmond, Sir John 214
Ripperda, Jan Willem 105
Robinson, Thomas 118
Roe, Sir Thomas 50–51
Romania 157, 170–71, 187, 205, 217, 250, 260
Rome, Ancient 22–3, 23–4, 54, 155
Roosevelt, Franklin D. 193, 206, 207, 208, 209
Roosevelt, Theodore 179
Rubens, Peter Paul 70
Rumbold, Sir George 142
Rundall, Sir Francis 219
Russell, Theo 184
Russia (Soviet Union) 68, 101, 145, 146, 165, 167, 169, 192, 238
   Afghanistan occupation 227–8, 234
   and Africa (late 1900s) 227
   American recognition of (1933) 196
   Anglo–Soviet relationship 99, 191, 192, 196
   China, relationship with 93–5, 196, 198, 219, 222, 223, 261
   Civil War 191
   and Cold War 217, 220–21, 227–8
   Comintern 133, 191, 192, 195
   Communism, collapse of 228–9

Crimean War 158, 165–6, 167–8
détente 224, 226, 227, 231
diplomatic culture 37, 73, 88, 98–101, 108–11, 113, 116, 171, 188
First World War 186, 189
Franco–Soviet relations 142, 196, 203
and Georgia 127, 240, 250, 257
and Houghton art collection 70
ideological diplomacy 195–6, 198, 214
imperialism 170–71, 195–6, 198, 213, 227
KGB 218, 227–8
League of Armed Neutrality 108, 117
and League of Nations 201, 203
and Middle East peace process 235
Molotov–Ribbentrop Pact 203
NATO–Russo Council 240
and nuclear power 223
Ochakov Crisis 137, 207
open diplomacy, call for (1900s) 188
People's Commissariat for Foreign Affairs 191, 192
Perso–Turkish frontier disputes (1800s) 158
personal diplomacy (1900s) 210–11
Quadruple Alliance 148
revolution, attempts to spread 191, 192
royal diplomacy (1900s) 178
Russian Revolution 191
Russo–Japanese War 179, 185, 186
Second World War 196, 205, 206–7, 209, 210, 211
Soviet bloc collapse 224
Treaty of Iazhelbitsii 57
Treaty of Khiakta 95
Treaty of Nerchinsk 94, 95
Treaty of Rapallo 191
Treaty of Tilsit 142, 143
United Nations membership 211
Western NGOs, distrust of 229
Rycaut, Paul 94, 115

Sadat, Anwar 243
Saddam Hussein 238, 239, 258
Sánchez, Oscar Arias 253
Sapiti, Andrea 28
Sardinia 49, 52, 69, 101, 110, 136, 139, 168
Satow, Sir Ernest 12, 180, 181, 255
Saudi Arabia 206, 208, 219, 234, 238–9, 242
Savary, General A.-L.-M.-R. 143
Saxony 55, 105, 145, 146, 207
Scaglia, Alessandro 56, 70

Schepper, Cornelius 55
Scheunemann, Randy 250
Schöpflin, Johann Daniel 100, 105
Scott, Ian 214
Seckendorf, Count 108
Second World War 192–4, 195, 200, 205–7, 209, 211
secret diplomacy 107, 110, 181, 188
Sedwill, Mark 258
Selden, John 76–7
Serbia 157, 186, 238, 259
Shepilov, Dmitri 220
Siam *see* Thailand (Siam)
Simon, Sir John 187–8
Skelton, Bevil 74
Soames, Christopher 221
Soviet Union *see* Russia
South Africa 215, 240
South America 154, 156–7, 166, 219, 245, 249
    see also individual countries
Spain 88, 127, 130, 146, 186
    Black Chambers and code-breaking 109
    Carlist Wars 166
    Coach Museum, Belém 111
    Cold War neutrality 221
    diplomatic culture 104, 112
    dynastic diplomacy 141–2, 143–4
    French power seizure (early 1800s) 143
    and French Revolution 139
    and Gibraltar 137
    ideological diplomacy (1900s) 195, 198
    independence and sovereignty (1800s) 154
    and Mexican loans (1800s) 156
    monopolization and autonomy 57
    Reformation and lack of foreign embassies 57–8, 60
    Second World War 209
    and slave trade (1800s) 160
    Spanish Civil War 195, 196
    Treaty of Basle 136
    Treaty of Rastatt 65
    Treaty of Seville 103
    United Nations membership 211
    War of Spanish Succession 64–5, 109, 112
Sparre, Baron 103
Spathar-Milescu, Nicolas 71–2
sport, diplomatic links with 12–13, 257
Squier, E. George 156
Stalin, Joseph 140, 192, 195–6, 199, 206–10, 219–20, 227, 260
Star Trek (TV series) 222

Staunton, Sir George 123
Stepney, George 115
Stresemann, Gustav 190–91
Stuart, Charles 154
Sudan 260
summit diplomacy 209–10, 229–30
Susman, Louis 175, 253, 258
Sweden 157, 168, 221
Switzerland 69, 146, 157, 209, 231, 237
Syria 15, 215, 234

Talleyrand, Charles Maurice de 145, 153, 174
Tanzania 215, 238
Temple, Sir William 74–5
terrorism 51, 213, 234, 237, 242, 244–5
Thailand (Siam) 75–6, 159, 178, 205, 209
Thatcher, Margaret 239, 243
Thirty Years War 27, 58, 63–6, 69, 80, 81, 88, 89–90, 133, 137
Thornton, Sir Edward 168
Tornochichi 90–91
Trench, Colonel Chenevix 171
Trench, Colonel Frederick 171
Truman, Harry 199
Turkey 68, 152, 160, 164, 167, 168, 169, 170, 171
    and Armenia 232–3
    Britain, first resident envoy in (1793) 123
    Chanak Crisis 200
    diplomatic culture 62, 68, 88, 95
    embassy attacks 238
    ethnic and religious considerations 246
    Europe, relationship with 51, 61, 65, 156
    free-trade agreements (1800s) 159
    Ottoman Empire 33, 35, 45, 54–5, 58, 157
    Perso–Turkish frontier disputes (1800s) 158
    post-First World War 148, 190, 201
    Second World War 206
    and slave trade (1800s) 160
    Treaty of Lausanne 189
    Treaty of Sèvres 189
    Western diplomacy, adoption of (1800s) 158
Turnbull, David 160
Tyrconnel, John, Viscount of 101

UK *see* Britain
Ukraine 238
United Nations 201, 209–10, 211–13, 226, 235, 240, 242, 253, 256, 259

United Provinces *see* Netherlands
Uruguay 249
US *see* America

van Dijkveld, Everard van Weede 73
Varè, Daniel 199
Vatican 221, 226
    papal diplomacy 25–32, 39, 52–3, 57, 64, 68, 75, 100
Venezuela 15, 41, 156, 206, 249, 251
Vergennes, Charles, Count of 98, 102, 107
Victoria, Queen 164, 177–8
Vietnam 126, 163, 214
Villars, Marquis de 80
Villeneuve, Louis, Marquis of 96, 115
Viry, Francesco, Count of 101
Visconti, Gian Galeazzo, Duke of Milan 44–5
Vorontsov, Count Simon 109, 137

Wade, Abdoulaye 233
Wake, Sir Isaac 73
Waldegrave, James, Lord 101, 102
Walker, William 153
War, Angus 218
The War of the Worlds (Wells) 222
Watzdorf, Friedrich, Count 114
Webb, Jim 254
Whitworth, Sir Charles 99
Wicquefort, Abraham van 83, 111–12
Williams, Anthony 239
Williams, Sir Charles Hanbury 98, 128–9
Williams, William 168
Wilson, Harold 200
Wilson, Hugh 193, 194
Wilson, Woodrow 188, 199, 201, 212, 236
Woodward, George 110–11
Wotton, Sir Henry 59
Wratislaw, Count 108
Wright, Sir Roger Curtis 92
Wyatt, Sir Thomas 59

Yoshida, Shigeru 195
Young, Andrew 215
Yugoslavia 193, 199, 226

Zaire 237
Zamboni, Giovanni 106
Zimbabwe (Rhodesia) 200–1, 229, 237, 260